Subverting the Republic

Subverting the Republic

DONALD J. TRUMP AND THE
PERILS OF PRESIDENTIALISM

Nicholas F. Jacobs and Sidney M. Milkis

University Press of Kansas

© 2025 by the University Press of Kansas
All rights reserved

Published by the University Press of Kansas (Lawrence, Kansas 66045), which was organized by the Kansas Board of Regents and is operated and funded by Emporia State University, Fort Hays State University, Kansas State University, Pittsburg State University, the University of Kansas, and Wichita State University.

Library of Congress Cataloging-in-Publication Data
Names: Jacobs, Nicholas F., author | Milkis, Sidney M., author
Title: Subverting the republic : Donald J. Trump and the perils of presidentialism / Nicholas F. Jacobs and Sidney M. Milkis.
Other titles: Donald J. Trump and the perils of presidentialism
Description: [Lawrence, Kansas] : University Press of Kansas, [2025] | Includes bibliographical references and index.
Identifiers: LCCN 2024042506 (print) | LCCN 2024042507 (ebook) | ISBN 9780700638840 cloth | ISBN 9780700638901 paperback | ISBN 9780700638857 ebook
Subjects: LCSH: Trump, Donald, 1946– | United States—Politics and government—2017-2021 | Abuse of administrative power—United States—History—21st century | Executive power—United States—History | Executive-legislative relations—United States | BISAC: POLITICAL SCIENCE / American Government / Executive Branch | HISTORY / United States / 21st Century
Classification: LCC E912 .J34 2025 (print) | LCC E912 (ebook) | DDC 973.933—dc23/eng/20250327
LC record available at https://lccn.loc.gov/2024042506.
LC ebook record available at https://lccn.loc.gov/2024042507.

British Library Cataloguing-in-Publication Data is available.
Authorised Representative Details: Easy Access System Europe
Mustamäe tee 50, 10621 Tallinn, Estonia | gpsr.requests@easproject.com

Dedicated with love and gratitude to

        Rachel Jacobs   Carol Milkis
        Benjamin Jacobs   Lauren Milkis
        Anderson Jacobs   David Milkis
                                    Jonathan Milkis

Contents

Preface, ix

Introduction, 1

1. The Modern Presidency and Executive-Centered Partisanship, 28

2. Trump, the Conservative Movement, and the Grand Old Party, 65

3. Unilateralism and the Trump Presidency, 108

4. Trump and the Separation of Powers, 151

5. The Presidency in Crisis: COVID-19, Racial Justice, and the 2020 Presidential Election, 200

Conclusion: The Future of the American Presidency, 231

Postscript, 266

Notes, 271

Index, 315

Preface

With this book, we join a number of our colleagues in seeking to explain how Donald Trump—a real estate mogul and reality television star, with no political experience—has become the central animating force of American politics. Ever since he and Melania Trump descended the escalator in Trump Tower to announce his presidential campaign, Trump has dominated talk radio, network and cable news, newspapers, popular magazines, and, perhaps most ubiquitously, social media. Even after failing to win reelection in 2020, attempting to overturn the results of a free and fair election, and retreating to his Elba, Mar-a-Lago, Florida, Trump overawes political life in the United States. This book was completed before his redemptive reelection in 2024, a development that foreshadows a recrudescence of the pathologies we analyze in the chapters to follow. As we explain in a short postscript on the 2024 election, a second Trump term will almost certainly aggravate the toxic partisanship that characterized his first four years in the White House. Trump's ability to galvanize his base, dominate the Republican Party, and subvert the norms and institutions of representative constitutional government will continue to test severely the foundations of the American republic.

Although many scholars and pundits first viewed Trump as a cult of personality, a one-off who would be frustrated and relegated to the dustbin of American history by a somewhat frayed but still resilient constitutional democracy, we saw a different type of presidency in the making. During the first few months of Trump's presidency, there was plenty of evidence to suggest that his administration would fail to navigate the complexities of the divided and separated institutions of American government. Just days into the administration, the White House's insistence that it had "alternative facts" to show that the crowd of President Trump's inauguration ceremony was larger than Barack Obama's seemed to portend that this was a presidency more concerned with building an alternative reality to inflate Trump's ego than with a collective effort to make America great again. But behind the scenes, the wheels were in motion. As we wrote in the autumn of 2017, just eight months into Trump's presidency, "Often overlooked among the disappointments and recriminations of Trump's frenzied beginning is his administration's aggressive and deliberate assault on the Liberal state.... Since day one, Trump has forcefully—and sometimes successfully—taken aim at the programmatic achievements of his predecessor."[1]

Nearly eight years later, few deny that Trump's presidency and its calamitous aftermath pose a serious threat to liberal democracy. Trump's second presidency, buttressed by a party remade in his image, has aroused fear that the United States is experiencing the worst political crisis since the Civil War. Indeed, warnings abound that Trump is a dangerous demagogue who has tapped into and aggravated a "cold civil war": Republicans and Democrats now view each other as existential threats to each other's way of life and are willing to bend the Constitution and win at all costs to impose their vision of a just America. A more disciplined and coherent Trump operation stands in wait, having learned the lessons of the tumultuous four years of his presidential term and dedicated to fulfilling its most ambitious and divisive goals.

In some ways, Trump's primordial ties to his followers—the Republican base—defy reasoned explanation. Max Weber stressed the religiosity of charismatic leadership, something Trump—the thrice-married and vulgar celebrity—seemed to intuit in seeking common cause with the Christian right and projecting himself as the "savior" of his party's base.[2] "Charismatic domination," Weber wrote, "means a rejection of all ties to any external order in favor of the exclusive glorification of the genuine mentality of the prophet and hero. Hence, its attitude is revolutionary and transvalues everything; it makes a sovereign break with all traditional and rational norms: 'It is written, but I say unto you.'"[3] As Tim Alberta details in *The Kingdom, the Power and the Glory*, evangelical Christians, believing *they* are under siege by a secular deep state, view Trump's vulgar rhetoric and iconoclastic leadership as necessary means to a righteous end.[4]

Yet Trump is not the first charismatic leader to challenge American constitutional government and claim the mantle of the voice of the People. Huey Long, Joseph McCarthy, and George Wallace all played the strongman and disrupted American politics. But Trump was the first right-wing populist to establish primordial ties with a national constituency and reach the White House. How did Trump reach the presidency? Why did American politics summon a Trump, rather than a progressive reformer like Franklin Roosevelt, at this transformative moment? How enduring will the changes he brought about be?

Although much ink has been spilled in seeking to answer these questions, we have written one of the few book-length studies that comprehensively examines Trump's presidency and its legacy. Without denying Trump's idiosyncrasies and acknowledging that certain features of our political time are unprecedented, we argue that his imprint on the American political landscape is a reckoning of institutional and constitutional changes—and failures—that have been decades in the making. Only by taking this long view, we argue, can scholars explain where Trump stands in the long train of democratic crises that have occurred throughout American history, how his presidency and its provocative aftermath are symptoms of long-standing changes in the relationship between the presidency and the party system, and why the presidency itself has become a polarizing institution.

Our core argument, tested in previous collaboration,[5] is that Trump's presidency and his enduring spell on the Republican Party are due to the rise of what we call executive-centered partisanship, which is deeply rooted in American politics. Both Democrats and Republicans depend on presidential candidates and presidents to pronounce party doctrine, raise campaign funds, campaign on behalf of their partisan brethren, mobilize grassroots support, and advance party programs through administrative action (and court appointments).

Presidential partisanship sits at the crosscurrents of two related developments. First, organizational and electoral reforms weakened the decentralized, patronage-based parties that dominated most of the nineteenth century. Throughout the twentieth century, insurgent movements pressured both political parties to alter the rules governing their presidential nomination process. Party leaders were removed as guardians of national party conventions, with power shifting to "the people" in selecting candidates for office and determining party priorities through direct primaries and open caucuses. This shift accelerated in the 1960s, propelled by civil rights and antiwar activists, culminating in the McGovern-Fraser Reforms of the early 1970s. Republicans quickly followed suit.

"Participatory democracy" did not empower the median voter—the target of pragmatic parties seeking national consensus. The weakening of traditional party organizations enhanced the influence of donors, interest groups, and social activists who scorned pragmatic politics and compromise that, historically, had been credited with forging majority coalitions in the United States. That is, reforms empowered the so-called party bases—the most militant and ideological voters, who see politics not as a venue for compromise or grand bargains but as an arena for those intensely focused on politics to struggle for control over the nation's identity.[6]

A second development enhanced the voice of the newly empowered "grass roots": the growth of executive prerogative. The modern presidency blossomed during Franklin Roosevelt's long term of office, in an era when decentralized parties still provided a check on presidential ambition. Roosevelt created the Executive Office of the President through the Executive Reorganization Act of 1939. That organic statute of the modern presidency established the White House Office (the West Wing) and important staff agencies like the Office of Management and Budget (OMB). By the 1960s, these institutional developments collided with the new politics of social protest and popular mobilization, encouraging presidents to form alliances with activists and outside groups who disdained the party "establishment." The joining of executive prerogative and partisanship subordinated decentralized and pluralistic party coalitions to more national and programmatic networks.

These two developments, combined, have led to a national struggle for American identity that reverberates powerfully through our own time. Battles over who belongs to the sovereign have disrupted the United States since the beginning of the republic. But the cataclysmic 1960s, especially the civil rights revolution and the right-wing counterrevolution that sought to erase it, transformed what was once episodic and regional into a national norm.

Since then, progressive and conservative movement activists—especially civil rights activists on the left and evangelicals on the right—have pulled the parties away from the center, fueling ideological polarization and legislative stalemate. Organized interests and movement activists increasingly demand executive action to further their aims. Consequently, presidents of both parties have sought to achieve their policy objectives and appeal to their party base using administrative powers rather than navigating a complex system of separated powers to pass legislation.

No single president is responsible for the rise of executive-centered partisanship. Lyndon Johnson, Richard Nixon, Ronald Reagan, George W. Bush, and Barack Obama all contributed to make this an entrenched feature of the modern presidency. We seek to explain how Donald Trump brought the merging of executive power and polarization to a dangerous culmination. Most scholars sensitive to this polarization stress the "radicalization" of the Republican Party. Ronald Reagan's enlistment of the Christian right into the Republican Party was instrumental in turning the GOP into a conservative party, with a right-wing movement wing. Trump and the MAGA movement, it seems, have turned it into a movement party with a fading institutional wing. Less opposed to the administrative state forged during the New Deal and more responsive to the demands of a multiracial nation, Democrats have evolved as a more pragmatic and diverse party. Nevertheless, we take issue with the position that the Democrats are best characterized as a "coalition of interest groups," immune to the movement politics that currently roils America.[7]

Since the 1960s, interest groups like labor and "neoliberal" business constituents have had to share power with a multitude of social movement organizations—representing the causes of civil rights, environmental protection, gun control, and consumer protection—that disdain pragmatism and the regular party apparatus. It is this conflict between establishment groups and "outside" organizations within the Democratic Party that resisted so fervently Joseph Biden's promise during the 2020 campaign to restore "normalcy" to a fractured nation. Indeed, as we show in the book's conclusion, Biden signed more executive actions during his first one hundred days in office than any president since Franklin Roosevelt. The cascade of executive orders, memorandums, and other administrative actions, which continued through the 2024 election season, demonstrated how intent the new president was to address many of the immediate concerns of his most progressive partisan allies.

The polarization that afflicted the Biden administration and the fact that Trump, in spite of facing four criminal indictments, emerged victorious in 2024 does not bode well for the resilience of democracy in America. We recognize that American institutions have been strained throughout history but have survived. The current struggle for the soul of American democracy is the latest episode in the never-ending quest to achieve the multiracial democracy promised by the Declaration of Independence and codified by the amendments added to the Constitution in the wake of the Civil War. Yet this reckoning with slavery and the civil rights revolution of the sixties were collective engagements that joined presidential leadership, vigorous party organizations, and social movements that pressed progress on political institutions from below. Alas, arousing unyielding resistance from progressive officeholders and activists, who believe it is necessary to fight fire with fire, Trump's disruptive first four years in the White House further instilled in the country the false hope that a single individual, even with the tools of mass communication and social media, could ever truly serve as the sole steward of the public welfare. Our hope is that this book persuades its readers to grapple with the perils of presidentialism, for until this misplaced faith in a presidency-centered democracy is disabused, the prospect of restoring the constitutional norms and institutions of the American republic will be an impossible dream.

Our collaboration grew out of a relationship formed at the University of Virginia, where the professional ties between mentor and student evolved into warm friendship and the fruitful sharing of ideas and research. Our partnership has been supported by colleagues and friends who have pushed us to clarify our arguments and defend them more systematically: Bill Antholis, Lawrie Balfour, Bill Galston, Will Howell, Desmond King, Frances Lee, Robert Lieberman, Sandy Maisel, Kal Munis, Rachel Potter, Katie Rader, Andy Rudalevige, Dan Shea, Stephen Skowronek, Anthony Sparacino, Sidney Tarrow, Daniel Tichenor, and Phil Wallach. A small army of research assistants was integral to the collection of evidence that allowed us to properly situate Trump in deep historical relief: Lukas Alexander, Linh Dinh, Charlotte Hoopes, Helena Kopans-Johnson, Maddie Silano, and Haley Stiles.

It has been a great pleasure to work with David Congdon, who showed faith in this book project from the start, patiently waited for it to reach its destination, and enlisted two very helpful reviews that provided insightful guidance for a final set of revisions that strengthened the manuscript. We are very grateful to John Kenneth White and Jeffrey Crouch for sharing their wisdom and detailed editorial suggestions with us.

Finally, we are deeply thankful for the constant love and support of our families, who now have endured our immersion in two book projects that have preoccupied us for the better part of eight years. These undertakings have been labors of love, but we are very happy to celebrate their completion by spending more time with Carol, Lauren, David, and Jonathan Milkis (and our beagle Iverson, the pride and joy the family); and Rachel, Benjamin, and Anderson Jacobs. Anderson was born as we were finishing up the final chapters of our first draft—a blessed interruption that reminded us of which things in life really matter.

Nicholas F. Jacobs
Vassalboro, Maine

Sidney M. Milkis
Charlottesville, Virginia

Introduction

On November 6, 2016, the American presidency changed forever. Flouting the polls, the pundits, and, really, common sense, Donald Trump won the election for president of the United States.

Trump defied not only the election forecasts but also our common understanding of what the presidency means in American politics. He was the first president who had never served in either elected or appointed public office.[1] Since the birth of mass democracy during the early part of the nineteenth century, the president has been viewed as the "tribune" of the people. Trump, however, captured the office with nearly three million fewer votes than his challenger. Although this was the second time in sixteen years that the Electoral College produced a president who lost the popular vote, Trump's bombastic campaign appeared to pose a novel challenge to the "resilience" of American democracy.[2] Thousands of protesters demonstrated at his inaugural, shouting "Not my president!" on the day that has come to emblematize American democracy. The emergence of the modern presidency during the early part of the twentieth century raised expectations that the executive office would be occupied by transcendent national leaders—"stewards of the public welfare," to use President Theodore Roosevelt's alluring phrase. But Trump campaigned on a polarizing platform, pledging to use the presidency to claw back power from the elites and undeserving, and give it back to "real" Americans.

And yet, despite violating expectations, norms, and precedents, after four years in office, Trump accomplished much of what he promised, or threatened. He denigrated expertise and the Washington establishment, even as public health experts and bureaucracy became more central to Americans' everyday lives during the COVID-19 pandemic. He used the president's power to reward, as his aides called them, his "loyal customers," redeploying national administrative power to "make America great again." As the dramatic events of January 6, 2021, exposed, President Trump concocted a vision of the nation at war with itself, twisting a tale of widespread fraud to prop up the "Big Lie" that he won the 2020 election. "We won in a landslide," he repeated. "This was a landslide ... we built the greatest political movement in the history of our country and nobody even challenges that.... We fight like hell. And if you don't fight like hell, you're not going to have a country anymore."[3] Perhaps more than any of his predecessors, Trump revealed the power of the president's words as he actively courted a movement to overturn a free and fair election—to win at all costs, even if it meant a violent attack on the nation's Capitol.

The Republic is sick. But while many have argued that it fell ill on Donald Trump's watch, the symptoms of our ailing constitution have deep historical roots. Trump changed the presidency, for sure, but most revealing was the institutional disease he laid bare—a presidential office imbued with immense power and partisan ambition that has long afflicted the American regime. Trump is a symptom, not the disease itself. Reforming the presidency, therefore, requires more than treating a symptom; it necessitates a comprehensive examination and restructuring of the institutional incentives and powers that have long been vulnerable to exploitation and abuse.

Of course, there is much about Donald Trump's presidency and his leadership of the Republican Party that is novel. However, his tempestuous term gave dramatic testimony to a development more than half a century in the making: the modern presidency disappoints our hopes, fails to live up to our expectations, and aggravates our divisions. Trump brought to a culmination long-term developments that pose a significant challenge to the idea that the president could represent the "whole people." All presidents claim a "mandate" to govern, but the fact remains that few presidents even come close to capturing a clear majority of voters. Since FDR's reelection rout in 1936, victorious presidents have averaged just 52 percent of the national vote (52.4 percent if you exclude the non–Electoral College victors). That is hardly evidence for a clear national mandate. Likewise, we tend to think that the White House, as Richard Neustadt warned in 1960, "is no place for amateurs."[4] That may have been true fifty years ago; however, since the Watergate crisis left the very experienced Nixon administration in disgrace, only one true Washington insider has managed to secure the presidency: George H. W. Bush in 1988. Dismissed as out of touch with rank-and-file Americans, he was badly defeated by the "outsider" Bill Clinton in his bid for a second term.[5] Finally, as American politics has become more complex and fractious, we expect presidents to cut through the Gordian knot—and manage the country's affairs in the national interest. As Harry Truman's placard on his Oval Office desk proclaimed: "The buck stops here." Yet presidents are factional leaders. Increasingly, as the nation has been mired in partisan gridlock, the president has been viewed by his most loyal supporters as the tip of the spear in the battle for their political causes. In many ways, Trump's provocative leadership marked a reification of the president's changing position in the American political order—a mirror of the nation's divisions and a lightning rod for conflicting visions of who we are and who we aspire to be. In this transformation, Trump did not create the fractures but laid them bare, amplifying tensions long simmering beneath the surface of American democracy.

Donald Trump rattled the national resolve. However, his blatant disregard for norms and institutions brought to full realization a joining of executive prerogative and partisanship that sows discord and fuels rancorous behavior. He capitalized on the accrual of ambiguous statutes and delegated authority to repurpose national administrative power in the service of a new form of conservativism—one that sought to redeploy rather than roll back the expansion of the liberal state during the 1960s.[6] Even in losing reelection, Trump remained a powerful figure by exploiting the erosion of constitutional forms. In recapturing the White House in 2024, he demonstrated the enduring potency of a presidency untethered from traditional constraints, wielded as a tool to exploit cultural and political divides that have roiled American politics for more than half a century. Trump did not break the mold of the modern presidency; he just helped us see how broken it already was.

This book is our effort to explain how and, more important, why Donald Trump's presidency played out the way it did, and why his second term of office will reinforce the evolving dynamics of presidentialism in modern American governance. We are not so bold as to claim we could predict some of the must unfathomable moments that made Trump's four years in office so disruptive, not the least of which was an armed uprising, encouraged by a sitting president, to overturn a free and fair election, the foundational rock of self-government. But Trump's incitement of the attacks of January 6, as with every other one of his actions, cannot be understood without taking account of the long-term institutional developments that have transformed the way the modern presidency operates. These changes have bequeathed a constitutional order that places presidents in the middle of the political storm, equips their office with vast power, and incentivizes them to listen to the most extreme voices in society. Since, unlike many scholars and political commentators, we see Trump as a symptom of this emergent political order, we were not surprised that his departure from office failed to cure the deep pathologies afflicting American government and politics. Whether or not Trump was reelected, the infirmities of presidentialism would have continued to threaten the constitutional foundations of the American republic. The 2024 election, which resulted in a more decisive Trump victory than he won in 2016, and a party remade in his own image in control of both congressional chambers, is very likely to exacerbate the profound challenge of restoring the constitutional norms and institutions of American constitutional government.

This is not to say that we are trying to normalize Trump or underestimate the danger his presidency posed to representative constitutional government. He seems to be exceptionally gifted at spinning lies and fomenting discord—a popular demagogue who, as Alexander Hamilton feared, "flatters [the people's] prejudices to betray their interests."[7] Nor do we downplay the importance of current developments that animate what many pundits have termed a "cold civil war." However, we seek to place the Trump administration's actions within a deeper institutional and historical context than do most accounts of his presidency—to better understand why his four years in office shook the foundations of American democracy and, perhaps most alarmingly, why it might happen again.

Our core argument is that Donald Trump's presidency should not be understood merely as a cult of personality; rather, his term in office should be taken seriously as a lesson in the fragility of American political institutions and the American Constitution. We view Trump's remarkable and unsettling ascent to the White House as the reckoning of institutional and constitutional pathologies that have been decades in the making. From aggressively redeploying the federal government's administrative powers, to using the tools of the modern presidency to undertake a hostile takeover of the Republican Party, Trump's presidency reveals the peril of a presidency-centered democracy that combines executive aggrandizement and polarizing struggles over the meaning of American identity. Moreover, the dynamics that impelled the Trump presidency are deeply ingrained in American democracy, embraced by progressives and conservatives, Democrats and Republicans alike. As a result, although future administrations may override or change much of what Trump might have accomplished in terms of substantive programmatic reform, his most important and troubling legacy is cultural and institutional. When institutional guardrails and norms are so routinely and flagrantly violated, there is no guarantee that democracy will endure. And until the misplaced faith in a presidency-centered democracy is decisively disabused, the hope of restoring the constitutional norms and institutions of the American republic will remain a chimera.

THE TRUMP PRESIDENCY IN HISTORICAL CONTEXT

How should scholars and students of American politics understand Donald Trump's presidency? We argue, first and foremost, that to understand Donald Trump, you need to understand the American presidency and its development through time. The presidency is a national institution that shares power with Congress and the Supreme Court. Congress has 535 voting members; the Supreme Court has 9. We should not conflate these complex organizations with the imperatives and motivations of its individual members. Rather, collectively, they form an institution that takes on a life of its own, is subject to its own set of rules, and exists independently of the persons and personalities who occupy it.

Nevertheless, we are especially prone to conflate the presidency, the most personal office, with the president. It was once common for scholars to peer into the minds of presidents to try and understand their true "character"—how their personality and orientation to power shaped their performance in office.[8] Several political scientists and psychiatrists have placed Trump on the couch, probing the psychological roots of his rage. As Leonard Glass, a professor of psychiatry at Harvard Medical School, anguished, "[Trump] acts like he's impervious, 'a very stable genius,' but we know he is rageful, grandiose, vengeful, impulsive, devoid of empathy, boastful, inciting of violence and thin-skinned. At times it seems as if he cannot control himself or his hateful speech. We need to wonder if these are the precursors of a major deterioration in his character defenses."[9]

Diagnoses of Trump's psychological needs and disorders make for titillating reads. But probing Trump's psyche, as fascinating as that may be, will not provide a comprehensive understanding of the enduring effect of his presidency on American political life. Of course, presidential character is important. After all, it was a deliberate institutional choice to make the presidency a unitary office. The decision regarding whether to make the executive plural or singular was the first issue to rouse the delegates at the Constitutional Convention and one of the most contentious issues that roiled the bitter contest between the Federalists and Anti-Federalists over whether the Constitution should be ratified. Fearing that a single executive would be, as Edmund Randolph of Virginia put it, the "foetus of monarchy," opponents of a strong presidency proposed instead a plural office, where a collective body, resembling a cabinet in a parliamentary system, would have had to work out disagreements before acting.[10] Nevertheless, most of the convention delegates and the defenders of the Constitution during the ratification struggle viewed a plural presidency as anathema to good governance. As Hamilton argued, "Decision, activity, secrecy, and dispatch will generally characterize the proceedings of one man in a much more eminent degree than the proceedings of any greater number; and in proportion as the number is increased, these qualities will be diminished." Hamilton also argued that plurality in the executive "tends to conceal faults and destroy responsibility," which would make it difficult for the public to hold their leaders accountable.[11]

The framers designed a unitary presidency that they believed would be more energetic and accountable than a collective body. It was always intended to be an office that might attract strong leaders who were "preeminent" in their "ability and virtue."[12] But, of course, the presidency is not just one person sitting behind the Resolute desk, exercising personal discretion. Presidents sit in the peculiar place of occupying an office that is, as Stephen Skowronek argued, "inherently hostile to inherited governing arrangements."[13] Over time, the executive office has been pivotal to major transformations of the foundational principles and institutions of American political life, with the country's most consequential presidents also playing a critical part in the development of the presidential office, embedded with powers far surpassing those envisioned at Independence Hall in 1787. Reimaging what powers and authority the presidency could wield, Theodore Roosevelt, Woodrow Wilson, and Franklin Roosevelt changed our understanding as to what the president can and should do, giving birth to the "modern presidency." The president became the center of politics and government—an executive that still depends on the constitution, but which seems altogether new.

This "modern" presidency, which was consolidated during the New Deal political order, transformed the country's collective understanding of what a president could accomplish. During Roosevelt's long tenure, the president, rather than political parties or Congress, became the principal agent of American democracy. Previous presidents had commanded their "political time"; as Skowronek argues, Thomas Jefferson, Andrew Jackson, and Abraham Lincoln were "reconstructive" presidents who were at the vanguard of regime change that redefined the social contract.[14] With the institutionalization of the modern executive, however, what was once episodic now became routine. Every president since has dwelled in FDR's shadow—or tried to out-Roosevelt, Roosevelt.[15] Presidents try to create new politics, remake their office, and transform

American government in the process. Regardless of their persona, whether liberal or conservative, presidents carry expectations for change and continuity.

Our account of the Trump administration begins from this point of departure: to understand any president, even one as distinctive as Donald Trump, you have to place their actions in an institutional context that is shaped by history. There are, of course, plenty of "as-it-happened" explanations of the former administration. Tales of palace intrigue fill the reports of seasoned Washington analysts such as Bob Woodward and Robert Costa (*Rage, Fear, Peril*),[16] Philip Rucker and Carol Leonning (*A Very Stable Genius; I Alone Can Fix It*),[17] and Maggie Haberman (*Confidence Man*).[18] These texts offer important and timely insights into the persona of the president, and their intrepid authors capture behind-the-scenes moments that supply scholars with important evidence about the state of the presidency. Newspapers and their investigative reporting are the first cut at history, but they miss the larger institutional story.

Failing to take account of the institutional and historical context of presidents leads to the false impression that the executive is but an amalgam of presidential thoughts, actions, and, now, tweets. But the presidency is much more than that. The presidency, as Jeffrey Tulis has argued, is a "layered text," which reflects major cultural and institutional changes in American history.[19] It is a complex institution, made up of various actors, many of whom may compete with the president himself for power. To understand any president, even one as iconoclastic as Donald Trump, we need to investigate how the institution of the American presidency has transformed over time: in coming to personify the entire governmental apparatus of the American state; in developing the capacity to implement major policy changes unilaterally; and in increasing its leverage over other institutions once considered largely independent, such as state and local governments, the courts, and bureaucracy. No more important development stands out as in need of further specification than how the presidency has become the fount of party responsibility—how both Democrats and Republicans have become dependent on presidential candidates and presidents to pronounce party doctrine, raise campaign funds, mobilize base supporters, and advance party programs.[20] There is hardly such a thing as a political party divorced from the popularity and performance of the sitting president. These institutional developments, we argue, are critical factors in explaining why Donald Trump was able to fundamentally influence the direction of American politics.

Journalists are not the only commentators who de-emphasize institutional developments. Trump's presidency raised significant constitutional issues and muddled the boundaries between law and lawlessness. Such actions—and two impeachments—produced extensive legal commentary that lamented how Trump revealed the striking vagueness of the legal and constitutional constraints on presidential power. As Susan Hennessey and Benjamin Wittes have argued, "The presidency itself, stripped down to its legal essence, is actually a pretty spare institution. The Constitution doesn't describe much about what a modern-day president should actually do. . . . These and countless other expectations of the modern presidency are extra-constitutional grafts onto the Constitution's bare-bones model."[21] Likewise, Bob Bauer and Jack Goldsmith suggest that the single greatest lesson to take from the Trump presidency is "how his conception of the office of the presidency and his actions in it have exposed gaps and ambiguities in the law and norms governing the office, and broader weaknesses in presidential accountability."[22]

However, Trump's exploitation of modern governing institutions is more than legal contrivance—the violation of some legal principle or the presence of loopholes in need of correcting. Legal analysis does not help explain why those laws were violated in the first place, why half the country excuses flagrant behavior, and why we are unlikely to see major reform to prevent presidential aggrandizement in the near future. Among those with institutional power and not just pens, few in Washington or the statehouses have any real incentive to stop the rising tide of presidentialism. Even though the Constitution is a historical document, placing the president's actions in legal or constitutional perspective is not the same as suggesting they are the result of a historical process and a part of an institutional logic. In almost every instance, Trump behaved the way he did not because the legal doctrine was weak or incomplete but because such power was seen as an appropriate response to the political opportunities bestowed by presidency-centered partisanship. Close all the loopholes, and there is still no countervailing political power that would have been able to stop Trump—or his successor. As such, strengthening the constitutional and legal constraints on the presidency requires that we consider how the presidency has developed into a perilous institution.

Indeed, a singular focus on legal authority belies any explanation for *why* power was exercised for the ends Trump and his Republican allies so dogmatically pursued. And an overreliance on legal reform fails to shed any light on what made Trump's presidency particularly dangerous: he and his political allies pushed the bounds of presidential power with such alacrity because previous presidents eroded the tenuous restraints on presidential power—the guardrails of constitutional government. Illegitimacy begets illegitimacy, which is not to excuse Trump or to draw a false equivalence between his and other administrations. Our account makes clear that no president has more forcefully exploited the fragile state of republican self-governance than his administration. Still, this disruptive behavior was not solely the result of the sinister motives of Trump's legal team and ambiguities in constitutional text.

The rise of executive-centered partisanship has upended constitutional norms, denigrated political parties as collective organizations, and undermined the separation and division of powers. With each drawn-out campaign for president, the public's hopes for some transcendent leader swells—a final "fix" to a government that is too corrupt, too inept, too unresponsive, and too removed from the concerns of everyday people. The person who best exploits those dashed hopes makes the best candidate; there is no room for a restrained vision of presidential leadership on the campaign trail. Once in office, what else is the president who promised to fix all that ails the nation to do than play the savior—to claim a "mandate" and carve out "new" powers because of the "unprecedented" nature of the times. Given the high stakes, the drama of Election Day does not subside to accommodate the exigencies of governing. Presidents must continue to mobilize, inspire, and rally the people. Such is the task of the current institution of the American presidency. Trump failed to live up to his own vision of transcendent presidential leadership not just because of personal flaws but because transcendent presidential leadership is defied by long-term systemic developments that discourage efforts to find common ground. Like his predecessors, Trump revealed the jarring disconnect between the institution's form and its reality—what people *expect* presidents to do and what deeply rooted dynamics compel them to do. This disjuncture reveals a crisis of legitimacy: Can—or should—any president live up to the task?

A CONSTITUTIONAL DISEASE?

Because the Constitution lacks a clear definition of what presidents are supposed to do, debates over the institution's powers go back to the beginning, embroiling even those who helped write the document in the first place.[23] The Constitution, for example, establishes the president as the commander in chief. But did this designation give George Washington the authority to ride at the head of a thirteen-thousand-man militia to put down insurrectionists in Western Pennsylvania who protested the federal government's excise tax on whiskey? Likewise, the Constitution seems to clearly place prosecutorial discretion within the executive, but did that mean that the administration of John Adams's persecution of dissident pamphleteers in pursuance of the Alien and Sedition Acts was constitutional? Even Thomas Jefferson recognized the serious constitutional questions his actions raised when, without clear constitutional authority to incorporate new territory, he spent $15 million to purchase the Louisiana Territory from the French, an act he admitted was "beyond the Constitution." It was up to the people, he argued, to censure his action if they deemed it did not serve the national interest.[24]

These debates emerged because America's constitutional framework reflects the two-part nature of the presidential office: the person, ideally an esteemed leader; and the office's formal powers, limited, albeit ambiguously, by constitutional processes and precedent. On the one hand, as Hamilton claimed, the framers thought that institutions such as the Electoral College would make it likely that the "office of the president will seldom fall to the lot of any man who is not in an eminent degree endowed with the requisite qualifications."[25] The office, Hamilton stressed, required a leader experienced in the art of "good administration"—a national leader who has risen above the "talents for low intrigue, and the little arts of popularity."[26] In fact, as they were designing the office, the framers had a clear vision for who would be the first president of the United States. It was tailor-made for a person of Washington's stature and respect. It would be foolish to simply conflate a "constitutional," or what we may also call a "legitimate," presidency with a weak presidency. The presidency was designed to be a preeminent office.

On the other hand, the framers of the Constitution recognized that "experience has taught mankind the necessity of auxiliary precautions." "Enlightened statesmen," James Madison recognized, "will not always be at the helm."[27] Although the opponents of the Constitution thought the president would be a monarch, in fact if not in form, its friends assured the public that "ambition would counteract ambition." The system of checks and balances, four-year terms, and Congress's power to impeach rogue presidents would protect the republican character of the executive office—a strong but accountable institution.

Institutions sometimes fail to produce their intended effect, and the framers of America's Constitution, ratified in 1788, are not beyond reproach. Although their design has withstood the test of time, their plans have not always played out as anticipated. Indeed, just twelve years after the forging of "a more perfect union," the Electoral College—"almost the only part of the system, of any consequence, which has escaped without severe censure," Hamilton wrote—threw the country into a constitutional crisis. The first peaceful transition of power from Adams to Jefferson—the "Revolution of 1800," as Jefferson called it—almost failed when the manner of tabulating votes, requiring each elector to cast two votes for president rather than select a party ticket, a provision enshrined in the Constitution to control the "mischiefs of faction," produced a tie between the Democratic Republicans' presidential and vice presidential candidates. This left a lame-duck Federalist Congress to decide whether Jefferson or his running mate, Aaron Burr, would assume the presidency. Only the entreaties of Hamilton, who sized up the would-be vice president as a dangerous demagogue, and his and Democratic Republicans' assurances that Jefferson would "temporize" in pursuit of his party's objectives, forestalled a coup by Federalist leaders who saw advantage in appointing Burr, a less principled and therefore a more pliable politician than the "fanatic" Jefferson. With the enactment of the Twelfth Amendment in 1804, which enabled electors to cast separate votes for president and vice president—clearing a constitutional path for the rise of a party system—presidents could no longer rise above factionalism. Effective presidents had to master the art of party leadership.

Adding to the burden of party leadership, the early years of the American republic confirmed the idea that the Constitution created an office that summoned ambitious politicians without providing clear authority to realize their desires. The constitutional executive lacks commanding authority over the purse and sword. Significantly, the president cannot declare war—the preeminent sovereign power held by monarchs and tyrants. Nor was the executive authorized to dissolve the legislature as some executives can, whereas the Congress can impeach and remove a sitting president. In fact, to do almost anything, the president must rely on other institutional actors within the system. Even Washington's squelching of the Whiskey Rebellion required securing from Supreme Court Justice James Wilson a certification that the situation was beyond the control of federal marshals and courts, and the thirteen-thousand-strong militia had to be dispatched to Washington after he requested it from state governors.[28] The textual ambiguities and institutional constraints contained throughout the Constitution collide with the political ambitions of savvy, ambitious presidents. It is this combustible mix of ambition and "auxiliary precautions" that makes grand presidential statecraft so alluring, and the failure to live up to growing expectations so destabilizing.

The presidency suffered many legitimacy crises during the first century of its existence, as legal boundaries set around the office gave way to the practical realities, first of territorial expansion and then of slavery and a devastating Civil War. Even in issuing the Emancipation Proclamation—an act "otherwise unconstitutional" but one that was "indispensable to the preservation of the constitution"—Abraham Lincoln recognized the lasting damage likely done by his extraordinary and glorious act: "Was it possible to lose the nation, and yet preserve the constitution . . . life and limb must be protected; yet often a limb must be amputated to save a life; but a life is never wisely given to save a limb."[29] The use of such a powerful metaphor amid a war that saw so many soldiers lose limbs revealed Lincoln's somber recognition that bold presidential decrees would leave an indelible mark on the presidential office.

Lincoln, of course, was not the first or the last president to disfigure the Constitution and weaken the restraints placed on presidential power—especially those most fragile and susceptible to the logic of war. "War," Madison recognized, "is in fact the true nurse of executive aggrandizement."[30] In testament to Madison's claim, the American presidency has been forged on the anvil of empire, with the hammer of violence. Throughout the nineteenth century, a sprawling frontier entangled the United States in conflicts and high-stakes diplomacy across the Western Hemisphere. Presidents John Tyler and James Polk pursued bloody military action and negotiated transcontinental borders in pursuit of America's Manifest Destiny. Both survived serious impeachment efforts for their presidential exploits in Mexico and Canada and on the land of Indigenous tribes. After the Civil War, President Ulysses S. Grant, inheriting a permanent standing army well practiced in war, fought tirelessly against Indigenous peoples, completing the nation's conquest over the American West with expulsion, exclusion, and genocide. President William McKinley—a reluctant imperialist—nevertheless set his sights on the territory of a competing Spanish empire and issued the call to "civilize and Christianize" the peoples of Cuba, the Philippines, Hawaii, and Samoa.

By the turn of the twentieth century, despite all the institutional complexity built into the American Constitution, the presidential office had grown to occupy a predominant place in the country's political order. At the peak of this imperial age, Woodrow Wilson celebrated what the president had become:

> The President can never again be the mere domestic figure he has been throughout so large a part of our history. The nation has risen to the first rank in power and resources. The other nations of the world look askance upon her, half in envy, half in fear, and wonder with a deep anxiety what she will do with her vast strength.... We can never hide our President again as a mere domestic office.... He must stand always at the front of our affairs, and the office will be as big and as influential as the man who occupies it.[31]

Wilson, the first and only academic political scientist to become president, did not just espouse academic theories of the office. He was guided by the experience of his predecessors, especially the formative tenure of Theodore Roosevelt, and contributed to the creation of the modern executive—the birthing, Tulis argues, of a "second constitutional presidency." Although Wilson, as much as we can know, hoped to keep the United States out of the Great War enveloping Europe, his presidency was dedicated to building an American state, which would not just rival the great empires of the world but also demonstrate that a nation founded in democratic principles and individualism could harness the collective spirit in service of national greatness abroad. Pushed by a long series of German submarine attacks to enter a struggle to "make the world safe for democracy," Wilson declared that it was "surely the manifest destiny of the United States to lead in the attempt to make [this mission] prevail."[32] Other early twentieth-century progressives, such as Randolph Bourne, recognized the interplay between America's new position in the global order and the emergent sense of an American "state"—one that fused civil society, government action, and executive power. "War," he discerned, "is the health of the State." War, or national emergencies interpreted as the "moral equivalent of war," elevated the presidency into a dominant and dangerous position that advocates of a modern presidency hoped would somehow transcend petty partisan politics and forge a foremost role for the national state at home and abroad.[33]

Wilson, despite waxing poetically about a "new world order," never harnessed the executive's powers to establish an enduring role for the United States in international affairs. Overestimating his strength to transcend partisan differences, he refused to include Republican senators in discussions that ended World War I and attempted to sideline them in the debate over American entry into the international organization he hoped would buttress a new world order: the League of Nations. Presidents could not yet advance treaties unilaterally—one of the clear limits on the office's powers—and Wilson left office in humiliating defeat. The election of 1920—animated by the Republican candidate Warren G. Harding's call for a "return to normalcy"—refuted Wilson's domestic and international idealism, and as time has passed, historians have come to better grips with the divisiveness Wilson's administration fomented, particularly around racial segregation, lynching, and violation of civil liberties.[34] The dream of elevating the president to a commanding position in the constitutional order would have to wait until a full-scale domestic crisis, the Great Depression, propelled Franklin D. Roosevelt to a landslide victory in 1932.

Roosevelt's unmatched tenure as president, which broke the venerable two-term limit (he was elected to a third and a fourth), did not eliminate the cultural and institutional boundaries that constrained presidential power. He was no dictator, as critics then, and now, allege. But the Great Depression and FDR's vision of presidential stewardship provided the opportunity to consolidate developments that began during the Progressive Era. Prior to 1932, only Abraham Lincoln could lay claim to such an extraordinary degree of faith that the American people placed in the office. In the midst of an economic calamity, FDR responded to the people's demand for quick, resolute action. His first hundred days in office have captured the imagination of every subsequent president-elect, and much of our modern-day vision of the potential for presidential leadership is drawn from the extraordinary power that he commanded over national politics. To combat the effects of the Great Depression, Congress delegated immense authority and administrative power to Roosevelt and placed the White House in the lead role over the direction of the country's political affairs, a position it has continued to occupy ever since. Indeed, Roosevelt's legacy was so critical to the development of the institution's current legitimacy crisis that it is fair to say that the current debate over the promise and peril of a presidential dominion can be traced back to the executive-centered construction of the New Deal order.

Many claim that Roosevelt's presidency was the beginning of the end for constitutional government: his aggressive deployment of new administrative powers and his centralization of federal responsibilities over issues as far-ranging as crop subsidies to public architecture turned the constitution "upside down," as the conservative legal scholar Michael Greve has remarked.[35] Progressive scholars, too, most notably the historian Arthur Schlesinger Jr.— once a strong defender of a powerful presidency—feared that the modern executive had become an "imperial" institution several decades after FDR laid down its course.[36] And yet, the dangers of the modern presidency did not emerge as a result of Roosevelt's or subsequent presidents' usurpation of power. The ills that plague contemporary American politics followed from a broad agreement among the Congress, the bureaucracy, and eventually the courts to expand executive power—a consensus that the president was truly the voice of the "whole people."

This constitutional and political consensus that helped give rise to American presidentialism was grounded in the view that Roosevelt's presidency, particularly his wartime leadership, matched the extraordinary domestic and international crises that dominated his long tenure. Roosevelt's inspiring rhetoric and his confident leadership in the face of the Great Depression and World War II epitomized what scholars, pundits, and most of the public believed a strong executive could achieve—how a presidency-centered democracy might meet the profound challenges of the twentieth century. One of the foremost historians of the post–World War II era, James MacGregor Burns, viewed the Roosevelt administration as the archetype for what "bold and creative national leaders" could accomplish; "democracy's most essential and priceless commodity," he exalted, was "the leadership of men who are willing to move ahead to meet emerging problems."[37]

Moved by this vision, Congress and the executive branch negotiated the development of the modern presidential office during the Great Depression and World War II with the creation of new programs, administrative agencies, and presidential institutions. Undergirding these developments was a new public philosophy. For nearly a decade, Roosevelt had curated a new social contract, but he gave clearest expression to it in his iconic State of the Union address of 1941—the Four Freedoms speech. Urging the country to give up its deeply rooted fear of centralized power, which reemerged with a vengeance in the aftermath of World War I, the president argued that America's traditional freedoms like speech and religion were inadequate to the task of safeguarding liberty. Throughout the world, democracy had fallen because of the failure to recognize two new "essential human freedoms." He argued for a refounding of the American regime and a reconstitution of its sacred creed. The time had come to pronounce a "second bill of rights"—presupposing a strong national state that could protect citizens' "freedom from want" and "freedom from fear."

Roosevelt's rights talk was neither rhetorical flourish nor wishful thinking. These charter commitments of the new American regime were accompanied by specific institutional developments—some enacted during his first two terms in response to domestic exigencies to fulfill freedom from want, which formed the foundation of the welfare state, and others that would come after he dared to break the two-term tradition as the country mobilized for war. In securing freedom from fear, Roosevelt envisioned a national security state, which would first achieve victory over fascism and then protect the rights of liberal self-determination against Soviet-supported communist regimes. These commitments, the charter of the modern American state, were subject not to partisanship but to "enlightened administration"—to the creation of an executive-centered administrative state that would supplant limited constitutional government, congressional supremacy, and a federal system that clearly demarcated state and federal responsibilities. Dwight Eisenhower, the first Republican president elected during the New Deal regime, epitomized the bipartisan legitimacy that underpinned the executive-centered administrative order. Two years after his 1952 landslide victory, he worked with the Congress to pass an expansion of Social Security, thereby rendering America's nascent welfare state more inclusive.[38] More telling of a bipartisan commitment to the fledgling national state was the creation of a national highway system, first proposed in 1944, which Eisenhower celebrated as "the biggest peacetime construction project ever undertaken by the United States or any other country."[39] Perhaps most important, against the powerful strain of isolationism in the Republican Party, Eisenhower also retained Roosevelt's and Truman's commitment to liberal internationalist institutions like NATO, the United Nations, and global financial institutions.

The expansion of the federal government in mobilizing for war and in taking charge of its new economic responsibilities privileged administration and expertise. War mobilization showed that the economy could be managed to achieve national prosperity. Wartime also revealed the folly of American retreat from world affairs and the need to establish a permanent class of diplomatic agents to guide its foreign policy. Eisenhower was no New Deal Democrat in disguise. But his administration harnessed the institutional muscle it inherited from the New Dealers and lent it legitimacy throughout the 1950s. For a time, a nation could believe that the president's interests were not *political*, subject to debate among elected officials, but *administrative*, the domain of policymakers, planners, and bureaucrats. A generation later, President John F. Kennedy best summarized this perspective, declaring: "Most of us are conditioned for many years to have a political viewpoint—Republican or Democratic—liberal, conservative, moderate. [But] most of the problems or at least many of them that we now face are *administrative problems*. They are very sophisticated judgments which do not lend themselves to the great sort of 'passionate movements' which have stirred the country so often in the past."[40]

Administrative reform was thus at the heart of the New Deal's constitutional refounding and the emergence of the modern institutional presidency. As FDR's Committee on Administrative Management—the Brownlow Committee, as it came to be called—urged, "The President Needs Help!" Under the new design the presidency was to become the "centerpiece of a liberal administrative state."[41] The development of a reconstituted presidency was hardly foreordained. The reorganization proposals aroused considerable disagreement and concern, even among Roosevelt's ardent allies in Congress. Enacted only after a bitter two-year struggle in Congress, the Executive Reorganization Act of 1939 granted the president some but not all the administrative powers that he wanted. For example, it exempted twenty-one regulatory commissions, which retained some independence from the White House. Nevertheless, Roosevelt's implementation of the reorganization act effected many of the Brownlow Committee's recommendations. It created the Executive Office of the President (EOP), which included the newly formed White House Office (the West Wing) and a strengthened and refurbished Bureau of the Budget. The administrative reform law also strengthened the chief executive's control over what was becoming a maze of departments and agencies. Because the creation of the EOP enhanced the president's capacity to manage the expanding activities of the executive branch, it hastened the development of the "administrative presidency," in which public policy is shaped on the president's behalf through executive actions, rulemaking by executive departments and agencies, and policy implementation.[42]

This initial act of "legiscide," as Theodore Lowi has referred to it, forever changed the terms by which Congress understood and debated its own powers. This is not to suggest that Congress became institutionally emasculated. Immediately following World War II, Congress sought to constrain the White House's control over the administrative state by enacting the Administrative Procedure Act of 1946, which established formal rules to govern rulemaking and review of agency decisions, granting civil servants a degree of autonomy from the president and political appointees. In the same year, Congress also passed the Legislative Reorganization Act, which increased its own capacity to oversee the modern administrative establishment—charging a revamped committee system to engage in "continuous watchfulness" of departments and agencies. Yet the increased capacity afforded to the White House atop a range of new programmatic responsibilities transformed what had been a modest office, particularly subject to the president's personal impulses, into an institution, which took on a life outside of the president's persona. Administrative reform gave the president and his partisan allies the power and the support staff to truly become the Constitution's national office capable of fulfilling the promise of security at home and abroad.

The further expansion of the welfare and national security states during the 1960s and 1970s accelerated the demise of local politics and foregrounded the nation's political conflict in Washington. As activists aroused by the civil rights movement denounced federalism as an antediluvian institution that sustained white supremacy and undermined constructive international engagement, House Speaker Tip O'Neill's famous observation that "all politics is local" lost much of its meaning. By the end of Ronald Reagan's two terms, the nationalization of partisanship had further enhanced the power of the president. Democrats and Republicans had come to depend on presidents and presidential candidates to raise funds, mobilize grassroots support, articulate the party's message, and advance party programs.[43] Consequently, the dimension of conflict that divided Democrats and Republicans during the New Deal—whether to expand or roll back the administrative state—was displaced by a struggle for its powers and resources. Liberals have sought to build administrative capacity to design and implement social welfare policies. Despite rhetorical appeals to "limited government," since the late 1960s conservatives have sought national administrative power as ardently as liberals, in the service of partisan goals such as enhancing national defense, homeland security, border protection, and local policing as well as establishing more market-oriented policies in education, climate change, and government service.

The consolidation of executive power at home and abroad raises profound questions about the fate of democracy in the United States. Is a strong administrative state compatible with an active and competent citizenry? Can the modern presidency, even with the tools of instant mass communications, function as a truly democratic institution with meaningful links to the public? These are the profound questions brought to the surface by Donald Trump's unlikely ascent to the White House.

PRESENT-DAY PATHOLOGIES AND THE TRUMP ADMINISTRATION

The current crisis confronting the American presidency has its roots in the New Deal reforms pursued by FDR and the culmination of presidency-centered government in the 1960s. During that tumultuous decade, the office Roosevelt and progressives sought to secure as the "steward of the public welfare" was pulled into the vortex of fundamental conflicts over what it means to be an American. The first challenge came from the New Left, which ramped up expectations for government and heightened the administrative responsibilities of the presidency, all while subjecting it to rampant criticism. Cynicism and distrust toward Washington were born of the social movements that vilified the liberal establishment for its compromises with corporate greed, white supremacy, and imperialistic adventurism in the developing world. This was exemplified most clearly in the tragic presidency of Lyndon Johnson, who achieved momentous reform but fell from grace amid the nation's reckoning with past and present injustices.

The cultural protests unleashed by the long civil rights movement, second-wave feminism, a nascent environmentalism, and student protests against the Vietnam War did not take place in isolation. Rather, these left-leaning social movements galvanized a reaction—a conservative counterprotest. Defenders of traditional family values and a woman's role in a two-parent household rallied around the call of the activist Phyllis Schlafly, who tied these "American" ideas to the existential struggle against communism. Barry Goldwater distributed Schlafly's book, *A Choice Not an Echo*, at rallies for his presidential campaign in 1964. Goldwater's appeal was largely confined to the South; however, the reaction to school desegregation spread across the country, particularly when desegregation was pursued through interjurisdictional busing, unleashing a tidal wave of opposition that helped galvanize the modern political movement to defend school choice and tax exemptions for religious schools. Richard Nixon began to forge a bond between evangelical Christians and the Republican Party in 1968; he promoted his personal relationship with the country's most popular preacher, Billy Graham, and promised to end the liberalization of sexual and racial mores. When Graham endorsed Nixon in 1968, telling audiences that "the very survival of the country may be at stake in this year's election," Nixon's response expressed his view that the modern presidency, built by progressive presidents and reformers, could serve conservative objectives.[44] "The days of a passive presidency belong to a simpler past," Nixon promised. "Let me be very clear about this: The next president must take an activist view of his office. He must articulate the nation's values, define its goals and marshal its will. Under a Nixon Administration, the presidency will be deeply involved in the entire sweep of America's public concerns."[45]

Nixon was the first Republican president who presumed to speak for the "silent majority"; however, the key inflection point for modern conservatives was the new Christian right's alignment with the Reagan administration and the Republican Party. The Reagan–Christian right alliance, although not without its tensions, transformed the Republicans into a decidedly right-of-center party, one that joined an attack on the liberal state with a redeployment of administrative power to fight communism abroad and support traditional values at home. As Bert Rockman has observed, "It was the Nixon presidency, particularly in the aborted second term, that became celebrated for its deployment of the [administrative presidency]," but "the Reagan Presidency intended to perfect the strategy and to do it from the beginning."[46]

The bipartisan embrace of presidentialism is a critical development in agitating the country's rancorous political conflict and growing cynicism. Polarization has periodically disrupted the American constitutional order, arousing perilous but restorative struggles over the meaning of our rights, but presidency-centered partisanship—born of the merging of executive prerogative and the battle over American identity during the 1960s—poses new challenges to the resilience of American democracy. The culture battles of the sixties for the soul of America led to the emergence of a more viscerally partisan politics, with the presidency fully implicated.

Donald Trump has both exploited and aggravated contemporary polarization. By routinizing the use of executive discretion to make good on campaign promises and placing the presidency at the vanguard of an enervating contest between activists on both sides of the ideological spectrum, the merging of executive prerogative and partisanship has raised the stakes of the conflict and aroused a winner-take-all contest. It is not just that the president cannot rise above the country's deep social divisions. The presidency foments them.

Since both conservatives and liberals fight for the power that comes with controlling a presidency-centered administrative state, presidential elections have taken on an especially divisive quality. Cue the 2020 US presidential election. The sitting president, Donald Trump, depicted the country as being in a lawless state of ruin and despair; only his reelection could "save America's soul."

Joe Biden, the Democratic contender, waged his own "battle for the soul of the nation," declaring on election night that his victory would usher in a "time to heal in America."[47] In 2024, nearly three-quarters of Americans believed the election was "vital to the future of US democracy," but they were split on who posed the greater threat.[48] Despite all their differences, of policy, temperament, and experience, Biden and Trump projected an image of American democracy with the president at the center—the lifeblood of the American state. Even after Kamala Harris succeed Joe Biden as the presidential heir apparent, she couched her campaign as a fight against "fascism." Their rhetorical excesses of "soul-saving politics" could have leaped from the pages of Woodrow Wilson, the Roosevelts, and other progressives who viewed the office as transcendent. In reality, the presidency has become a principal cause of America's "cold civil war."

OUTLINE OF THE BOOK

The rest of this book analyzes how Donald Trump's use of presidential power exacerbated the pathologies plaguing America's presidency-centered democracy. Trump, and the conservative groups that championed his cause, understood how dramatically altered the presidency had become by 2016. Echoing the entreaties of Richard Nixon, Donald Trump mobilized a conservative base—a "silent majority"—by promising a forceful and purposeful use of the American presidency in their cause. While Trump's embrace of presidential power seemed novel, it was a difference in degree, not type. Conservative presidencies, especially since that of Richard Nixon, have galvanized the foot soldiers of the Republican Party by heralding a vision of a presidency-centered state dedicated to "traditional values" and "American exceptionalism."

In chapter 1, we elaborate on the brief historical sketch we have drawn here by situating Trump's presidency in the stream of American political development. In particular, we emphasize how the fracturing of America during the 1960s was a critical juncture that unleashed the antinomian forces that gave rise to an embittered partisanship that, ironically, amplifies expectations for a unifying, transcendent leader. While the genus of presidentialism in the United States can be traced back to the Progressive Era and the reforms enacted during FDR's protracted presidency, Trump principally benefited from the mix of movement politics and administrative government that emerged from the social tumult of the 1960s and early 1970s. In this regard, Trump is not so much the heir to FDR as he is the student of Richard Nixon and his acolytes who embraced presidential power to transform the Great Society into a conservative state. Like Nixon, Trump did not wish to bring about the "deconstruction of the administrative state" so much as transform the existing programmatic commitments he inherited in service of conservative causes. Just as it is important to understand the Kennedy and Johnson administrations to make sense of Nixon's crusade, we similarly emphasize developments within American politics that took place during the George W. Bush and Obama administrations to shed light on Trump's presidency.

A general weakness of presidential studies is that scholars tend to treat presidential administrations in isolation—clear signposts of when power changes. But we believe it is necessary to draw out the similarities and differences Trump has with his immediate predecessors to explain the groundswell of populist enthusiasm he captured to secure the Republican nomination and presidency. We emphasize the growing schism within the conservative movement, which has its roots in Barry Goldwater's capture of the Republican nomination, but which took on real force as a response to the Bush administration's foreign endeavors in the Global War on Terrorism, its "compassionate" immigration programs, and its commitment to free trade. During the Obama administration these once intraparty disagreements evolved into a full-fledged movement against modern progressivism and a complicit Republican "establishment."

With that context in mind, chapter 2 takes a closer look at Trump's influence on the Republican Party, perhaps the most consequential legacy of his presidency. It begins with Trump's campaign for the Republican nomination. Few scholars or pundits anticipated that an outsider, with no government experience, would so quickly and thoroughly rout the Republican establishment. Yet the evidence is difficult to deny. The Republican Party had by that point become ripe for Trump's plucking. Drawing on survey evidence going back to 2006, years before Trump's ascendance, we document the widening gulf between Republican officeholders and party officials and a radicalized base that Trump eventually exploited.

The 2016 presidential election was just the beginning. Using the tools of the modern presidency, Trump continued his conquest of the Republican Party once in office. From day one, Trump leveraged his atavistic connection to the GOP's most reliable and passionate supporters to remake the party organization in his own image—fully interjecting himself in the electoral fate of his co-partisans and imprinting his own brand of conservatism, distinguished by protectionist trade policy and a draconian immigration program, on Republican Party politics. Even after his failure to win reelection in 2020, the Trump wing of the Republican Party remained empowered in Congress and the states.

Trump's takeover of the Republican Party would not have been possible had he only championed the causes of his base come Election Day. As we document in chapter 3, his conquest succeeded because of a relentless administrative campaign to make good on his campaign promises—even the most polarizing pledges many scholars and pundits dismissed as rhetorical flourish. He closed borders, separated migrant families, and built sections of a border wall (although Mexico never did, as he promised, pay for any of it); he weakened his predecessor's namesake reform, Obamacare, and stripped federal civil rights guarantees from transsexual youth, victims of sexual assault, and children brought to the country as undocumented migrants; he saw the passage of huge tax breaks for corporations, while making it harder for so-called blue states to raise revenues for services its citizens supported; and he appointed three Supreme Court justices who shifted the balance on the court toward greater acceptance of public action that advances conservative policies in national security, protection of the homeland, policing, and civil rights.

In short, Trump was the "disrupter in chief" his bombastic campaign anticipated. He thus proved to his supporters that he was "their guy." Although previous presidents, especially Barack Obama, had sought to mobilize the base through administrative action, Trump's White House embellished the strategy. Throughout this chapter, we build on six years of research on the Trump presidency's administrative program. What distinguishes our account of Trump's relationship with the Republican Party is the close attention we pay to changes in the presidency and partisanship since the sixties that have joined executive power, social activism, and existential struggles over American identity. Our account depicts Trump's tumultuous four years in the White House as a complex interplay between top-down and bottom-up politics—the mobilization of grassroots support and partisan fury that animated the Trump administration's war on—and repurposing of—the "deep state"

The power afforded to Trump through the development of America's presidency-centered administrative state is largely responsible for the immediate policies achieved during his four years in office. Therefore, some may reasonably wonder why it matters, when so much of Trump's policy program was knocked down by the courts or was rescinded in the early months of the

Biden administration. In chapter 4, we consider the *institutional* consequences of Trump's unilateralism, which are likely to be more enduring than his policy accomplishments. Unilateralism, we show, not only mobilized the base and brought policy change but also accelerated the long-term damage to the norms and institutions of American politics and government that constrain presidentialism and sustain democratic resilience.

Our analysis highlights the Trump administration's relationship with three institutions that have been fundamentally transformed by the development of the modern presidency. We begin with Congress, where Senator Mitch McConnell and other leading Republicans were critical, if sometimes reluctant, partners in advancing Trump's programmatic and institutional initiatives. But this was not a partnership of equals. Republicans in Congress, believing their political fate was wedded to Trump's, failed to defend their traditional institutional imperatives or their long-standing party principles. This institutional alliance between the White House and Congress allowed Trump to move beyond administrative action. Trump's nearly unprecedented success in nominating judges to the federal bench significantly advanced long-standing commitments of the conservative legal movement to the unitary executive doctrine, which has sanctioned presidential efforts to control the bureaucracy. Although the judiciary restrained some of the Trump administration's most egregious excesses, it did not challenge, and in some cases embraced, the pillars of modern presidential power. Indeed, it often provided a legal road map to help guide the Trump administration toward its programmatic destination—a set of plans that will see the light of day during a second Trump administration. We close the chapter by considering the Trump presidency's influence on federalism and document how states sometimes resisted and sometimes bolstered the president's causes. The joining of executive power, social activism, and partisan conflict over the past sixty years has pulled state governments—especially governors and attorneys general—into fierce partisan struggles centered in the national capital over American identity.[49] Trump's presidency heightened intergovernmental conflict and further divided the nation, making social welfare policies more contingent on where one lived, and preempting state power when it challenged his MAGA program.

We fear that the raw factionalism of Trump's impeachments confirms that the transformation of the party system since the late 1960s has severely weakened the ability of Congress to hold the president accountable for abuses of power. The partisan fury of Trump's two impeachments was not in itself novel.

Yet, the framers of the US Constitution could not have envisioned how the fusion of presidential power and ritualized partisan combat would make the public, and its representatives, recklessly coarse to constitutional norms during Trump's impeachment proceedings and Senate trials. The damage to the guardrails of American democracy was dramatized by the refusal of Trump and his political allies to accept the verdict of the 2020 election. As he had threatened during the campaign, claiming he had to protect the integrity of the vote, the president, citing specious evidence and bizarre conspiracy theories, became the first president to obstruct a peaceful transfer of power. Indeed, the failure to hold Trump's administration accountable for either of these two episodes—especially after January 6—prompts our call to fundamentally reconsider the power and responsibility afforded to modern presidents.

In important respects, the pathologies of modern presidential politics were born of crises that expanded executive prerogatives. Chapter 5 therefore focuses on the Trump administration's response to the COVID-19 pandemic and the ways in which it systematically advanced its priorities under the cover of a severe public health and economic crisis. The Trump administration's response to the worst national crisis since the 1930s made all too clear how emergencies have encouraged presidents to pursue partisan objectives with the dubious claim that they are protecting the national interest, in the name of "We the People." While the architects of the Constitution were influenced by Lockean notions of "prerogative power," most of the framers believed these times of necessity must be rare, and ultimately subject to public judgment.[50] For the bulk of the country's history, the public's verdict on the appropriate role of the presidency has led to the rise and fall of various regimes, giving political development its cyclical rhythm. However, with the consolidation of an executive-centered administrative state during the New Deal, necessity and executive discretion have become routine.

The relationship between executive power and emergency governance is an ancient topic of political science. "Constitutional dictatorship," as Clinton Rossiter famously argued, may be endemic to republican forms of governance.[51] But Trump's response to the worst public health crisis since the "Spanish flu" ravaged the country in 1918 showed how contemporary partisan rancor, vast presidential power, and emergency governance have metastasized into a new governing pathology. Other presidents would have responded differently, perhaps with greater success in stemming the spread of the virus; other presidents might have attempted to centralize administrative power aggressively in fighting the pandemic, rather than deflecting responsibility to states and private entities. Nevertheless, Trump's actions were not irresolute; they were defined by a purposeful pursuit of partisan objectives: a denigration of bureaucratic expertise and an attack on the deep state; the politicization and racialization of federal administrative procedures to crack down on legal and undocumented immigration; a campaign of "law and order" to quell civil rights demonstrations; and a punitive form of federalism, defined by partisan attacks against "blue states."

Finally, the conclusion seeks to come to terms with cultural, political, and constitutional legacies of the Trump presidency and its aftermath. Because the Trump White House so relentlessly reshaped the administrative state, his successor, Joe Biden, had no option but to aggressively deploy vast executive power. During the campaign, Biden promised to restore civility to American politics and celebrated his ability to broker legislative compromises with Congress. However, even before public health and racial crises engulfed the nation, progressives were determined to pressure the Biden administration to use executive power aggressively in the pursuit of progressive objectives. Arguing that Trump had set important new precedents in using administrative power, approved by the courts, that justified bold unilateral action to advance progressive causes in matters such as climate change, they urged the Biden administration to fight fire with fire.

Although Biden's leadership style differs starkly from Trump's, he struggled to escape from the political and institutional forces that sustain executive-centered partisanship and have embroiled the country in polarizing battles over public health measures and expansions to the American welfare state. Biden undid much of Trump's most provocative agenda and refused to engage in the same bare-knuckle political brawls that the former president relished. He embraced the ideal of a multiracial America, firmly rejecting right-wing nationalism. But rescinding Trump's executive orders could not restore the norms and institutions of liberal democracy. The displacement of party politics by executive administration has made both parties ever reliant on partisan administration to fulfill their collective goals. In ceding greater authority to the White House, partisan rancor has not subsided, trust in governmental expertise has not returned, and faith in constitutional restraints, once heralded by conservative politicians, has been severely tested.

Curing the sickness of the Republic will not be easy. The spread of illegitimate rule is pervasive; it certainly goes beyond the persona that is Trump. While largely moot after Trump's reelection, our analysis casts deep skepticism on the idea that holding Trump accountable through the Justice Department and the courts would have buttressed the foundation of American constitutional government. A speedier trial or more resolute investigator would have done little to address the root causes of the issues we identify. Indeed, we may have avoided a constitutional catastrophe: What would it mean to inaugurate an imprisoned former president who captured the popular and Electoral College vote in a national election? Restoring the executive office's legitimacy will require political leaders and the American public to rethink what we expect and desire from the presidency—whoever occupies the office. At a time when Americans make ever more demands on government and trust it less, it remains very uncertain that any president may come to this realization and help lead a movement to reform America's presidency-centered democracy. The start of any such an effort requires, as we attempt in this book, grappling with the question of whether the American people can expect so much of executive power and still claim to be engaged in anything resembling self-government.

1. The Modern Presidency and Executive-Centered Partisanship

We have diagnosed the malignancy that enabled the rise of Donald Trump to the White House as executive-centered partisanship. But what is new about presidents or parties?

The United States has had a presidency since the ratification of the US Constitution in 1788 and the unanimous election of George Washington in 1789. Soon after, the tradition of ritualized, organized partisan opposition began. However, while partisan competition is unavoidable, executive-centered partisanship is an emergent phenomenon, sitting at the crosscurrents of two related phenomena in American political development. The first development is a consequence of organizational and electoral reforms that weakened the decentralized, patronage-based parties that dominated most of the nineteenth century. This allowed Trump to capture the Republican nomination without having any loyalties to the Republican Party. This would have been impossible in an earlier period of party organization, but throughout the twentieth century, both parties were pressured by insurgent movements to alter the rules governing their presidential nomination process—ostensibly to give more power to "the people" in selecting candidates for office and in determining party priorities. As Trump dramatically demonstrates, however, the pursuit of "participatory democracy," culminating with the enactment of the McGovern-Fraser reforms in the late 1960s and early 1970s, did not empower the median voter. Rather, the weakening of traditional party organizations enhanced the influence of donors, interest groups, and social activists who scorned the pragmatic politics and compromises hitherto credited with forging majority coalitions.[1]

The effect of those reforms has been enhanced by a second development: the creation of a presidential institution, formed in pursuance of the Executive Reorganization Act of 1939, and the development of an administrative state during Franklin Roosevelt's protracted presidency. With the Executive Office of the President, consisting of the White House Office (the West Wing) and important staff agencies like the Office of Management and Budget (OMB), the president could form alliances with activists and outside groups who disdained the party "establishment," thereby subordinating decentralized and pluralistic party coalitions to the more national and programmatic networks that shape contemporary partisan politics.

THE MODERN PRESIDENCY AND THE ASSAULT ON POLITICAL PARTIES

The empowerment of the modern presidency alongside a weakened, more "democratic" party system allowed Trump to seize power and wield authority in direct contradiction of the goals and expectations of a constitutional presidency. As noted in the introduction, many of the most important characteristics of the executive date from the Constitutional Convention and the earliest days of the Republic. During the nineteenth century, too, significant presidential patterns and practices took shape. What marked the twentieth-century transformation of the executive was the emergence of the president, rather than Congress or political parties, as the leading instrument of popular rule. Acting on the modern concept of presidential power, Theodore Roosevelt and Woodrow Wilson inaugurated the practices that strengthened the president as a popular leader, closely associated with the rise of rhetorical leadership. Roosevelt and Wilson also took the first steps to construct an administrative presidency, which gave the president more control over the executive departments and agencies and more power to carry out policies with formal congressional authorization.[2] It then fell to Franklin Roosevelt to consolidate or institutionalize the changes in the executive office that were initiated during the Progressive Era by establishing rhetoric and administration as the pillars of a reconstituted presidency. After Roosevelt's long tenure, this new understanding of executive responsibilities led even conservative Republican presidents to wield the powers of the office in the manner of their liberal forebears.

Redefining Liberalism and Presidential Power: The New Deal

The consolidation of the modern executive presupposed a departure from traditional constitutional principles and institutions. The relationship between the presidency and the American party system has always been difficult. The architects of the Constitution established a nonpartisan president who, with the support of the judiciary, was intended to play the leading institutional role in checking and controlling the "violence of faction" that the framers feared would rend the fabric of representative democracy. Even after the presidency became a more partisan office in the early nineteenth century, its authority continued to depend on the ability to transcend party politics. The president is nominated by the party, but unlike the British prime minister, the president is not elected by it.

The inherent tension between the presidency and the party system reached a critical point during the 1930s. The twofold emergencies of economic depression and the rise of authoritarian regimes across Europe raised profound questions about the adequacy of America's traditional natural rights liberalism of John Locke and the framers, which emphasized the need to limit constitutionally the scope of the national government's responsibilities. As an alternative, the New Deal presupposed a modern liberalism that became the guiding public philosophy of the modern American era, entailing a fundamental reappraisal of the concept of rights. As Roosevelt first indicated in a 1932 campaign speech at the Commonwealth Club in San Francisco, effective political reform would require, at a minimum, the development of "an economic declaration of rights, an economic constitutional order," grounded in a commitment to guarantee a decent level of economic well-being for the American people. Although equality of opportunity had traditionally been promoted by limited government interference in society, Roosevelt argued, recent economic and social changes, such as the closing of the frontiers and the growth of industrial combinations, demanded that America now recognize "the new terms of the old social contract."[3]

Pronouncing a new doctrine does not begin change on its own. Establishing a new constitutional order requires a reordering of the political process—a remaking of political institutions that change the incentives and logic of American politics. The forging of a new liberalism presupposed that the traditional patterns of American politics, characterized by constitutional mechanisms that impeded collective action, would have to give way to a more centralized and administrative government. The traditional party system forged during the first three decades of the nineteenth century was marked by muted competition between localized, patronage-based organizations that buttressed the decentralizing institutions of American government: Congress, states, and localities. These parties provided presidents with a stable basis of popular support and during political upheavals the opportunity to pursue transformative change; however, by the end of the nineteenth century, as Stephen Skowronek has argued, "the tenacity of this highly mobilized, highly competitive, and locally oriented democracy" thwarted attempts to construct a national state on American soil, even in the face of the disruption caused by the Industrial Revolution, massive demographic shifts, and the growing importance of world affairs.[4] The Great Depression and President Hoover's unalterable commitment to preserve the traditions and practices of the old order in the face of mass suffering served only to discredit them. As Roosevelt put it, "The day of enlightened administration has come."[5] In Roosevelt's view, the party system, which was poorly organized for the daunting challenges of twentieth-century America, would have to be transformed into a national, executive-oriented system organized on the basis of public issues.

In this understanding, Roosevelt was no doubt influenced by the thought and practices of Woodrow Wilson. The reform of parties, Wilson believed, depended on extending the influence of the presidency. The limits on partisanship inherent in American constitutional government notwithstanding, the president represented the party's "vital link of connection" with the nation: "He can dominate his party by being spokesman for the real sentiment and purpose of the country, by giving the country at once the information and statements of policy which will enable it to form its judgments alike of parties and men."[6] Wilson's words spoke louder than his actions; like all presidents after 1800, he reconciled himself to the strong fissures within his party,[7] especially the Democratic Party's intransigent positions on racial inequality.[8] Roosevelt, however, was less willing to work through existing partisan channels; more important, the New Deal represented a more fundamental departure than did Wilsonian progressivism from traditional Democratic policies of individual autonomy, limited government, and states' rights.

Franklin Roosevelt's relationship to the Democratic Party was more attuned to the partisanship of his cousin Theodore Roosevelt. Imagining a reconstituted executive as the "steward of the public welfare," TR emphasized national administration and indifference, if not hostility, to party politics. As one of FDR's aides, Ernest Cuneo put it, "FDR ran against only one opponent his whole life—Teddy Roosevelt, his relative." He admired his cousin's New Nationalism, formulated in the aftermath of his presidency when he led an insurgent movement as the candidate of the Progressive Party campaign of 1912; his attack on the Republican Party; his iconoclastic defense of autonomous executive power; and his commitment to building a strong national state, which Wilson's New Freedom made impractical.[9]

While president-elect, FDR began preparations to modify the partisan practices of previous administrations. For example, convinced that Wilson's adherence to traditional partisan politics in staffing the federal government was too dependent on placating partisan loyalties, Roosevelt expressed to Attorney General Homer Cummings his desire to proceed along somewhat different lines, with a view, according to Cummings's diary, "to building up a national organization rather than allowing patronage to be used merely to build Senatorial and Congressional machines."[10] Roosevelt followed traditional patronage practices during his first term, allowing the chair of the Democratic National Committee (DNC), James Farley, to coordinate appointments in response to local party organizations and Democratic senators. The far-flung organization of the Democratic Party contributed to Roosevelt's success in pursuing programmatic reforms—providing him campaign resources, structuring the incentives of other powerful leaders, and imposing discipline on elected representatives. However, the strong but fragile relationship between the president and the party "establishment" during his first term would be severely tested after his triumphant reelection campaign. Roosevelt won every state except Maine and Vermont and captured over 60 percent of all votes cast, to that point the greatest popular vote landslide in American history. Democrats in the House strengthened their already-historic supermajority over Republicans, 334 to 88, and the Democratic coalition in the Senate maintained its filibuster-proof majority, 74 to 22—the most lopsided Senate since immediately after the Civil War.

Yet those Democratic congressmen and senators did not set off for Washington in 1937 eager to rubber-stamp FDR's grand designs. While the 1936 elections are properly understood as a "realigning" force in American politics—one of those rare moments when a majority of American voters supported a president and his party to move the nation in a new direction—the Seventh-Fifth Congress challenged Roosevelt's stewardship of the country in ways that would have been unthinkable during the president's first four years in office.[11] The political and programmatic achievements of Roosevelt's first term had begun to transform the Democratic Party, hitherto an uneasy coalition of Southern conservatives and Northeastern "machine" bosses dedicated to local self-government, into a national programmatic party. Yet the transition was hardly complete; it depended on a truce between the regular party organization and New Dealers that would be sorely tested and eventually broken during Roosevelt's second term.

The president's political aide Stanley High anticipated this confrontation in an article titled "Whose Party Is It?" (1937). He argued that FDR's triumphant reelection campaign was but a prelude to a forthcoming battle for control of the Democratic Party. The traditional Democratic Party, High observed, had little use for the labor unions, civil rights groups and liberal intellectuals who advocated for New Deal programs. These liberal constituencies and the Brain Trust, which was forging the New Deal within the White House and newly created administrative agencies, in turn, had no particular devotion to the Democratic Party, save its use as a vehicle to advance the "President's Program." The popularity of Roosevelt and his program as well as the severity of the Depression had brought these two "factions" together, a "happy union" that held through the 1936 election. However, the union was one of convenience, and it was not likely to endure. The issue, therefore, High wrote, is "to determine whether the Democratic Party as it has always been or whether it is now to become a liberal party."[12]

After 1936, Roosevelt took extraordinary measures to strengthen the reformist faction of the Democratic Party. For example, the recommendations of Farley and other party regulars in Congress and the states were not followed as closely. Beginning in 1938 especially, as Edward Flynn, who became the DNC chair in 1940, indicated in his memoirs, "the President turned more and more frequently to the so-called New Dealers," so that "many of the appointments in Washington went to men who were supporters of the President and believed in what he was trying to do, but who were not Democrats in many instances, and in all instances were not organization Democrats."[13] From a political point of view, this departure from conventional patronage practices resulted, as the distinguished scholar of public administration Paul Van Riper noted, "in the development of another kind of patronage, a sort of intellectual and ideological patronage rather than the more traditional partisan type." The decentralized party system existed for and because of the traditional spoils system, but this new form of ideological patronage would revamp the executive branch so that its personnel would support the transformation of America's liberal tradition.[14]

In addition to revamping the patronage system, Roosevelt worked to establish the White House as the vital center of party counsels. Wilson had taken care to consult with congressional party leaders in the development of his policy program, but Roosevelt relegated his party in Congress to a decidedly subordinate status. He offended legislators by his use of press conferences to announce important decisions and, unlike Wilson, eschewed the use of the party caucus in Congress. Roosevelt rejected as impractical, for example, the Wilsonian suggestion of Rep. Alfred Phillips Jr. "that those sharing the burden of responsibility of party government should regularly and often be called into caucus and that such caucuses should evolve party policies and choice of party leaders."[15]

These changes in party practices, not surprisingly, targeted the most recalcitrant wing of the Democratic Party: Southern Democrats. The Roosevelt administration acted in 1936 to abolish the Democratic National Convention rule that required support from two-thirds of the delegates for the nomination of the president and vice president. This rule had been defended in the past because it guarded the most loyal Democratic region—the South—against the imposition of an unwanted ticket by the less habitually Democratic North, East, and West.[16] To eliminate the rule, therefore, would weaken the influence of Southern Democrats (whom Thomas Stokes, a liberal journalist, described as "the ball and chain which hobbled the Party's forward march") and facilitate the adoption of a national reform program.[17] "The abolition of the two-thirds rule will enable the Northern and Western Democrats to control the Party, nominate its candidates and write its platform," lamented Senator Josiah Bailey of North Carolina soon after the 1936 Democratic convention. "All of this will come out in 1940."[18]

The most dramatic aspect of Roosevelt's attempt to remake the Democratic Party was his twelve-state effort, involving one gubernatorial and several congressional primary campaigns—most from Southern or border states—to unseat conservative Democrats in 1938. Such intervention was not unprecedented; William Taft and Woodrow Wilson had made limited efforts to remove recalcitrant nominees from their parties. But Roosevelt's campaign took place on a scale that had never before been seen and, unlike previous efforts, made no attempt to work through the regular party organization. Roosevelt's purge campaign, Farley charged, violated "a cardinal political creed" of American politics "that the President keep out of local matters."[19] The president's action was viewed as such a shocking departure from the norm that the press labeled it the *purge*, a term associated with Adolf Hitler's attempt to weed out dissension from Germany's National Socialist Party and Joseph Stalin's elimination of disloyal members from the Soviet Communist Party.[20] Roosevelt's "purge" was a far more benign form of despotism, and yet the "campaign for liberalism," as he called it, was a jarring departure from the traditions of party politics in the United States.

After the 1938 purge campaign, the columnist Raymond Clapper noted that "no President ever has gone as far as Mr. Roosevelt in striving to stamp his policies upon his party."[21] For a time, Roosevelt was hopeful that his efforts would not isolate the Southern wing of the party but instead bring them into a liberalized Democratic coalition. Claiming Warm Springs, Georgia, as his second home and showing reluctance to intervene in race relations, Roosevelt and his New Deal programs were very popular throughout the South—none more admired than the Tennessee Valley Authority, which brought electricity to thousands in one of the most impoverished regions of the country. Roosevelt believed that conservative democracy in that section of the country was not really an economic conservatism; rather, it was firmly established in reaction to the Populist movement at the end of the nineteenth century by the exploitation of racial issues. The president's silence on antilynching legislation and his emphasis on building an *economic* constitutional order that improved the material well-being of most whites and Blacks represented his hope that the South could be allied to a new liberal coalition.[22]

Most of Roosevelt's anointed candidates were defeated, and his hope that the South could be reconstructed on the basis of a national program of economic reform was disappointed. In the dozen states in which the president acted against entrenched incumbents, he was successful in only two—Oregon and New York.[23] Anticipating the massive realignment of Southern politics that would occur in the aftermath of the expansion of the liberal state during the 1960s and 1970s, Roosevelt lost all the battles he fought in the Southern and border states. Nevertheless, this unprecedented presidential effort to remake his party clarified the factional disputes in the Democratic Party and set the course for its development as a national programmatic party that would expand the central government's power. Moreover, Roosevelt's assault on the regular party organization presupposed that the sheltering of New Deal liberalism required executive-centered partisanship. Going so far as to claim that he would prefer to have liberal Republicans than conservative Democrats elected to the Congress, the president's purge campaign was a dramatic testament to the ideal that, as one Roosevelt aide put it, "the President, and not either party, was now the instrument of the people as a whole."[24]

Roosevelt's ambitious partisan effort began the process of transforming the Democratic Party from a local to a national and programmatic organization. At the same time, the New Deal made party organizations less important. Roosevelt's partisan leadership ultimately was based on forging a personal link with the public that would better enable him to make use of his position as leader of the nation, not just of the party that governed the nation.[25] For example, in all but one of the 1938 primary campaigns in which he participated personally, Roosevelt chose to make a direct appeal to public opinion rather than attempt to work through, or reform, the regular party apparatus. This strategy was encouraged by earlier reforms, especially the direct primary, which had begun to weaken the grip of party organizations on the voters. Radio broadcasting also had made direct presidential appeals an enticing strategy, especially for as popular a president with as fine a radio presence as Roosevelt. After his close associate Felix Frankfurter urged him to go to the country in August 1937 to explain the issues that gave rise to the bitter Supreme Court–packing controversy, dedicated to a constitutional revolution that would sanction the New Deal redefinition of the social contract, Roosevelt, perhaps anticipating the purge campaign, responded, "You are absolutely right about the radio. I feel like saying to the country—'You will hear from me soon and often. This is not a threat but a promise.'"[26]

In the final analysis, the benevolent dictatorship that Roosevelt sought to impose on the Democratic Party was more conducive to corroding the American party system than to reforming it. His prescription for party reform—extraordinary presidential leadership—posed a serious if not intractable dilemma. On the one hand, the decentralized character of politics in the United States could be modified only by strong presidential leadership; on the other, a president determined to alter fundamentally the connection between the executive and the party eventually would shatter collective party responsibility.[27] Roosevelt felt that a full revamping of partisan politics was impractical, given the obstacles to party government that are so deeply ingrained in the American political experience. That he lost most of the purge contests could only have reinforced this view.

Moreover, Roosevelt and his New Deal allies did not view the welfare state as a partisan issue. It was a "constitutional" matter that required eliminating partisanship about the national government's obligation to protect individual men and women from the vagaries of the market and the abuses of big business. The reform program of the 1930s was conceived as a second bill of rights that New Dealers meant to establish as much as possible in permanent programs beyond the vagaries of public opinion and elections. The new rights that Roosevelt pledged the federal government to protect included "the right to a useful and remunerative job" and "the right to adequate protection from the fears of old age, sickness, accident and unemployment."[28] These new rights were never formally ratified as part of the Constitution, but they became the foundation of political dialogue, redefining the role of the national government and requiring major changes in American political institutions.

Two Pillars of a New American State: Freedom from Fear and Freedom from Want

As Theodore Lowi wrote in his classic treatment of liberalism, the New Deal led to the development of a modern welfare state and a transition from legislative to executive-centered government.[29] In the process, the Democratic Party was to be used as a means to provide presidents greater control over the welfare state so that the executive department would be freed from the "provincialism" of localized parties. Parties had once been key to the delivery of public goods in response to local and state interests. Roosevelt's redefinition of the social contract, which had long emphasized individual privacy and limited constitutional government, formed a new understanding of rights, so that the economic security of the American people became a new obligation of experts and administrators who served under the presidency. The idea of constitutional policy is embodied by the Social Security program, enacted by Congress in 1935, which was framed as a new self-evident truth that transcended partisanship—not something that could be taken away depending on which party was in office, or which faction controlled the new Social Security Administration. This feature of New Deal–style, executive-centered democracy is seen vividly in how most citizens—even in the wake of the Reagan Revolution—refer to Social Security: it is a programmatic right that, as FDR foretold, "no damn politician can scrap."[30]

Nevertheless, this displacement of partisan politics by "enlightened administration" required in the short run a major partisan effort to generate popular support for the new economic constitutional order. To a point, this made partisanship an integral part of New Deal politics, for it was necessary to remake the Democratic Party as an instrument to free the councils of government, particularly the president and bureaucracy, from the restraints of traditional party politics and constitutional understandings. As the vanguard of this effort, Roosevelt claimed extraordinary personal power to remake systematically the terms of partisan politics and government. But, as we noted in the introduction, Roosevelt's administrative reform program was dedicated to remaking American political institutions—in forging a new political order that bequeathed new powers to both Democratic and Republican presidents who styled themselves leaders of the "whole people." In the aftermath of Congress's enactment of New Deal programs, partisanship centered more on executive administration and the new beneficiaries of the law who had a direct connection to the government's largesse, to the detriment of Congress and other establishment figures who helped design and champion the law's passage in the first place.

While the defense of national administration infused reform during the Progressive Era, as Daniel Carpenter has shown, the early architects of the administrative state, celebrating expertise and "independent" regulatory commissions, emphasized "bureaucratic autonomy."[31] With the Executive Reorganization Act of 1939, Roosevelt and his political allies sought to strengthen the president's influence over the departments and agencies that sprawled during his first term, a consolidation of executive power that he insisted was necessary to secure the programmatic rights championed by the second bill of rights.

Our discussion of the New Deal administrative state in the introduction acknowledges that the consolidation of the modern executive was fiercely resisted, arousing a highly contentious, two-year battle between New Dealers and a conservative coalition of Southern Democrats and Republicans. Nevertheless, although the original legislation was compromised in important matters—most notably, the independent regulatory commissions retained some of their autonomy—the reorganization act is appropriately viewed as the organic statute of the modern presidency. It created the Executive Office of the President (EOP) and moved several existing agencies under its umbrella. In addition to the White House Office (the West Wing) and the refurbished and strengthened Bureau of the Budget, the new EOP included the National Resources Planning Board, a long-term planning agency that first proposed the idea of consecrating New Deal programs as a second bill of rights and took the lead in Roosevelt's pioneering efforts to poll test the New Deal social contract.[32] The transplanted bureau began to acquire much greater power, eventually assuming responsibility to oversee the formation of the president's domestic program. By the end of Roosevelt's tenure as president, it had grown from fewer than fifty employees to more than five hundred.

Because the creation of the EOP enhanced the president's capacity to manage the expanding activities of the executive branch, it was an "epoch making event in the history of American institutions," wrote one of its architects, Luther

Gulick, and "perhaps the most important single step in the institutionalization of the presidency."³³ Most significant, just as the purge campaign advanced the rhetorical presidency, the 1939 reforms hastened the development of the administrative presidency, in which domestic and foreign policy is shaped on the president's behalf through executive orders, personal diplomacy, rule-making by executive departments and agencies, financial oversight, and discretion in implementation.³⁴ Moreover, the refurbished EOP was adopted and enlarged by FDR's successors, Republicans and Democrats alike. For a time, the modern presidency achieved a status above party conflict; its cachet was nonpartisan leadership. Politics was now a search for pragmatic solutions to the challenging responsibilities that America had to assume, at home and abroad, in the wake of the Great Depression and World War II.³⁵

Roosevelt's commitment to executive-centered democracy was expanded and given more elaborate institutional form during World War II. His 1941 State of the Union address, stating his support for the Lend Lease Act, which for all intents and purposes ended America's neutrality in the global conflict, pronounced the four freedoms that became a charter for the New Deal. To the traditional freedoms of speech and religion, he added the "freedom from fear," to derive from "a world-wide reduction of armaments to such a point and in such a fashion that no nation will be in a position to commit an act of physical aggression against any neighbor," and the "freedom from want" (a shorthand for the second bill of rights), requiring a commitment "to economic understandings which will secure to every nation a healthy peace-time life for its inhabitants." These new freedoms justified changes that intensified the concentration of power in the national government, its administrative apparatus, and the president. By the end of his long tenure in the White House, Roosevelt and the New Deal thus brought about two, seemingly contradictory developments that continue to shape partisanship in the United States. On the one hand, Democrats became more unified around a liberal program dedicated to greater federal interventionism in domestic politics, including policies to promote ethnic and racial equality and, in the aftermath of World War II, a greater role for the United States in world affairs.³⁶ On the other hand, the programmatic and national objectives of the Democratic platform gave rise to an executive-centered administrative state, which subordinated partisanship to the political and programmatic ambitions of the White House.

From the end of World War II to the late 1960s, party politics was subordinated to a policymaking state, where partisan conflict and resolution were largely displaced by a new understanding of rights and the delivery of services associated with those rights.[37] With the expansion of executive authority to secure those rights, traditional decentralized party organizations lost influence. Gradually, the president became the depository of party responsibility, depriving leaders at the state and local levels of the power to choose candidates, whip their party's membership into line, and control the policy agenda. In the aftermath of this transformation, party organizations lost their power to moderate—or broker—elections and government action. The New Deal state was better equipped to provide domestic and international security—to uphold freedom from want and freedom from fear. At the same time, it weakened those organizations that moderated political ambition and constrained party conflict.

THE AMERICAN STATE AND DEMOCRATIC UPHEAVAL

Contemporary executive-centered partisanship is not a direct lineal descendant of the New Deal and the consolidation of presidential power; it is also a product of how the Great Society and sixties-era populism recast New Deal institutions. Contemporary partisanship combines the New Deal's embrace of presidential leadership with a widespread faith in an unfiltered national, majoritarian democracy that arose amid the populist upheavals of the 1960s. "Sixties civics," as Hugh Heclo called it, gave rise to a new, more antinomian strain of executive-centered partisanship.[38] The proliferation of social movements in the 1960s exposed the Democrats and Republicans to social activism that disrupted their coalitions and intensified the assault on party organizations.[39] Combining distrust of the government and a passion to expand its responsibilities, these activists envisaged the American state as a multicultural society whose government would actively protect the rights of women, immigrants, and African Americans, and promote a free society abroad through free trade, diplomacy, and a commitment to human rights that proscribed imperialism.

Although John F. Kennedy promised a New Frontier, his election in 1960 and his pursuit of a more expansive domestic agenda appeared to sanctify the pragmatic administration governing the welfare and national security states. As discussed in the introduction, Kennedy celebrated the displacement of party conflict and "passionate movements" by a bureaucratic state that managed "administrative problems."[40] Reifying these developments, the Harvard sociologist Daniel Bell heralded the "end of ideology."[41] But civil rights leaders, antiwar protesters, and the women's liberation movement rejected the working arrangements of the New Deal state for its egregious accommodation of racism, sexism, and corporate greed and the imperialism it pursued under the banner of protecting global freedom. Inured to America's simmering racial divisions and inequalities, neither Kennedy nor Bell foresaw the powerful social movements that would soon pressure the presidency to abandon incremental reform and throw American politics "off-center."

The assassination of Kennedy was therefore a tragic but revealing inflection point in the development of a more "democratic" state. This new vision manifested itself most fully in the social causes championed by Lyndon Johnson's Great Society. When Johnson became president, aides like Bill Moyers and Richard Goodwin urged him to listen to the aspirational voices of sixties activism. Johnson was an ambitious politician who achieved success through the pragmatic wielding of institutional power.[42] However, less than six months after taking office, he gave a commencement address, drafted by Goodwin, that, far from recommitting his administration to the technocratic, elite-dominated, corporate liberalism of his predecessors, echoed the criticisms boiling up on the left. Johnson told the graduating students:

> In your time, we have the opportunity to move not only toward the rich society and the powerful society, but upward to the Great Society. The Great Society rests on abundance and liberty for all. It demands an end to poverty and racial injustice, to which we are totally committed in our time. But that is just the beginning. The Great Society is a place where every child can find knowledge to enrich his mind and to enlarge his talents. It is a place where leisure is a welcome chance to build and reflect, not a feared cause of boredom and restlessness. It is a place where the city of man serves not only the needs of the body and the demands of commerce but the desire for beauty and the hunger for community. It is a place where man can renew contact with nature. It is a place which honors creation for its own sake and for what it adds to the understanding of the race. It is a place where men are more concerned with the quality of their goals than the quantity of their goods. But most of all, the Great Society is not a safe harbor, a resting place, a final objective, a finished work. It is a challenge constantly renewed, beckoning us toward a destiny where the meaning of our lives matches the marvelous products of our labor.[43]

The Great Society testified to Johnson's outsize ambition—his desire to tap into the radical liberal ferment of the 1960s, presupposing a departure from, rather than an embellishment of, the New Deal political order. Whereas Franklin Roosevelt and his New Deal allies had advanced reforms to bring about the day of "enlightened administration," the Great Society launched a new phase in the development of American liberalism that would imbue the national state with moral fervor. Yet in seeking to satisfy the New Left's "hunger for community," Johnson seemed to disregard how a newly empowered executive office was in tension, if not incompatible, with the New Left's reform aspirations.

This tension between executive administration and movement politics would play out most dramatically in the signature Great Society policy: the War on Poverty's community action programs (CAPs), which were codified by the Economic Opportunity Act of 1964. Johnson and political aides like Goodwin and Sargent Shriver, who headed the War on Poverty, envisioned CAPs as a new type of government agency that would respond to the New Left's pervasive condemnation of New Deal–style bureaucratic politics. In empowering local communities to develop and deliver social welfare programs, the Great Society reimagined the meaning of effective governance—it would amend the sprawling machinery of federal bureaucracy that had, as the New Left's manifesto, the Port Huron Statement, charged, "developed indifference to human affairs."[44] By creating new avenues of political participation and neighborhood advocacy, CAPs sought to reinvigorate the grassroots institutions that might strengthen the frayed connection between the people and their government—to ameliorate, in particular, the declining sense of civic responsibility and governmental efficacy that plagued impoverished homes. Community action programs were therefore to be an important intervention in addressing the "quest for community," as Robert A. Nisbet, a renowned conservative sociologist, phrased it.[45] Johnson's hope, however, was not to diminish the national state, as Nisbet prescribed, but rather to pioneer a new form of top-down, bottom-up politics that would ameliorate the torpor of the New Deal party system. Indeed, by federal law, CAPs had to be organized by a public or private nonprofit agency, *not* a political party or elected official.[46]

Community action programs thus sought broad-based participation, but in doing so the poverty programs inspired highly emotional, radical condemnation of existing institutions: attacks on the schools for failing to educate; derision of the police departments for racial biases and violence; blaming the local party machine for years of political neglect; liberation from the paternalistic welfare counselors who presumed to impose "middle-class" values on their clients. Such a response, far from being unwarranted, accurately expressed the frustration felt by many of these communities at the seeming indifference of political elites to the immense problems they faced. Schools were not performing adequately; cops were prejudiced; local social welfare officials were rigid and formulaic. What matters, however, is not only the accuracy of these claims but also the political consequences of the institutional arrangements meant to address and respond to those discontents. As Allen Matusow notes, "Community action was supposed both to elicit the cooperation of local institutions and reform them—to promote community consensus and to risk conflict. Naively, the planners hoped for a creative synthesis in which the institutions would respond positively to protest, and the protesting poor would accept the necessity of compromise. These hopes were soon blasted."[47]

Hoping to build a new progressive coalition in the vein of FDR, Johnson deployed the tools of the modern presidency in the service of the highly mobilized constituencies that became prominent during sixties uprisings: women, racial minorities, and immigrants. These constituencies were further strengthened by the antiwar movement, which imbued Great Society liberalism with a new form of globalism that promised to replace imperialist adventures like the Vietnam War with a renewed commitment to human rights. However, the attempt to realize the Great Society exposed the liberal state's central fault lines, and with violent upheaval in Vietnam and in the nation's urban core, the pragmatic center that buttressed the New Deal disintegrated.

The 1960s left many social and antiwar activists feeling alienated from the "establishment," but they remained active in government during the 1970s through "public interest" groups, dedicated to remaking rather than dismantling administrative politics. Celebrating "participatory democracy," these public lobbyists gained access to the regulatory process, opened up the courts to further litigation, and democratized congressional procedures. Consequently, programmatic liberalism was extended to new policies such as affirmative action, environmental and consumer protection, and the desegregation of schools. As Paul Pierson argues, these policies gave rise to an activist and polarized state centered on "a range of profoundly contentious issues. . . . The character of these issues made compromise difficult, and created incentives for polarizing forms of mobilization."[48]

The "new" liberals also transformed the presidential selection process, affirming E. E. Schattschneider's insight that "new policies create new politics."

Between the late 1960s and early 1970s, the old local and state party-based convention system of presidential nomination was upended by a system of direct primaries and open caucuses. The new plebiscitary system exposed the rear guard of the New Deal establishment to the insurgent campaign of South Dakota's antiwar senator George McGovern, the Democratic presidential candidate in 1972. Accepting the nomination, he stood before a convention infused with the moral fervor of the civil rights and antiwar movements and heralded a new liberal state: "It is the time for this land to become again a witness to the world for what is just and noble in human affairs. It is time to live more with faith and less with fear."[49]

Although Richard Nixon defeated McGovern in a landslide election, McGovern's vision ultimately came to fruition after decades of civil rights reform and massive demographic shifts matured into an electorally viable progressive coalition. The centrist politics of Jimmy Carter and Bill Clinton, which prevailed for a time in the wake of McGovern's electoral disaster, ultimately gave way to the election of the country's first African American president. As important as economic issues were to Barack Obama's insurgent campaign in 2008, he defeated his more establishment rivals, most notably Senator Hillary Clinton, by mobilizing what Jesse Jackson called a "rainbow coalition" of minorities and their white allies, youth, immigrants, and the LGBTQ community.

CONSERVATIVE STATE BUILDING

Given Republicans' rhetorical attack on government, it is not surprising that scholars and public commentators tend to equate conservatism and antistatism. "In this present crisis, government is not the solution to our problem," Ronald Reagan famously declaimed in his first inaugural address, "government is the problem."[50] And yet, animated by the causes of law and order and patriotism, conservatives have relied on presidential prerogative and administrative power to uphold private property, protect "middle-class" values, secure the homeland, and fight foreign threats by building up the nation's military. Moreover, rather than rolling back the government to unleash the power of the free market, conservatives have devised novel policies that subsidize private interests and inject business practices into social welfare programs. In fact, Republicans have surpassed Democrats in fusing executive prerogative and partisanship—accelerating the declining influence of party organizations that might moderate the most dangerous populist tendencies of the New Right.

With his call for a more militant conservatism during the 1964 campaign, Senator Barry Goldwater of Arizona advanced the contemporary conservative movement's rightward shift. Fellow crusaders rejected Roosevelt's new freedoms as portending a "hellish tyranny" that would destroy self-reliance at home and compromise with freedom's enemies abroad. As the Republican presidential candidate, Goldwater rejected pragmatism in apocalyptic terms: "I would remind you that extremism in the defense of liberty is no vice." "And let me remind you also," Goldwater intoned, "that moderation in the pursuit of justice is no virtue."[51]

It fell to Nixon to tie the conservative anticommunist crusade to the powers of the modern presidency. Barry Goldwater, as he enjoyed pointing out, ran as the 1964 Republican presidential candidate on FDR's 1932 policy platform of sound currency, balanced budgets, and a reduced federal payroll. Nixon would take America off the gold standard, use federal fiscal policy to impose price controls, expand the federal bureaucracy, and repurpose, not cut, federal programs.

Nixon was not a liberal in sheep's clothing. He was a strategic conservative who fulfilled his campaign promises through aggressive administrative tactics to remake inherited domestic commitments. To the surprise of many, he did not immediately dispense with LBJ's signature antipoverty program but rather reconstituted it to give business interests greater influence over the deployment of federal funds while diminishing the role of activists in urban planning. Moreover, he transformed the Bureau of the Budget into the new Office of Management and Budget, adding a cadre of presidentially appointed assistant directors of policy who stood between the OMB director and the bureau's civil servants. Consequently, the budget office became one of the presidency's most important instruments for planning new programs, administering old ones, and setting the public agenda.

Finally, Nixon strengthened the National Security Council and established a new Domestic Council to further centralize foreign and domestic policymaking in the White House. Nixon's commitment to politicizing the executive branch resulted in a doubling of the size of the White House Office, which swelled from a full-time staff of 203 under Johnson to 522 comparable employees by the end of Nixon's first term.[52] Although Nixon's efforts to further consolidate presidential power by overhauling executive departments and agencies during his second term were thwarted by a Democratic Congress and Watergate, his deployment of conservative administrators in a revamped structure that would be more responsive to the expanded White House Office paved the way for Reagan's conservative administrative presidency.[53]

Goldwater's rhetoric and Nixon's instrumentality thus laid the groundwork for a conservative state—a bastion of institutions, norms, policies, and relations that promoted a new conservative worldview. As Goldwater's nomination and campaign showed, conservative activists scorned the social welfare policies of the liberal state. Yet viewing populist insurgency as a force that could disrupt the liberal political order, conservatives sought to install policies that would mobilize support for the Republican Party. Conservative social movements developed that pressured Republican leaders to use state power in the service of their objectives. Conservativism thus evolved from an attack on the administrative state to a strategy that involved the creation of parallel organizations to *redeploy*, rather than dismantle, the levers of national power.[54]

The development of a redeployment strategy required grassroots as well as formal institutional support. Leading that charge was the "Sweetheart of the Silent Majority," as she was later anointed, Phyllis Schlafly, a crusader for government support of "traditional values."[55] Schlafly burst onto the scene in 1964 with a powerful tract denouncing Eastern establishment "kingmakers" who sought to prevent Goldwater's nomination.[56] Her book *A Choice Not an Echo* sold over three million copies that year, and Schlafly came to embody a living refutation of liberals' claim that conservative women were powerless in the Republican Party. Schlafly was a successful lawyer, prolific writer, and mother of six, who was ensconced in the halls of power.

When congressional Democrats sent the Equal Rights Amendment (ERA) to the states for ratification in 1972, Schlafly organized thousands of women in successful opposition—the first true demonstration of modern conservative social movement politics.[57] Schlafly and her newly established Eagle Forum collected donations from around the country to organize women in defense of "pro-family" government policies. She argued that the ERA would require women to register for the draft, that single-sex bathrooms would be eliminated, and that same-sex couples would be allowed to marry.[58]

The ERA was just one of many issues conservative activists viewed as evidence of America's crumbling moral order and erosion of traditional values.[59] Schlafly demonstrated the power of antiliberal movement politics and tied it to Republican electioneering. Her antifeminism and sermonizing on moral decay resonated with religious conservatives, particularly evangelical conservatives, who became the core constituency of the New Right.[60] As with the civil rights movement, the rise of a conservative countermovement has roots that extend further back than the 1960s.[61] But the sixties produced a litany of causes that galvanized conservative Christians: mandatory sex education, court rulings prohibiting school prayer, and the inclusion of controversial authors like Malcom X and Allen Ginsberg in public school reading curricula. The increased presence of gay rights advocacy and a general liberalization of sexual mores on television and film further evidenced the conservative claim that, in the words of the Moral Majority leader Jerry Falwell, "America, our beloved country, is sick" and under "concerted attack by ultraliberals."[62] Parochial school attendance increased throughout the decade, as those "in search of another country" fought to establish separate institutions outside of the federal government's new civil rights regime.[63]

In the South, white evangelical conservatives resisted the dismantling of Jim Crow, denounced the "troublemaking" of African American preachers like Martin Luther King and his followers, and established private religious schools that critics called "segregation academies" because they excluded nonwhite students. Conservative evangelical leaders suggested that private evangelical schools held special appeal to parents who wanted their children "to study under born-again teachers in a Christian environment with academic excellence."[64] Critics, by contrast, charged that many of these private institutions were formed primarily as "white-flight schools" to enable white parents to have their kids instructed apart from African American children at precisely the same time as federal and state governments mandated desegregation of public schools.[65]

Tellingly, Thomas Road Baptist Church established its Lynchburg Christian Academy only a few months after Virginia's commissioner of education ordered all public schools in 1966 to implement far-reaching integration plans. The African American clergy at Lynchburg, which was billed in the local news as "a private school for white students," protested "the use of the word 'Christian' in the title of a school that excludes Negroes and other non-white people."[66] Proponents of racial justice and school desegregation pressed the federal government to challenge and sanction this proliferation of segregation academies. Christian school officials responded that they were not trying to thwart racial desegregation; instead, they explained, they were resisting government efforts to regulate licensure, hiring practices, admissions, and curriculum standards that they considered intrusive. During the 1970s, the Internal Revenue Service (IRS) regulations governing tax-exempt status for private schools became the focal point of this conflict.[67]

The rise of conservative social activism was thus directly associated with the strong cultural reaction to sixties liberalism, yet the different strains of the religious right eventually found common purpose in fighting for the "rights of the unborn." A year after Schlafly's anti-ERA crusade began, the Supreme Court ruled in *Roe v. Wade* that the US Constitution guaranteed women the right to an abortion through the second trimester. The case unleashed a firestorm of protest, and conservatives who had taken notice of the ERA fight turned to similar tactics.[68] *Roe* proved to conservative leaders how important it was to transform American political institutions, and their eyes fixated on the presidency as the wellspring of institutional reform. Tolerating the onslaught of changes was a moral crime, and politics offered a venue for the country's redemption. Evangelicals joined with other causes such as the antitax crusades in the West, hawkish neoconservative intellectuals in the East, and Schlafly's Eagle Forum to establish the New Right movement in American politics.

In response to the mobilization of Christian conservatives, President Nixon spied an opportunity to make partisan use of a reconstituted executive office. The modern presidency, he believed, could harness the energy of conservative activists to strengthen the party's collective position. Stoking fears that America's role in the world was declining, Nixon sounded the trumpet of patriotism to arouse support for his Vietnam policy. The Vietnam War crippled Lyndon Johnson's presidency and the support of his most progressive allies, yet Nixon believed that the war provided an opportunity to remake the modern presidency, forged by liberal presidents, into the leading edge of a revitalized conservatism. Ten months after becoming president, Nixon sat behind the resolute desk to announce a new policy in the war—a plan to ensure "peace with honor," but one with indefinite timetables and a recommittal of American resolve. At the end of the address, after giving token acknowledgment to the students and antiwar demonstrators—the idealists—the president stared straight into the camera and called out to those who did not join the growing antiwar demonstrations: "If a vocal minority, however fervent its cause, prevails over reason and the will of the majority, this Nation has no future as a free society.... And so tonight—to you, the great silent majority of my fellow Americans—I ask for your support."[69]

Just as communism posed an international threat to America's freedom, so the failure of public officials to keep the streets safe prepared the way for tyranny at home. To conservatives, urban crime and rioting during the "long hot summers" of the 1960s demonstrated the false promise of government assistance and a loss of faith in the rule of law. "Security from domestic violence, no less than from foreign aggression," Goldwater warned, "is the most elementary and fundamental purpose of any government," a condition of citizens' loyalty.[70] Goldwater thus preached the gospel of law and order that would become a rallying cry for conservatives' redeployment of state power. As with foreign policy, it was Nixon, not Goldwater, who sutured the promise of law and order to state power. Goldwater viewed domestic unrest as a disease of heightened expectations; the welfare state denigrated the human spirit and created a legacy of government dependence inimical to free society. In contrast, Nixon prescribed conservative management of social welfare policy: "The next President must unite America . . . and bring its people together once again in peace and mutual respect. . . . This requires leadership that believes in law, and has the courage to enforce it."[71] Nixon, the first president who presumed to speak for the "silent majority" while staying the course in Vietnam, summoned both Democrats and Republicans to join him in restoring the balance between the "peace forces" and the "criminal forces" in the country. Speaking before the 1968 Republican convention in Miami, Florida, he told the nation:

> Let those who have the responsibility to enforce our laws and our judges who have the responsibility to interpret them be dedicated to the great principles of civil rights. But let them also recognize that the first civil right of every American is to be free from domestic violence, and that right must be guaranteed in this country.[72]

Nixon's pledge to restore law and order not only implicated the politics of race but also was a direct attack on what many in the New Right perceived to be a radical judiciary, more committed to a liberal agenda than to convicting criminals. Throughout the 1960s, the federal courts had gradually expanded the rights of criminals and transformed local police department procedures. At the start of the decade, the Supreme Court, led by Chief Justice Earl Warren, ruled in favor of Dollree Mapp, whose home police raided in search of a fugitive. There police discovered certain "lewd and lascivious books, pictures, and photographs." Rather than ruling on whether such materials were obscene or whether they were protected on First Amendment grounds, the Court ruled that any evidence gathered without a specific warrant was inadmissible in court.[73] In *Gideon v. Wainwright* (1963), the Court ruled that Florida, and all states thereafter, must provide public defenders to those accused of capital cases.[74] And, most famously, in 1966, the Court mandated that it was incumbent upon police officers to make sure that criminals are aware of their rights against self-incrimination and public counsel—their Miranda rights.[75]

Conservatives drew a direct line between a judiciary stacked with appointees from Kennedy and Johnson (never mind that Warren was an Eisenhower appointee) and post–New Deal liberalism, which was weak on crime and permitted the lawlessness that preyed on the central city.[76] In May 1969, less than four months after his inauguration, Nixon had his opportunity to make good on his law-and-order pledge. The appointment of Warren Burger to serve as chief justice was an unambiguous message from the White House. As an appellate judge, Burger promoted positions on crime that paralleled Nixon's, echoing the candidate's declaration that the Warren Court had strayed too far, excusing criminals from any responsibility by neglecting the "moral basis of the criminal law."[77] In a dissenting opinion issued two months before the announcement of his appointment, Burger, in what has always been a common tactic of marginalized jurists, directly struck at the Court's Miranda decision:

> The seeming anxiety of judges to protect every accused person from every consequence of his voluntary utterances is giving rise to myriad rules, sub-rules, variations and exceptions which even the most alert and sophisticated lawyers and judges are taxed to follow. Each time judges add nuances to these "rules" we make it less likely that any police officer will be able to follow the guidelines we lay down. We are approaching the predicament of the centipede on the flypaper—each time one leg is placed to give support for relief of a leg already "stuck," another becomes captive and soon all are securely immobilized. Like the hapless centipede on the flypaper, our efforts to extricate ourselves from this self-imposed dilemma will, if we keep it up, soon have all of us immobilized. We are well on our way to forbidding any utterance of an accused to be used against him unless it is made in open court. Guilt or innocence becomes irrelevant in the criminal trial as we flounder in a morass of artificial rules poorly conceived and often impossible of application.[78]

Nixon openly celebrated Burger's insights on the "anxiety of judges" and coupled it to the larger argument for conservative presidential leadership. Ironically, Burger later would write the opinion ruling against Nixon's claim of "executive privilege," thereby requiring the president to turn over the secret White House tapes concerning the Watergate scandal, which lead to the impeachment proceedings that forced him from office. Burger, too, would oversee the Court's most contentious cases of the decade, further welding the future of conservatism to control of the White House and its powers of judicial appointment: *Roe v. Wade* (abortion rights), *Lemon v. Kurtzman* (proscribing reimbursement for parochial schools), and *Swann v. Charlotte-Mecklenburg* (constitutionality of busing). Burger thus helped to construct court majorities in opposition to the conservatives who celebrated his appointment. Yet, far from discouraging activists, these cases spurred conservatives to dedicate themselves to forming entirely new organizations such as the Federalist Society that could counter liberal hegemony in law schools and on the courts.[79]

For a time, Watergate torpedoed the burgeoning connection between the Republican presidency and the New Right. In 1980, however, the movement found its prophet. While running for president, Ronald Reagan made his conservative bona fides clear, and the GOP's platform compatible with the New Right's message: the GOP no longer was to support the ERA; the party platform added planks calling for constitutional amendments to protect "unborn children" and to appoint judges "who respect traditional family values"; and under a Reagan presidency, Christians could be guaranteed that the IRS would stop its investigation of private schools for civil rights offenses.[80] Reagan's harsh rhetoric denouncing communism for its godlessness and lack of spiritual foundation made the New Right an ardent supporter of the GOP's foreign policy in Central America and Eastern Europe. This was not mere rhetorical flourish. In a range of administrative initiatives, Reagan further welded presidential power to conservative activism—from issuing the Mexico City policy that prohibited funding for international nongovernmental organizations that provided or counseled abortions, to preempting state-level regulations on business and environmental protections, to funding a secretive campaign to support anticommunist guerrillas in Nicaragua.

The cultural conflicts spurned by the conservative counterrevolution thus embraced the political strategy of presidential management. Regulation writing, grant administration, budget planning, personnel selection, and rhetorical prowess are consequential forms of power in the modern American state. As Richard Nathan, a former Nixon aide, recognized, "Operations is policy."[81] Nixon and Reagan laid the groundwork for using presidential power in the service of movement objectives. Instead of cutting spending, the federal government increasingly relied on contractors to rapidly build up the nation's armaments, further extending the Sunbelt's reliance on America's military-industrial complex.[82] Goldwater had once proposed doing away with the New Deal edifice by automatically cutting taxes every five years, starving the beast, and fully privatizing popular agencies like the Tennessee Valley Authority. Under Nixon and Reagan, conservative policy came to embody the principle of devolution and decentralized administration.[83] Instead of grants for purposes deemed worthy in Washington, states, armed with federal waivers that encouraged a repurposing of social welfare programs, would decide how best to spend federal tax dollars. As the budgets busted, Republicans abandoned their centuries-long opposition to deficit spending and followed their president's lead in enacting supply-side tax cuts, redistributing the nation's economic largesse to the top earners in the hope of encouraging more investment (Reagan's vice president, George H. W. Bush, labeled this conservative adventure in fiscal policy "voodoo economics" during the 1980 Republican primaries).[84] Decades of congressional acquiescence or "delegation" to the executive branch abetted the president's reach in unilaterally advancing conservative policies, often through innovative administrative changes that evaded congressional control.[85]

The growth of national administrative power under Nixon, Reagan, and Bush bestowed bipartisan legitimacy on executive-centered partisanship. Put simply, liberals and conservatives fought for the soul of the New Deal state that Franklin Roosevelt anointed in his Four Freedoms address: conservatives embraced the national security state and a war on crime (freedom from fear) while liberals devoted more attention to the welfare state (freedom from want). Yet the events of September 11, 2001, and the subsequent war on terror brought the foreign and domestic executive closer than they had ever been before, blurring the line between the two. Creating a permanent condition of crisis that posed novel threats to civil liberties and the rule of law, the idea of "homeland security" became ubiquitous.[86] Republicans have accepted this state of perpetual war, and George W. Bush exploited his party's ideology and organization to extend the conservative administrative state into a preventative war against terrorist states, or the "axis of evil." Barack Obama's adoption of a "surge" strategy in Afghanistan in 2009 and use of covert drone strikes reveals a resemblance rather than a contrast with his predecessor. However, the partisan rancor over Obama's refusal to define his objectives as a war on terror and the enemy as "radical Islamic terrorism" indicates that the Democrats took a different approach to national and homeland security—an approach defined by multinational rather than unilateral action, surgical strikes rather than massive troop deployments, and diplomacy rather than brinksmanship.

In the wake of 9/11, George W. Bush built on his conservative predecessors' legacies to further enshrine the new presidency-centered orthodoxy of the GOP. With his party in control of both the House and the Senate, Bush simultaneously pursued an aggressive supply-side economics—passing the largest tax cuts in history in 2001 and 2003—and an increase in the national government's programmatic responsibilities: the expansion of Medicare in a way that attended to conservative objectives; the creation of a new governmental department, Homeland Security, which Republicans sought to make their signature commitment; and, consistent with this ambition, the launching of wars in Afghanistan and Iraq.

The Bush administration viewed the Medicare drug benefit, which cost more than $50 billion annually, as a first step in generating public support for the further diversion of Medicare services to the private sector in the future.[87] It delegated delivery of the program to competing, private insurance companies to enhance their power. The policy was designed this way to give a conservative cast to national government activism. Delegation to private actors subtly redeploys state power to recast rather than dismantle this particular social program. Bush's effort to "reform" Social Security during his second term had a similar aim. This reform, the president claimed, would yield beneficiaries a better rate of return on their contributions, but the federal government would still force people to save, restrict the investment choices they would make, and regulate the pace at which they could withdraw their money at retirement. While Congress ultimately balked at the president's proposal, Bush relied on a series of unilateral orders to strengthen state control in making decisions over abortion access, stem cell research, and LGBTQ rights. In doing so, the president capitalized on a decades-in-the-making ideological transformation in which conservatives grew comfortable with the idea of "big government" so long as it was their version of big government.

Bush's presidency-centered partisanship was reaffirmed in the 2004 election. Eschewing the "soft focus" issues that dominated Reagan's 1984 reelection campaign—"It's morning again in America"—the Bush White House made personal leadership a partisan issue. The president's strong leadership in Iraq and the war on terror, campaign strategist Matthew Dowd argued, was championed by the campaign not to elevate Bush as a commander in chief who stood above partisan conflict but, instead, to highlight the Republicans' advantage over Democrats on matters of national security.[88] John Kerry's campaign, for its part, emphasized the Democratic nominee's military service in Vietnam. The Democratic convention focused on presenting him as the candidate who displayed the "strength required of a leader in post-9–11 America."[89]

Kerry's electoral chances suffered when a group calling itself the Swift Boat Veterans for Truth sponsored a devastating television ad claiming that Kerry lied about actions in Vietnam that earned him medals. Legally, the group was a nonprofit, tax-exempt 527 organization that had no official tie to the Bush campaign, but the White House kept a deafening silence for more than a week after the assault was launched on Kerry's war record. In other ads, the group denigrated Kerry's patriotism, claiming that the Massachusetts senator, who became an outspoken critic of the Vietnam War, dishonored troops with his 1971 Senate testimony alleging American atrocities in Vietnam. The commercials reopened scars left raw by the cultural conflicts of the 1960s, serving the Bush administration's ambition to expand a Republican base dedicated to traditional values.

Republicans amplified the loyalty issue by characterizing Kerry's erratic support for the war in Iraq as "flip-flopping," which also appeared to defy his campaign's emphasis on strength of character. Like many Democrats in Congress, Kerry justified his vote for the 2002 Iraq resolution by claiming that he was merely voting to authorize the president to decide whether to go to war. Kerry maintained throughout the campaign that he would have cast the same vote even after seeing how frustrating the situation became in Iraq. After all, he said, "I believe it's the right authority for the president to have."[90] In that sense, Kerry's acceptance of executive aggrandizement was not all that different from Bush's.

The extraordinary Bush-Cheney get-out-the-vote effort infused executive-centered partisanship with innovative appeals to the party's base supporters. Rather than merely focusing on swing voters, the campaign's grassroots organization, in coordination with the Republican party committees, emphasized mobilizing "lazy Republicans" who were predisposed to vote for the GOP at all levels but who were unreliable in their voting habits.[91] The grassroots organization was extremely successful in locating, targeting, and turning out these Republicans. The focus was on Bush as a wartime leader. As Dowd put it, "People want someone they can count on in tough times, and Bush filled this paternalistic role."[92]

The 2004 election, widely regarded as a referendum on the Bush presidency, appeared to sanction his approach to homeland security and the war on terror. In fact, the White House's mobilization and expansion of the Republican base emphasized a personal connection with the president. Much grassroots organizing was run out of the Bush-Cheney campaign office, although the Republican National Committee played an important ancillary role. Campaign officials admitted that they bypassed uncooperative or incompetent state and local party organizations and created new political operations to maximize the effectiveness of their grassroots efforts.[93] The success of the grassroots effort in Ohio, which provided Bush with his margin of victory in the Electoral College, was due in large part to the "volunteers' admiration for and loyalty to George W. Bush."[94] Significantly, as Dowd acknowledged, "both parties' organizing force focused on President Bush, the Republicans in defense of his leadership; the Democrats in opposition—hostility—to it."[95]

Just as Reagan laid the philosophical and political foundation that enabled the GOP to become a solidly conservative and electorally competitive party by 1984, so did Bush help to enlarge the party's ranks of core supporters by 2004. With crucial support from the Republican organization, Bush won 51 percent of the popular vote to Kerry's 48 percent, and his party gained three seats in the House and four in the Senate. Reagan never converted his personal popularity into Republican control of Congress or a majority of states; Bush approached his second term with his party in charge of the House, the Senate, and most governorships. Indeed, the Republican Party controlled more governing institutions than at any time since the 1920s.

Beyond its immediate effectiveness in securing Bush's reelection, the Republicans' White House–inspired mobilization effort in 2004 might have provided a plausible blueprint for a revitalized party politics that could draw in more people—one that was less about whether to expand or dismantle government than about the fresh, bracing question of what objectives the government should serve. Nevertheless, the centrality of the Bush White House in policymaking, as well as in mobilizing support and framing issues in the 2004 campaign, meant that presidential politics ultimately subordinated partisan responsibility to executive primacy. As Karl Rove, the architect of Bush's political strategy, argued at the time, the executive-centered parties that have emerged since the 1980s are "of great importance in the tactical and mechanical aspects of electing a president." But they are "less important in developing a political and policy strategy for the White House." In effect, parties serve as a critical "means to the president's end."[96]

Moreover, by the end of the Bush era, the Republican Party had built a militant conservative base whose constituencies set their collective sights on the instruments of executive power. These new foot soldiers, most notably the sectarian Christian right and Tea Party conservatives, determined to redeploy rather than roll back administrative power, rallied around their belief that liberalism had so corrupted the country that the national government had responsibility to support "family values," a view that permeates proposals to restrict abortion and undermine the Supreme Court ruling on same-sex marriage; to require work for welfare; and to impose standards on secondary and elementary schools. Most relevant to the 2016 campaign and the Trump presidency, in the wake of the 9/11 attacks and the Great Recession of late 2007 to 2009, the main target of conservative activists became radical Islamic terrorism and undocumented immigration.

Democrats and Republicans thus no longer fought over whether there should be a large national government, tasked with extensive responsibilities. The struggle that had dominated the Roosevelt years had been replaced by a battle for the services flowing from national administration. Conservatives, no less than liberals, as Heclo puts it, became "policy-minded," and so they have remained. The waning of the traditional decentralized party system brought on by the merging of grassroots mobilization and executive prerogative has had the twofold effect of nationalizing policy debate and centering that debate on the ends the newly empowered national state should serve. During the 1960s and early 1970s, the locus of party politics shifted from the cities, counties, states, and Congress to the presidency. Democrats and Republicans came to depend on presidents and presidential candidates to raise funds, mobilize grassroots support, articulate the party's message, and advance party programs.[97]

THE CULMINATION OF EXECUTIVE-CENTERED PARTISANSHIP

By the early twenty-first century, the development of presidency-led, movement politics had been nearly a century in the making, preparing the ground for the election of America's first African American president. During his 2008 candidacy, Barack Obama envisaged his campaign as a progressive crusade that marked a new stage in the fusion of executive power and partisan politics.

Seeking to mute the backlash that might be aroused by the election of the first Black president, he pledged to bring Americans together and to overcome the raw partisanship that had polarized the country for nearly two decades. Yet Obama and his leading advisers also saw enormous potential in the national party politics that George W. Bush had practiced. Obama's organizational strategy, which combined Internet-based recruiting of volunteers, the use of data files to carefully target potential loyalists, and old-fashioned door-to-door canvassing, elaborated on the tactics that had worked successfully for Bush and the GOP in 2004. Just as the Bush-Cheney machine of 2004 resulted in a wide-ranging Republican victory, the Obama-Biden campaign of 2008 yielded not just a decisive triumph at the presidential level but also substantial gains in House and Senate races. This success was in large measure the result of voters' unhappiness with Bush, who had mired the country in an unpopular war and a severe financial crisis. But Obama's sophisticated grassroots campaign linked a vast network of volunteers, elicited enormous enthusiasm among potential supporters, and mobilized the highest voter turnout since 1968. A former community organizer, Obama built an innovative information age grassroots organization, Obama for America (OFA), dedicated to linking him directly with a widely scattered but potentially powerful "coalition of the ascendant," as the journalist Ronald Brownstein has aptly termed it: millennials, environmentalists, racial minorities, feminists, the LGBTQ community, and educated white professionals, especially single women.[98]

Candidate-centered campaign organizations had been a staple of American politics since the Eisenhower administration.[99] But Obama was the first president to keep his electoral machine intact as the vanguard of a movement that would free him from the constraints of the Democratic "establishment" and connect him directly to the new progressive coalition he envisioned. Hoping to reap the benefits of their party-building efforts during the election, Obama campaign officials announced in January 2009 that the new administration intended to maintain the grassroots campaign in order to press the president's agenda and lay the groundwork for his reelection. The now renamed Organizing for America (OFA) would be housed in the DNC, headed by Virginia governor Timothy Kaine, who had endorsed Obama's candidacy early in the 2008 primary fight and provided critical support for his general election campaign. Dubbed Barack Obama 2.0 by insiders, the plan called for hiring full-time organizers to mobilize the Internet-based grassroots network forged during the presidential campaign, which had generated a database of thirteen million email addresses and tens of thousands of phone bank volunteers and neighborhood coordinators.

Although some state-level Democratic officials were enthusiastic about embedding Obama's machine in the DNC because they viewed OFA as a potential grassroots arm of the party apparatus, others expressed concern that it could become a competing political force that revolved around the president's ambitions, while diminishing the needs of other Democrats.[100] Just as the 2004 Republican campaign was directed by Bush-Cheney strategists, so was the 2008 Democratic grassroots effort run out of the Obama-Biden headquarters. The architects of the Obama campaign relied almost completely on their own staff, money, and organization not only to compete in battleground states but also to make incursions into traditional Republican territory. And just as the Bush-Cheney machine relied on volunteers whose principal loyalty was to the president, so did the Obama-Biden grassroots organization rest in the volunteers' deep admiration for the Democratic standard-bearer.[101] As two liberal bloggers fretted toward the end of the 2008 campaign, "Power and money in the Democratic Party is being centralized around a key iconic figure. [Obama] is consolidating power within the party."[102]

Obama's aides, including his highly regarded campaign manager, David Plouffe, denied that Obama 2.0 was merely a permanent campaign to advance the president's fortunes. They insisted that the grassroots network's purpose was to deliver on the reform that Obama and his party had promised during the 2008 campaign. Moreover, the president's political aides assured their partisan brethren that Obama 2.0 would be a force in mobilizing support for Democratic candidates in the 2010 congressional and state races.[103] Congressional Republicans' near-unanimous resistance to the president's main initiatives during his first term—an economic stimulus package, a financial reform program, and Obama's signature accomplishment, a national health care bill—appeared to confirm the need to sustain a strong Democratic organization.

The Patient Protection and Affordable Care Act proved especially polarizing. National health care reform had been the holy grail of progressive politics since the New Deal, and Republicans, spurred by the emergence of the grassroots Tea Party movement, were determined to defeat it. When GOP recalcitrance continued despite the Obama administration's willingness to compromise on key features of his plan, most notably a public health care option that would compete with private providers, the president's politics, hitherto "ruthlessly pragmatic," took a decidedly partisan turn.[104] The final push for health care reform featured Obama in a series of campaign-style rallies in Pennsylvania, Missouri, Ohio, and Virginia, where an impassioned president repeatedly taunted Republicans for failing to take on the responsibility of expanding coverage and reducing health care costs. Beyond making public appearances at rallies and town hall meetings to whip up support for reforms among Democrats, Obama deployed OFA to pressure members of Congress into supporting the legislation. In the immediate aftermath of Obama's multistate swing, health care reform was passed into law through the unorthodox—and esoteric—budget reconciliation process, which exploited the Democrats' firm control of both chambers of Congress. Although the Republicans' unwillingness to compromise gave eloquent testimony to their partisan approach to legislating, Obama's leadership throughout the debate—and his acceptance of the use of the reconciliation process, which circumvented the filibuster rules of the Senate, to enact health care reform—revealed a partisan streak of its own. The *New York Times* concluded that "in the course of this debate, Mr. Obama has lost something. . . . Gone is the promise on which he rode to victory less than a year and a half ago—the promise of a 'postpartisan' Washington in which rationality and calm discourse replaced partisan bickering."[105] Shaped by a polarized party system, the signal legislative achievement of the president's first two years became the only major social welfare program ever to become law without a single Republican vote.

The partisan rancor generated by the fight over the health care legislation, which took place amid the stubborn persistence of high unemployment, would haunt the Democrats at the polls. In 2010, the Republicans gained sixty-three seats in the House to reclaim control of the lower chamber—the worst defeat for a president's party in an off-year election since 1938. In the Senate, the GOP added six seats, leaving Obama and the Democrats with a slim majority of fifty-one seats. And yet, this shellacking did not discourage Obama from seeking to build what he termed a "new foundation for American politics."[106] The White House began to prepare OFA, which was active in both the health care fight and the 2010 campaigns, to mount a strong ground game to reelect the president. Moreover, after Obama and congressional Republicans reached an impasse on fiscal policy that almost brought the government into default, the White House launched the We Can't Wait campaign, dedicated to advancing policies that the president and his progressive allies supported through unilateral executive action.

Most of these initiatives were designed to strengthen the "coalition of the ascendant." During the final two years of his first term, Obama took measures that authorized the Environmental Protection Agency to implement greenhouse gas regulations that were stalled in the Senate; issued waivers that released states from many of the requirements of No Child Left Behind, which Congress had failed to reauthorize, only to bind them to the administration's own education policies; and bypassed the usual confirmation process to make four recess appointments that Senate Republicans had been filibustering.[107] Finally, confirming the adage that policy makes politics, Obama announced in June 2012 the Deferred Action for Childhood Arrivals (DACA)—an executive initiative that granted relief to an entire category of young immigrants, as many as 1.7 million people, who would otherwise have been subject to deportation. Obama thus elided Republican opposition to the Dream Act, the administration's bill designed to provide a conditional pathway to citizenship for immigrants who were brought to America illegally as children. This measure not only contributed to the president's successful reelection campaign, which saw Hispanics support him by an overwhelming margin, but also, given the importance of the Latino vote to the future of American politics, might have contributed significantly to the development of a new Democratic majority, albeit one that appeared to be a presidential, rather than a party-wide, coalition.[108]

Although the president paid dearly in the coin of public opinion for the partisan nature of the battle over health care reform and the We Can't Wait campaign, his grassroots organization outperformed that of his opponent, former Massachusetts governor Mitt Romney, in the 2012 presidential election, providing the edge in a bitterly contested campaign. Working hand in glove with the Democratic Party and liberal advocacy groups, "Obama's Family" evolved into a "well-oiled machine."[109] As one volunteer put it, "There were differences between 2008 and 2012. Everyone was excited in 2008; in 2012 people may have been less passionate, but they worked just as hard. It was more businesslike this time. It wasn't just a bunch of excited people on a major quest to make history. This time it was more about: 'This is important and we're going to do it whatever it takes.'"[110] That sense of mission would continue into Obama's second term. Soon after the election, OFA was recast for a third time as Organizing for Action, which was established as a nonprofit social welfare organization that would mobilize grassroots support for the progressive causes championed by Obama and his coalition: implementation of the Patient Protection and Affordable Care Act, immigration reform, climate change legislation, the advance of LGBTQ rights, and gun control. He promised his followers that removing his organization from the Democratic National Committee would strengthen its potential as a grassroots advocacy group.[111] Such a move also advanced an *executive-centered* Democratic Party.

Like Republican presidents Ronald Reagan and George W. Bush, Obama's commitment to partisan administration revealed that modern presidents can circumvent partisan gridlock by exploiting executive power for partisan purposes. Taking a longer historical view, however, Obama's special relationship with OFA marked a new stage in the century-long development of presidential partisanship. Organizing for America was a pioneering organization that held the possibility of a new party system that joined executive prerogative, street-level politics, and collective responsibility. At the same time, the very effectiveness of this personal organization, combining a fiercely devoted activist core with a technically sophisticated campaign organization, had sometimes presented the illusion that the president could campaign and govern independently of Congress, the bureaucracy, and the regular party organization.

Even some of OFA's most sympathetic allies feared that its commitment to transformative change had been subordinated, if not extinguished, by its personal loyalty to the president. As Joe Szakos, the founder and executive director of Virginia Organizing, the leading progressive grassroots group in a key battleground state, explained, "Obama's *family*, for all its strengths, was not well equipped to orchestrate the building of a reform coalition. OFA could not be a reliable leader, or even partner, of such a coalition" because "the hierarchy of the group and the fact that they are fundamentally about advancing the president's agenda make it very difficult to establish a close, enduring, working relationship with it."[112]

Progressive advocacy groups viewed OFA as an unreliable but potentially powerful ally; Democratic officeholders, although they cheered its policy advocacy, tended to be jealous of its familial relationship with the White House. The uneasy relationship between the White House and Democratic legislators underscored a long-held contention on Capitol Hill that Obama's political operation functioned purely for the president's benefit and not for his party's, an indictment that became especially bitter after the Democrats lost control of the Senate in the 2014 midterm campaign. Obama allies retorted that the president had shared with the Senate campaigns part of his massive lists of volunteer data and supporters' email addresses, considered by his advisers to be sacred documents. But as had been clear throughout the Obama presidency,

OFA's personal allegiance to Obama was not portable, and the president's battle cry during the 2014 campaign—that he was not on the midterm ballot, but his policies were—did little to extend his personal organization's loyalty to the Democratic Party.[113] Obama thus presided over a greater loss of congressional seats for his party than any two-term president since World War II.[114]

Just as the 2010 elections encouraged Obama to pursue Democratic causes unilaterally, so did the 2014 midterm, which placed the president in opposition to a hostile Republican House and Senate and further encouraged him and his grassroots political machine to emphasize the administrative presidency. Indeed, soon after the election, Obama announced an expansion of the deportation relief he provided in the Dreamers initiative, extending protection to an additional 4.3 million unauthorized immigrants.[115] Concurrently, OFA roused its members to support the White House initiative and, more generally, to shift their focus almost exclusively to administrative politics. As OFA's executive director Sara El-Amin wrote in an email of December 12, 2014, "The last month has been a [big deal] for those of us who want to see meaningful action to fix our broken immigration system. But it came towards the end of a frustrating year. House leaders had more than 500 days to hold one simple vote on bipartisan, comprehensive reform, and they failed to act, making it clear that they were just running out the clock on this Congress. That's why President Obama refused to wait any longer." The frustrations Obama and OFA experienced owed in large part to the fiercely divided polity that confronted them. But their response to this bitter factionalism—the celebration of partisan presidential unilateral action—raised the fundamental question of whether the executive of a vast administrative state, even with the tools of instant communication and social media, can truly function as a democratic institution with meaningful links to the public.[116]

THE PERILS OF EXECUTIVE-CENTERED PARTISANSHIP

Although concerns about the president's outsize influence on the course of American politics had drawn the attention of scholars and some elected officials for decades, the election of Donald Trump raised the old alarm to a previously unheard level. As we will detail in the ensuing chapters, Trump's remarkable and odds-defying ascendance to the presidency in 2016 appeared to complete the fusion of centralized administration and partisanship. Although Obama and Trump could not have been more different in their underlying political philosophies and policy objectives, the style of politics they practiced nevertheless reflects two key features of contemporary executive-centered partisanship: a detachment from party organization and a vision of the White House as the vanguard of a movement. As such, while the contents of Obama's and Trump's messages were radically divergent, their presidencies further ritualized the independent and plebiscitary nature of presidential politicking. Trump never could claim an independent grassroots machine as organized or as institutionally sophisticated as Obama's. However, Trump perfected the unmediated rhetorical strategy of Obama and succeeded in galvanizing his base supporters through direct appeals over social media and more than three hundred rallies held across the United States in the primary and general campaign season. These rallies, which became a critical forum during Trump's presidency, were energizing spectacles that produced an image of the president as the leader of a movement and mobilized his supporters with the same fervor and passion as liberal activists under OFA. Obama saw himself as the leader of a new "coalition of the ascendant"; Trump and his strategists positioned him as the steward of a "coalition of restoration" composed of blue-collar, religiously devout, and nonurban whites who felt that traditional Republican politicians had forsaken their needs and demands.[117]

Indeed, as president, Trump surpassed Obama in attending to his base. From the first days in office, his efforts to mobilize support for his controversial plans to make America great gain involved unrelenting appeals to core supporters. Despite pleas among fellow Republicans to act "more presidential," Trump relished his administration's unapologetic support for, as one White House aide put it, the former businessman's most "loyal customers."[118]

The culmination of presidential partisanship did not make the president of the United States all-powerful. As Trump's provocative four years in office showed, the federal courts, the states, and Congress still resist executive aggrandizement. But there is no denying that the locus of political authority had dramatically shifted away from these institutions. Even if there were nods toward an imperial presidency from the founding, and even as periodic crises have caused the president's power to swell, the messianic fervor that now swarms around the presidential office lacks historical precedent. Jefferson, Lincoln, FDR—none were so bold to claim, as Trump did on the night the Republican Party ceded him the nomination: "I alone can fix it." And not even years of scandal, partisan bickering, or criminal investigations changed how Trump and his base celebrated presidential power; as he said on the eve of his first federal indictment while running for reelection: "I am the only one that can save this nation."[119]

Such bold, unsubstantiated rhetoric, reminiscent of Louis XIV's audacious claim to central authority—"L'E'tat, c'est moi"—was startling testimony that the checks placed on presidential power have become less reliable; the collective fate of party members has increasingly come to depend on the president's personal successes once in office; and institutional loyalties have been severely challenged, if not displaced, by partisan priorities. As both political elites and average voters have come to view the White House as indispensable to the attainment of partisan objectives, there is little desire among the president's co-partisans to reclaim power. To do so, they fear, would weaken their party in the high-stakes cultural and policy battles that roil executive-centered partisanship. By the same token, the president's partisan opponents tend to arouse the base with reflexive opposition of the White House's program. Put simply, both parties crave presidential power, while half the country hates the president.

2. Trump, the Conservative Movement, and the Grand Old Party

When Donald Trump announced his candidacy for the Republican nomination on June 16, 2015, few scholars or pundits anticipated that an outsider, with no government experience, would so quickly take over the Republican Party. But the evidence is difficult to deny. While his first run for president featured sizable opposition, Trump enjoyed the overwhelming approval of the GOP throughout his presidency. On average, 87 percent of Republicans approved of President Trump's performance in office; indeed, as figure 2.1 details, his approval rating among GOP loyalists never wavered once he was anointed the party's standard-bearer, never dipping below 78 percent. Almost as soon as he captured the White House, most of the establishment Republicans who closed ranks around the Never Trump movement either deserted the cause or were marginalized. The intellectual bulwark against Trump's "America First" conservativism, the *Weekly Standard*, closed shop—unable to sustain an offensive (or readership) against a president as popular with the GOP base as Trump proved to be.

While much of Trump's appeal can be explained by his demagogic exploitation of what many scholars and pundits call the "cold civil war"—the development of a partisan sectarianism in which Democrats and Republicans have come to view their opponents as existential threats to their way of life—Trump's conquest of the Republican Party is more than a cult of personality.[1] From the very start of his presidency, Trump set in motion a coordinated campaign to remake the Republican Party in his image. Consequently, despite Republicans' losing forty seats and control of the House during the 2018 midterm elections, the Republican National Committee (RNC) pledged its "undivided support" for the president nearly two years before Election Day—the result of an unprecedented merger between a president's reelection committee and the national party apparatus. The White House also mobilized its base supporters in a campaign to take over the state party committees. Over four years, many of Trump's most ardent critics, including Senators Bob Corker (R-TN) and Jeff Flake (R-AZ), chose not to run for reelection rather than face hostile primary challenges from the wing of their party that displayed staunch allegiance to the White House. Other former adversaries within the GOP not only softened their tone but enthusiastically promoted their partisan in chief. Senator Lindsey Graham (R-SC), who once labeled Trump the "the world's biggest jackass" and openly admonished the fact that "my party has gone batshit crazy," put a fine point on the Republican Party's new reality a year prior to the 2020 presidential election: "If we undercut the president, that's the end of his presidency and the end of our party, and we deserve to be punished if we give in now."[2]

Trump's organizational strategy was abetted by a decades-long transformation in the way the American party system works. As we discussed in chapter 1, throughout the twentieth century both parties faced pressure by insurgent movements to alter the rules governing their presidential nomination process, ostensibly to give more power to "the people" in selecting candidates for office and in determining party priorities. Party leaders were removed as guardians of national party conventions, with power shifting to "the people" in selecting candidates for office and in determining party priorities through direct primaries and open caucuses. This shift accelerated in the 1960s, propelled by civil rights and antiwar activists, culminating in the McGovern-Fraser reforms of the early 1970s.[3] Republicans, animated by conservative activists' countermobilization, quickly followed suit.

"Participatory democracy" did not empower the average, middle-of-the-road voter. Rather, the weakening of traditional party organizations enhanced the influence of donors, interest groups, and social activists who scorned the pragmatic politics and compromises hitherto credited with forging majority coalitions.[4] Gradually, the president became the repository of party responsibility, depriving leaders at the state and local levels of the power to choose candidates, whip their party's membership into line, and control the policy agenda.[5] The party, in effect, sacrificed collective responsibility to the ambition and program of the president.

Therefore, as remarkable as Trump's domination of the Republican Party might seem, his conquest fits a pattern endemic to modern presidential politics. In securing the nomination, with barely a majority of his own party's primary supporters, he instantly seized the mantle of party leader. His partisan leadership marks the apotheosis of a century-long development in American politics: the rise of an "executive-centered partisanship," with Democrats and Republicans alike relying on presidents and presidential candidates to pronounce party doctrine, raise campaign funds, campaign on behalf of their partisan brethren, mobilize grassroots support, and advance party programs.

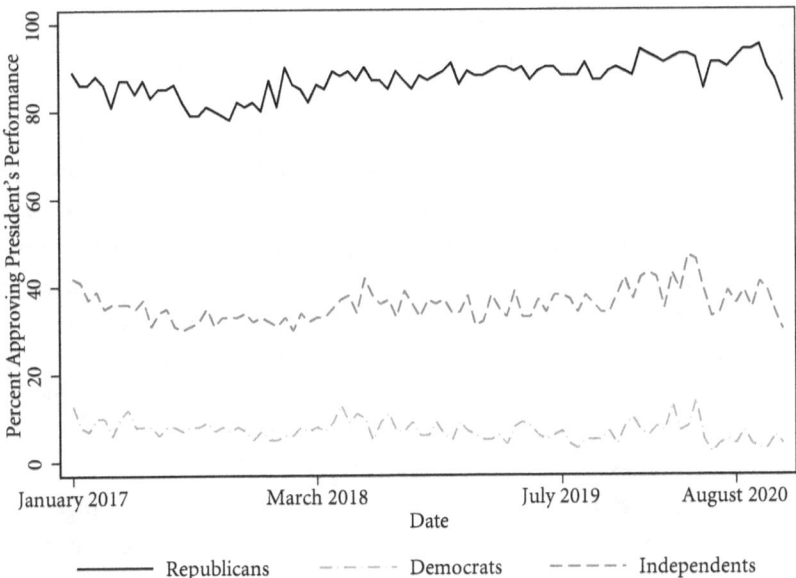

Figure 2.1. Donald Trump's approval ratings among Republicans, Democrats, and Independents from January 2017 to January 2021.
Source: Gallup. *Credit:* Created by authors.

Although his domination of the Republican Party has deep historical roots, Trump stands out from other presidents—particularly Republicans—for his administration's extraordinary effort to restructure the party organization. Trump seized the advantage given to presidents in controlling the party national committee. Whereas previous Republican presidents had seen some value in relying on the national party apparatus to build a diverse majority coalition, Trump engaged the RNC in a polarizing struggle against the "deep state." Moreover, he and his political allies methodically captured state party organizations throughout the country, even in heavily blue areas.[6] This "Trumpification" of the Republican Party was closely tied to the Trump White House's mobilization of the base. As we detail in this chapter, Trump surpassed his Republican predecessors in leveraging his atavistic connection to the GOP's most reliable and passionate supporters to advance his own political fortunes—fully interjecting himself in the electoral fate of his co-partisans and tying the success of Republican Party officials to his personal successes. His charisma was further routinized by the four-year campaign to place loyalists in positions of power in the RNC and the Republican state party organizations.

Consequently, Trump's domination of the Republican Party involved a combination of top-down and bottom-up politics—mobilizing and empowering conservative activists who had become core constituencies of the party's base.

Trump did not create the contemporary Republican Party—but he exploited divisions within the GOP that were long in the making and rallied the party's most loyal supporters who were primed for his candidacy. In truth, the current state of the Republican Party represents the joining of a conservative movement and a charismatic leader. Conservatism, of course, defies any easy definition. One scholar—and partisan—of the conservative movement describes it as an ideological association consisting of four "diverse and often factious components": libertarians, traditionalists, religious evangelicals, and neoconservatives.[7] Trump does not belong to any of these constituencies, but he has nevertheless succeeded in unifying the Republican Party. He did so by preaching a sectarian nationalism in defense of "real America." Tinged with nativist and isolationist strains, this fractured the Republican establishment and galvanized the party's historic base of white, largely evangelical voters. Just as important, he embraced causes such as trade protectionism and "traditional family values" that presupposed using, rather than deconstructing or retrenching, government power. As we detail in chapter 3, Trump's deliberate and well-executed strategy of mobilization to remake the Republican Party organization in his own image was joined to an aggressive understanding of the administrative presidency. But this forceful display of unilateralism presupposes a fragile party system, one in which institutional guardrails have eroded, allowing presidentialism to overshadow collective party goals and traditional coalition-building strategies—our focus for the remainder of this chapter.

NEVER TRUMP?

How did a political "outsider" with no experience running for elected office capture the ultimate prize in the American political system? With a lot of help, some fortunate timing, and a little luck.

Fighting for the Republican Nomination

Presidential campaigns are a complex mix of spectacle and contentious politics. An entire cottage industry exists to serve the needs of ambitious politicians who fight for the office every four years. Pollsters, insiders, fundraisers, and marketing groups vie to provide the keys to the kingdom. Although few people are as quick to take all the credit as Trump, the fight for the 2016 Republican nomination and presidency depended on a vast network of groups and individuals with extensive experience in national politics. Kellyanne Conway, the first woman to manage a successful presidential campaign, was already a long-sought-after pollster in mainstream Republican politics before she joined the Trump campaign; Conway's affinity for Trump was rooted in her deepening resentment toward the GOP establishment and its supposed indifference to blue-collar voters. Trump hired Paul Manafort as campaign chairman—a longtime Republican Party operative who had been working the ins and outs of the esoteric nominating convention bylaws since Gerald Ford was running for renomination in 1976.[8] As his deputy campaign manager, Trump tapped David Bossie, the chairman of the interest group Citizens United, whose notorious documentary *Hillary* was part of a long-standing effort to tarnish the Clinton family name, and the plaintiff in a landmark Supreme Court case that paved the way for the creation of super PAC fundraising organizations in 2013. David Urban—ranked as a "top lobbyist" for four years in a row by *The Hill*, a Washington, DC, insider publican—joined as a senior adviser. These professionals joined two of the most high-profile names affiliated with the Trump campaign—"America's Mayor," Rudy Giuliani, and Roger Stone, who worked on the campaigns of nearly every Republican presidential candidate since Nixon and had been encouraging Trump to run for president as early as 1998. Trump's campaign was no bootstrap operation.

With all this organizational capacity, we might not want to be so quick to judge the Trump campaign as an insurgent force that vanquished a unified Republican establishment—the image that Trump supporters, as well as Trump defectors, tried to paint. Although many Republicans and conservative intellectuals opposed Trump's candidacy, especially before he became the party nominee, Trump was ultimately successful because he tapped into a deep schism in the Republican Party, which was long in the making. To be sure, there was strong resistance to Trump's nomination after he had won the party's primary contests decisively. But it was not unprecedented, and the level of opposition never reached the point of a serious third-party candidacy, tantamount to Strom Thurmond's Dixiecrat opposition to the Democratic nominee, President Harry Truman in 1948 or the "independent" candidacies of George Wallace in 1968 and H. Ross Perot in 1992. Never Trumpers were vehement in their opposition to Trump. But as Robert Saldin and Steven Teles have thoroughly documented, their opposition was more about Trump's style than substance.[9] With the looming threat of a Clinton presidency, most Never Trumpers jumped back on the bandwagon during the general election—assuaged in no small part by Trump's promise to be the steward of important Republican causes, none more consequential than the list of preapproved judges he promised to appoint. The main policy dispute that lingered once Trump was ensconced in the White House pertained to national security issues, aroused by neoconservative elites like Bill Kristol who lamented Trump's neo-isolationist creed. Nevertheless, most partisans stayed true on Election Day: 88 percent of self-identified Republicans voted for Trump (in comparison to 89 percent of Democrats who voted for Clinton).

Tapping into the disaffection of the Republican base, Trump stood apart from most of the GOP "establishment" during the primary and general election campaigns, carefully cultivating an image of the outsider. Conway played an important role in maintaining enthusiasm among Trump's inner circle following her rise to campaign manager in July 2016. In Trump, she saw the chance to build a conservative movement similar to Barack Obama's progressive crusade eight years earlier. As Conway recalled telling Trump the day she started: "People believe that this election is not about you—it's about them. And when you say 'I, I, I' you sound like her: 'I'm with her,' 'Ready for Hillary.' She should just shortcut all of her slogans to say 'Me, me, me, me, me.' . . . You've built a whole movement, and people feel like they're part of it. Mr. Trump, people have stood in the rain for three hours just to say they were there when you were there."[10]

Conway's comments reveal that the campaign's overarching goal was to treat the Republican base as a movement and to anoint Trump as its long-sought-after leader. An iconoclastic businessman and reality television star, Trump exhibited a political mastery for branding policy positions—build the wall, make America great again (MAGA), "crooked Hillary." Moreover, claiming he was the leader of a movement to protect the country from the ravages of globalism and the radical left, he was as energetic as he was divisive. Trump's mass rallies were especially effective in harnessing that movement energy, and people standing in the rain to attend his rallies become the dominant metric by which the Trump campaign understood its own potential. National polls had him behind Clinton, and Clinton's fundraising juggernaut and super PAC alliances eventually outspent the Trump campaign by over $560 million—nearly twice of what was spent in support of Trump from all sources.¹¹ Trump overcame this fundraising deficit on the ground, capitalizing his support in key battleground states that, if mobilized, might allow him to win the Electoral College. As textual analysis of Trump's campaign rhetoric would later demonstrate, his message sealed a deeply emotional and visceral bond with "ordinary Americans."[12] Like Barack Obama's efforts to create a new grassroots movement, Trump's raw personality and charisma energized his campaign and fused it to the party's base. "Trumpers" openly celebrated the fact that theirs was a self-named insurgency to reclaim power. As Conway recalled, the campaign

> really mastered the art of putting Donald Trump where he was best, which was in these big rallies, these huge settings in swing states, in front of the people. . . . Donald Trump does best when he's with the people. He can take his message directly to the American people and cut through the noise or through the silence, whatever the case may be. It was a masterful way of doing it, . . . because it was low-cost; it was high-energy.[13]

Although the style and substance of Obama's and Trump's leadership were radically divergent, their method of communication nevertheless further ritualized the independent and plebiscitary nature of presidential politics. Just as Obama relied on OFA and direct mass appeals to mobilize support for his candidacy and programs, so Trump stood apart from most of the GOP "establishment," basing his campaign on cable television, social media, and mass rallies. And, while Trump's rally-centered strategy was criticized early on as inefficient and unreflective of mass opinion, this criticism was quickly brushed off after he sustained his base level of support as primary and caucus votes were cast. Between the launch of his campaign in the summer of 2015 and his first official campaign rally in Manchester, New Hampshire, Trump held 187 rallies until he wrapped up the nomination in June 2016, oftentimes several in one day, for an exhausting average of 3.6 rallies per week.

Trump's victory in New Hampshire—where he held seventeen major rallies alone—more or less ended the talk that his candidacy was a joke. After Trump beat out the runner-up, Ohio governor John Kasich, by 55,000 votes, his campaign never lost its early momentum, even as it struggled to increase its support in the party to a true majority. As figure 2.2 illustrates, the Trump campaign never outperformed its early delegate lead, measured here as a percentage of all delegates who had been awarded at that time in the nomination

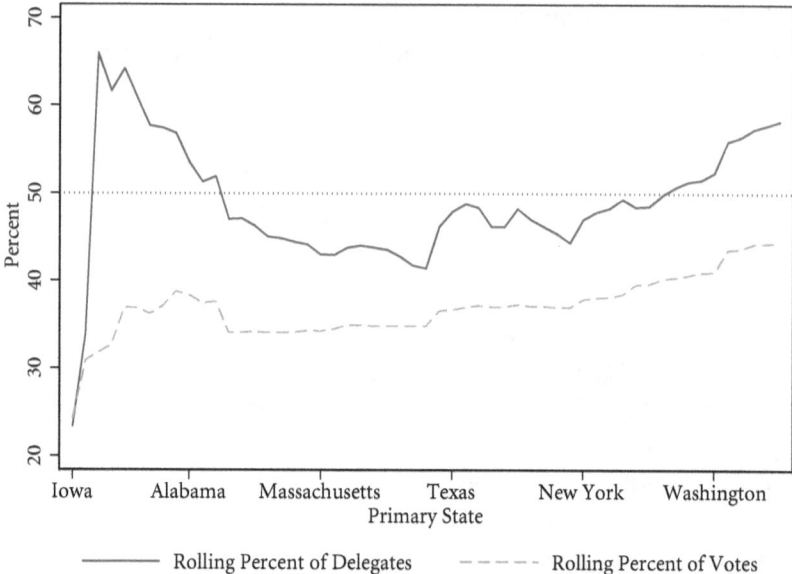

Figure 2.2. Percentage of delegates and votes Donald Trump received in the 2016 Republican nominating contest from the Iowa Caucus (February 1, 2016) until June 7. Each point represents Trump's totals as a percentage of votes and delegates awarded through that moment in the campaign.

Source: Author calculations from state secretaries of state offices. *Credit:* Created by authors.

contest. In fact, it was not until May 10 that Trump officially had a majority of selected delegates, and it would not be until May 26 that he secured a majority of delegates who would eventually cast ballots at the nominating convention.

Although delegates are the political currency by which nomination contests are decided, what is telling for our purposes is the gap between the delegate outcome and the percent of votes Trump received in the primary races. In short, although Trump did eventually secure a delegate majority, he did so while winning just 44 percent of all votes cast in the various primary and caucus contests within the states. In fact, it was not until April 19 that Trump would finally win a contest with a majority of Republican party voters: in the New York primary. Before that, he had averaged just 32 percent of the vote in each of the previous state nominating contests, while increasing his delegate lead to nearly 50 percent.

Two aspects of the Republican nominating process account for this fact; both are reflective of the democratizing trends we discussed in chapter 1. First, Trump performed best in those states where delegations were over-represented in the Republican Party, when compared to their actual population. Consider as an example the fact that South Dakota sent 29 delegates to the RNC in 2016—about 1 percent of the total delegate allotment; but South Dakota has just two-tenths of 1 percent of the American population. The reason delegates are not distributed in strict proportion to state population is because the Republican Party rewards reliable red States. It rewards the base. Consequently, states, such as California, New York, and Illinois get fewer delegates than they should, were allocations made strictly according to population, while staunchly red states such as North Dakota, Montana, Wyoming get more. Although Trump did not win all those deeply red states (he lost badly in Wyoming, the most overrepresented state), all in all, Trump's campaign performed comparatively better in those states that were *overrepresented* in the distribution of delegates.

The disproportionate allocation of delegates to staunchly Republican states was compounded by a second factor. Trump performed better than average in states where delegates were disproportionately awarded to the plurality winner, regardless of how many delegates they had to allot. In other words, Trump won in states that gave winners an extra "boost" in the delegate prize. This was a deliberate strategy and reflects the shrewdness of the Trump campaign, which invested in these particular states as opposed to running a national race for the presidency. For example, although Trump won just 35 percent of the vote in New Hampshire, he earned almost half of that state's delegates. While most states awarded their delegates in strict proportion, Trump's early victories in Alabama (43 percent of the vote, 71 percent of the delegates), Tennessee (38 percent of the vote, 57 percent of delegates), Mississippi (47 percent of the vote, 62 percent of delegates), Illinois (38 percent of the vote, 78 percent of the delegates), and Missouri (41 percent of the vote, 71 percent of the delegates) allowed him to overperform in the delegate race compared to his actual support among Republican primary voters. The fact that the Republican Party still has some states that award delegates on a winner-take-all basis was a further boon to his nomination strategy; before New York's winner-take-all primary, where he won over 59 percent of the vote, Trump won a plurality—not a majority—of votes in each of these states, but walked away with all the delegates: South Carolina (32 percent of the vote), Florida (45 percent of the vote) and Arizona (46 percent of the vote). The rules that favored the winners of states, meant to solidify the party's support behind a nominee and give the appearance of a unified GOP, worked to Trump's advantage as he navigated a field of seventeen candidates, twelve of whom competed for delegates.

These rules meant that on the eve of the Republican National Convention, Trump did not command a majority of Republican primary voters, but he did capture the nomination. As expected, a number of conservative media outlets, some members of the conservative intelligentsia, and a few elected Republicans remained lukewarm if not avowedly hostile to Trump's nomination. But it is hard to measure just how much influence these high-profile objectors had. The *National Review*'s 70,000 strong readership paled in comparison to the late Rush Limbaugh's nearly-20-million listeners. And unlike establishment conservatives, who failed to find a viable alternative candidate, Limbaugh's audience knew who to follow: "For the longest time," Limbaugh said in March 2016, " the Republican party has told us that they can't win with just Republican votes. . . . Donald Trump has put together a coalition. Whether he knows it or not, whether he intended to or not, he's put together a coalition that's exactly what the Republican party says that it needs to win, and yet look [at] what they're [Republican leaders] doing. They're trying to get Trump out of the race, because they're not in charge of it."[14]

Exploiting the calendar, state-by-state variation in nomination rules, and longstanding rifts inside the GOP, Trump won the nomination decisively. Perhaps this should not be as surprising as it was because the nomination system he exploited was deliberately established to empower "the people" over the establishment. Eight years earlier, Obama's outside strategy established him as the leader of a new progressive "coalition of the ascendant." And in 2016, Trump's "people" spoke, leading a "coalition of restoration" comprised of blue-collar, religiously devout, and non-urban whites who were frightened about demographic and social change.[15] Although Trump's populist crusade triumphed in the primaries and caucuses, it remained to be seen whether the majority of Republican partisans and a sufficient number of the shrinking but pivotal "independent" voters would rally around Trump on Election Day.

Revenge of the "Deplorables"

Las Vegas oddsmakers thought Trump's takeover of the GOP was unlikely to pay off on Election Day: a $100 wager would have netted you $275 on November 6, or $2,500 if you placed your bet the night the Republican National Convention ended![16] Yet academic political science would have discouraged those tempted by such a payday. Across eleven of the major and most respected models for forecasting presidential elections, just two indicated that Trump would beat Hillary Clinton in the general election: Helmet Norpoth's Primary Model and Alan Abramowitz's Time for a Change Model. All the rest, in addition to almost every leading media outlet, predicted a victory for Hillary.[17]

To be fair, according to the forecasters themselves, most of the models were accurate—"impressive to extraordinary" by historical standards.[18] Hillary Clinton did receive more of the votes cast on Election Day than Donald Trump; however, she failed to conquer enough territory to win the Electoral College.

These Electoral College dynamics, however, should not have been so overlooked. Although the Electoral College has, since 2000, produced two winners who failed to win the popular vote, it has been more common for an incoming president to receive less than a *majority* of votes cast. Having received 47 percent of the popular vote, Trump's less-than-majority support approximated those cast for nine previous elected presidents since 1900—nearly one-third of election results during that period. Trump had larger public support than Richard Nixon in 1968, Bill Clinton in 1992, and Woodrow Wilson in 1912. Presidential elections in America tend to be fairly close affairs. Even the most recent electoral "landslide"—Ronald Reagan's rout of former vice president Walter Mondale in 1984—garnered less than 10 percent more popular votes than Donald Trump's victory. Ten presidential elections since 1896 have fallen within a margin of three points (the usual margin of error in national polls).[19]

Of course, calculating average results over a long period of time cannot gauge the shock most people experienced as they watched election night returns late into the evening. Few expected a former reality television star who ran a scorched-earth campaign to be elected president. Even the Trump campaign seemed surprised. The mood at the contenders' respective celebration parties spoke volumes about the most die-hard's perception of Trumps' chances. Clinton had rented out a massive convention center, fit with the symbolism of a glass ceiling, and had invited thousands to join what was expected to be a historic victory celebration; thousands more could attend and catch a glimpse of the various celebrity invitees on the webcast the campaign set up. Less than two miles away at a much smaller Manhattan hotel, just a few hundred Trump supporters attended—perhaps all of those in Manhattan. But as reporter after reporter noticed, struggling to make news of Trump's "celebration," hardly anyone was wearing the signature red MAGA hat, which was the hallmark of Trump's rallies. These disparate moods were, of course, reflective of what major news sites, polling firms, and even both campaigns thought they knew from a wide spectrum of data all pointing toward a Clinton victory.

However, as state results were tabulated, the moods of the two camps dramatically shifted and more red hats were adorned. The Associated Press called West Virginia right after the polls closed. This was no surprise. But Trump's margin of victory in this reliably red state (6 points higher than Mitt Romney's in 2012) and the enthusiasm for his candidacy (a turnout that was nearly 10 points higher) were early portents of what one pundit called a "complete earthquake."[20] In the battleground states of North Carolina and Florida, the exit polls were unclear on who would prevail, but they showed Clinton hemorrhaging votes in comparison to Obama's 2012 performance. Around 11:00 p.m., they were called and added to Trump's Electoral College lead. All eyes then turned to the Democrats' "blue wall" states of Michigan, Wisconsin, Minnesota, and Pennsylvania, all of which had voted for the Democratic presidential candidate since 1992. Trump was outperforming Romney in those states, and turnout was up. Between August and November, Trump had held eighteen rallies in these states alone. His investment paid off. Although Clinton, despite underperforming by 6 points, managed to hold on to Minnesota, she lost Pennsylvania and Michigan by razor-thin margins. Wisconsin, which had not voted for a Republican since Ronald Reagan in 1984, sealed the deal; twenty-three of Wisconsin's seventy-two counties, which had voted Democratic four years earlier, flipped. At 2:31 a.m. on November 9, the Associated Press called the race for Donald Trump.[21]

The movement-style politics that pushed Trump over the top in the Republican nominating contests carried over into the general election. Defying the received wisdom that candidates should run to the center in the general election, Trump ran a polarizing campaign. In truth, as noted in chapter 1, presidential campaigns had been tapping into and reinforcing a polarized electorate since George W. Bush's pioneering mobilization strategy in the 2004 campaign. Expanding and mobilizing the parties' base supporters, not persuading a shrinking pool of independents, had become the key to success in the polarized politics of the twenty-first century.[22] Leveraging new technologies to microtarget voters, exploiting campaign finance laws to raise unlimited donations, spending unlimited funds on voter mobilization activities, and merging social media analytics with advertising platforms, Trump's campaign zeroed in on the places, and not just the voters, that counted.

The key to such mobilization was Trump's populist style of rhetoric that divided the electorate into winners and losers, victims and the powerful, the people and the elite. Trump's campaign, championed by Steve Bannon's "alt-right" *Breitbart News*, displaced the traditional conservative emphasis on rugged individualism and redefined it under the administration's compelling but elusive "Make America Great Again" slogan. America once was great but no longer. When Hillary Clinton, in an extemporaneous description of Trump's base supporters labeled them as "racist, sexist, homophobic, xenophobic, Islamophobic"—all in all, a "basket of deplorables"—Trump's supporters embraced the term.[23] Clinton's dismissal of Trump loyalists as uncouth bigots resonated because it aptly represented their perception—and perhaps the reality—of how the establishment political class treated them. The campaign quickly issued new flags, bumper stickers, and buttons reading "Proud Deplorable."

Believing that Clinton's basket of deplorables included "people of faith," conservative evangelical leaders, who had long felt marginalized in American political culture and politics, threw their unequivocal support to Trump, a thrice-married and onetime New York liberal.[24] Trump himself openly wore the "deplorable" label, especially after a 2005 video of him caught what amounts to an admission of sexual impropriety and possibly even assault: "When you're a star, they let you do it. You can do anything. . . . Grab 'em by the pussy. You can do anything."[25] As Ralph Reed—chairman of the Faith and Reform Coalition—would later recount, Trump's transgressions mattered little alongside his promise to "protect Christianity." Paying court to evangelical leaders, Trump pledged to stack the federal courts with nominees who would oppose abortion, stand up for the traditional family, and protect Christian schools from the Department of Education.[26] Likewise, Liberty University president Jerry Falwell Jr., Focus on the Family's James Dobson, and the Family Research Council's Tony Perkins all closed ranks, despite Trump's personal travails. "We're not electing a pastor-in-chief," Falwell explained to Fox News, echoing the expediency his father expressed in championing the candidacy of Ronald Reagan. "Sometimes you have to be pragmatic. You have to choose the one with the best chance of winning and who is closest to your views."[27]

As Michael Zoorob and Theda Skocpol have shown, the Christian right's support was more than symbolic. With more than two thousand volunteers and two hundred paid staff working out of thirty field offices, the Faith and Freedom Coalition carried out a massive mobilization and outreach campaign. Moreover, the efforts of Christian right national leaders were reinforced at the community level by a network of local congregations that delivered a message depicting true believers as part of a beleaguered "Christian nation"—and liberals as responsible for the country's moral decline.[28]

Many Republicans lamented Trump's populist rhetoric and transactional faith. In particular, they wondered how the party could be so inured to the country's massive demographic shifts. Trump's rhetoric, they argued, alienated two of the largest group of voters Republicans had tried to win over after Obama made them central to the Democratic Party's emerging base: young college-educated professionals and ethnic minorities. The RNC's own "autopsy report," which party leaders issued following Romney's loss in 2012, suggested as much. Noting that Republicans had lost the popular vote in five of the previous six elections, the report lamented that "public perception of the Party is at record lows. Young people are increasingly rolling their eyes at what the party represents, and many minorities wrongly think that Republicans do not like them or want them in the country."[29]

However, Trump's populist campaign strategy credited another, less publicized weakness the RNC report emphasized. While the 2012 autopsy report noted that Republican outreach to minority voters—especially Latino voters—was of paramount importance, it also stressed economics and a deepening perception in the minds of the American voter that the GOP had forsaken the American working class. In fact, while most media attention focused on outreach to ethnic minorities, a concern of economic elitism was the first issue the party identified in the report: "We have to blow the whistle at corporate malfeasance and attack corporate welfare.... We should speak out when CEOs receive tens of millions of dollars in retirement packages, but middle-class workers have not had a meaningful raise in years." Trump's outreach to blue-collar, non-college-educated workers thus comported in important ways with the GOP's playbook.[30]

Indeed, Trump was not the only candidate who espoused "populist" rhetoric on the campaign trail during the Republican nomination contest. Other self-styled outsiders, such as Carly Fiorina, Ben Carson, and Scott Walker, also tried to seize the mantle of populist leader who could take on the establishment in the name of "the people." Moreover, these assaults on the establishment had bipartisan resonance. Bernie Sanders, a self-described democratic socialist, nearly won the nomination of a party he refused to join by taking the Democratic establishment to task for rigging the system against working-class Americans. Significantly, about one in ten Sanders supporters in the Democratic primary ended up voting for Trump in the general election. What distinguished Trump from other contenders for the populist mantle was his audacious disregard for civic norms and institutions. Politics had become a nasty business by the end of the Obama presidency, and Trump forged a primordial bond with the Republican base by expressing in unapologetic—often vulgar—terms its visceral contempt for politicians and government.

No other candidate, in other words, came close to the way Trump's campaign braided populist discontent and fundamental struggles over identity—what it means to be an American. Populist outsiders such as George Wallace and H. Ross Perot had run consequential campaigns as third-party candidates; however, Trump's capture of the Republican Party and election to the presidency represented an unprecedented challenge to the rear guard of the party establishment. By 2016, the "gatekeepers" who had sustained parties as collective organizations had been so weakened by reforms that presumed to "democratize" fundraising and the presidential selection process that they were unable to protect the Republican brand from a clever demagogue who mocked conservative principles and institutions.[31] Conservative intellectuals may have, at an earlier time, stood on principle and encouraged partisans to vote for the lesser of two evils. But Republican candidates had so willingly profited from the base's anti-intellectualism for many years—especially in opposing Barack Obama, a Harvard-educated law professor—that by 2016 the cognoscenti's arguments carried little weight.

Similarly, scholars and pundits had long emphasized the importance of interest groups in sustaining the status quo; however, with the rise of movement politics loosed by the sixties, more transactional groups such as unions and corporations had lost ground to social activists and more ideological interest groups such as the National Rifle Association (NRA).[32] Trump did not have the endorsement of any "established" group, which he celebrated as a badge of honor. Nor was the fragmented media capable of fending off a bombastic reality TV star. To the contrary, even those outlets hostile to Trump's candidacy were infatuated by the boost in ratings achieved in covering his campaign; the competition for these ratings enabled Trump to dominate the airwaves and thus control the agenda of the campaign—to benefit from what political scientists identify as the "second face" of political power.[33] In sum, Trump won because the traditional guardians against demagoguery and political adventurism had already lost.

BUILDING THE PARTY OF TRUMP

The work of transforming the Republican Party began the day Trump descended his golden escalator and unleashed a no-holds-barred campaign against undocumented immigrants, "radical Islamic terrorists," and domestic criminals. "I am," he proclaimed at the 2016 Republican National Convention, the "law and order candidate."[34] His masterful portrayal of the charismatic leader—a strongman who would command the MAGA movement—did not stop on Election Day. Rather, the president-elect took off on a "thank you tour" during the transition period, showing how he intended to continue to hold mass rallies after he occupied the White House. Just weeks after his inauguration, Trump returned to the campaign stump, appearing in Melbourne, Florida, on February 18. Proclaiming that the people at the rally were a part of "a great movement, a movement like has never been seen before in our country or probably anywhere else," Trump explained why he felt compelled to see his most loyal supporters in person: "I . . . want to speak to you without the filter of the fake news." Invoking comparisons to some of his most consequential predecessors, the new president continued, "Thomas Jefferson, Andrew Jackson, and Abraham Lincoln and many of our greatest presidents fought with the media and called them out oftentimes on their lies. When the media lies to people, I will never, ever let them get away with it."[35] In the seven campaign-style rallies after he took office, the president landed some of his hardest blows against the media—energizing his supporters and renewing their faith that the president spoke for them, and them alone.

Whereas Obama transformed his 2016 grassroots campaign organization, Obama for America, into a nonprofit advocacy group that promoted the president's policies, Trump set out on a permanent campaign to sustain the momentum of his Make America Great Again crusade. During his first year in office, Trump averaged about one campaign-style rally a month (complete with cable news coverage and live feeds through his personal Twitter account). In the lead-up to the 2018 midterms, the president made forty-six separate appearances between March and November (almost one per week); between December 2018 and the end of the 2020 campaign, Trump held sixty-four political rallies, even continuing to court his base amid a deadly pandemic. Twenty-six—more than a third—of these campaign-style events took place in the final two months preceding Election Day. The unmediated connection between the president and the people is a hallmark of the modern presidency, but with the tools of instant communication and the blurring of news and entertainment, Trump gave new meaning to the "permanent campaign."[36] When asked by reporters on Air Force One as he flew to the Melbourne rally whether it was a little early to resume campaigning, the newly elected president responded: "Life is a campaign. Making our country great again is a campaign. For me, it's a campaign; to make America great again is absolutely a campaign."[37] Indeed, even Trump's inaugural address was a rallying cry to his antinomian followers:

> You came by the tens of millions to become part of a historic movement, the likes of which the world has never seen before. At the center of this movement is a crucial conviction, that a nation exists to serve its citizens. Americans want great schools for their children, safe neighborhoods for their families, and good jobs for themselves. These are just and reasonable demands of righteous people and a righteous public.[38]

All Eyes on the Next Election: 2018 Midterms

A vital object of Trump's permanent campaign was to retain unified Republican rule, an imperative given the rise in executive-centered partisanship. Bringing that development to a culmination, Trump obliterated the line between the Republican Party and the White House. The 2016 election was all about Trump, and through fundraisers, campaign rallies, and his Twitter account he was determined to make the 2018 congressional elections a plebiscite on his first two years in office. On the campaign trail, he clearly defined the midterm election as a referendum on his presidency. "I'm not on the ballot," he acknowledged at one campaign rally. "But in a certain way, I'm on the ballot. So, please go out and vote."[39]

To some extent, Trump's personalization of the midterm elections fit a pattern of twentieth-century presidential politics. Since Theodore Roosevelt first gave form to the modern executive office, presidents have become the repository of party responsibility. So positioned, however, few presidents have been able to prevent their party in Congress from suffering loses in the first midterm election (figure 2.3). Presidents Calvin Coolidge, Franklin D. Roosevelt, and George W. Bush are unique among modern presidents for seeing their party pick up seats in both chambers following their initial inauguration. Trump is a part of a larger class of presidents who expanded his majority in one chamber (the Senate, by one seat), although this was still a rare occurrence. However,

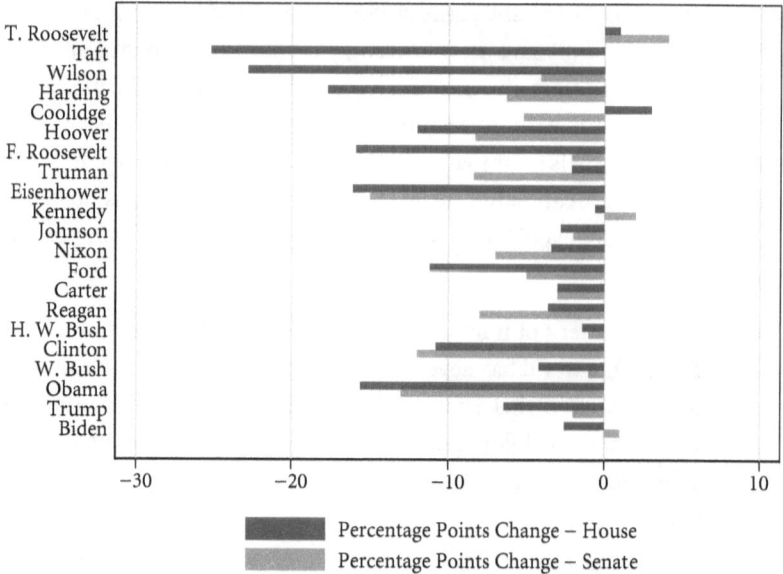

Figure 2.3. Percentage of seats in both the House of Representatives and the US Senate that the president's party in Congress lost or gained after their first midterm election.

Source: US House and US Senate Historian Office and Author Calculations. *Credit:* Created by authors.

the results of elections to the lower chamber were more representative of historical trends: the Republican Party lost forty seats and majority control of the House of Representatives.

Midterm elections are determined by many factors, including the president's performance in office, trends in economic growth, and the relative strength of each party when the president first takes office.[40] But the constant flipping between Democratic and Republican majority control of Congress since the late 1960s is also a consequence of increasing polarization, straight-ticket voting, and the consolidation of national party messaging that focuses on presidential politics and popularity.[41] In essence, as Obama's two terms dramatically demonstrated, executive-centered partisanship tends to sacrifice the collective fortunes of the party to the president's personal ambitions and programs.[42]

Trump's domineering presence in the 2018 elections thus followed a pattern endemic to executive partisanship, and, as history would suggest, his interventions had mixed results. In 2016, Trump outperformed the Republican candidate for the House seat in just 28 of the 211 contested races that a Republican won, or about 13 percent of races. Republican members were more electorally popular than their party leader in those contested races: Republican candidates won their district, on average, with 62.1 percent of the vote; Trump, in comparison, secured on average 56.5 percent of the vote in those same districts. Clearly, Republican voters in 2016 were much more supportive of the Republican congressional candidates than they were the Republican presidential nominee.[43]

Nevertheless, the outcome of the 2018 midterms suggests that the Trump campaign and the prerogatives of the modern presidency have forged a leaner and more united Republican Party. In effect, the Republican Party's support was increasingly confined to those places—rural and outer-ring suburban areas—where Trump performed well in 2016. Of the 170 contested races that a Republican won in the 2018 midterms, the president's 2016 numbers outperformed the Republican candidate in ninety-four districts, or 55.3 percent. Trump won those districts with an average 58.8 percent of the vote, while Republican congressional candidates averaged 59.1 percent of the vote. Trump had thus tied the fate of Republican candidates more closely to his political fortunes.

Of course, numbers tell only part of the story—especially numbers taken from midterm returns, as compared with presidential election years. Still, Trump leaned in heavily during the 2018 primary season. More than any president since Franklin Roosevelt's failed 1938 purge campaign, Trump sought to influence the outcome of several high-profile intraparty contests. It is difficult to systematically evaluate the president's influence in this process because incumbents have a choice when faced with a primary challenge. They can choose to run or retire. Two of the president's loudest critics in the Senate, Jeff Flake (AZ) and Bob Corker (TN), chose to retire rather than face primary opponents. In the fight to replace Corker, the open-seat contest between Marsha Blackburn (a Republican congresswoman) and Phil Bredesen (a Democratic two-time ex-governor) proved to be much closer than anticipated. About a month before the election, Trump visited Tennessee to campaign on behalf of Blackburn. "A vote for Marsha is really a vote for me," the president avowed, "and everything that we stand for. It's a vote for 'Make America Great Again.'"[44] While Trump won Tennessee in 2016 with more than 60.7 percent of the vote, Blackburn took office with 54.7 percent of the vote cast. Whether this victory was because of Trump or in spite of him is an open conjecture; however, there is no question that he turned the contest into a referendum on his brand of conservatism.

Trump made similar appeals in Arizona during the general election, but there the Republican candidate, Martha McSally, lost to Rep. Kyrsten Sinema, a Democrat. McSally faced a more competitive primary contest than did Blackburn, campaigning against two Republican contenders who styled themselves as the Trump candidate: Joe Arpaio, the incendiary former sheriff of Maricopa County, whom Trump pardoned; and Kelli Ward, a former state senator who had tried to unseat Trump's nemesis John McCain in a 2016 primary contest. While Trump remained neutral in the primary contest, most political observers at the time acknowledged that McSally adopted a rhetorical style similar to Trump's and was careful not to criticize the president's administration, lest he endorse Arpaio or Ward.[45] McSally lost in a state that Trump previously won, while Ward won a divisive intraparty contest to chair the Arizona Republican Party. Subsequently, the Republican governor of Arizona appointed McSally to the US Senate to fill the remainder of the late senator John McCain's term.

The Arizona race shows the power of Trump's endorsement, even in its absence. In two noteworthy cases, however, Trump's endorsement of a preferred Republican candidate in a primary contest proved futile. In Alabama's special election for US Senate in 2017, the president came out in support of Luther Strange—over the more "Trump-like" candidate running for the nomination. Strange took over Jeff Sessions's seat after Trump appointed Sessions attorney general, but he faced a strong challenge from the outspoken former state supreme court justice Roy Moore. Moore had earlier gained nationwide notoriety for his refusal to support the US Supreme Court's decision to legalize same-sex marriage and for his vocal support of Trump's racist birther conspiracy, which claimed that President Obama was not a natural-born citizen. Moore won the primary, but despite gaining the president's support, he lost the general election.[46] In West Virginia—the only other Senate race where Trump made a clear intervention during a Republican primary—the most "Trump-like" candidate, Don Blankenship, also failed to secure the president's personal endorsement. Instead, Trump came out in support of the two other challengers, equivocating between the two in a last-minute tweet.[47] The ultimate victor, Patrick Morrisey, failed to beat out the Democratic incumbent, Joe Manchin, in a state where Trump garnered 68.5 percent of the vote in 2016. Manchin, nevertheless, certainly felt the pressure from Trump's base. During the 115th Congress (2017–18), he voted in line with President Trump's priorities in the Senate nearly 61 percent of the time, and he provided a critical vote to confirm Trump's second Supreme Court pick, Brett Kavanaugh.

Although the president's aggressive intervention in the 2018 contests was a mixed blessing for Republicans, he declared victory. As Trump proclaimed in a postelection press conference: "Candidates who embraced our message of low taxes, low regulations, low crime, strong borders, and great judges excelled last night. They excelled. . . . On the other hand, you had some that decided to 'let's stay away.' They did very poorly. . . . I feel just fine about it."[48] The losses Republicans suffered in the House, as well as in many state and local races, cast serious doubt on the president's self-serving interpretation; nevertheless, his analysis did not prompt any vocal criticism from fellow Republicans, who accepted—even if reluctantly—the president's authority to weigh in on party contests and make Republican races all about him.

Trump's mastery of the Republican Party continued even after he left office. In part, this was due to his primordial relationship with the base; just as important, the 2020 election left the country badly divided. The Republicans suffered critical defeats in Senate races, largely due to Trump's influence. Republican Senate candidates lost in Arizona and Colorado, and on the eve of the January 6 riot, after weeks of electioneering missteps by Trump and his allies, Democrats picked up two more seats in Georgia. In the House, however, Republicans recovered fourteen seats, leaving Democrats with a very slim majority. Historically, no Democratic president in the last century has entered office with as few co-partisans in the legislature as Joe Biden. Not surprisingly, given the president's low approval rating and the troubled state of the economy, the Democrats lost the House in 2022, albeit by much smaller margins than anticipated, and they picked up one seat in the Senate, giving them a slender majority in the upper chamber. Trump's polarizing presence in the campaign diminished prospects of a "red wave," but it also prevented a blue one. The University of Maryland's Critical Issues poll found that nearly as many people said the 2022 election was a referendum on Trump as said it was a referendum on Biden.[49]

All Politics Is Local . . . and about Trump

Barack Obama and Donald Trump practiced executive-centered partisanship; however, Trump pursued a carefully calculated strategy to transform his party's national, state, and local organizations. Whereas Obama constructed a parallel organization alongside the Democratic National Committee to advance his partisan objectives, Trump decided to merge his reelection campaign and the RNC's election efforts. Rather than stand apart from the Republican apparatus, his objective was to remake its national and state committees in his own image. President Trump set about this task immediately, becoming the first president in history to file reelection paperwork with the Federal Elections Commission on Inauguration Day. More than a symbolic gesture, the decision allowed Trump to maintain a separate campaign office (in Trump Tower), perpetually blurring the line between campaign functions and official presidential obligations.

After four years of party building, the 2020 elections reflected a party remade in Trump's image. Split-ticket voting is a hallmark of a party system that diffuses power and does not rotate around the star of presidential campaigns.[50] Indeed, when Trump was first up for election, Republican members of Congress were able to distinguish themselves from their party's nominee at the top of the ticket (figure 2.4); down-ballot Republicans won in more districts carried by Clinton than did Democratic House candidates running in districts carried by Trump. Specifically, in 2016, 43 congressional districts split their support between a House member of one party and the presidential candidate of another; of those, the majority, 29, went for Hillary Clinton while sending a member of the GOP to Congress. By 2020, that number had shrunk to 16 split seats; just 9 congressional districts went for Biden but chose a Republican candidate for the House. Historically, this is the lowest number of split seats in the last five elections (2004: 59 split districts; 2008: 86 split districts; 2012: 26 split districts). And the Senate paints a starker pattern. In the presidential elections in 2016 and 2020, just one state sent the senator of a different party from that which won the popular vote statewide: Susan Collins, from Maine, in 2020.

Looking more closely at the split delegations, the evidence suggests that, although some Republican candidates were successful in distinguishing themselves from Trump in 2016 or 2018, other constituencies solidified their support around the party's standard-bearer. Of the 206 contested House races that a Republican won in 2020, the Republican candidate averaged 62.1 percent, while Trump averaged 59.7 percent—slightly worse than 2018 but better than 2016. Trump outperformed just 30 Republican congressional candidates, or 14.56 percent of contests. All of this suggests that, despite a global pandemic, impeachment, and four years of political brinksmanship, Trump nevertheless increased his support in some parts of the country, while Republicans—primarily in California, New York, and parts of Texas—struggled to build a brand distinct from the Trump-era GOP.

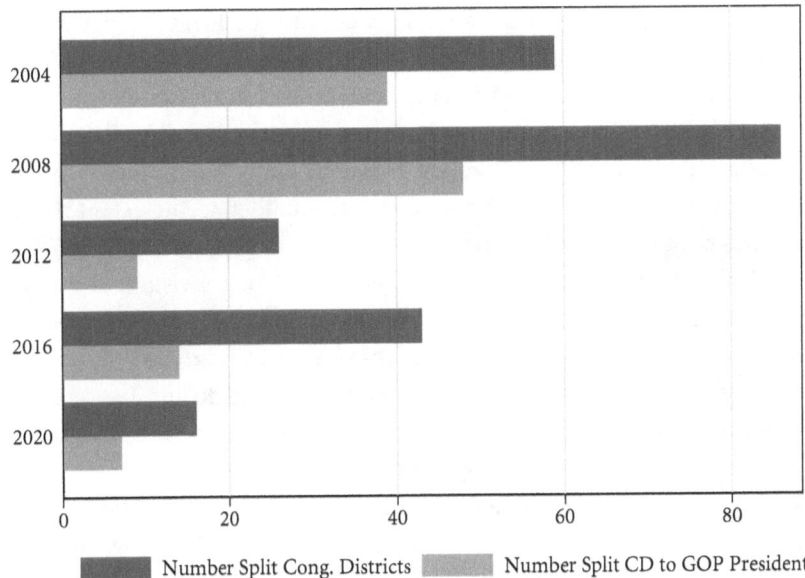

Number Split Cong. Districts   Number Split CD to GOP President

Figure 2.4. Decline in the number of congressional districts split between the presidential vote (district-wide) and the party of the winning member to the US House from 2004 to 2020. The total number of split districts (dark gray) is above the subset of districts that had a Democratic House victory and a Republican presidential district-wide victory.

Source: Presidential vote share of House districts from DailyKos.com. Credit: Created by authors.

The decline in split-ticket voting is partly a consequence of Trump's involvement in the 2018 and 2020 congressional primaries. Trump's record in picking primary winners is undeniable, even when looking at the narrower set of open-seat contests (Trump normally bragged about his overall win rate, which included uncontested and incumbent-dominated primary "contests"). Considering just open contests, his overall record in 2018 stood at 88 percent, greater than that of the NRA, the Chamber of Commerce, the Koch network, or any other major advocacy group that sought to influence the direction of the Republican Party.[51] In 2020, Trump's influence rose. In the twenty-three primary contests for House, Senate, and governor, Trump backed just one unsuccessful insurgent—Lynda Bennett in North Carolina's Eleventh Congressional District.

Ostensibly, Trump's personal campaign for reelection and intervention in several primary contests was the latest iteration of the modern candidate-centered campaign. The presidency has always had an uneasy relationship to the American two-party system and, since at least FDR, the parties have sought to escape the constraining effects of party organization by establishing their independence from or seeking to control the formal party organization once taking office. Trump's strategy, however, was to nominally strengthen the Republican Party apparatus by sealing its agenda to the White House's messaging. In this way, Trump was an attentive party-builder, to the extent that the party was built up in his own image.

Much of Trump's work as a party-builder took a less visible, and potentially more insidious, dimension than his more bombastic Twitter appeals or rally appearances. These organizational changes centralized the White House's control of Republican Party messaging and fundraising during Trump's presidency, especially in the lead-up to the 2020 presidential election. In addition, Trump's firm grip on the party apparatus completed the rout of Never Trumpers, all but assuring an uncontentious 2020 Republican convention. As such, these tactics worked well beyond mere "branding." Trump's engagement with the RNC and state party organizations marked a relentless campaign to institutionalize various aspects of Trump's political tactics and program—to make the GOP organization subservient to his personal ambition.

For example, successful presidential candidates are traditionally given the right to select their committee chairpersons; Trump followed suit by appointing Ronna Romney McDaniel as GOP chairwoman. The connection to Utah Republican senator Mitt Romney (her uncle and a vocal Trump critic) is not nearly as important as the fact that McDaniel comes from Michigan—an essential battleground that Trump won in 2016 and narrowly lost in 2020. McDaniel loyally oversaw the reorganization of the RNC to strengthen the president's reelection chances. Unanticipated at the time, she also remained in power while Trump sought to capture the 2024 Republican nomination. McDaniel was key to ousting dissent within the party during Trump's term; despite the lack of a vocal opposition in the congressional rank and file for much of his four years in office, the iconoclastic president, registering the opposition of a shrinking but stubborn band of Never Trumpers, recognized the possibility of a primary challenge. Several prominent Republican governors—most notably, Larry Hogan of Maryland and former governor John Kasich of Ohio—repeatedly raised the possibility. The RNC, however, sought to ensure that any possible primary challenge would be doomed from the start.

In addition to McDaniel's unwavering support, the campaign staff in Trump Tower and the RNC orchestrated a state-by-state campaign to place Trump loyalists in powerful positions within the state party organizations, allowing them to change party rules governing the selection of delegates for the national convention. McDaniel's experience as a state party chair proved invaluable in this respect, as the Trump machine succeeded even in states where the president performed poorly in 2016. For example, Jim Lyons, the Trump-backed candidate for state party chairman in Massachusetts, defeated the candidate supported by the vocal Trump critic and popular Republican governor, Charlie Baker. Once in charge of the state party, Lyons, with the active support of the Trump campaign, successfully pushed through a rule change that would make any presidential primary race a winner-take-all contest—thus limiting the delegates that a primary challenger to the president might accumulate and making less likely a fractious convention. This rule change was, in part, motivated by the threat of former Massachusetts governor Bill Weld—the Libertarian Party's vice presidential candidate in 2016—who announced in 2019 that he would challenge Trump for the 2020 GOP nomination.[52] Similar efforts took place in New Hampshire and Iowa.

Just how important these prophylactic measures were to the Trump administration became clear when Nick Trainer, a White House political operations director, left in December 2018 to head up the innovative Delegate and Party Organization branch of the campaign, with the goal of "organizing the state, county and local Republican parties; managing the delegate selection and ballot access process; and executing the national convention whip operation."[53] Trainer ably orchestrated the presidential campaign's direct intervention in state party leadership fights to control the Republican organizations in the key battlegrounds of Florida and Michigan. In other critical swing states, like Arizona and Colorado, the president's primordial relationship with the base, stoked by administrative action on polarizing issues such as immigration and trade, empowered Trump loyalists to secure leadership positions by mobilizing grassroots support. With several successes already to his name, Trainer and his three regional directors carried out a plan to ensure that no delegate at the 2020 Republican National Convention would be opposed to the president's reelection.

The short-term motivation for Trump's party-building efforts—to control the optics of the 2020 Republican National Convention in Charlotte, North Carolina (another important swing state)—was confounded by the pandemic, which forced the president to abandon plans for a mass gathering. However, the ruthless and carefully planned operation to take over state and local party organizations ensured that Trump's influence on the Republican Party would continue beyond his reelection campaign. Trump's message to would-be supporters in 2016 was that he would shake up the Republican establishment; the theme of 2020 was Trump's populist takeover of establishment organizations. The RNC hoped that a unified Republican Party, absent the internal dissent and personal squabbles that marred Trump's coronation at the 2016 Cleveland convention and his general election campaign, would send precisely that message. While no incumbent president has failed to garner his party's nomination since the Democrat Franklin Pierce in 1856, modern electoral history suggests that drawn-out primary fights exacerbate existing divisions within the party and weaken the party's general election appeal. Ronald Reagan's challenge to Gerald Ford (1976), Ted Kennedy's run against Jimmy Carter (1980), and Pat Buchanan's campaign to unseat George H. W. Bush (1992) were all reflective of the incumbent's vulnerability, and it is very likely that efforts to fend off these primary challenges weakened the incumbent's general election performance. To that end, Trainer and his aides dove into the rules that govern the state-by-state delegate allocations, keeping close tabs on the contests for the influential state chairmanship slots and laying out plans to organize at local meetings where the convention-goers would be picked.[54]

The determined campaign to take control of the state party organizations complemented efforts to restructure the Republicans' national organization. During the 2016 campaign, national committee staffers and novice Trump organizers routinely clashed on the campaign trail over small but vital matters of campaign infrastructure: yard signs, phone bank volunteers, canvassers, and bumper stickers.[55] To limit conflict and duplication, and to efficiently mobilize a cadre of necessary volunteers for 2020, the president's personal campaign organization formally merged with the RNC's campaigns staff. The RNC and Trump fundraising arms joined efforts in 2016, creating the Trump Victory Leadership Team, which raised an additional $108 million, independently of the president's personal campaign. But the finance strategy developed for the 2020 campaign—simply Trump Victory—signified the challenge of tying the president's highly personalized political style and reelection campaign to a collective partisan effort.

At one level the creation of this new joint fundraising committee was a clever circumvention of federal campaign finance limits placed on individual donations to political parties, by allowing individual donors to "stack" their contributions. Between 2016 and 2020, Trump Victory, for instance, created contribution agreements between Trump's campaign, the RNC, and forty-six state parties. While individuals can donate only so much to any one campaign ($5,600 per election cycle), national party ($35,500 per year), and *each* state party ($10,000), state parties can donate unlimited amounts to the national party. So, in effect, an individual donor, distributing their wealth across each of these entities, every year, could donate over $817,800 to Trump Victory through these fundraising agreements. Trump Victory could then determine how to distribute the funds.

The ability to stack donations increases the amount of money in presidential campaigns and the influence of large donors. The Trump 2020 campaign did not invent "stacking"; Hillary Clinton used this fundraising strategy effectively in the 2016 campaign. Relying heavily on "free media," Trump had sixteen state-level agreements for his first presidential campaign.[56] But, once in office, Trump's control of the joint fundraising activities of the national and state parties further unified the RNC's messaging strategy for other high-profile races in 2020 (Republicans were defending twenty-two of the thirty-four Senate races up for election) and provided Trump operatives with greater influence in directing national party resources to battleground states that were necessary for a Trump reelection. In the two-plus years following Trump's election, the joint fundraising committee raised $38.5 million to be used in Republican contests across the United States.[57]

The consolidation of the Republican Party's financial arrangements further impressed Trump's personal style of politics and his America First brand of conservatism on the party. Staffers for the joint RNC-Trump organization rotated in and out of the White House, including top-level communications directors, who made clear that the RNC viewed opposition to President Trump as a useless distraction. Campaign directors even sought to limit the extent to which major donors could influence other Republican races and coordinate independent efforts with conservative organizations operating outside the party establishment. For example, the RNC distanced itself from the Koch network, a once prominent organization in mainstream Republican politics that refused to endorse Trump in 2016; once he was ensconced in the White House, the Koch organization openly clashed with his administration over its trade and immigration policies. After it was reported that the network indicated it might openly support Democratic candidates in certain midterm races, McDaniel made a personal appeal to key Republican donors to stop working with the Koch organization, particularly as it related to the tradition of data sharing between party organizations and outside conservative groups. "I want to be very clear," McDaniel wrote in a memorandum leaked by *Politico*, "the RNC proved in 2014 and 2016 that the Party is the only entity which can be trusted with the data Republican candidates need to win up and down the ballot—and this week proves why it is NECESSARY that the Party keep building on our successful operation."[58] While the RNC did not demand that Republicans refuse Koch donations in the future, the rift demonstrated the national committee's commitment to centralizing campaign operations in support of the president—in an era marked by the proliferation of outside groups that compete with the party organization to provide services for candidates running for office.

The RNC's stated opposition to the Koch network's independent efforts was not reflective of the Trump campaign's refusal to accept outside support. Formal coordination between campaigns and independent expenditures committees (super PACs) is legally forbidden; however, during the 2018 midterms, four of the ten largest organizations supporting conservative candidates self-identified as committees that formed specifically to support President Trump's agenda: America First Action, Restoration PAC, Future45, and the Committee to Defend the President spent a collective $51.36 million in the 2017–18 midterm cycle. The largest of these, America First Action, targeted House races with clear implications for President Trump's Electoral College strategy, spending $7.4 million in Minnesota, $2.8 million in Indiana, and $2.4 million in Michigan. In 2020, $313 million in outside money from these groups supported the Trump campaign.

As a first-time candidate, Trump repudiated outside fundraising, staking his reputation on the fact that he won a "populist" campaign in 2016 over Hillary Clinton, who, relying heavily on "independent" organizations, outraised and outspent him in the election. But as president, Trump learned that these groups could support candidates who lacked Trump's ability to capture media attention, and he encouraged these organizations to raise and spend money in key legislative races. In addition to regular appearances on behalf of the Trump Victory fund, the president often spoke before donors to these super PACs, who regularly hosted events at the Trump International Hotel in Washington, DC, only blocks away from the White House.[59] Just as the Trump administration captured the party organization, so it fostered outside groups and cultivated megadonors who supported the transformation of the Republicans into the party of Trump.

Trump's permanent campaign thus shored up data collection and fundraising efforts—especially among the megadonors who were skeptical of Trump's 2016 candidacy. The early launch of his reelection operation gave the president his desired advantage over potential Republican rivals and a head start to what was expected to be a hard-fought general election campaign. Nearly a year and a half before the 2020 election, Trump's principal campaign committee reported raising nearly $98 million, almost four times more than the leading Democratic fundraiser, Bernie Sanders. Barack Obama, in contrast, raised just $4.1 million in his first two years in office; George W. Bush raised $3.1 million during his first two years. Although Joe Biden had a monetary advantage—including an almost two-to-one advantage in outside committee expenditures—the turn of fortunes did not happen until the final month before Election Day.[60]

Through his heavy-handed approach to remove independently inclined Republican officeholders and dominate state party organizations, Trump went far to purge the remnants of the Never Trumpers who opposed his reelection or supported the election of more moderate Republicans to Congress and state and local governments. While some congressional and gubernatorial Republicans continued to express concern about Trump's visceral partisanship in matters pertaining to the coronavirus, immigration, and the protests against unjust police practices, those voices had become very frail vestiges of collective partisan responsibility. As Daniel Galvin concluded in his study of Trump's relationship with the GOP, "Although divisive issues that generate public dissent from Republicans will undoubtedly continue to emerge, the main storyline of Trump's party leadership through early 2020 has been his domination and personalization of the Republican Party."[61]

The consequences of Trump's party-building tactics are likely to be enduring. Tellingly, Trump's allies within the national, state, and local Republican Party organizations were the loudest and most active proponents of the "Big Lie" following his loss in the 2020 presidential election.

THE 2020 CAMPAIGN AMID NATIONAL CRISES

Even before the COVID-19 pandemic and the widespread social protest movement galvanized by the murder of George Floyd, 2020 was set to be a tumultuous year. The public health, economic, and civil rights crises exacerbated the cultural divisions and partisan unrest that had ushered Trump into office four years earlier. This time, however, Donald Trump was not an outsider running against the establishment; fully ensconced in office, having campaigned for reelection since his inauguration, Trump had the full force of the American presidency to aid his reelection campaign. Moreover, as a result of the rule changes Trump pursued while in office, there were few sites of organized, independent party influence left to refute Trump's outlandish Election Day claims. Indeed, state and local party organizations, remade in Trump's image, were empowered to amplify the Big Lie and remake their states' electoral machinery—"reforming" voting laws in the name of "electoral security" and fully exploiting the opportunity to shore up Republican victories with new redistricting maps.

No president has so manipulated the country's institutional structure for their personal benefit. Andrew Johnson, having assumed the presidency following the assassination of Abraham Lincoln, attempted to build his own post–Civil War coalition by doling out pardons to ex-Confederates and rushing the entry of Southern states back into the Union. But he was a president without a party; Republicans and Democrats alike scorned his attempt to break free of the traditional party system.[62] Richard Nixon's audacious pursuit of personal and political self-interest seemed to set the standard. Seeking to bypass the traditional party apparatus, he formed a personal reelection campaign (the Committee to Reelect the President, or CREEP) that abused the powers of the modern presidency to gain dirt on his political enemies, most notoriously in its effort to burglarize the Democratic National Committee, housed in the Watergate office building. More dangerous were the White House's efforts to pressure the Department of Justice, the FBI, and the CIA to cover up the campaign's nefarious activities.

Nixon paid a severe price for his abuse of power, becoming the first—and still only—president to resign the office. His decision to give up power testified to the integrity of some independently or institutionally minded members of Republican Party. A delegation of Republicans led by Senator Barry Goldwater, considered the conscience of his party, told the president that he was surely to be impeached and convicted. No more than sixteen to eighteen senators, Goldwater informed him, would vote against impeachment.

In contrast, by the 2020 election, the Republican Party was dominated by Trump and MAGA supporters in Congress and the states. The only president to be impeached twice, his party nevertheless remained enthralled with him.

The culmination of executive-centered partisanship—marked by the joining of presidential prerogative, social activism, and party polarization—was a perfect storm that severely threatened a pillar of American democracy: the peaceful transfer of power. Nixon's denigration of the Constitution and democratic process took place behind closed doors—only the White House tapes brought his crimes to light. Trump's assault on republican government took place largely in public. He attacked the legitimacy of the 2020 election process with campaign rallies, televised appearances from the White House, and his popular Twitter feed.[63]

Trump also had threatened not to accept the results of the 2016 election; indeed, he claimed that save for massive voter fraud, he would have won the popular vote as well, prompting the creation of a presidential commission tasked with the quixotic responsibility of finding the evidence of those illegal votes.[64] But unlike in 2016, when Trump's remonstrances would have been limited to bald-faced lies, he held the power of the modern executive in 2020. Deploying the two pillars of the modern presidency—rhetoric and administration—Trump exalted the Big Lie to millions of supporters and pressured public officials to prevent Joe Biden from assuming the office he won in a free and fair election. Complicit in this plot was the Republican Party, remade as a Trump party. A year after Biden's inauguration, a survey showed that nearly three-quarters of Republican respondents said they didn't believe he was rightfully elected to the White House; the same polls also found that an overwhelming majority of Republicans—80 percent—saw the January 6 riot as a legitimate "protest."[65]

The Lead-Up to Election Day

In most election years, the line between an incumbent president's governing strategy and campaign is blurred—indeed, for the past sixty years, that line has been virtually obliterated. Trump, in effect, never stopped campaigning. As we will detail in chapter 3, Trump and his political allies in the executive branch surpassed Obama in deploying administrative power for partisan causes. Whereas Obama's resort to unilateralism became paramount after his party's losses in the 2010 midterm elections, Trump, with the complicity of the Republican majority in Congress, embraced partisan administration from the start. At first glance, it might seem that the day-to-day technicalities of bureaucratic management would undermine a movement-style politics that nourishes a passionate base. Yet, a great deal of American government now takes place within the confines of the administrative state. And while it lacked the fanfare of a momentous bill signing or the president's bully pulpit, executive administration was the primary way in which Trump sought to fulfill his promises to his base. In fact, in policy areas where there was formerly broad public consensus among elected politicians, the administrative presidency allowed Trump to pursue highly charged partisan initiatives that lacked broad support. As an example, table 2.1 compares the policy positions of Trump and non-Trump Republicans, according to the 2020 Cooperative Congressional Election Study (CCES). It shows the policy positions of those who "strongly approve" of Donald Trump's performance in office, as compared with those Republicans who were less enthusiastic about his leadership. The two-to-one split in party approval between those who identified as Trump Republicans and those who had reservations about the president—mostly between "strongly approve" and "somewhat approve"—is analogous to post-2020 polling among Republicans. Although the data measure attitudes and support in the lead-up to the 2020 election, we use it to supplement our main contention that Trump's administrative policies animated and responded to an activist faction within the GOP.

Two conclusions are apparent from the general comparison across the five administrative actions Trump pursued. First, they speak directly to the Trump base; there is a clear difference in support among Republicans when it comes to Trump's administrative agenda. Moreover, since we cannot determine positions among Republicans prior to the administration's actions, these figures most likely represent a low estimate of how the Republican Party's base differed from establishment candidates and most elected leaders. As we elaborate on in the next chapter, these numbers are reflective of how the president won over many of the Trump-hesitant.[66] Second, these numbers demonstrate the deep divide in the larger American polity over Trump's actions. Except for free trade, none of Trump's administrative agenda commanded majority support. Yet contemporary elections are about enlarging and mobilizing the parties' bases, and the Trump campaign believed, as it had in 2016, that a strategic mobilizing strategy could win a majority of Electoral College votes.

Although the terms of that campaign changed dramatically in March 2020, as a global health crisis and a national grassroots protest against police brutality transformed the political terrain that the Trump team had been planning to traverse, the White House never strayed from its fierce partisan tactics.

Table 2.1. Policy Positions on Donald Trump's Administrative Policies, 2020 CCES

	All Americans (%)	Non-Trump Republicans (%)	Trump Republicans (%)
Tariffs on $200 billion worth of goods imported from China	62.28	75.55	89.66
Withhold federal funds from any local police department that does not report to the federal government anyone they identify as an illegal immigrant	47.71	60.43	87.24
Strengthen the Environmental Protection Agency enforcement of the Clean Air Act and Clean Water Act even if it costs US jobs	59.8	47.88	24.77
End the Department of Defense program that sends surplus military weapons and equipment to police departments	46.91	28.86	16.2
Allow employers to decline coverage of abortions in insurance plans	44.83	61.91	79.02

Note: Data are weighted; the unweighted sample includes 61,000 individuals—including nonvoters—who were asked the policy questions. Among those, the unweighted sample included 9,851 Republicans who we identified as "Trump Republicans" and 5,363 Republicans who had some degree of reservation about the president. To be sure, just 1,554 of those Republicans, or 10 percent, disapproved of Trump's performance in office.

Unlike many past presidents, who viewed national crises as an opportunity to rally the nation, Trump viewed COVID-19 and Black Lives Matter as threats to his reelection prospects. On March 30, Trump stood alongside the CEOs of major American corporations and implored Americans, "Stay calm. It will go away. You know it—you know it is going away, and it will go away. And we're going to have a great victory."[67] For a short time, pundits agreed: the same day Trump sought to wish away a life-threatening pandemic, the *Economist* predicted that he would beat the likely Democratic nominee, Joe Biden, in the Electoral College 275 to 263.[68] This was not a call into the wind. The Primary Model—one of two that correctly predicted Trump's 2016 victory—forecast a Trump landslide. Given Biden's lackluster performance in the early primaries, and the success of Trump in preventing an intraparty challenge to his nomination (Bill Weld failed to make serious inroads in New Hampshire, where Trump cruised to victory with 86 percent of the vote)—Trump had a 91 percent chance of winning reelection.[69] All signs pointed to four more years.

For a time, COVID and racial unrest failed to disrupt Trump's campaign machinery. With the approach of the 2020 election, Trump rallies, which resumed in the middle of the pandemic, became more meticulously produced than the spontaneous and thinly staffed events of his first presidential campaign. Although the rallies were no longer covered by cable networks, the campaign turned them into "giant, roving field offices that vacuumed up personal data from rallygoers, registered new voters, and signed up his most enthusiastic supporters as volunteers."[70] Trump also remained an active force on Twitter, stoking the culture wars and mobilizing his base to combat Democratic governors, who took the lead in issuing stay-at-home orders and mask mandates early in the pandemic.

Although public health experts—and a majority of the American public—chastised Trump's response to the pandemic, the 2020 election dramatically confirmed the president's spell over the Republican Party. For the first time since its first presidential campaign in 1856, the GOP failed to adopt a platform. Instead, the RNC passed a resolution before the scaled-back national convention convened in Charlotte, North Carolina, at the end of August pledging "to enthusiastically support the president's America-first agenda."[71]

With the fealty of his party assured, the Trump team reprised the strategy that propelled them into the White House in 2016. As he had four years earlier, Trump brushed off concerns about the fundraising advantage Democrats once again assumed at the national level as an "anxious army of small donors," outraged over the president's provocations in the face of a severe national crisis, overcame the early advantage of the Trump Victory campaign. Never mind that Senate Republicans also faced the "fundraging" wrath of Democratic voters: in the fourteen most competitive Senate races in 2020, Democrats raised more money in eleven states.[72]

More telling, Trump and his political allies insisted, was the size of their rallies—held throughout the country, including in COVID-19 hotspots. Trump's rallies, thereby, took on greater significance—not just for cementing loyalty between Trump and his most avid supporters but also demonstrating the president's disregard for the social distancing and public health measures that public health officials in his administration supported. The Trump campaign took special delight in comparing the vitality of its mass rallies and elaborate ground game with the isolation of its opponent. Biden, following the recommendation of public health experts, campaigned "virtually"—holding events via the now-ubiquitous ZOOM webinar. Even without the pandemic, Trump was likely to paint Biden—though just four years older than he—as an old man, unaware and out of touch. COVID gave more edge to this indictment: the narrative of "Sleepy Joe" who wouldn't "leave his basement."[73]

It is hard to overstate the significance of COVID-19 in understanding the eventual outcome of the 2020 presidential race. It touched on nearly every issue and every aspect of President Trump's final year in office. Trump's flippant remarks about the "Kung flu" and "China virus" were further evidence of his brash demeanor and callous disregard for unifying language—even in the midst of a national crisis. Throughout the year, he seemed more interested in blaming Democratic governors for the massive loss of life than in promoting the information his own health agencies were disseminating.

Pundits and historians always speculate about an "October surprise" that might change the dynamic of the campaign. But when Trump tested positive for COVID in early October, "surprise" fails to describe the political theater that ensued: the carefully choreographed portrayal of Trump being helicoptered to nearby Walter Reed Hospital; the seating chart arrangement showing "close contacts" at the White House event held days before to celebrate the nomination of Supreme Court Justice Amy Comey Barret; and perhaps the most dramatic photographic moment, Trump's triumphant but somewhat unsteady return to the White House. Still medicated and fragile, Trump nevertheless managed a theatrical return: disembarking from Marine One and walking the staircase to the South Portico entrance, where he turned to face the cameras, removed his mask and gave his signature two thumbs up. Just days before he was in intensive care as the result of a disease that, as he had falsely claimed at a September campaign rally, "affects virtually nobody."[74] As was later reported, Trump's chief of staff was "consumed with fear that Trump might die." Other aides, including Dr. Anthony Fauci and Robert Redfield, the director of the Centers for Disease Control and Prevention, were convinced the whole experience would change Trump's attitude—persuade him, in the closing days of the campaign, that without a vaccine, the need to remain vigilant was paramount.[75] But, as he had done so many times before, Trump stood in defiance of common expectations (and public health guidance) and assured his followers not to be afraid of the disease—promising them, as if everyone could expect the same level of care as that received by the president of the United States, "You're going to beat it. We have the best medical equipment. We have the best medicines. All developed recently. And you're going to beat it."[76]

The crisis atmosphere of the 2020 campaign was compounded by a dramatic surge in social protest in the name of racial justice. In late May 2020, the country awoke to raw, unedited video of a Minneapolis police officer, Derek Chauvin, murdering a Black man, George Floyd. Floyd's death was not the first to be captured on video. And Floyd was not the only Black person shot and killed by police in 2020 (there were eighteen police shootings of unarmed Black persons that year). But the dislocation caused by the coronavirus pandemic created a social and political environment ripe for massive protest. Thousands of protests, from small towns to large urban cities, engaged an estimated twenty-six million Americans: young, old, white, Black.

While the protests spread throughout the country—and eventually the world—an overwhelming number of Americans supported the demonstrators and accepted a truth long denied, or resisted, that Floyd's death was a sign of systemic racial injustices. A Monmouth poll released a week after the protests began found that 57 percent of Americans—including a majority of white people—said the anger that led to the protests was completely justified. Even among self-described conservatives, 65 percent said the protesters' frustrations were at least partly justified. These sentiments were especially striking among younger individuals surveyed, with 52 percent of Republicans under fifty-five indicating they believed the killing of Floyd was evidence of a broader problem.[77]

As impressive as these massive and widespread calls for social justice appeared at the moment, they were quickly overwhelmed by campaign politics. Standing against the tide, Trump doubled down on his "law-and-order" mantra. One of his first actions as president had been to pull back on the Obama administration's vigilant oversight of police departments that violated the rights of citizens in their jurisdictions. After the Floyd protests, Trump declared himself "your president of law and order" and threatened to treat protesters, whom he called "terrorists," with "dominating" force.[78] Trump believed, as Nixon did, that most voters supported his commitment to "traditional values." Living not only in rural and exurban areas but also in working-class suburbs, these voters and potential voters had developed an atavistic relationship with Trump.[79] To rally them, he carried his resistance to the protests beyond rhetorical bluster to include deployment of federal forces to Portland, Oregon; Washington, DC; and other cities to quell demonstrations. Federal agents had broad authority to enforce federal laws—for example, to protect a federal courthouse under siege in Portland—even against the wishes of local authorities. But Homeland Security forces appeared to cross that line as they roamed widely around American cities, intruding on local policing.[80]

As we will discuss more in chapter 5, the administration viewed the coronavirus and social demonstrations as threats not only to its reelection prospects but also to Trump's larger vision of conservative nationalism. The transformation of Republican Party politics, the economic and social disruption caused by the pandemic, the surge of social unrest, and the pragmatic imperative to conduct an election in the middle of a public health crisis all created a combustible atmosphere that Trump exploited to stoke his base. Like 2016, the Trump campaign bet on itself—that the refusal to play to expectations or apologize for its mistakes would continue to energize his strongest supporters and bring voters out to the polls.

Still, the Trump team hedged its bets. Trump's rhetoric and commission on electoral security had laid a foundation for sowing doubt in the integrity of the 2020 outcome; with the approach of Election Day, Trump amplified this conspiratorial view. Four years earlier, he played coy about whether he would concede the race. But in 2020, he made specific, unfounded claims about features of the election adopted by many states in response to the pandemic. To adhere to public health recommendations, an unprecedented number of voters cast their ballot by mail. Rejecting the advice of some of his campaign team, Trump refused to encourage his supporters to do so. Instead, the president warned these public health measures would enable "thousands and thousands of people sitting in somebody's living room signing ballots all over the place."[81] Given the high number of absentee ballots, which most states and local election registrars were legally required to count after voting on Election Day ended, it was inevitable that Trump's election night lead would dissipate as Democratic voters—highly attentive to public health measures—were more likely to mail in their ballots than were Republicans. Anticipating a post–Election Day wave, Trump warned of "ballot dumps" and "illegal votes."[82] Republicans worried that all the president's talk of illegal votes and a fraudulent election might discourage Trump supporters from voting. Maybe they were right. Trump received eleven million more votes than he did in 2016, but Biden won back votes in critical swing states—Michigan, Wisconsin, Pennsylvania—and pulled out surprises in Georgia and Arizona.

The Plot That Failed

Trump's concerns with electoral fraud were more than campaign rhetoric. In the immediate aftermath of losing the election, the Trump campaign filed forty-two legal challenges, asking the courts to invalidate ballots because local and state officials had violated election rules, largely those governing the validation of mail-in ballots.[83] Given the unprecedented number of voters casting absentee ballots, state officials were severely strained by having to handle the large number of legal or procedural questions that arose during the count. But in each alleged case of malfeasance, the courts—including the Supreme Court of the United States, which had three Trump-appointed justices—found no illegal or unconstitutional action.

Still, the president kept up the ruse: "[Biden] only won in the eyes of the FAKE NEWS MEDIA," Trump tweeted on November 15, nearly two weeks after Election Day. "I concede NOTHING! We have a long way to go. This was a RIGGED ELECTION!"

On the morning of January 6, the president made his way up to the podium on a makeshift stage in front of the White House lawn—the final, last-ditch effort to "stop the steal." "Make no mistake," Trump told the crowd, "this election was stolen from you, from me and from the country."[84] The only hope for redemption, the president claimed, was his heretofore obsessively loyal vice president. Throughout the morning, speakers at the "Save America" rally concocted an incoherent and baseless claim that the certification of the Electoral College ballots at the other end of Pennsylvania Avenue could be preempted. Vice President Mike Pence had the constitutional authority—nay, obligation—they insisted, to declare Trump the rightful winner. "All Vice President Pence has to do is send it back to the states to recertify and we become president and you are the happiest people," Trump argued before an adoring crowd of supporters. "When you catch somebody in a fraud, you're allowed to go by very different rules. So, I hope Mike has the courage to do what he has to do."[85]

The Big Lie, the provocative measures advocated to redress the purported fraud, and the surge in populist anger that followed agitated a severe constitutional crisis, only part of which involved inciting a mob to storm the Capitol. These verbal and physical assaults on the legitimacy of constitutional rule were only conceivable in the incendiary political environment that Trump had deliberately fueled. This is not to claim the unfathomable demonstration of violence and intransigence on behalf of a sitting president and his supporters was overdetermined. However, Trump's schemes were part of a systematic effort to disrupt and transform established norms and institutions, the culmination of the convergence of presidential aggrandizement and movement politics during his administration—a fateful development over sixty years in the making.

Placing Trump in the long stream of American political development does not gainsay the unprecedented danger he and his most loyal political allies pose to representative constitutional government. Despite the RNC's effort to cast the attack on the capital as "legitimate political discourse," there is no "sympathetic" reading of the facts leading up to January 6.[86] In the immediate aftermath of the 2020 presidential election, Trump and a special legal team he convened to challenge the results concocted a seemingly viable tale of the vice president's authority to challenge the validity of Electoral College votes sent to the Congress for certification. Led by Rudy Giuliani and John Eastman—a legal scholar affiliated with the Claremont Institute—the White House dedicated immense energy to crafting a fictitious legal path starting with a plan to toss the election to the House of Representatives. If either candidate, with Pence's complicity, failed to garner 270 votes, then each state delegation would cast a single ballot for one of the two candidates; since Republicans controlled twenty-seven state delegations, there was a high likelihood that this would result in a Trump victory. However, once it became clear that Vice President Pence would not join the coup—not until the morning of January 4—Trump implored him to simply delay the count and send the electoral ballots back to the states. There, in states such as Georgia and Arizona that Republicans controlled, the legislatures would appoint an alternative slate of electors to cast ballots for Trump.[87]

This second option was no afterthought. Trump, Eastman, and Giuliani had a conference call with over three hundred state legislators from key states on January 2, prepping these loyal supporters on talking points and legal procedures to "decertify" their states' election results. "You are the real power," Trump told them. "You're more important than anything because the courts keep referring to you, and you're the ones that are going to make the decision."[88] As the January 6 rally date drew closer, former Trump aides and advisers, including former chief White House strategist Steve Bannon, established a so-called war room at the famed Willard Hotel, across the street from the White House.[89] There, they coordinated with Alex Jones, who had long given extremist paramilitary groups a platform to speak on his notoriously conspiratorial radio show, *InfoWars*. They solicited hundreds of thousands of dollars to advertise the event across the country, with the effect that nearly a hundred thousand Trump supporters descended on Washington, nearly two months after Election Day.[90]

At the vanguard of these "patriots" were the Proud Boys, an alt-right group Trump had defended throughout 2020, as they protested pandemic restrictions and intimidated and attacked Black Lives Matter protesters. The group began to style itself as a Trump militia after the president gave it a shout-out in his first debate with Biden, telling its members to "stand back and stand by." This one quote, according to the testimony of Proud Boys leaders, increased membership exponentially, and for a time the quote made it onto T-shirts with the group's distinct black and yellow pattern. When "President Trump tweeted about the January 6 rally and told attendees, 'Be there. Will be wild,'" the Proud Boys and their alt-right comrades—the Oath Keepers—viewed the tweet as a call to arms. Indeed, the Proud Boys' plans for the January 6 attack began to take shape a day after that December 19 tweet.

Eastman, among others, tried to portray these events as "what-if" situations; they were crafted at the behest of Trump, he acknowledged, but nobody in a real position of power believed the president's plans would be realized. Regardless, when Eastman and Giuliani spoke on the morning of January 6— immediately before Trump—they were not speaking in "what-if" terms:

> Eastman: We've got petitions pending before the Supreme Court that identify in chapter and verse, the number of times state election officials ignored or violated the state law in order to put Vice President Biden over the finish line. We know there was fraud . . . and all we are demanding of Vice President Pence is this afternoon at 1:00, he let the legislatures of the state look into this, so we can get to the bottom of it and the American people know whether we have control of the direction of our government or not!
> Giuliani: Who hides evidence? Criminals hide evidence. Not honest people. Over the next 10 days, we get to see the machines that are crooked, the ballots that are fraudulent, and if we're wrong, we will be made fools of. But if we're right, a lot of them will go to jail. Let's have trial by combat.[91]

On the morning of January 6, Trump made clear who would decide the future of his movement. One person, Trump supporters were told, could make Trump the winner: Mike Pence. And so, as the hour approached 1:00 p.m., just as Republican senators Josh Hawley (MO) and Ted Cruz (TX) were objecting to certifying the vote on the Senate floor, demonstrators outside the Capitol broke through the police barricades. Some, shouting, "Hang Mike Pence!" and "Bring out Pence," raced to the Senate chambers, where Capitol Police had, moments earlier, evacuated the vice president and then the rest of the Senate chamber.[92] If there was any doubt who would be blamed for Trump's plot that failed, Eastman emailed a Pence aide, as the vice president hid in a secure room: "The 'siege' is because YOU and your boss did not do what was necessary to allow this to be aired in a public way so that the American people can see for themselves what happened."[93]

In the aftermath of the siege, a congressional investigation, backed with the full support of the Department of Justice, pieced together many of the facts that led up to the assault on the People's House. Building on these hearings and their own investigations, Special Counsel Jack Smith, and Fulton County, Georgia, district attorney Fani Willis brought criminal indictments against Trump and his accomplices. Text messages between the White House chief of staff, Mark Meadows, and others—including Sean Hannity and Donald Trump Jr.—suggest that the White House neither anticipated nor intended violence.[94] But what has always been clear, because Trump and his closest allies always said it publicly, is that they were determined to find a way for Trump to maintain power after he failed to get enough votes—no matter what damage they did to the Constitution and American democracy.

Yet, as we will detail in the conclusion to this book, neither the former president's party nor his loyal base supporters held him accountable. As visual memories of the mob attack faded and political realities caught up with Republican members of Congress, Trump unabashedly returned to the scene to peddle his lies. A year after the attack, questions of voter fraud and illegal ballots continued to dominate the political news cycle. Seeking to put an end to the Big Lie, Republicans such as Senator Mike Rounds (SD) cut to the chase: "The election was fair, as fair as we've seen. We simply did not win the election." In response, Trump characteristically unleashed a tirade of recrimination: "He found the election to be ok—just fine. Is he crazy or just stupid? . . . I will never endorse this jerk again."[95]

Readers of the *New York Times*, or those who primarily got their news from Twitter, may have thought the former president would fade away. But this was not to be. Just a few short weeks after January 6, Trump was openly welcomed and celebrated at Republican establishment events. He continued to fundraise and speak at forums hosted by sympathetic organizations; six months after *leaving* office, he raised over $80 million in new contributions.[96] Fox News—even if it, as Trump said after the network refused to fully buy into his claims of fraud, "forgot what made them successful"—still gave a platform to Trump.[97] And Republican candidates for office eagerly sought his endorsement and personal appearance in support of them on the campaign circuit. In fact, in what may be a first, the RNC—still under the leadership of Rona McDaniel—openly promoted the former president's new social media website, Truth Social, after he was banned from Twitter.[98] On a near-daily basis in the lead-up to the app's launch, the RNC blasted its supporters with email after email encouraging people to sign up. Trump did not disappear; he created his own alternative reality, and a large majority of his party are currently living in it.

CONCLUSION: THE GRAND NEW, OLD PARTY

By the morning of January 6, even before the violence and discord of the Capitol riot would severely test, and ultimately confirm, the influence Trump would continue to have in his post-presidency, it was clear that the Republican Party was no longer the party of constitutional, limited government—the pillar of orthodox, or Reagan, conservatism. During Donald Trump's presidency, Republican leaders, pressured by the party's activist base, pushed government deeper into individuals' private lives and local communities: deploying federal agents throughout America's cities to uphold law and order, raising tariffs and generating tax loopholes to protect failing industries from the free market, preempting state control of public education and the environment, bankrolling the militarization of local police, nearly doubling the nation's debt in four years, and eroding the constitutional independence and prestige of the judiciary and the Justice Department. The final barrage was Trump's assault on the Constitution's much revered and lauded tradition of securing the peaceful transition of power—a tradition dating back to the "Revolution of 1800"—the last, and previously only, time the ownership of the presidency was in so much doubt.

Anyone able to see past the endless distraction of Trump's 2016 presidential campaign would not find this surprising; Trump did what he said he was going to do, despite lacking any governing experience and encountering sizable resistance from party leaders during the 2016 Republican primaries. His commitment to a MAGA agenda strengthened Trump's primordial relationship with his base and enabled him to maintain his firm grip on the GOP, even as he presided over his party's loss of the House, Senate, and White House; plotted to overturn the result of a free and fair election; and perpetuated the Big Lie, which became a loyalty test for Republicans running for office. Trump's capture of his party's apparatus was dramatically displayed in the months after the election as Republican-controlled states investigated election "fraud" and enacted laws that not only would impose new restrictions on access to the ballot but also subordinate nonpartisan election officials to highly partisan state legislatures.

In the final analysis, Trump's dominance over the Republican Party was a result of a top-down, bottom-up politics that all presidents since Lyndon Johnson have had to navigate. His braggadocio and machismo aside, Trump always seemed to recognize who had the real power: his base. He was led by "his most loyal customers" as much as he led them—a combustible relationship that fueled America's cold civil war. Nevertheless, Trump's takeover of the Republican Party was not just a matter of his personality—as much as he exhibited the traits of a Weberian "charismatic leader." Rather, this chapter demonstrates that Donald Trump was the culmination of long-standing developments in the party system, which have led presidents to capture the attention of the American electorate every four years. Presidents and primary voters have converged to make parties vehicles for the movement politics modern presidents must seek to manage. What distinguished Trump was his eagerness to serve a movement—and the alacrity with which he fundamentally disrupted American politics and society to do so.

3. Unilateralism and the Trump Presidency

Standing before the delegates at the 2016 Republican National Convention, Donald Trump boasted that he "alone" could fix America's problems. At the time, scholars and pundits laughed at such self-aggrandizement, arguing that Trump's inflated ego blinded him to the resilience of the Constitution's balance of powers. "I can't really imagine him on a white horse, but that seems to be what he's telling us," responded Hillary Clinton, who then launched a new campaign slogan, "Working Together," in direct response to Trump's braggadocio.[1]

Yet once Trump assumed office, we learned that this bravado was not rhetorical bluster. The president and his advisers immediately set to work to "erase" Barack Obama's legacy, exploiting the precedents that Obama himself had left behind when he relied on executive action to carry out his policies after Democrats lost control of the House in the 2010 midterms.[2] Trump promised, as his controversial chief strategist Steve Bannon put it, the "deconstruction of the administrative state."[3] Following the formula of executive-centered partisanship practiced by Democrats and Republicans since the late 1960s, Trump grasped the levers of administrative power with alacrity. His administration cannot lay claim to many major legislative achievements; however, as we detail in this chapter, he can be credited, or blamed, for aggressively exploiting administrative power to fulfill his campaign promises. Moreover, far from satisfied with reversing Obama's achievements, Trump "redeployed" the powers of the administrative state to pursue traditional commitments of Republican statism advanced by Ronald Reagan and George W. Bush: national and homeland security, law and order, protection of "family" values, and market-based approaches to social welfare policy. This stands in contrast to some presidential scholars, who insist that conservative presidents, while embracing presidential power, nevertheless use it to attack the ramparts of the administrative state.[4] Here, we emphasize that Trump repurposed aspects of traditional administrative politics to advance long-standing conservative goals *through* administration, not in opposition to it. Indeed, Trump's efforts to administer his Make America Great Again platform recast conservatism in his own image. Dedicated to strengthening the "coalition of restoration"—composed of blue-collar, religiously devout, and nonurban whites who felt that traditional Republican politicians had forsaken their needs and demands—Trump's executive actions imposed draconian immigration measures and aggressive protectionism that divided the beleaguered GOP establishment but mobilized base supporters.

While there is no single way to assess a president's success in office, it is true that Trump comes down near the bottom of the list on most traditional measures. He lacked a comprehensive legislative agenda and, apart from the Tax Cuts and Jobs Act of 2017, never put his personal stamp on major legislation. With the Republicans' failure to achieve their pledge to repeal and replace the Affordable Care Act, there would be no "Trump-Care." Nor did Trump's rhetoric offer a positive vision of what his presidency might accomplish. Breaking with the precedent of new presidents' invocation of shared American values and appeals for national unity, his inaugural address painted a dystopian portrait of "American carnage" marked by "the crime and the gangs and the drugs." Most of Trump's public speeches were stream-of-consciousness rants at campaign-style rallies that excoriated the mainstream press as the "enemy of the people" and scorned his political opponents as radical leftists intent on "dismantling and destroying the American way of life." Unlike previous presidents who at least presumed to be uniters rather than dividers, Trumps speeches and tweets were laced with ripostes that made the long-festering partisan polarization that had roiled the nation for nearly four decades more intractable and acrimonious.

Nevertheless, Trump left office with a significant policy legacy. Although he was a fierce critic of Obama's "major power grabs of authority," believing they were "the easy way out," Trump became an enthusiastic defender of the administrative presidency.[5] The administrative presidency may lack the fanfare of momentous bill signings and dazzling rhetoric, but as we detail in this chapter, executive administration gave practical effect to Trump's incendiary rhetoric. More to the point, partisan administration was an important mobilizing force that built support within the Republican Party and maintained base-level enthusiasm among the president's most ardent supporters. By *administration* or the *administrative presidency*, we mean Trump's unilateral efforts to leverage the federal bureaucracy for his personal and partisan goals. These tools included staffing agencies with loyalists, abetted by changes to personnel policy; moving funds between different agencies with limited, if any, congressional oversight; the use of formal and informal rulemaking; and direct presidential control over federal policy that undermined standard operating procedures within departments and agencies.

The politicization of the bureaucracy did not begin with Trump. With the consolidation of the modern presidency during Franklin Roosevelt's long reign, these personnel, financial, and regulatory tools enabled presidents and their appointees to short-circuit the separation of powers in carrying out domestic and foreign policy, thus facilitating the transfer of power from Congress to the executive.[6] Nevertheless, as we suggested in previous chapters, Trump marks a culmination of partisan administration that began to take root during the cataclysmic changes wrought by the culture wars of the sixties. Both Democratic and Republican presidents have centralized power in the White House since the Nixon years, attenuating protocols and institutions that maintained departments and agencies as neutral sites of public policy; however, the Trump administration represents the strongest expression to date of this denigration of "bureaucratic autonomy."[7] By conventional measures, Trump did not rely on the administrative presidency any more or less than expected.[8] Yet his unflinching use and public celebration of unilateralism threatened to alter the character of American democracy. Overseeing a provocative merging of administration and partisan mobilization, Trump seized the instruments of administrative control to rally his party around a new, more populist brand of American conservatism—a model that Republican officeholders or those aspiring to hold office have felt compelled to follow as they have sought the former president's endorsement in primaries or jostled to be his would-be successor.

As we have documented elsewhere throughout this book, the former president's dominance over party affairs after he retreated to Mar-a-Lago is evidence of more than a cult of personality. We extend that idea further in this chapter by showing that Trump's partisan success is attributable, in large part, to his ability to achieve base-pleasing policies through unilateral action and administrative rules. While there is truth in many analyses that have viewed Trump's executive aggrandizement as animated by "authoritarian" or "despotic" tendencies on the American right, few have recognized that the opportunities for such an aggressive form of conservative nationalism are the result of historical institutional developments long in the making. Consequently, the opportunities for a repeat performance, even among a less charismatic or bombastic president, remain a great threat to the resilience of American democracy.

UNILATERALISM, EXECUTIVE POWER, AND THE TRUMP WHITE HOUSE

The relationship between presidential power and bureaucratic management has always been a difficult one to negotiate. On the one hand, the overarching principle of America's constitutional order is popular sovereignty. All governmental power flows from the people, and its exercise is always conditional on their consent. And yet, the entire structure of administrative government is predicated on the idea that some decisions are best left to experts. There are scientific and objective standards for what works and what does not, regardless of what the people think. This commitment to merit and expertise undergirds civil service procedures that provide most personnel in departments and agencies some protection from political influence.

To achieve this balance, we traditionally think that Congress and the president may negotiate on the broad contours of the government's goals, crafting legislation to promote such policies as consumer and environmental protection, encourage some immigration while restricting entry by others, or declare "homeland security" to be a new national priority. But afterward, the details are worked out elsewhere, subject to oversight procedures, budget writing and appropriations bills, formal rulemaking, and appointments and promotions. Under Lyndon Johnson's direction, Congress created a new Department of Housing and Urban Development, staffed with experts and administrators who coordinated dozens of programs at the local, state, and federal levels for slum clearance, public housing, rental assistance, and antidiscrimination enforcement. During the Nixon administration, Congress dedicated vast new sums of money for environmental cleanup and bestowed new regulatory authority on the Environmental Protection Agency (EPA) to restrict new pollutants into the country's air and rivers. As we all learned during the worldwide COVID-19 pandemic, federal agencies such as the Food and Drug Administration and the Centers for Disease Control and Prevention followed meticulous, predefined procedures for ensuring that new vaccines were safe and effective—procedures influenced not just by the White House but also by elected representatives in congressional subcommittees and politically appointed officials at the heads of those agencies. Unlike other advanced representative democracies, such as the United Kingdom, France, and Germany, where highly trained experts are granted constitutional protection from political interference, the American administrative state—layered uneasily atop a political culture highly suspicious of centralized power—has long sought to balance the independence of experts and the responsibility of elected representatives to hold those experts accountable.

Since the emergence of the federal administrative state in the late nineteenth century and early twentieth century, politicians and bureaucrats have openly struggled to keep those seemingly competing principles in balance with one another. Regardless of their ideological orientation, presidents of both parties have challenged the "neutral competence" of the federal civil service. With the rise of partisan administration in the 1960s, liberals and conservatives alike have often viewed the "administrative state" with at least some scorn—an obstacle to remaking American politics in their own image. As Arthur Schlesinger Jr. once opined, John F. Kennedy was routinely thwarted by a "great deadweight on executive innovation," given the bureaucracy's "infinite capacity to dilute, delay, obstruct, resist, and sabotage presidential purposes."[9] Conservative presidents, most notably Nixon and Reagan, were enthusiastic about lambasting "wasteful, muscle-bound government" and "big bureaucracy."[10]

Still, despite many high-profile and dramatic standoffs between presidents and federal agencies, the balance has usually held. Administrative agencies were never the "transmission belts" of presidential orders or congressional intent (especially during times of divided government).[11] Nor were presidents and their political appointees fully free to control what took place inside the halls of various departments and federal agencies. Bureaucrats, Rachel Potter has shown, routinely leverage their vast knowledge of procedure and intra-agency rules to delay presidential and congressional meddling in making new regulations.[12] Beyond civil service protections, there was always power in information, fact-finding, and evidence-based reporting. The Court's oversight of "arbitrary and capricious" executive action checked the most ambitious plots to harness the full extent of the modern administrative state.

The historical record demonstrates that the Trump administration fit into this long-standing pattern of presidential administration—to a point. The recent history of administrative action displayed in figures 3.1 and 3.2 begins with Dwight Eisenhower's presidency, several years after the administrative convulsions brought about by World War II and military demobilization subsided, which provide a good baseline for evaluating the management practices since the consolidation of the modern presidency. We include a variety of instruments presidents, including Trump, have used to manage federal policy. The most recognizable of these is executive orders—a practice dating back to

George Washington's administration. But executive orders are just part of the administrative measures that presidents have deployed. Presidents also rely on memorandums, which are similar in function to executive orders, except that they do not have the same level of reporting or statutory authorization requirements. Then there are proclamations and other addresses. Many are celebratory, issued in commemoration of some event, but others might signal important policy change. Signing statements proclaim a president's view that certain parts of a law are unconstitutional and the White House's intention not to enforce these faulty provisions. In figure 3.1 we have tallied the orders, memorandums, proclamations, and signing statements that relate to changes in the federal government's operations.

These figures show that all presidents since World War II have relied heavily on administrative action to pursue their objectives—a sign that unilateralism has become a routine feature of modern presidential leadership. Indeed, the arsenal of presidential administration has grown, with the increasing use of more flexible measures such as memorandums to make policy. Rather than reduce the White House's reliance on unilateral action, for which Trump excoriated the Obama administration, Trump's executive aggrandizement on average surpassed his predecessor's in almost every possible way. Just as important, while Trump bragged in a 2016 presidential debate that he would take on all the "waste, fraud, and abuse all over the place" and "cut so much your head will spin!," many of his administrative actions presupposed repurposing, rather than curtailing, the bureaucracy. Significantly, although these figures only go up through 2021, Trump's aggressive administrative actions appear to have prompted the Biden White House, determined to change the trajectory of Trump policy, to rely extensively on unilateral action to do so.[13]

This is not to say that Trump was an effective administrator in the vein of modern public administration scholarship. As Michael Livermore and Richard Revesz write, "The reason that the Trump administration's approach to regulation is dangerous is not because of attempts by political appointees to influence agency decision making. Political oversight of agencies is a normal and expected part of the contemporary presidency. The problem is that the administration has rejected the system of norms, conventions, and practices that have evolved over the past several decades to channel that political influence."[14] The violation of long-standing protocols did not lead merely to chaos, however. Rather, the Trump White House sidestepped those norms and practices to use administrative power strategically to obtain its objectives.

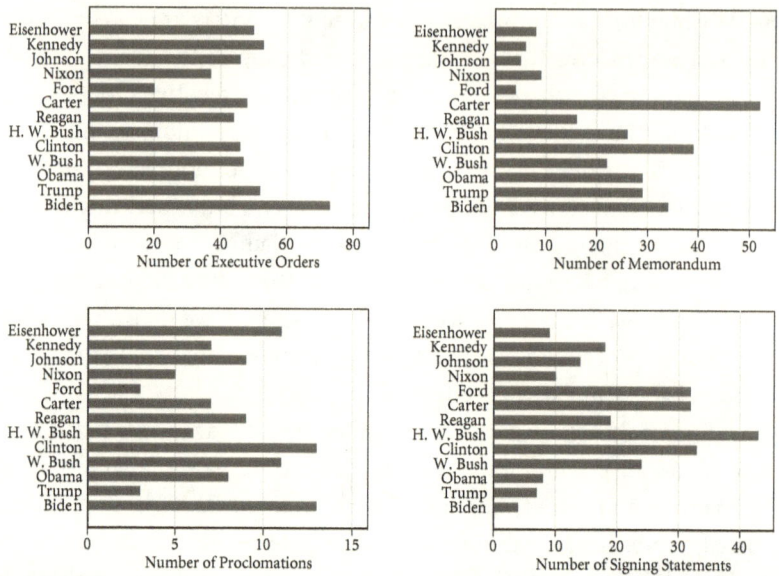

Figure 3.1. Historical comparison of the use of various administrative tools—executive orders, memorandums, proclamations, and signing statements—by US presidents from Dwight Eisenhower through Donald Trump, within the first calendar year of holding office.

Source: The American Presidency Project and author calculations. *Credit:* Created by authors.

Rather than deconstructing the administrative state, the numbers seem to suggest that Trump was deliberate in *redeploying* key aspects of federal administration in the service of conservative goals. And while redeployment is a long-standing conservative approach to managing the administrative state, Trump's indifference, if not downright hostility, to the principles of bureaucratic management gave further momentum to this stratagem.

Consider how the redeployment strategy helps to explain the Trump White House's approach to regulatory policy, which was celebrated, even by Never Trumpers, as admirably "deregulatory."[15] Although the rules-writing process entails complex negotiations between Congress, the various agencies, the president, and interest groups, the White House has gradually amassed an upper hand in regulatory politics. Formed during the final year of Jimmy Carter's presidency and expanded during Ronald Reagan's tenure, the White House Office of Information and Regulatory Affairs (OIRA), located in the Office of Management and Budget (OMB), manages a regulatory review process, which

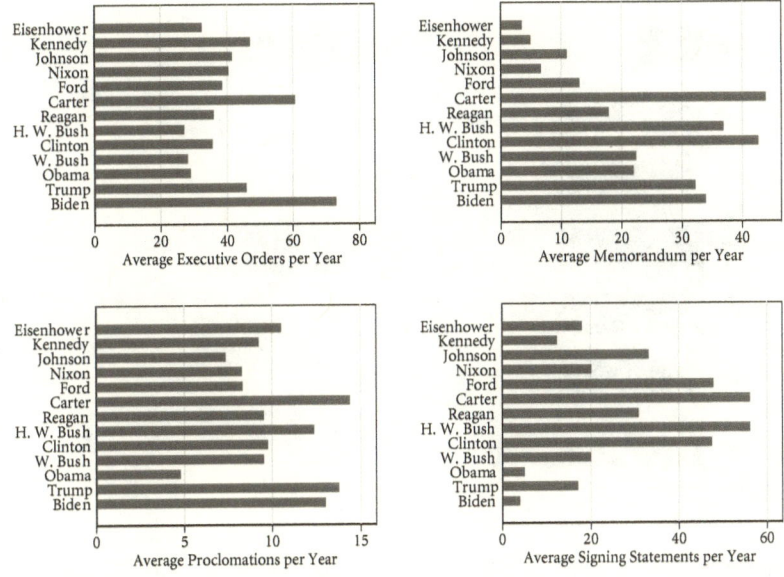

Figure 3.2. Historical comparison of the use of various administrative tools—executive orders, memorandums, proclamations, and signing statements—by US presidents from Dwight Eisenhower through Donald Trump, averaged over the number of years they held office.

Source: The American Presidency Project and author calculations. *Credit:* Created by authors.

is the primary procedure presidents use to control executive departments and agencies. Through the process of regulatory review, presidents can propose changes to agency rules or reject them.[16] This institutional innovation was an extension of a long-running, bipartisan desire to circumvent bureaucratic independence and put the president's personal stamp on regulatory action.[17]

Consequently, we can consider the total amount of change to the federal regulatory code as a measure for understanding the president's effort to change the trajectory of regulatory politics. But not all rules are equal. Some are quite small and mundane, which would inflate a simple count. In 1993, President Clinton signed Executive Order 12866, which further institutionalized the regulatory review process enacted under Reagan by requiring agencies to submit "economically significant" rules for review.[18] There is a further classification scheme, which includes economically significant rules but also includes any change that would "create a serious inconsistency or otherwise interfere with an action taken or planned by another agency."[19] Together, we can use these two

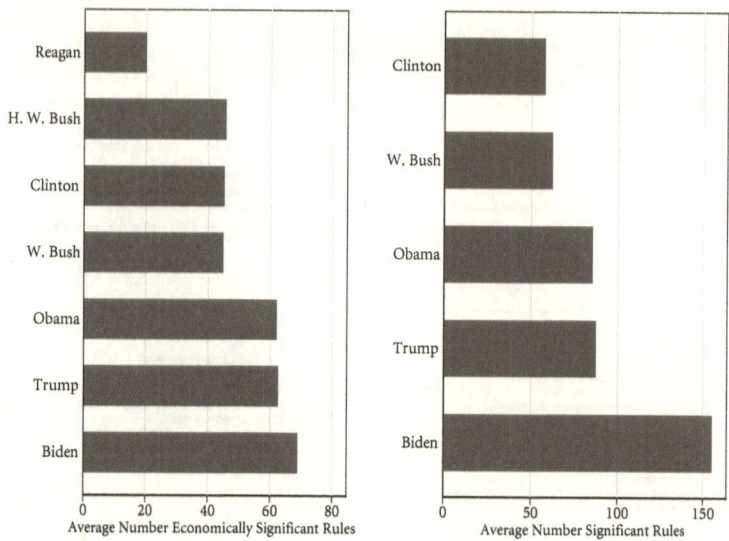

Figure 3.3. Average number of rules finalized per year by US presidents from Ronald Reagan to Joe Biden, categorizing rules into "economically significant" and "significant" as defined by Executive Order 12866.

Source: Reg Stats, Regulatory Studies Center, George Washington University. *Credit:* Created by authors.

classifications to visualize how Trump fared in comparison to his predecessors and to the first year of Joe Biden's administration. Figure 3.3 suggests that aggressive rulemaking has increased over time—regardless of party.

What explains these trends, given the Republican Party's decades-long commitment to ending "big government"? Given Trump's own pledge to "drain the swamp," some might argue that the failure to limit government growth is evidence of Trump's claim that a "deep state" conspiracy prevented his administration's boldest reforms for remaking American government. And, it is true that a significant portion of Trump's deregulatory agenda was blocked by the courts; according to the Institute for Policy Integrity at New York University, Trump is the only president since Clinton (when counting began) to have lost a majority—57 percent—of major rules challenged in court.[20] But well before Trump concocted farcical tales about bureaucratic power, mainstream conservatives had chosen to join, not fight, administrative government; not every rule change rolled back government. Many of those conservatives—including Trump's second attorney general, William Barr—were leading intellectual figures in developing a strategy to use, rather than dismantle, administrative power—so long as it was subject to an independent, forceful, and conservative presidency.

During the Reagan administration, officials within the Department of Justice (DOJ) and other intellectual circles, such as the newly formed Federalist Society, began to see the president's control of administrative power as deeply rooted in the nation's history and constitutional logic. Since the start of the twentieth century, conservatives had primarily thought of the administrative state as a constitutional perversion—a creeping Leviathan that lacked legitimacy at every turn, the work of progressives who viewed the constitutional system as antiquated and incompatible with administrative government. However, after the Nixon administration demonstrated that the presidency could be used to advance conservative causes by redeploying, rather than deconstructing, federal power, these new intellectuals abandoned the traditional conservative line.

Before this turn, traditional conservatives preached a doctrine of strict enumeration, congressional supremacy, and nondelegation; new conservatives found expansive presidential power lurking in the text of Article II. Enamored of the promise of Reagan's conservative commitments—and deflated by the thought that Democrats had controlled Congress since 1955—leaders of the conservative legal movement shifted course and argued that the president had the authority to control the entire executive branch. The "unitary executive" doctrine has serious implications for Congress's ability to perform its oversight duties—to hold the modern executive accountable, as the Legislative Reorganization Act of 1946 put it dramatically, by engaging in "continuous watchfulness" over the bureaucracy. As Reagan's legal counsel justified a unitary executive, "Our majoritarian democracy may work better if, when Congress is significantly divided, a President can exercise strong leadership to effect the will of the majority that elected him."[21]

Writing in the aftermath of Reagan's presidency, Steven Calabresi, who worked in the Reagan White House, and Kevin Rhodes bestowed academic credibility on the unitary executive doctrine in the *Harvard Law Review*. Drawing on Justice Scalia's dissent in a case in which the majority opinion upheld Congress's powers to appoint independent counsels to investigate the president, they argued that the unitary executive was consistent with the Framers' plan for the separation of powers, which proscribed the creation of "independent entities" within the executive department. "Article II does not create parity among executive officials," they argued; it gives all executive power to "a

President."[22] "Such an interpretation," they wrote, which denies that Congress, or the judiciary, has the power to fragment executive power, "facilitates the recapture of the Framers' vision of three competing, co-equal, and coordinate departments—no single one of which was given the *exclusive* role of maintaining the constitutional plan."[23]

At one level, the historical and textual arguments are quite academic and seemingly uncontroversial. But, as Stephen Skowronek has noted, presidential dominion over the executive branch was joined to larger, more fundamental debates over public authority and legitimacy. Ironically, conservatives' objectives echoed arguments that had initially motivated progressives' desire to see a stronger presidency:

> It [the theory of the unitary executive] justified the release of presidential power within the executive branch as a restoration of responsibility and accountability in government. . . . All the conservatives needed to do to tap this sense of democracy was to constitutionalize the public voice, to tie the fact that the President is the only officer in American government who represents the nation as a whole more closely to the notion that the selection of the President had become, in effect, the only credible expression of the public's will.[24]

Consequently, the unitary executive could not be dismissed as "situational constitutionalism," with conservatives and Republicans abandoning their processual commitments once ensconced in power.[25] Rather, as these deeply theorized and researched attempts to legitimize a unitary executive demonstrate, modern conservativism has come to the view that the current position of the president as the vital center of American democracy is embedded within the original constitutional structure. As such, conservative intellectuals found much to admire in Trump's "I alone can fix it" mantra. He fit squarely within the mainstream of conservative intellectual orthodoxy on questions of presidential power and control.

A case in point is Trump's pick for attorney general, William Barr, who he tapped to head the DOJ after the firing of Jeff Sessions. Although Sessions had been a loyal Trump supporter—the first senator to endorse his candidacy in 2016—he infuriated the president by recusing himself in the investigation of possible Russian interference in the 2016 election, leading to Deputy Attorney General Rod Rosenstein, in his role as acting attorney general, appointing Special Counsel Robert Mueller to carry out the inquiry. In a 2019 address to the Federalist Society, which could be viewed as an audition to become the next attorney general, Barr gave a constitutional defense of Trump's excoriation of Sessions's recusal: "The implications of the Framers' decision are obvious. If Congress attempts to vest the power to execute the law in someone beyond the control of the President, it contravenes the Framers' clear intent to vest that power in a single person, the President."[26]

For Barr and others who defended the president's claims to unilateral power, such as those at the Claremont Institute (where John Eastman, the lawyer who devised the plan to overturn electoral ballots, was a senior fellow), the "implications" extended to numerous attempts to resist Trump's administrative decrees. It was justification for resisting the "constant harassment" by Congress: evading congressional approval of appointments, stonewalling Congress's "demands for testimony and documents," and refusing to comply with the "avalanche of subpoenas" that came from duly elected representatives at the other end of Pennsylvania Avenue. Again, Barr's fervent defense of a unitary executive was not merely an opportunistic power play; these words echoed the younger Barr's concern with "congressional incursions" into the "executive branch prerogatives" that motivated his work as assistant attorney general during George H. W. Bush's presidency.[27] Given the conservative movement's long curation of a unitary executive, Trump—the would-be destroyer of the administrative state on the campaign trail—had every incentive to take refuge in its powers. To the victors go the administrative spoils!

We have noted that Trump's heavy reliance on administrative action was not unusual, even for a self-proclaimed enemy of the deep state. However, we would be missing the forest for the trees if we confined our analysis to a simple count of administrative actions. While Trump's unilateralism is not a deviation from the prevailing conservative stratagem, Trump smashed constitutional guardrails that had previously constrained even the most expansive views of presidential authority. Reagan's White House largely sought to legitimize the unitary executive with the idea that presidential authority was heightened during prolonged periods of congressional gridlock and divided government, which defined the entirety of Reagan's tenure. As the only representative official elected by the entire country—usually by a majority of the vote—presidents had the special responsibility to overcome the ineffectiveness of a government stymied by separate partisan realms. Regardless of whether these are accurate claims or normatively desirable, they do not apply to Trump, who lost the popular vote and enjoyed Republican majorities in the House and Senate during his first two years in office.

Trump's claims to unilateralism were couched in a politics of fear, alleging that domestic and international enemies—immigrants, Black Lives Matter protesters, "radical Islamic terrorists"—posed an existential threat to the American way of life. His tarring of liberals and recalcitrant civil servants as illegitimate and his contempt for public institutions bore little resemblance to conservatism, traditionally understood. Indeed, by the end of his administration, Trump seemed to drop any pretense that conservatism stood for limited government. Reagan—a onetime New Deal Democrat—had sought to return significant responsibilities of the national state to the states. Trump, despite his relative inexperience, recognized the opportunity an expansive federal state presented and relished the exercise of partisan administration that joined presidential prerogative, partisan polarization, and social activism. To "erase Obama's legacy," Trump nourished stronger partnerships with right-leaning activists than had previous Republican presidents and congressional leaders. Consequently, his plebiscitary politics, animated by a direct relationship with the conservative base, was a harsher, more unfiltered version of the partisanship than Reagan, Bush, and Obama pursued.[28]

SECURING THE STATE: FREEDOM FROM FEAR

The average voter, of course, is not a conservative intellectual, schooled in the debates of the Constitution's framers or a subscriber to the Federalist Society's weekly podcast. But that does not mean that Trump's ascendence boils down just to his charisma, xenophobia, or demagoguery. There has to be a reason why so many found his views of presidential leadership attractive—especially on the right, where virtues of constitutional restraints, balance of powers, and rule of law are frequently preached (if seldom followed).

Part of the answer lies in the Trump administration's aggressive use of presidential power in the service of tangible causes (table 3.1). The redeployment of administrative power to make America great again tapped into a pervasive, multifaceted sense of fear, which was instilled in the Republican Party's base prior to the rise of Trump. Previous Republican presidential candidates Mitt Romney, John McCain, and George W. Bush had each tried to keep this faction of conservative activism at arm's length. Bush offered them compassion; McCain, a return to the idea that America had an important role to play upholding freedom abroad; Romney, a classic, well-groomed fiscal conservatism. Trump's

Table 3.1. Redeploying the State through Unilateral Action

Freedom from Fear: Homeland Security State	*Freedom from Want:* Welfare State
Immigration: Muslim ban, rescind DACA, "the Wall," sanctuary cities, family separation, stay in Mexico	*Informal Rulemaking*: loan service/debt and Title IX guidelines in Department of Education
Fiscal Priorities: Expand federal government spending: DHS, DOD, VA	*Formal Rulemaking*: Rescind labor protections for federal contractors
Trade Negotiations: Tariff increases, NAFTA	*Waivers*: Medicaid waivers for work requirements
Operations: Partial hiring freeze exempting military personnel	*Permits*: Offshore drilling exemptions

right-wing populism played into people's fears: undocumented immigrants, competition with China, unrest in big cities, "radical Islamic terrorism." Even when echoing a core conservative commitment that Republican presidents had stressed since Richard Nixon's 1968 presidential campaign, Trump's boast that he was the "law-and-order candidate" at the 2016 Republican convention foretold a would-be strong man determined to devote all the resources of the federal government to crack down on crime, deport undocumented immigrants, and show no mercy in preempting terrorist threats at home and abroad.

Once in office, Trump found ample discretion in the institutions and procedures dedicated to securing American's "freedom from fear." Franklin Delano Roosevelt had envisioned this promise of a new world order, buttressed by international institutions such as the United Nations and the World Bank, as a pillar of the New Deal state; Trump's salve for fear was an unwavering commitment to "America First," which scorned liberal internationalism. On the home front, this neo-isolationism meant dealing harshly with one of the most vexing political issues of the time: undocumented immigration. Trump provocatively stoked fear on the campaign trail, exaggerating tales of chaos on the US-Mexico border and the contribution that undocumented immigration made to crime rates. He claimed, without substantial evidence, that immigrants were the ones "bringing drugs" and "bringing crime" ("they're rapists"). The boisterous chants of "Build that wall" at Trump's campaign rallies substituted for a policy white paper, and tougher border security adumbrated the myriad problems that Trump addressed: bad trade deals, wage loss, terrorism, and the denigration of traditional values.

True to his leading campaign promise, or threat, Trump's executive actions on immigration policy became the most celebrated cause of his partisan administration. Abetted by precedents set during the George W. Bush and Obama administrations that allowed the presidency to amass considerable power to set national immigration policy, Trump fused the logic of a unitary executive to primordial fears of foreign "others." Trump did not manufacture this fear—it had been stewing since the traumatic events of 9/11. Following the deadliest attack in US history, the Bush administration, with bipartisan support in Congress, created the Department of Homeland Security (DHS)—the largest law enforcement agency in the federal government—which was given sweeping powers to vet foreigners as they entered the United States. For example, in 2002 Congress delegated authority to DHS to "establish national immigration services and priorities."[29] The Supreme Court sanctified this plenary power in 2012 with a 5-to-3 decision overturning a number of Arizona statutes that conflicted with federal prerogatives. Federal law on immigration reigned supreme, the majority opinion argued, and the president and immigration officials enjoyed "broad discretion" to enforce inherently underspecified and ambiguous immigration statutes.[30]

When Trump entered the Oval Office, therefore, he found a set of tools, honed by his predecessors, which he then used to disrupt the country's immigration procedures. Trump appointed a few establishment Republicans, such as General John Kelly—the first secretary of DHS—who resisted some of the White House's most provocative anti-immigration measures; however, the president empowered Stephen Miller, placed in the West Wing as a senior adviser, as the tip of the spear of his draconian immigration policy. Miller had established close ties with anti-immigration groups while working as communications director for Alabama senator and Trump's first attorney general, Jeff Sessions. Lending key staff support to Miller and Sessions was Gene Hamilton—former general counsel to Senator Sessions—who was appointed counselor to the attorney general. While in Congress, Sessions, Miller, and Hamilton had worked effectively to thwart bipartisan efforts to enact immigration reform; now, empowered by a populist president, they were determined to use the expansive powers of the presidency to redeploy the deep state in the service of sectarian nationalism. They drafted a raft of executive orders that fired up Trump's base and established a blueprint to unilaterally carry out the signature commitment of the president's America First program.

Just five days after Trump took office, on January 25, the White House released the first of these orders with the goal of "enhancing public safety in the interior of the United States."³¹ The order set new priority guidelines for federal immigration officials but, most significantly, threatened legal and fiscal consequences for any subnational jurisdictions that refused to volunteer information or commit suspects to federal immigration officials. Claiming that the new order would "ensure that jurisdictions that fail to comply with applicable Federal law do not receive Federal funds, except as mandated by law," the policy angered many Democrats and even some Republicans, who were conflicted by their professed belief in federalism and their desire to curb illegal immigration. The legality of Trump's crackdown on sanctuary cities was never resolved, and the White House never deprived uncooperative localities of any funding. In an attempt to publicly shame some of these municipalities, the administration constructed lists of local police agencies that refused to comply with any DHS extended detention requests; three weeks later, however, citing numerous errors in the list, DHS suspended publication.³²

The administration's awkward intervention into state and local policing was part of a broader law-and-order campaign. Trump issued two additional executive orders during his first year that were meant to encourage state and local police officers "to do their job." In late March, the DOJ announced that it would drastically scale back its use of consent decrees, which had become a major instrument under the Obama administration for investigating civil rights complaints levied against local police departments.³³ And, in late August, Trump announced an executive order that revoked a January 2015 order prohibiting the sale of military-grade munitions and equipment to local and state police forces.³⁴ In a further maneuver meant to reverse his predecessor's effort to reform criminal justice, the administration also overturned an Obama-era order that would have slowly ended the federal government's reliance on for-profit prisons.³⁵

Trump's interventions in states and localities were but the start of the president's "law-and-order" program to curtain immigration. Immediately following the administration's crackdown on sanctuary cities, Trump issued a second immigration order, which required DHS to begin to "identify and, to the extent permitted by law, allocate all sources of Federal funds for the planning, designing, and constructing of a physical wall along the southern border."³⁶ The Republican-controlled Congress did not appropriate any funds for Trump's border wall. Indeed, it was a key point of controversy in the logjam that stymied most legislative initiatives. But Trump, determined to fulfill a signature campaign promise, used executive power to send a strong signal to his base: to demonstrate that, protestations of the Washington establishment aside, work on the barricade had begun and was already showing signs of curtailing undocumented immigration.[37]

Beyond its campaign to crack down on undocumented immigration, the Trump White House also directed border and customs agents to restrict the entry of those seeking asylum in the United States. Executive Order 13769 *immediately* suspended the US Refugee Admissions Program for 120 days; suspended the entry of Syrian refugees indefinitely; and suspended entry, for at least 90 days, of travelers from Iran, Iraq, Libya, Somalia, Sudan, Syria, and Yemen.[38] More than seven hundred travelers were detained, having had their visas revoked en route to their destination, and up to sixty thousand visas were "provisionally revoked," as individuals—including many students and family members of American residents—remained at their points of departure. Two days later, after widespread protests at the nation's airports, the administration denied that it had ordered a "Muslim ban," citing the fact that Executive Order 13769 did not block entry from the other thirty-three Muslim-majority countries in the world.[39] Nevertheless, less than a week after implementation, federal judge James Robart, a George W. Bush appointee, stopped its enforcement.

Not to be deterred, one month later the White House reissued the order, modifying what it deemed the most legally precarious positions.[40] Many legal scholars dismissed the administration's claim that it had wide-ranging authority over refugee policy and that it was just following the example of six of the preceding seven presidential administrations.[41] However, the Supreme Court, without dissent, stayed the lower court injunction on the new order and allowed the temporary six-month ban to take effect. By the time the Supreme Court issued a final ruling on the case, Trump's first Supreme Court appointment, Justice Neil Gorsuch—who owed his seat to majority leader Mitch McConnell blocking Barack Obama's nomination of Merrick Garland—had joined the tribunal. In a 5-to-4 decision, in *Trump v. Hawaii*, the conservative majority claimed that the Immigration and Nationality Act of 1952 "exudes deference to the President in every clause"; this broad grant of authority was not compromised, Chief Justice John Robert's opinion argued, even though he acknowledged that Trump had made many statements expressing his desire to impose a "Muslim ban."[42]

Two years later, Roberts switched sides and, joined by the four liberal justices, issued a ruling that blocked the Trump administration's order to rescind Deferred Action for Childhood Arrivals (DACA), an Obama-era program that protected undocumented Dreamers, who had been brought to the United States as children, from deportation. However, his opinion hardly imposed a major constraint on the president's authority to remake immigration policy unilaterally. In fact, even though it labeled the Trump administration's actions "arbitrary and capricious," the Court tacitly recognized the president's authority to unilaterally terminate the policy so long as, in the future, the president provided the rationale to do so at the time of repeal.[43] In effect, the justices offered the administration a legal road map for repealing DACA, which the Trump administration soon embraced in the middle of his reelection campaign.[44]

The DACA saga testifies to the promise and perils of presidentialism in a polarized age. Hoping that a firm policy on border control might encourage a bipartisan agreement on comprehensive immigration reform, Obama pursued an aggressive deportation strategy during much of his first term; immigration rights groups anointed him the "deporter in chief." But, failing to reach an agreement with the Republican Congress, Obama, seeking a rapprochement with progressive activists, took dramatic administrative action toward the end of 2011 to protect Dreamers from deportation. Although the interdepartmental memorandum issued by Secretary of Homeland Security Janet Napolitano specified that the directive "conferred no substantive right, immigration status or pathway to citizenship," it did establish a process to allow qualifying individuals to gain protection from deportation for two years, and specified that those Dreamers granted deferred action could apply for work authorization.[45] Three years later, after the 2014 election, which saw the Republicans win control of the Senate, Obama extended deportation relief to the parents of permanent residents and citizens (Deferred Action for Parents of Americans [DAPA]). These programs, rooted in the president's power of "prosecutorial discretion," became the source of passionate partisan conflict that Trump exploited in the Republican primaries and general election. Immigration rights groups, despairing of legislative reform after Republicans took control of both congressional chambers in 2014, strongly advocated for such bold administrative action; however, this solution for partisan "gridlock," which had become a leading feature of executive-centered partisanship, left immigration rights exposed to the retaliatory unilateral action of President Trump and the aggressive conservative statists who occupied the White House in 2017.

Just as Obama crafted this policy as a bold strategy of administrative partisanship, so Trump, eager to partner with anti-immigration activists, sought to unilaterally suspend it. The fate of close to eight hundred thousand undocumented immigrants—the Dreamers who came to the United States as children and are in the country illegally through no fault of their own—thus became a volatile and highly scrutinized example of the mischiefs of executive-centered partisanship.

Trump's decision to suspend the program, which followed his rescission of the more expansive DAPA initiative, was not merely an attempt to placate his conservative base. While the decision to suspend DACA clearly resonated with his pledge to strengthen the country's immigration laws, ramp up border security, and cut down on both legal and illegal immigration, this action posed serious political risks for the administration. Although many of Trump's first executive actions were related to his hard-line campaign promises on immigration, when pressed specifically on the popular DACA initiative, the president and his administration demurred.[46] Given Trump's vitriolic oratory on the campaign trail, it is easy to dismiss his pledge to "show great heart" to the Dreamers after taking office as empty rhetoric. Yet, his delay in rescinding the DACA program immediately after entering the White House was enough to encourage ten states' attorneys general to threaten to sue the federal government over its continued support.[47] Faced with a September deadline, then secretary of homeland security John Kelly repeatedly traveled to Capitol Hill throughout the summer to warn of the program's impending termination.[48] The warnings were not without cause or precedent. When Obama attempted to expand DACA by adding parents of US citizens and legal residents to the program, legal challenges almost immediately led to a court injunction on the administrative action. Consequently, the Trump administration was stuck between the proverbial rock and a hard place: end the popular DACA program to appease his most loyal supporters or uphold the policy, reneging on one of his most high-profile campaign promises, and suffer a legal threat that might terminate the program immediately. Instead, in a calculated political maneuver, Trump sought to appear *simultaneously* hard on immigration and in favor of any number of legislative proposals likely to pass the Congress over the fate of affected individuals.

We emphasize the political calculus here, despite the fact that the Supreme Court eventually decided that Trump acted unconstitutionally in ending the DACA program—a fact we will explore in greater depth in chapter 4. The Court's slap on the wrist should not elide the fact that DACA was born of presidential administration and the Trump White House, bowing to its base supporters, risked ending a popular initiative through executive fiat. There was no prospect, then, that the effort to appease both sides in the rescission of DACA would lead to a ceasefire in the political war zone that Trump occupied. Indeed, when considered in the context of his other anti-immigration actions, the DACA maneuver merely threw salt in the wound of Trump's opposition. The rescission of DACA came less than two weeks after the president pardoned Joe Arpaio, the former Arizona sheriff who drew intense criticism for his aggressive pursuit of unauthorized immigrants, which earned him a criminal contempt conviction. Moreover, in defending the rescission order, Trump and Attorney General Sessions both used the trope of anti-immigrant activists, arguing that those in the country illegally are lawbreakers who hurt native-born Americans by usurping their jobs and pushing down wages.

The most provocative action the Trump White House pursued in the war over immigration policy was the family separation policy. Shortly after taking office in January 2017, Trump called for an end to the "catch-and-release" policy for immigrants at the southern border. Under this enforcement regime, families contesting deportation or applying for asylum were generally released from detention quickly and allowed to remain in the United States until their cases are resolved. This policy adhered to the Flores Agreement, approved in a 1997 federal appeals court in California, which barred prolonged child detention.[49] The Trump administration's pursuit of a zero-tolerance policy led to contentious debate in DHS about how to deter border crossings from Central America, which, to the White House's dismay, after a brief plunge when Trump first took office, were once again growing due to terrible political and economic conditions in migrants' home countries. In March, administration officials, pressed by Stephen Miller and his allies in the DOJ and DHS, began considering the harsh remedy of family separation, with parents placed in custody and children held by the Office of Refugee Resettlement (ORR) in the Department of Health and Human Services (HHS), hitherto tasked with sheltering minors who came to the United States alone.[50] Secretary Kelly, seeking to arbitrate the contentious debate between immigration hawks rallied by Miller and careerists in HHS who questioned the morality and feasibility of such a final solution, assured agitated Senate Democrats that mothers and children would not be separated at the border.[51]

Kelly's diplomatic efforts were undermined by immigration hawks ensconced in the West Wing. Over the next several months, Miller engaged various government officials (DHS directors and staffers, the Customs and Border Protection commissioner, Immigration and Customs Enforcement [ICE] officials) in communications over how to resuscitate proposals to start a family separation policy. These efforts gained support on the ground in July, when Jeff Self, the Border Patrol chief in El Paso, Texas, acted on general orders emanating from the White House stipulating that he and other sector chiefs should work with their counterparts at DOJ to crack down on border crossings in service to the president's agenda. Self, embracing ideas that had been percolating in DHS and DOJ, decided that the best way to serve that mission was to start referring parents traveling with children for prosecution, placing their children in the care of ORR. Federal officials would later call this program, eventually extended to New Mexico, a "pilot"—even as they maneuvered to make this experiment the model for a national policy that separated families. The proponents of family separation claimed, without evidence, that it was carried out to protect children from "trafficking"—schemes in which minors were either kidnapped or paired with random adults to gain both parties easy access to the United States. However, private documents revealed that the real purpose was based on Miller's conviction that to deter desperate families from seeking sanctuary in the United States it was necessary "to take their children away." As a border agent acknowledged in defending expanding the pilot program, "Although it is always a difficult decision to separate these families, it is the hope that this separation will act as a deterrent to parents bringing their children into the harsh circumstances that are present when trying to enter the United States illegally."[52]

The pilot program provided ample evidence of the serious problems separating families at the border would create. Inadequate resources compounded the terrible trauma the policy inflicted on migrant families. Public defenders and advocates observed that cell blocks at the federal courthouse were overrun by detainees, many of them distraught parents who had their children taken away and had no idea where they had been sent. Richard Durbin, the acting US attorney in El Paso, who established standards that would not prosecute low-culpability families with children, learned that border agents ignored his guidelines. Although he rejected two-thirds of the cases referred to his office by the Border Patrol, Durkin found that it was very difficult to reunite families. By the time parents were returned to immigration custody, many of their children had been sent to ORR shelters in different states. The Office of Refugee Resettlement, which had not been warned of the pilot program, was forced to deal with shelters that were inundated with inconsolable children; moreover, because the Border Patrol did not form a database that would trace where migrant youth were sent, their parents and the public defenders and aid societies that tried to help them had a terrible time finding their children. Upon separation, many migrants were pressured to sign deportation papers with the promise that their children would be returned once they were deported; yet once returned to their home country, they were subjected to agonizingly long periods of separation during which obtaining information about their separated children was very difficult if not impossible.[53]

Concerned about the stress that family separation placed on the immigration system and published reports that began to expose the policy's combination of ineptness and cruelty, Kevin McAleenan, the Customs and Border Protection commissioner, ended the El Paso pilot program. However, in spite of all the problems that policy lab revealed, Miller and his ally in DOJ, Gene Hamilton, relentlessly pressured DHS to establish family separation as a national policy. When John Kelly, anointed as the president's new chief of staff, left DHS and was replaced by the less formidable Kirstjen Nielsen, Miller and Hamilton filled the power vacuum. As Hamilton got a willing Sessions to codify DOJ's commitment to a draconian zero-tolerance policy, Miller, with the help of DHS chief of staff Chad Wolf, circumvented senior DHS staff and resistant civil servants in forging a network of support for family separation in the beleaguered department.

Nielsen, an assistant to Kelly at DHS who shared his skepticism about the feasibility of family separation, resisted signing off on a nationwide policy for a time. But dramatic news reports surfaced in late March 2018 that a caravans of one thousand to fifteen thousand asylum seekers from Honduras, Guatemala, and El Salvador had formed, and twenty-four-hour news coverage of them traveling through Mexico to the United States gave immigration hawks the leverage they needed to get Nielsen, who was being lambasted by the Trump and right-wing activists for tolerating lax border security, to cooperate.[54] Echoing the speeches he wrote for Trump during the 2016 campaign, Miller said that unless the Trump administration was willing to separate families, the moral, legal, and logistical complications notwithstanding, the Central American deluge would be the "end of the country as we know it." Summoned to the White House Situation Room for a meeting convened by Miller, which included Sessions and HHS secretary Alex Azar, Nielsen saw that further resisting the White House's plans to pursue an extreme deterrence policy would completely isolate her politically, threatening her career ambitions. A few days later, on May 7, the DHS secretary signed a memo instructing the department's personnel to prosecute all migrants crossing the border illegally, including parents arriving with their children, who would be placed in HHS shelters.[55]

All the danger signs that plagued the El Paso and New Mexico pilot program were magnified when family separation was transformed into a national policy. Detention centers quickly were overrun, leading to dangerous and unsanitary conditions for migrant families. Children were wrenched from the arms of their parents and placed in separate detention spaces that only added to their trauma. Immigration and Customs Enforcement agents, who were responsible for transporting migrant children, quickly shipped them off to HHS's ORR, with no system in place for reuniting families. With little time to prepare for this onslaught, ORR struggled mightily to care for inconsolable children in overcrowded conditions who were not formally part of the agency's responsibility. When ORR facilities, which consists mostly of foster homes and a few small shelters housing only up to thirty-six children at a time to ensure that each child still received individualized care, filled up, children were sent to less responsible private companies that eagerly accepted multimillion-dollar government contracts. These profit-driven organizations housed children in huge facilities such as a former Walmart, which at one point was used to detain more than one thousand children. Large-scale institutions, which had long since been eliminated from the domestic child welfare system because they were found to be traumatizing and unsafe, were now key players in the Trump White House's zealous plan to discourage migrants from coming to America.[56]

Even as court cases and news reports began to expose the immorality and practical failures of family separation, the Trump administration was reluctant to abandon it. In fact, evidence was uncovered that the White House intentionally, with the complicity of DHS, abetted a broken system to ensure that its program was horrific enough to deter desperate families in Central America from seeking asylum. Soon after the start of zero tolerance, Matt Albence, a top official at ICE, expressed concern that if the parents' prosecutions happened too quickly, their children would still be waiting to be picked up by HHS in Border Patrol stations, making family reunification possible. He saw this as a bad thing. Receiving reports that reunifications had occurred in several Border Patrol sectors, Albence immediately sought to block the practice from continuing, contacting at least one sector directly while also asking his superiors—ICE commissioner Tom Homan and BCP commissioner Kevin McAleenan—for help. "We can't have this," he wrote to colleagues, underscoring in a second note that reunification "obviously undermines the entire effort" behind zero tolerance and would make DHS "look completely ridiculous." Albence and others proposed "solutions" such as placing parents whose prosecutions were especially speedy into ICE custody or in "an alternate temporary holding facility" other than the Border Patrol station where their children were being held. This appears to have prevented family reunification in a few cases.[57]

The Trump administration's family separation policy stands out, even amid the most nativist presidential program since the 1920s, for its cruelty and provocation. But it must be seen as a grimmer version of the calculus that governs the politics of fear. For Trump and Miller, the battle to fend off a cavalcade of immigration from Central America with a harsh response would mobilize the base—the core of a strategy to form a united and passionate coalition that would enable the Republican Party, given its advantages in what might be called a constitutionally gerrymandered system, to capture the Electoral College, the Senate, and the courts—and, during pivotal moments, even the lower House chamber. The appeal of sectarian nationalism tapped into fears that Trump loyalists were at risk of losing their country; the power of the administrative state enabled the Trump White House to respond to these acculturated beliefs.

After receiving Nielsen's pending memo authorizing the controversial border program, Gary Tomasulo, who was then the senior director for border and transportation security on the National Security Council, sent an email to the deputies and lower-level staffers who would be tasked with carrying out immigration policy, telling them that their bosses had agreed to the new zero-tolerance prosecution and separation policy and that they needed to develop plans to support it. It mattered little to the Trump administration and his immigration czar, Stephen Miller, that some of the subordinates to the cabinet secretaries who were responsible for carrying out zero tolerance—especially civil servants—had raised moral objections. In the email, obtained by NBC News, Tomasulo told the deputies and other subordinates that their bosses "acknowledged that there are no easy solutions, but remained committed to collectively do everything possible to develop innovative solutions that leverage the full resources, capabilities, and authorities of the U.S. government."[58]

Eventually, the Trump administration was forced to recalibrate it administrative border strategy. Nielsen's efforts to obfuscate the alarms family separation was setting off around the country were pierced in June when *ProPublica* published a stunning leaked audio of separated children crying for their parents inside a government facility. The heartbreaking cries of innocent children begging to see or at least talk to their families, mocked by the overseeing border agents, made all too clear that the targets of zero-tolerance policy were not criminal traffickers or kidnappers but children, who were pawns in immigration hawks' grim calculations.[59] By that point, the Trump administration had separated more than four thousand children from their parents under zero tolerance and earlier local initiatives. Facing a national and international public outcry for its inhuman treatment of migrant families, even some of Trump's staunches allies on immigration, such as Senator Ted Cruz, condemned zero tolerance.[60]

A few days later, accepting the need to change course, President Trump issued Executive Order 1831, which ended his administration's family separation policy. The order was hardly a mea culpa. It placed the blame for the immigration crisis on Congress's failure to pass legislation to fix the border crisis. However, implying skepticism that immigration reform of any kind would be passed by a gridlocked legislature, the order also recommitted the White House to its zero-tolerance policy, and its pledge to maintain family unity in the continued pursuit of that policy by "detaining alien families together" hardly promised a more humanitarian treatment of asylum seekers.[61] "The president doesn't get any Brownie points for moving from a policy of locking up kids and families separately to a policy of locking them up together," said Karen Tumlin, director of legal strategy at the pro-immigration National Immigration Law Center. Eventually, as we shall see later, Trump sought a way out of this conundrum by weaponizing protective tariffs—the other pillar of America First—to force Mexico to detain families while they awaited some resolution of their pleas for entry to the United States.[62]

Sanctuary cities, building the wall, the "Muslim ban," the rescission of DACA, and the family separation policy were among the most high-profile, publicly visible changes to immigration policy. They garnered extraordinary media coverage, but the contours of the modern administrative state also created multiple, subtler avenues for the exercise of presidential power. Across his four years in office, seemingly benign changes added up and seeped through departments and agencies that hold secondary, and even tertiary, responsibility for immigration policy. For example, collaborating with anti-immigration activists who staffed positions throughout the federal bureaucracy, Trump deployed the full force of the executive branch to implement his desired policies, from revising the rules that the Department of Housing and Urban Development uses to curtail rental assistance to unauthorized migrants; to delaying and often suspending the enlistment of foreign national military recruits; to

DHS's expansion of the "public charge" rule to prevent less fortunate migrants from coming to America and to deter legal and undocumented immigrants from accessing health, housing, and food assistance benefits; to establishing a new form of information sharing between the Office of Refugee Resettlement, which sits within HHS, and ICE, housed in DHS, that put those who sought to take custody of migrant children at risk of deportation.[63] The White House also instructed ICE officials to arrest unauthorized immigrants deep in the US interior, even targeting sensitive sites long viewed as off-limits to immigration enforcement, such as courthouses and churches.[64] Later in his administration, Trump officials would team up with the group Federation for American Immigration Reform (FAIR) in an effort to recruit local governments and sheriffs' offices to participate in heightened immigration enforcement, under a controversial program known as 287(g), which delegated authority to arrest and detain foreign nationals. Under Trump, the number of participating police departments increased from the mid-30s to more than 140.[65]

The Supreme Court reinstated DACA, and the election of Joe Biden to the presidency ultimately put an end to some—but not all—of the Trump era's most transformative polices. Still, the political damage done by Trump's unilateral adventurism could not be erased by another president's executive rescissions. Lives were dramatically uprooted, and fear was widespread. That is reason enough to second-guess the powers bestowed on the modern president in the name of securing the state. More long-lasting, and more deleterious to the goal of sustaining constitutional government, is the fact that these actions sapped the government of its root legitimacy.

SERVICING THE STATE: FREEDOM FROM WANT

Homeland security and immigration politics was the first priority of Trump's executive partisanship, but his onslaught on the federal workforce—the lifeblood of the administrative state—was a close second priority. As we detailed earlier, every president since FDR has understood that they could pursue their policy goals, in part, by reorganizing the executive branch and modifying the workplace rules of the federal civil service.[66] Yet, for President Trump, "deconstructing" the federal civil service was not a means to an end—it was a core commitment of his partisan strategy. His attacks on the bureaucracy weakened the independent authority that federal officials have long leveraged to reform domestic policy commitments and served as a rallying cry to mobilize the base.

Like his assurance that he would build a wall at Mexico's expense, Trump's promise to "drain the swamp" might be dismissed as empty campaign rhetoric. Yet just as the slogan "Build the Wall" foretold disruptive immigration politics, so the clarion call to drain the swamp reified Trump's aggressive assault on the civil service in the name of achieving a unitary executive. His administration thus tapped into conservatives' disdain for government—playing on tropes of bureaucratic inefficiencies, red tape, and insider deals. But unlike the previous Republican presidents' assaults on "neutral competence," Trump's attack on the deep state celebrated his business acumen. Never mind that he had received millions in public assistance throughout his career for his business ventures; he bragged that his "deals" qualified him as the only one who could fix a system that sacrificed the livelihood of American workers on the altar of free trade.[67]

Just as Trump's unilateralism in the service of DHS was joined to partisan statecraft, so his administrative actions in domestic policymaking were one bit substantive, two bits performative. Even before he took office, the administration sought to clarify its tough-outsider position by inserting itself in a high-profile negotiation with Lockheed Martin over the costs of the F-35 Joint Strike Fighter jet. By Trump's own account, the estimated $700 million in savings was merely a drop in the $3.85 trillion bucket of federal expenditures for fiscal year 2016.[68] And yet, the incoming administration portrayed its contretemps with Lockheed as a prime example of how it would use its managerial powers to intervene in federal contracting negotiations. The F-35 drama was just a precursor to a more sweeping departure from Republican orthodoxy: partisan administration that intruded on the marketplace.

At the beginning of his term, Trump issued a set of executive orders to support companies that "hired American" and to provide "Federal financial assistance awards and Federal procurements [to] maximize the use of materials produced in the United States, including manufactured products; components of manufactured products; and materials such as steel, iron, aluminum, and cement."[69] Later on in his presidency, he ordered the Department of Energy to force utility companies to purchase electricity from coal and nuclear power plants, which had struggled to compete with alternative, and cheaper, sources of energy.[70] Couching his words in the language of national defense, Trump also resurrected a long-dormant idea of establishing a national industrial policy—plans that would have seen more daylight had Trump been reelected, and which continue to inform Trump's policy legacy.[71]

The most visible feature of Trump's MAGA platform that departed from Republican orthodoxy was his commitment to America First protective tariffs. Even though a majority of Americans might have been, in the abstract, supportive of trade protectionism, Trump's imprint on Republican partisanship was most dramatically demonstrated in his battles with the GOP establishment over tariff policy. During the 2016 Republican primary contests, trade was a distinguishing position of then candidate Trump. While Trump's positions on immigration (especially a proposed Muslim ban) received top media attention, his rhetoric on the debate stage emphasized the need to impose protectionist trade measures. Often, he was the only candidate speaking about the issue, indeed, more than any Republican candidate since the 1920s.

These defining issues of Trump conservatism were joined in the president's threat in June 2019 to deploy tariffs as a surrogate barrier to the surge of Central American migrants coming to the United States through Mexico. The objective of this diplomatic brinkmanship was to pressure Mexico to support the Trump administration's successor to the failed family separation program. Announced in a December memo by DHS secretary Nielsen, the Migration Protection Protocols—a policy proponents and critics dubbed "Remain in Mexico"—required that individuals (mostly from Central America) entering the United States from Mexico, illegally or without proper documentation, could be returned to Mexico for the duration of their immigration proceedings. Defying critics who denounced the policy as a dire threat to the health and safety of asylum seekers, Nielsen proclaimed:

> Today we are announcing historic measures to bring the illegal immigration crisis under control. We will confront this crisis head on, uphold the rule of law, and strengthen our humanitarian commitments. Aliens trying to game the system to get into our country illegally will no longer be able to disappear into the United States, where many skip their court dates. Instead, they will wait for an immigration court decision while they are in Mexico. "Catch and release" will be replaced with catch and return."[72]

Unhappy with Mexico's enforcement of this new initiative, the White House threatened to slap tariffs as high as 25 percent on all goods from Mexico unless it thwarted the transit of undocumented immigrants and refugees to the United States. Trump thus connected MAGA policies that caused unrest among his partisans in Congress, especially the Senate, but mobilized his base. In a resolution that the president's supporters heralded as an important victory for the "disrupter in chief," the Mexican foreign minister and the US secretary of state reached an agreement that obligated "Mexico [to] take unprecedented steps to increase enforcement to curb irregular migration," including the deployment of its national guard to its southern border. Mexico further guaranteed that it would hold any migrants "while they await adjudication of their asylum claims." Although some of Trump's supporters expressed skepticism that the "Remain in Mexico" policy would resolve the border crisis—warning that the administration's weaponizing of tariffs risked harming the economy and undermining a trade deal to replace NAFTA—the episode testified dramatically to how Trump's America First program had become an all-consuming dimension of conflict that would be a major issue in the 2020 election.[73]

Though the dramatic "Remain in Mexico" deal captured the headlines, the Trump administration aggressively deployed tariffs throughout his term in office. Invoking seldomly used provisions of US trade law, the White House was able to impose tariffs without congressional authorization or legislative debate. Trump relied on legislative authority granted during the heyday of presidentialism—the Trade Expansion Act of 1962 and the Trade Act of 1974—to declare that foreign imports, like hordes crossing the Mexican border, represented a threat to US national security, which allowed him to raise tariffs to protect American industries and workers.[74] The Trump administration emphasized that the tariffs were necessary in order to target unfair Chinese trading practices. But, with the stroke of a pen, the president's trade war also targeted major US allies, such as Japan, South Korea, and Germany.[75] Moreover, as we might expect given the underlying logic of executive-centered partisanship, Trump targeted imports that were especially salient to the coalition Trump forged during the 2016 campaign. For example, the largest tariffs focused on agricultural products and goods manufactured primarily in Midwestern states—key areas of Trump support, and a part of Trump's brand as a defender of rural America. Blending MAGA partisanship with crass politics, Trump's Commerce Department issued thousands of waivers to the tariff increases, benefiting companies with the knowledge—and legal support—to navigate the shifting regulatory landscape.

Neither diplomatic brinkmanship with Mexico nor the imposition of tariffs on China and allies in Europe and Asia deterred the administration from taking aim at the bête noire of Trump's working-class base supporters: the North American Free Trade Agreement (NAFTA), which the Clinton administration, with bipartisan support, pushed through the Congress in 1993. On May 18,

2017—less than five months into office, Trump announced that he would renegotiate a seminal deal. While the treaty with Canada and Mexico had long been viewed by the far left and far right with scorn, Trump was the first president to fully denounce it. Part partisan symbolism, part innovate policy, the new trade deal—the United States-Mexico-Canada Agreement (USMCA)—did not truly blow up the status quo as he promised. In fact, a year of negotiations produced a new trade agreement that preserved many elements of the original treaty. Still, just replacing NAFTA with a new brand signaled to Trump's base that he fulfilled one of his most important campaign promises.

The new agreement, which Congress, in a rare display of bipartisanship, approved in late 2019, marginally helped farmers by loosening Canadian protections of its dairy market; USMCA also promised to help American automakers by imposing a minimum wage requirement on manufactured goods and establishing stricter "rules of origin" requirements for assembled products. Determined to make trade a core Republican commitment, Trump did not invite any Democrat to the signing ceremony, even though the USMCA was hammered out with Democrats in Congress, who succeeded in getting labor and environmental protections added to the agreement.[76] Regardless of economic effect, Trump declared a major victory for his America First platform. This was not merely rhetorical flourish. Perhaps the most important provision of the new agreement, still lying in wait (maybe for Trump's second term), allows any of the participating countries to void the entire treaty if another successfully negotiates a free trade agreement with a "non-market country." Such a measure would limit China's ability to enter and influence the structure of Canadian and Mexican markets without US involvement. The Trump administration, therefore, managed to reach a deal with Canada and Mexico that enlisted them in the president's most important objective: "an aggressive agenda of increasingly squeezing China out of global supply chains while pressing for structural change in Beijing."[77]

Trump's America First rendition of conservatism threatened to alienate important Republican constituents. Although satisfying the demands of traditional GOP stalwarts in some areas, Trump's cultivation of a "coalition of restoration" also estranged pragmatic business interests, which constituted an important part of the Republican coalition forged by Ronald Reagan and George W. Bush. Beyond concerns about his protectionist policies, his controversial comments in the wake of violent demonstrations that erupted in Charlottesville, Virginia—appearing to condemn in equal measure the actions of neo-Nazis and those who confronted them in the streets—forced the administration to shut down two presidential advisory councils after corporate leaders repudiated the president's comments. Jamie Dimon, the chief executive of JPMorgan Chase and a member of the White House's Strategy and Policy Forum, echoing the sentiments of many corporate leaders, stated in a note to employees: "Constructive economic and regulatory policies are not enough and will not matter if we do not address the divisions in our country. It's a leader's role, in business or government, to bring people together, not tear them apart."[78]

Trump's combustible joining of sectarian and economic nationalism put him in tension with corporate America. However, he offered some compensation to business interests in deploying administrative power to deliver on long-standing conservative objectives: deregulation of environmental protection, support of traditional values, and an effort to undermine bureaucratic independence. Here, as with the president's oft-touted but dubious claims that he slashed the federal regulatory code, private interests were willing to overlook Trump's adventures in economic nationalism for progress in other areas.

In subsequent chapters, we will explain how the Trump presidency also leveraged institutional imbalances to remake other core policies of the American state, but the Trump administration's interventions in health, education, and welfare—as important as they were—paled in comparison to its assault on Obama-era environmental protections. Faced with divided government for the majority of his presidency, Obama routinely relied on executive orders and presidential memorandums to strengthen federal protections of the environment and to counter the effects of man-made climate change. Trump used those same instruments to reverse many of those orders. Still, as we have emphasized, the rolling back of environmental protections does not simply suggest that Trump led a "deconstruction of the administrative state." Rather, even in an area where conservatives abhor state power, Trump deployed administrative power to reorient national priorities. We can see this in how his administration used state policy to encourage natural resource extraction and to limit what states and localities could do to impede economic development in the name of mitigating climate change.

Perhaps no issue galvanized environmentalists and their political enemies more forcefully than the long-standing debate over the Keystone XL Pipeline, a policy battle that took on even more drama with another proposed project: the Dakota Access Pipeline. President Obama equivocated throughout his presidency, acknowledging the trade-offs between local conservation and the pipelines' economic benefits. After painful vacillation and consultation with Secretary of State John Kerry, Obama finally halted the project, with a wistful plea for a return to the progressive principle of "neutral competence":

> For years, the Keystone pipeline has occupied what I, frankly, consider an overinflated role in our political discourse. It became a symbol too often used as a campaign cudgel by both parties rather than a serious policy matter. And all of this obscured the fact that this pipeline would neither be a silver bullet for the economy, as was promised by some, nor the express lane to climate disaster proclaimed by others.[79]

Trump, however, embraced the overinflated position of the pipeline projects, using the pomp of a full-throated presidential denial to rally his base. Four days after taking office, in a widely publicized ceremony inside the Oval Office, Trump reversed the Obama administration's Keystone XL order, approved the other divisive pipeline project—Dakota Access—and further stated in a memorandum that they would have to be made with American steel.[80]

Administrative partisanship over environmental issues was greatly intensified by the White House's announcement that it would pull the United States out of the 2015 Paris Climate Accord—a decision that suspended payments on the $3 billion that the United States had pledged to climate change efforts in industrializing countries. Alongside these major public reversals, the Trump administration also pursued a less publicized series of executive actions to disrupt the Obama-era regulatory framework for enacting environmental rules. These included an order that overturned rules requiring that recipients of federal funds seeking to build in flood zones consider the risk of flooding and design accordingly; the order, ironically, was signed two days before Hurricane Harvey formed in the Gulf of Mexico—eventually decimating parts of the greater Houston area with torrential rain.[81] The overarching purpose of this action, however, was not to roll back federal involvement but, instead, to ensure that "the Federal environmental review and permitting process for infrastructure projects is coordinated, predictable, and transparent"—to redirect policy, that is, from environmental protection to the rapid expansion of the national government's role in the development of the nation's infrastructure. Moreover, at the order of the president, the Department of the Interior undertook an initiative to permit energy exploration in the Arctic National Wildlife Refuge in Alaska for the first time in more than thirty years.[82] Congress has sole authority to determine whether oil and gas drilling can take place within the refuge's 19.6 million acres, but seismic studies and gauging how much oil is below the ground represent a necessary first step. Under the auspices of the Trump administration, Interior Department officials modified a 1980s regulation to permit such tests. This sub-rosa push to open up the refuge, occurring as longtime drilling proponents occupied key positions in Interior Department, marks an important redeployment of policy in a debate that has raged for decades.[83]

As with environmental policy changes, Trump sent clear overtures to the Republican base by flexing his administrative muscle in America's ongoing culture wars. Given his well-known indiscretions and three marriages, Trump took special precautions to maintain his alliance with the Christian right. Like Ronald Reagan, who had used administrative shows of force to bring the Christian right into the Republican fold, Trump also made clear that the White House was a welcome home for evangelicals. White evangelicals voted overwhelmingly for him (81 percent) in 2016, and Trump returned their gratitude. In a presidential first, Trump tweeted an order in July 2017 that transgender people would be barred from the military—an action that the evangelical activist Tony Perkins of the Family Research Council had been urging for months. This initiative raised the perplexing question of whether a presidential tweet had legal standing; but the White House sanctified the policy on August 25 by releasing a memorandum directing the Department of Defense to implement Trump's transgender ban on military personnel.[84]

Although the campaign to ban transgender individuals from the armed forces received great national attention, more central to the heart of Trump's social agenda was an executive order that took aim at Obama-era regulations intended to protect gay people from discrimination and ensure that women have access to birth control. Appearing in the Rose Garden flanked by Vice President Pence, who had strong ties to the Christian right, and Paula White, a Christian televangelist, who was the president's spiritual adviser, Trump issued an order that directed Attorney General Sessions to provide guidelines for reinterpreting religious liberty protection in law. The order also instructed federal agencies to vigorously protect religious liberties and consider issuing new rules to address conscience-based objections to health care mandates regarding birth control.[85] Given pending lawsuits involving the DOJ's birth control regulations, the president's order had no immediate effect on policy. But, as the *New York Times* reported, "It did start a flurry of activity across the government—prompting agencies to draft new policies that chipped away at the Obama-era mandates." A preview of partisan administration that continued through Trump's term to shift the priorities of rights-based protection from minorities, women, and the LGBTQ community to people of faith, these early initiatives "pointed to a fundamental repurposing of the federal bureaucracy to promote social conservative priorities."[86]

The enduring consequences of such executive action remained unclear, yet the appeal to the conservative base was palpable. Echoing the sentiment of many social conservatives, Richard Land, president of the Christian Southern Evangelical Seminary in North Carolina, who had worked with Republican administrations since Reagan, marveled that he "never has felt his advice and input were more welcome in the White House since Trump became president." He described regular, ongoing, and continuing dialogue in emails, phone calls, and meetings. "I've been coming here for three decades," related another conservative activist at a White House dinner on the eve of a National Day of Prayer. "I no longer feel like the redheaded stepchild at the family reunion or the company picnic. I feel like a respected colleague and guest."[87] As we will discuss in chapter 4, the uneasy but formative relationship between Trump and the Christian right would be consummated by his appointments to the Supreme Court, which continued to consecrate conservative causes pertaining to abortion, gun rights, and the loosening of environmental protection during the Biden administration.

MANAGING THE DEEP STATE

Undergirding the redeployment of administrative power that rattled the resolve of federal civil servants, the Trump administration engaged in managerial reforms, thus confirming the Nixon-era realization that "operations is policy"—and bringing to a culmination the determination of its Republican predecessors to recast the modern presidency as an administrative weapon that could serve conservative objectives.

Within three days of taking office, Trump issued his first presidential memorandum instituting an across-the-board hiring freeze for the entire federal government.[88] Purposefully, however, the freeze exempted military personnel, and like Ronald Reagan's first-year moratorium, the memorandum carved out broad exemptions for any employee whom an agency head or cabinet secretary deemed "necessary to meet national security or public safety responsibilities." The freeze therefore shifted resources between departments and agencies and inserted policy activists in key administrative positions to advance the redeployment of domestic policy. Several weeks later, the White House continued its tinkering with the structure of the federal hiring process, this time by ordering the head of each administrative agency and department to submit a plan to reorganize their office. The new plans, which were incorporated into the following year's OMB report, were to take account of whether certain responsibilities under the agency's auspices should be devolved to state or local government; whether the private sector would more efficiently source the task; whether there was a redundancy with another agency; whether the costs of the agency's programs were justified by the public benefit it provided; and whether the agency's staff and programs were "redundant" with another agency or program in the executive branch.[89]

Beyond attention to redundancies, OMB director Mick Mulvaney ordered that agencies had to follow the president's proposed plan in submitting their budget proposal for fiscal year 2018, even though no laws required them to do so. Agency heads had to plan *as if* Congress were to follow through on the near $1.4 trillion cuts to the White House's nondefense discretionary budget over ten years.[90] Preliminary reports were due by October 1, 2017. In the meantime, the OMB sought legal authority to augment its hiring freeze; lower retirement benefits for federal workers; abolish cost-of-living adjustments for current and future enrollees in the Federal Employees Retirement System; reduce cost-of-living adjustments by 0.5 percent for contributors to the Civil Service Retirement System; and increase individuals' payments to their federal retirement plans, without an offsetting salary increase (effectively a 6 percent pay cut).[91]

President Trump not only sought to tighten the White House's control over a restructured federal civil service but also took administrative actions that exceeded efforts that began during Reagan presidency to impose new, more burdensome rules on the regulatory process. In January 2017, the White House issued an executive order mandating that every executive department or agency had to identify two regulations it wanted to repeal for every new regulation it proposed; moreover, the agency had to calculate the fiscal effect of these one-in, two-out transactions and ensure that, for a given year, the agency would not increase the regulatory-financial burden on the American economy.[92] Although some critics suggested that such reform was little more than a gimmick, the White House sustained its regulatory framework, taking measures to ensure that every agency proposal was carefully vetted by presidential staff. Less than a month later, Trump ordered every agency to begin developing a Regulatory Reform Task Force, using existing agency resources. Each task force was instructed to identify and report to the OMB regulations that eliminated jobs or inhibited job creation; were outdated, unnecessary, or ineffective; imposed costs that exceeded benefits; or created a serious inconsistency or otherwise interfered with regulatory reform initiatives and policies.[93] The White House further tightened its control over the regulatory review process by issuing an executive order subjecting all measures that intersected with the US tax code or relied on the IRS for implementation to review within the Department of the Treasury.[94] In pursuance of this order, the OMB developed a plan to establish a "regulatory cost allowance" for every part of the executive branch. Consequently, beginning in 2018, "no regulations exceeding the agency's total incremental cost allowance [set by the OMB would] be permitted in that fiscal year, unless required by law."[95]

It is tempting to brush aside Trump's unilateral attack on the bureaucracy, indeed, the entire corpus of his partisan administration, as temporary reversals, subject to rescission by the Biden administration. However, as the public administration scholar Donald Moynihan has argued, "As long as one party in a two-party system is no longer invested in good government, the quality of government will erode. Career officials value the opportunity to develop and use their expertise. If every election risks throwing up a President whose goal is to frustrate such opportunities, it will be increasingly difficult to attract a talented workforce motivated by public service."[96]

Moreover, the impact of these efforts to drain the swamp reverberates beyond the federal service. Since the 1980s, a significant amount of government service has been handled by contractors who are often exempt from certain requirements affecting civil service employees. In 2014, President Obama issued a wide-ranging order that would have required any company competing for a federal grant of more than $500,000 to disclose whether it had violated one of fourteen federal labor laws and myriad other state labor laws within the previous three years. While not creating any new protections on its own, the order, depending on how one interpreted it, either would blacklist any company not found in compliance with the law or would provide lucrative inducement to get companies to comply.[97] The Trump administration revoked many of these rules, and the White House placed all other contractor-labor relations subject to the "Fair Play" standards under formal review.[98] The Trump assault on labor standards was not always easy to reverse. For example, using the formal rulemaking process, which inoculates administrative actions against immediate rescission, the Department of Labor issued new regulations pertaining to independent contractors, limiting the types of employees subject to the Fair Labor Standards Act. In March 2022, after the Biden administration attempted to delay the rule's implementation, the US District Court for the Eastern District of Texas invalidated Biden's withdrawal of the rule.[99]

In addition to changing the bureaucratic rules of the game, the Trump administration's attack on the deep state entailed unprecedented efforts to politicize and place the president's personal stamp on the bureaucracy. As many tell-all books on Trump's tempestuous term have reported, the president's jousts with the civil service were somewhat hobbled by internecine fights in the West Wing that precipitated the exit of many White House officials: his national security adviser Michael Flynn, whose rapid departure foreordained the scandal over Russia's interference in the 2016 election; his chief of staff Reince Priebus; press secretary Sean Spicer; his chief strategist—and principal conduit to his "alt-right" constituency—Steve Bannon; and his iconoclastic foreign policy adviser Sebastian Gorka. Yet, the chaos at the center of the administration severely hampered the process of staffing important positions in the departments and agencies, thus abetting the deinstitutionalization of federal administration. Indeed, aides like Stephen Miller—the point person in the White House's efforts to redeploy state power—viewed disruption as a critical means to MAGA ends.

Trump thus deliberately sought to neutralize resisting civil servants and to hollow out the bureaucracy in order to elevate the role of his West Wing advisers, who included his daughter Ivanka Trump and son-in-law Jared Kushner. A report from the White House Transition Project issued eight months into his presidency showed that the Trump administration had the worst record in forty years in staffing its political appointments. The blame for this failure to fill critical leadership positions did not lie with Congress, as the pace of Senate confirmations matched that of the past three presidential administrations. Rather, it seemed to be a symptom of Trump's mischievous attempt to task the White House as the vanguard of an effort to drain the swamp and rebuild the executive branch in his own image.[100]

In examining the institutional determinants of presidential unilateralism, and its political consequences, one conclusion rises to the top. Trump's redeployment of state power clearly reveals to whom Trump felt most beholden and where from the start of his administration he and his political allies sought to take the Republican Party. Activists who took hold of the Republican nominating system saw Trump-the-candidate as an untested but promising disrupter. In 2020 and beyond, they could point to numerous examples of a president who would bend the rules and take no prisoners in order to deliver on the promises he made during his provocative ascent to the White House. Trump, they now argued, was the legitimate heir of a movement whose followers, including the ostensibly antigovernment Tea Party activists, expected the president to uphold law and order and defend "traditional" values.

CONCLUSION: RALLYING THROUGH REGULATION

The rise of executive-centered partisanship has fully exposed the tension at the heart of the modern presidency. The promise of "enlightened administration," although never realized, has become a delusion as presidents have become the tip of the spear of partisan combat since the 1970s. Presidents presume to represent the elusive national interest; in reality, they have become leaders of factions in a fractured nation, exploiting the vast powers of the modern executive office to mobilize loyal partisans and to advance their party's programmatic objectives. Maintaining a lingering commitment to the liberal administrative state, Democrats sometimes extol the virtues of bureaucratic management and expert rule. However, they also have become practiced at the art of partisan administration.[101]

Placing Trump's unilateralism in historical context, we have argued that he is not an aberration. Rather, unapologetic about his belief that the modern presidency gave him "the right to do whatever I want," his partisan administration is best viewed as a logical extension of institutional and cultural developments that long predate his rise to power.[102] Starting with Richard Nixon, Republican presidents have courted conservative activists with tactics and policies that would not roll back the administrative state but redeploy it for conservative objectives: national and homeland security; "traditional" values; law and order; and market-based domestic policy. However, Trump brought this conservative state building to a culmination—eschewing any efforts to reach across the aisle, he forged a primordial relationship with the Republican base.

We close this chapter by delving a bit deeper into the top-down, bottom-up politics that shapes current polarization. It is commonplace among academics and journalists to bemoan the sorry state of political knowledge in this country, and so it is reasonable to ask whether Trump's movement is merely a cult of personality or at least in part driven by symbolic and policy objectives. We have documented the details of Trump's unilateralism; it remains to be seen if the average Trump voter really cared about the details of executive branch operations.

Given the growing importance of movement politics in presidential partisanship—and Trump's reciprocal relationship with the Christian right, anti-immigrant activists, gun rights advocates, and alt-right groups, it is not always apparent who is leading whom. Did Trump create a new, dominant faction in the Republican Party, or did he cultivate visceral ties with a group of conservative activists who already accepted "Trump-like" positions? To what extent did Trump tap into conservative presidentialism, and to what extent was he converting traditional conservatives to embrace executive aggrandizement?

The data we present in table 3.2 provide some preliminary answers to these questions. They confirm that Trump's capture of the Republican Party was less hostile than is commonly believed. We begin with a set of questions asked over a twelve-year period from the Cooperative Election Study (CES, formerly the Cooperative Congressional Election Study), based at Harvard University. Each year the CES asks thousands of Americans a set of detailed questions on policy proposals that were debated in the previous year, in addition to standard questions about their age, income, and who they voted for.

Only the 2016 CES/CCES asked individuals about their primary vote. Using Markov Chain Monte Carlo (MCMC) procedures, we estimate Trump primary voters in years prior to and after the 2016 primary elections. That is, using what we know about Trump primary voters in 2016, we developed models to predict whether someone surveyed in earlier and later years shares similar features to Trump primary voters—"would-be" Trump voters. As in 2016, we consider these individuals to represent the core constituency of Trump's base. We can then compare these "base" voters to other, non-Trump-voting Republicans, as well as the representative samples of the American public we have for each of the years surveyed.

Looking back before the official rise of Trump, our evidence suggests that Trump was tapping into a conservative base curated by previous Republican presidents and social movements. Prior to Trump's candidacy, we see clear divides between Republicans and Democrats—not surprising in this era of heightened partisan polarization. However, on several key issues, from trade

Table 3.2. Percentage Favoring Policy Positions on Donald Trump's Administrative Policies, 2008–20 CES

	All Americans (%)	Non-Trump Republicans (%)	Trump Republicans (%)
2008: Extend NAFTA	49.19	55.55	51.66
2014: Identify and deport illegal immigrants	56.50	71.32	76.31
2014: Raise fuel efficiency for average automobile	69.36	59.39	53.72
2016: Ban Muslims from immigrating to the United States	25.51	35.74	55.69
2016: Give Environmental Protection Agency power to regulate carbon dioxide emissions	66.01	46.02	33.60
2018: 25% tariffs on imported steel and 10% on imported aluminum	38.38	56.60	59.19
2018: Withdraw the United States from the Trans-Pacific Partnership (TPP)	41.06	58.16	76.07
2018: Withdraw the United States from the Paris Climate Agreement	40.84	74.02	80.89
2018: Repeal the Clean Power Plant Rules	43.42	68.01	72.53
2018: Ban immigrants from Iran, Somalia, Sudan, Yemen, Syria, and Libya from coming to the United States for ninety days	52.94	87.66	90.47
2018: Requirement that for each new regulation enacted, two must be cut	49.52	78.70	82.45
2020: Withhold federal funds from any local police department that does not report to the federal government anyone it identifies as an illegal immigrant	47.71	71.19	77.48
2020: Repeal the entire Affordable Care Act	46.45	76.93	80.85
2020: Declare a national emergency to permit construction of border wall with Mexico	40.97	74.63	81.47
2020: Provide permanent resident status to Dreamers (DACA)	57.20	35.48	32.40
2020: Ban transgender people in the military	34.85	58.94	66.48

Note: Data are weighted; the unweighted sample includes 274,600 individuals, sampled independently from one another in 2008, 2014, 2016, 2018, and 2020.

policy to environmental protections to harsher immigration restrictions, Republicans were largely united. Those we estimate might have been predisposed to vote for Trump in 2016 actually held more mainstream positions on trade policy, such as favoring the extension of NAFTA. Still, especially as they relate to immigration, Trump's positions were established inside mainstream Republican Party politics before Trump took office.

However, in 2016, breaks within the Republican Party emerged between those individuals who self-reported voting for Trump in the Republican primaries and all other self-identifying Republicans. Two of Trump's signature positions—a declared "Muslim ban" and his attack on the regulatory powers of the EPA—were translated into highly celebrated executive orders within days of his inauguration. Trump's base was the main audience for these actions. His primary supporters were especially distinctive in their position on environmental issues, with less than a third supporting a heightened role for the EPA, compared with roughly 40 percent of non-Trump voters. There were also important differences between non-Trump and Trump voters on immigration, with only 35 percent of the former favoring a Muslim ban in 2016, while more than half of the latter supported such a measure.

These intraparty divisions became much less salient during Trump's presidency. For example, the 2018 survey showed overwhelming support among all Republican voters for a ban on immigration from six Muslim nations. The CES survey evidence strongly suggests that Trump's sectarian nationalism captured the Republican Party. His most "loyal customers" were aware and supportive of his administrative maneuverings; moreover, these base supporters became a more dominant faction of the Republican Party after 2016.

Two conclusions are apparent from the general comparison across the administrative actions Trump pursued and for which we have survey data. First, these initiatives were not merely policy; they were acts of partisan fanfare that contributed to the mobilization of a passionate following. And, since we cannot precisely determine positions among Republicans prior to the administration's actions, these figures most likely represent a low estimate of how the Republican Party's base differed from establishment candidates and most elected leaders and the degree to which Trump won over many of the Trump-hesitant. Second, these numbers reveal how Trump's partisan administration sharply divided the country and transformed the GOP into a leaner and more ideologically committed party. With the exception of protective trade measures, none of Trump's administrative agenda commanded majority support in the mass public.

The administrative presidency, therefore, forged with the hope of establishing the modern executive as the steward of the public welfare, has given institutional form to partisan polarization. Though it lacks the fanfare of a momentous bill signing or the president's bully pulpit, executive administration was the primary way in which Trump sought to fulfill his promises to his base. In fact, in policy areas where there was formerly broad public consensus among elected politicians, the administrative presidency allowed Trump to pursue highly charged partisan initiatives that lacked broad support. Theories of presidential behavior stress the need for a president, once ensconced in the office, to appeal to the median voter. Trump's partisan administration summoned a vocal and highly mobilized minority faction.

Trump's eager deployment of executive power also reflected a strategy to obviate divisions within his party over America First conservatism. Indeed, Trump's estrangement from the GOP establishment over the tenets and policies of sectarian nationalism resulted in some striking evidence of how presidents now dominate their party's "brand"—how they can denigrate parties as collective organizations with a past and a future. Although Trump's harsh positions on immigration and trade might not have won over the median voter, he forged strong ties with the GOP's base through tweets, mass rallies, and administrative action—dramatically transforming GOP loyalists' views on issues such as the "wall" and tariffs.[103]

Trump's remarkable rise to the White House has frequently been viewed as idiosyncratic; however, it has left a deep imprint on parties and governing institutions. His provocative executive-centered partisanship represents but a new stage—perhaps a final reckoning—of a development that has been deeply interwoven in the fabric of American politics. Ronald Regan, George W. Bush, and Barack Obama each demonstrated that modern presidents, especially when motivated by programmatic incentives, can exploit national administrative power for partisan purposes. Obama, in fact, developed more creative tactics that framed administrative partisanship as more routine. His administration made extensive use of informal measures such as policy memos and waivers that since the Reagan administration have been gradually supplanting executive orders and regulations, which require more complex administrative procedures and are subject to more resistance from Congress and the judiciary.[104] The Trump administration brought those informal but policy-consequential administrative tactics to a new level.

In making unilateral policymaking a central feature of his presidency, Trump dramatically exposed the false promise of modern presidential leadership—how the hollowing out of political parties, populist revolt, and administrative aggrandizement have rendered the prospect of transcendent presidential leadership an improbable, and mischievous, aspiration. Far from transcending the divisiveness and sectarian interests that form the core of party politics, presidents are now expected to take center stage in a partisan battle for the services of the American state. The Reagan, Bush, and Obama presidencies raised a concern that became a glaring alarm during Trump's presidency: the joining of presidential prerogative and partisanship creates the false illusion that the executive of a vast bureaucratic state, even with the tools of instant communication and social media, can truly function as a representative democratic institution with meaningful links to the president's party and the public.

4. Trump and the Separation of Powers

All presidents claim a mandate to achieve their legacy. Since Andrew Jackson first asserted that his election was a testament to the will of "the people," each president has bought into the idea that there is something special that follows their selection—that it is the only time the nation, as a whole, speaks with one voice and chooses their leader.[1] On Inauguration Day, the president echoes their voice and claims the mantle of national leadership.

Few, however, have so brazenly claimed the presidential mandate as Donald Trump. At his inaugural ceremony, standing before other elected representatives and judges, each of whom also enjoyed some constitutional mandate, Trump belittled the "establishment" and bespoke a nation wracked by "political carnage." With his election, Trump proclaimed, the day had come when "the people" would "start winning again, winning like never before." Steve Bannon, one of the architects of Trump's campaign and likely coauthor of his inaugural address, said that much of Trump's rhetoric was in homage to Andrew Jackson's claim that the president was the protector of the people. Like Jackson, Trump declared that his presidency would overcome the barriers set up against popular government. Neither Congress, the courts, nor the states would thwart the will of "the people," "starting right here, and right now," the new president said, "because this moment is your moment: it belongs to you."[2]

Seizing the mantle of popular leadership is to be expected, but even Jackson's inaugural referenced the Constitution and the limits it imposed on executive power, and even Jackson expressed "reverence" for "the examples of public virtue left by my illustrious predecessors."[3] Trump did not revere constitutional constraint. Rather, constitutional sobriety was a thin veneer that protected the power of "a small group in our nation's Capital," the real victors, who perpetually "reaped the rewards of government while the people have borne the cost."[4] Trump's interpretation of his presidential mandate thus foreshadowed the tumultuous four years that would follow. As Robert Dahl argued, presidential mandates have often been a self-serving "myth"—a claim by the leader of a faction to speak for the whole nation. Previous claims of a presidential mandate weakened democratic deliberation and exacerbated the country's political divisions. However, Trump's term of office revealed that the relentless pursuit of a faux presidential mandate could fracture the nation and threaten constitutional norms and institutions. As we have shown in previous chapters, Trump represented the culmination of executive-centered partisanship that combined presidential prerogative and militant partisanship. He presumed to speak and act for the People, an ambition abetted by partisan loyalties displacing institutional allegiances.

This governing philosophy strikes at the core of America's constitutional presidency, where each branch of the national government and the states are endowed with powers to circumscribe the power of any one of the other institutions. As James Madison wrote in *Federalist* No. 51, "ambition must be made to counteract ambition"—presupposing that the "interest of the man must be connected with the constitutional rights of the place."[5] Institutional conflict is encouraged by such a scheme. Gridlock, failed nominations, and contested claims of executive prerogative: these are nothing new, and they do not reflect a system gone awry, however frustrating. Beyond the division of power between the departments of the central government, the separation of authority between multiple governments with overlapping jurisdiction has accentuated the Constitution's centrifugal force. States' resistance to central authority has been an enduring part of America's federal republic.

But Trump's claim of a presidential mandate posed a serious challenge to this "compound republic."[6] To presume to speak for the whole people as a factional leader often leads presidents to claim prerogative power—to slice through the Gordian Knot of American constitutional government. This claim is all the more audacious—and destabilizing—when made by "minority" presidents. Trump's "mandate" came from 46.1 percent of votes cast. To be sure, this is not a rare occurrence, and it says little about Trump's personal views of the presidency. In the postwar period, six other presidents claimed a popular mandate though they failed to win a majority of the popular vote. Indeed, even when presidents can claim a majority, it is often slim.[7] The reality is that no president can ever lay claim to an unassailable presidential mandate; those elected to the highest office must compete with rival powers in a complex institutional structure that gives hundreds of different actors legitimate claims to represent "the people." Each branch and each government has some claim to power; however, exercising that power requires cooperation among a multitude of diverse interests. Ostensibly, a system of divided and separated powers encourages collaboration—constitutional government can only work if the disparate institutions it empowers can find some way to navigate a labyrinthian political system.[8]

Emphasizing the importance of institutional loyalties, the framers dreaded the "mischiefs of factionalism." Ironically, however, political parties and vital party competition, prior to succumbing to the force of presidentialism, have been central to each major constitutional development in American political history.[9] Without strong party organizations that can combine divided branches and separated governments, constitutional government is prone to legislative paralysis, unchecked sectional conflicts, and the emergence of unaccountable government agencies and programs that compose a veritable fourth branch of government. Political parties as collective organizations with a past and future have provided a measure of cohesion, ameliorating what Hugh Heclo called "institutional estrangement."[10] The party system in the United States has created incentives for presidents and partisans in Congress to find common agreement; to encourage decentralized political approaches for enacting national change through the states; to limit the delegation of responsibility to what Abraham Lincoln called an "eminent tribunal"; and to balance the needs of expertise with public accountability in the bureaucracy.

But once the president could establish a direct, unmediated relationship between himself and a partisan base through direct primaries and a nationalized media landscape, collective partisan responsibility gave way to executive-centered partisanship. As we showed in chapter 3, the emergence of the president as the repository of party responsibility also had an important effect on administrative government. With partisan loyalties eclipsing institutional attachments, the use of unilateral executive power as a partisan weapon became an important and troubling manifestation of presidentialism. The hollowing out of party organizations fueled the rise of an executive-centered administrative state, which encouraged the president not only to speak on behalf of the whole people but to govern in their name as well.

Consequently, the rise of executive-centered partisanship and its maturation during Donald Trump's presidency also threatened to fundamentally alter the dynamic of the constitutional system of checks and balances. The purpose of this chapter is to examine how the Trump administration—and the culmination of a party system remade by presidentialism—transformed the incentives, organization, and practices of Congress, the courts, and states.

As previous chapters have highlighted, although Trump posed a novel and more dangerous challenge to representative constitutional government, his disruptive occupation of the White House was in part symptomatic of the incentives cultivated by and the demands placed on presidential partisanship. In effect, Trump's presidency illustrates three overarching and enduring developments that characterize the perils of presidentialism for a constitutional system that is sustained through the division and separation of powers.

First, the president has become the central actor in the legislative process. Although the president is not all-powerful, a disproportionate amount of congressional action can be attributed to the "legislative presidency." Congress as an institution and the individual members that compose it take their cues from the White House. Partisanship is not a new feature of the prevailing order, and parties still govern with an eye toward satisfying core constituencies. But the process for managing conflicts within the party coalition is increasingly centralized.[11] Legislative committees—the traditional vestibules for channeling organized interests—are less important than party leaders in Congress who enjoy stronger ties with the White House.[12] Negotiations among partisans are channeled through the presidency, and the president plays a leading role in organizing minimal winning coalitions. Beyond agenda-setting powers, traditionally conferred by the claim of a presidential mandate and stipulated in the national spectacle that has become the State of the Union address, the presidency has become an active participant in crafting and steering the party program. This is true even in budgetary and appropriations processes, which were once jealously guarded congressional terrain. Increasingly, Congress does not appear to be an autonomous institution but rather a junior partner in a partisan alliance. Policy, as a result, is particularly reflective of the president's personal goals and the president's core constituency.

Second, the rise of executive-centered partisanship aggravates the disconnect between presidential power and legislative authority to such a point where the foundation of constitutional government is continually shaken. Presidents are expected to manage party affairs and advance partisan objectives, but they lack the formal means to command legislative action. As we document in chapter 3, when presidents cannot forge a legislative coalition to enact party programs, they seek, indeed are encouraged by their partisan brethren in the House and Senate, to govern by executive fiat. This is especially true in times of divided government, which has become a more routine state of affairs in a fractured nation. Another consequence is that the judiciary is increasingly politicized as it is forced to broker disputes between the branches and to respond to the litany of complaints from the states about presidential overreach. While the courts have long played an important role in buttressing the constitutional guardrails of America's constitutional system, executive-centered partisanship weakens the political legitimacy of the judiciary by drawing it into the vortex of partisan combat. The imperative for executive action has thus raised the stakes of judicial nominations, leading to all-consuming struggles to control a politicized court—battles that have consequences that endure beyond a president's term.

Finally, presidentialism and nationalized partisanship have weakened federalism as a constraining institution. Conservative and even progressive presidents once exalted the virtues of decentralized government and the need for local solutions to local community problems. But given changes in the structure of party competition, presidents no longer feel pressure to pay lip service to, let alone govern according to, federal principles. Whereas once presidents were beholden to state and local party leaders—particularly in securing nomination and renomination, this task has been supplanted by a media-churning plebiscitary system of direct primaries and caucuses. Like the separation of powers, federalism still exists in form; however, its constitutional function of cultivating decentralized power has been displaced by a centralized partisanship that threatens to transform state and localities into sites of national partisan conflict.[13] The geographic divisions between "red" and "blue" are less reflective of distinctively local circumstances than of partisan conflicts that estrange Republicans from Democrats at the national level.[14] When states and localities exert an independent influence on contemporary presidential affairs, it is largely through the courts—often the consequence of highly partisan state attorneys general suing the White House to advance their party's national objectives.[15]

The rest of this chapter expands on each of these observations, showing how the Trump administration brought these trends to a dangerous culmination. As a case of executive-centered partisanship in the legislature, we focus on the policy history of the Tax Cuts and Jobs Act (TCJA) of 2017, signed into law in the final month of Trump's first year in office. We then discuss how the dynamics of executive-centered partisanship influence the judiciary, particularly as it manifests in the increasingly politicized nomination battles over the president's appointments. We also consider how judicial politics during the Trump administration was shaped by legal developments in the theory of the unitary executive, and how the politicization of the courts has led to precedents that will continue to have consequences well after Trump leaves office. Finally, we consider federal-state relations during the Trump administration and consider how developments within American federalism—often described as the emergence of a "presidential federalism"—both facilitated and limited the policy objectives of the Trump administration.

CONGRESS-PRESIDENT RELATIONS DURING THE TRUMP ADMINISTRATION

In the original understanding of "republican government," it was Congress, not the president, that was supposed to hear and respond more immediately to the voice of the American people. Congress was charged with national representation; the executive, with administration. Even with the century-long rise of executive-centered partisanship, the importance of congressional representation to the overall functioning of the American constitution cannot be overstated. As David Mayhew reminds us, Congress is responsible for the essential task of sustaining the rule of law—the foundation of a constitutional republic: "Congress through its operations across history has probably helped legitimize—and keep legitimized—the U.S. regime out there among the public. We don't readily see that effect, but it is likely there."[16] That effect is profound—central to the remarkable stability the US constitutional system has enjoyed in comparison to almost every other country of the post-Enlightenment, liberal order. Congress matters not only for channeling the diffuse preferences out there in the mass public and putting them into workable legislation; as the most decentralized, and in a classical sense the most democratic, institution, Congress is expected to do the painstaking work of forging a popular consensus in a large and diverse society.

The transformation of president-Congress relations that has played out for nearly a century is momentous. It is a first-order conflict in the attempt to continually reestablish political legitimacy in a country that seeks to represent a diverse people—determining whether a sense of "We, the People" is nurtured and given a voice in the councils of power. As the disruptive events of January 6, 2021, powerfully reminded a horrified nation, it is Congress that certifies the electors' choice for the presidency and begin the people's business at the start of a new presidential term.

The rise of executive-centered partisanship has not emasculated the legislative branch; nor has it eviscerated the constitutional responsibility of Congress to represent the consent of the people. Throughout the twentieth century, Congress has had a consequential effect on the development of national politics, often by responding to what it perceived as presidential overreach. Immediately following World War II, as we noted in the introduction, Congress sought to reestablish control over the administrative state, enacting the Administrative Procedure Act, which established formal rules to govern rulemaking and review of agency decisions, granting civil servants a degree of autonomy from the president and political appointees. Congress also passed the Legislative Reorganization Act, which increased its own capacity to oversee the modern administrative establishment—charging a revamped committee system to engage in "continuous watchfulness" of departments and agencies. Up until the 1960s, Congress remained the guardian of this new "policymaking state," where partisan conflict and resolution were largely displaced by the ideal of expert-led, "neutral competence," channeled through the labyrinth of congressional subcommittees and fueled by a congressionally led appropriations process.[17] Presidents, expected to lead from the center, reinforced this dynamic, and Congress maintained a semblance of institutional balance.

However, that fragile arrangement could not withstand the groundswell of progressive and conservative activism that exposed the mid-twentieth century's political fault lines. With violent upheaval in Vietnam and in the nation's urban core, the ideal of a presidency-driven "policy state" disintegrated. A new band of highly mobilized constituencies—women, racial minorities, and immigrants—joined together with academics, media, research foundations, and public interest litigators, such as Ralph Nader, to demand democratic control over the administrative state. As R. Shep Melnick described the change, a government that once placed a premium on the congressional powers of "taxing and spending" transformed itself into one that now required outside groups to "mandate and sue" in order to achieve policy goals. And in the process, the initiative for government action shifted to highly mobilized constituencies, for whom "building public programs by exposing government's failures was the formula . . . to show that something is wrong and to demand (usually indignantly) that the situation be corrected."[18]

Distrust in government, from both the left and the right, did not hamstring the government. Indeed, expectations for the government to redress a growing number of boundless societal problems soared, whether the "hunger for community" or the "tangle of pathology" that perpetuated poverty amid a prosperous society.[19] But as Congress, hamstrung by intractable party differences and weakened institutionally, lost its position as the preeminent representative institution, presidents stepped into the void. To be sure, presidential prerogative had often been justified during domestic and international crises as necessary to galvanize purposeful action. Mayhew views presidential legislative leadership as indispensable to effective government action during these times. "Skill in congressional maneuvering is a key item in the White House job description," he writes. "It always has been. Presidents need to relish it and know how to do it. Coalitions, sometimes odd ones, need to be coddled and built. Congress, to operate effectively, often needs such sensitive intrusion."[20]

We do not dispute the fact that presidents have often played a critical role in maneuvering laws through Congress. At the same time, we contend that executive-centered partisanship marks a departure from the normal working relationship presidents have had with Congress. The growing importance of presidentialism in party politics has weakened Congress as an institutionally independent branch capable of constraining executive power. From this perspective, President Trump's relations with Congress are symptomatic of systemic developments that have played out for more than half a century.

One way to understand this change is to consider how often presidents get what they want from Congress, particularly from members of their own party. Using a measure developed by *Congressional Quarterly* in the mid-1950s, figure 4.1 illustrates how often each member of the House of Representatives and the Senate votes in agreement with the president, on every single vote for which we know the president's position. The data make clear that support for the president's legislative agenda, even among members of his own party, is never guaranteed. For most of the second half of the twentieth century, during the era of the so-called textbook Congress, with the legislature armed with strong committees and a substantial staff, Democratic and Republican presidents could only readily count on members of their own party to support them 60 to 70 percent of the time. As the dynamics of executive-centered partisanship took on greater force, however, support became much more common. Dissenting members have become the exception, as Senators and members of Congress of the president's party both routinely support the president's position 90 percent of the time.

Moreover, the rise of executive-centered partisanship has not just meant that support has coalesced around presidents and their legislative co-partisans. Figure 4.2 shows that opposition has grown as well. Particularly in the US House, members of the opposition party seldom support the president on legislative matters. Presidents can expect members of the opposition party to rally behind them less than 20 percent of the time. Some of this, as Frances Lee has

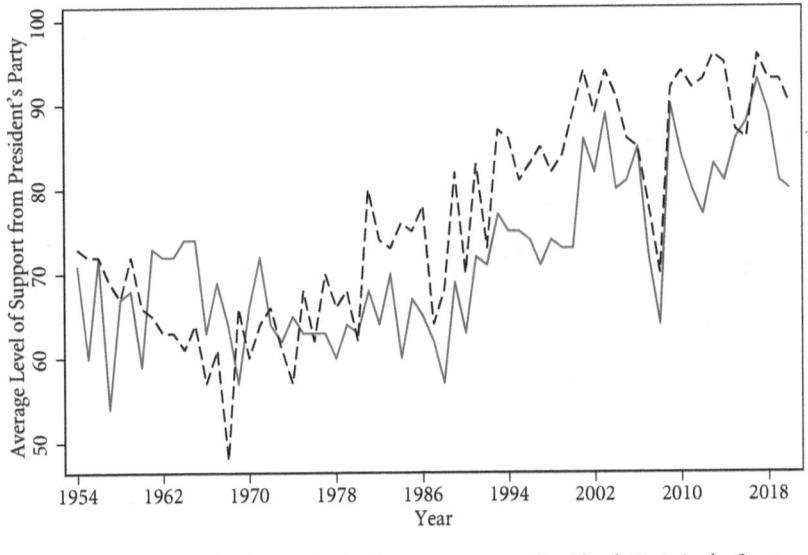

Figure 4.1. Percentage of votes in which members of the House of Representatives and the Senate from the president's party voted in agreement with the president, from 1954 to 2022.
Source: CQ Almanac: Presidential Support Scores, CQ Press. Credit: Created by authors.

convincingly shown, stems from the fact that since the demise of the New Deal coalition during the tumultuous sixties, congressional majorities have been very unstable. Consequently, members of the minority party see little reason to work with the prevailing power; the optimum strategy in a fractured nation is resistance, with the not unlikely prospect that political circumstances with soon tilt in their favor.[21] Presidents, especially, have become a target for the opposition party. Representing a faction rather than anything resembling the national interest, presidents no longer can transcend partisanship as stewards of the public welfare. With at least half the nation intractably opposed to the president (see chapter 2), it only seems rational for the "out party" to do all that it can to thwart the president's agenda.

For all his bellicosity, Trump's relations with Congress were paradigmatic. During his four years in office, Republicans in the House of Representatives supported Trump 86 percent of the time; Republican senators voted with the president 93 percent of the time. Opposition from Republicans was greatest during the final two years of the Trump administration, when he faced

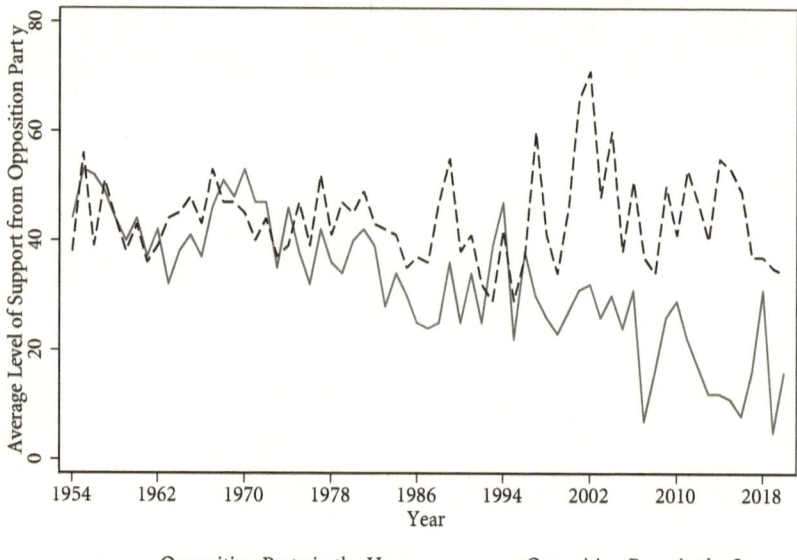

Figure 4.2. Percentage of votes in which members of the House of Representatives and the Senate from the opposition party voted in agreement with the president, from 1954 to 2022.

Source: CQ Almanac: Presidential Support Scores, CQ Press. Credit: created by authors.

a divided Congress, and Republicans were in the minority in the House of Representatives. Republican opposition was heightened in response to several spending measures introduced to offset the effects of the COVID-19 pandemic in 2020, which Trump, after long negotiations, supported. Likewise, opposition to the president's agenda fits the historic pattern of executive-centered partisanship. House Democrats supported Trump, on average, 17 percent of the time—the historical low-water mark for the opposition party in the US House. Democratic senators were slightly more supportive, largely owing to Senate rules, which required some level of support to cross over the filibuster threshold on several major pieces of legislation. Still, Democrats supported Trump's position on just 36 percent of legislative roll call votes during his presidency—another historical low. Partisan lines were so well entrenched that Trump rarely resorted to the veto; even during divided government, with Democrats in control of the House after 2018, the president used the veto power judiciously, when Congress was unlikely to override his action. As we discuss in chapter 3, the White House reserved most of its political capital for the flurry of polarizing executive orders Trump issued during his term in office. Privileging administration over legislation, Trump issued ten vetoes in 4 years, prevailing on all but one—the fewest number of vetoes since William McKinley's presidency, 120 years earlier.

Legislative Fight over the Tax Cuts and Jobs Act of 2017

The numbers tell an important story and allow us to situate Trump's relationship with Congress in historical context. But numbers alone do not tell the full story of executive-centered partisanship's effect on constitutional norms and institutions. On the one hand, if the president is going to claim a mandate to govern, it makes sense that members of his own party would rally behind the mandate, while the opposition party would dig in its heels. That is what we expect of parliamentary systems, where prime ministers and majority coalitions claim mandates to govern. To some extent, the clear partisan cleavages in the legislative agenda reflect a party system that has reduced the friction between the various branches of government and made legislation more reflective of the people's choice for president. On the other hand, a majority did not elect President Trump; the Senate gives more voice to individuals living in small states; and gerrymandering, incumbency advantages, and uncontested races for the House of Representatives make it nearly impossible to discern what the national majority is even in the "people's house." Moreover, the data indicate that Republicans were more likely to support Trump because their electoral fortunes were tied to the success of the president's, but legislative outcomes are also increasingly reflective of the president's particularistic policy goals, which can be exceptionally partisan and divisive.

A telling example of these consequences is seen in the Trump administration's crowning legislative achievement: the Tax Cuts and Jobs Act of 2017.[22] The Republican-led effort to reform the federal tax code epitomizes partisan politicking in an era of ideological polarization.[23] Passed without a single Democratic vote in a Republican-led Congress, the 185-page bill was signed at the tail end of Trump's first year in office. Celebrated as the first major tax overhaul since Ronald Reagan's Tax Reform Act of 1986, the TCJA delivered on the Republican Party's decades-long promise to overhaul the federal tax code by slashing the corporate tax rate by 14 points, increasing the size of the deduction granted for new business assets and real estate development, and eliminating the tax penalty imposed by the Affordable Care Act of 2010—the individual mandate—threatening the viability of "Obamacare."

As tax cuts have been a core Republican commitment since the Reagan administration, support for the bill should have been high. And it was; every Republican senator voted for it, and every Democratic senator voted against it. Passed as a budget reconciliation measure—an increasingly common parliamentary device in the age of executive-centered partisanship—there was no need to secure a bipartisan agreement to get past the sixty votes needed to overcome a filibuster. In the House, every Democrat voted against it, and just twelve Republicans bucked the president's wishes. Amounting to just 5 percent of the Republican caucus, this level of opposition was still well within the bounds of modern president-Congress relations. But zeroing in on this opposition is revealing for how the actual content of legislation changes under the dynamics of executive-centered partisanship.

In doubling the standard deduction and increasing the percentage of low-income Americans who pay no income tax at all, the TCJA added trillions to the federal debt; the annual deficit eclipsed $1 trillion two fiscal years after passage, even before the COVID-19 pandemic's emergency spending. Given that the law was a product of intraparty negotiation, this was the result not of bipartisan compromise but of an overwhelming desire to eke out a legislative victory for President Trump before the 2018 midterms, regardless of the party's lip service to fiscal prudence. The reform bill also limited one of the most regressive and upwardly redistributive features of the American tax code, the state and local tax (SALT) deduction.

Significantly, SALT benefits were highly correlated with President Trump's geographic electoral support. SALT deductibility allows residents of every state to deduct from the federal tax liability what they paid in local and tax taxes, but this benefit had been concentrated in two main areas of the United States, the upper Northeast and the West Coast. Two states—California and New York—accounted for 33.6 percent of all SALT deductions claimed on individual tax returns in 2016. Moreover, the gap between blue Democratic-voting states and red Republican-voting states increased in the twenty years preceding the 2016 election. That is, the SALT deduction was increasingly confined to Democratic states. In 1996, itemizers in states that voted for the Democratic presidential candidate took an average SALT deduction of $5,559, while individuals in states that voted Republican deducted 22.5 percent less, or $4,308. Twenty years later,

Democratic states claimed an average SALT deduction of $12,866, while Republican states claimed just $8,693, a 32.43 percent difference.

This is not to say that the SALT deduction was a Democratic policy. Millions of Republican Trump voters live in blue states. Over 40 percent of Trump voters in 2016 lived in states that ultimately cast votes for Hillary Clinton. In California and New York, Trump voters took the SALT deduction as eagerly as Clinton voters. Indeed, because Republican voters are, on average, wealthier than Democratic voters, it is likely that more Republicans took SALT deductions prior to its rescission under the new tax law.

Given the complex interaction between the geographic distribution of SALT benefits and partisanship, politicians have a choice in how they frame this issue. There is no straightforward narrative, and there are competing political pressures that may lead citizens and elites alike to favor or disprove of SALT, regardless of prior ideological commitments.[24] Frames matter, because that is how individuals evaluate policy and hold leaders accountable for the policy's redistributive consequences. And frames go beyond the single measure of partisan support in the legislature—they are the essence of what that support is ultimately about.

In seeking to rescind SALT, the Republican Party could have appealed to the broad set of voters in the middle of the electorate who might oppose the deductions on redistributive grounds: SALT deductions tend to favor wealthier citizens. Most Americans oppose policies whose benefits disproportionately go to the wealthy.[25] It is important to note that the Trump administration compromised its position on SALT deductions in the months leading up to the final bill's passage. The White House initially proposed to fully repeal the SALT deduction on the grounds that it would significantly reduce the TCJA's effect on the federal debt; as originally planned, repealing the SALT deduction alongside several others (including mortgage interest) would have increased revenues by $1.3 trillion over a ten-year period, amounting to a 10 percent decrease in projected US debt levels.[26] Making the rich pay their fair share, reducing the federal deficit—what's not to like?

That is not how the debate played out. Instead of making a bipartisan, consensus- building appeal for support, Trump consistently, and provocatively, galvanized backing for SALT's repeal by making it a partisan issue, emphasizing how SALT deductions favored profligate blue states. Red Trump-supporting America would win; blue Trump-opposing America would pay. As the president argued in an interview with Sean Hannity, states like California and New

York "are being subsidized by states like Indiana and Iowa.... They're being penalized. And it's not fair."[27]

Caught up in the call-and-response of presidential partisanship, other actors—Democrats and Republicans alike—took Trump's bait. New York governor Andrew Cuomo labeled the effort to repeal the SALT deduction as the president's latest salvo in an ongoing "economic civil war" between blue and red states.[28] By framing the policy change in partisan terms, proponents of the bill masked how SALT overwhelmingly benefited high-income households. Opponents of repealing or capping the tax benefit reacted in kind, stressing that higher state taxes in blue states supported social welfare measures denied red state citizens. Downplaying the inconvenient fact that 76 percent of all SALT claims go to individuals and families making more than double the US average income, Democrats decried the president's sacrifice of underserved communities to reward those who had supported him in the last election.[29] The political scientists Jacob Hacker and Paul Pierson compared this "new spoils system" with the "decades after the Civil War, when the GOP used the proceeds of high tariffs that aided Northern industry (while hurting the solidly Democratic South) to pay generous pensions to Union veterans concentrated in Republican states."[30]

Trump's influence on party politics can be gauged by revisiting the partisan dynamics of the SALT deduction during Reagan's presidency. Prior to the TCJA, prospects for eliminating SALT deductions reached their highest point with the election of Ronald Reagan and his proposals that made up the eventual Tax Reform Act of 1986. Repealing the SALT deduction was just a small component of Reagan's mammoth tax reform plan, but it drew considerable attention and aroused intense opposition because of its relationship to the president's broader governing philosophy.[31] Whereas liberals had previously questioned the utility of the SALT deduction because it limited the revenues flowing to the federal government, they took umbrage at Reagan's charge that the policy "helps subsidize high-tax states." Democratic New York governor Mario Cuomo—Andrew's father—assailed the president for pitting states against one another. When Cuomo traveled to Washington, DC, to make a personal appeal to Congress, his crusade monopolized Reagan's attention for several weeks, distracting the president's effort to navigate his complex tax reform package through Congress.

The White House had stressed that SALT's repeal conformed with Reagan's promise to renew the nation's commitment to limited government. Pat

Buchanan, the fiercely partisan White House communications director, defended the repeal of the SALT deduction on the grounds that it would prevent the effort of those "neo-socialist" states to "redistribute the wealth."[32] However, following Cuomo's march on the capital, which New York's Republican senator Alfonse D'Amato supported, Reagan shifted to a less partisan rhetorical strategy. Retreating from the front lines of SALT deductions, the White House emphasized that the president's plan would reduce tax rates and limit specialized deductions, the core commitment of his plan to reform the economy. In framing the debate over state and local tax deduction as a partial reprieve from high state taxes that benefited the middle class, Cuomo and the New York congressional delegation built a formidable coalition of states that undermined Reagan's partisan strategy. Middle-class taxpayers, not blue states, were the true beneficiaries of SALT deductions, they argued.[33] This message, which had bipartisan appeal, transformed the debate over state and local tax obligations into a policy conflict that left the public unfazed; as public opinion research has demonstrated, unclear partisan signals leave most individuals unable to construct fully formed opinions on a complex political issue.[34]

Whereas Republicans and Democrats in Congress thwarted Reagan's efforts to frame tax reform as a divisive partisan issue, their resistance was buttressed by federalism. As Senator D'Amato's opposition illustrates, local and state loyalties resisted national partisan strategies and policies. But over the past four decades, executive-centered partisanship and the growing importance of national advocacy groups have dovetailed the states. As a result, SALT deduction and many other policy debates, hitherto rooted in regional and state differences, have been transformed into national partisan struggles that pit loyal supporters of the president against the White House's intractable opponents. New York's Republican delegation, which was so essential to saving the SALT deduction during President Reagan's tax reform fight, had lost much of its influence in a Congress sharply divided between red and blue America. In 1986, Republican representatives made up nearly half the New York's state delegation to the House, but by 2016, the GOP share had fallen to just one-third.

Consequently, resistance to the Trump administration's plan to repeal the SALT deduction fell to a highly marginalized and geographically out-of-place faction within the GOP. Among the most vocal was Representative Peter King (R-NY) who, in an interview with *Fox News Sunday* bluntly affirmed the political rationale: "[SALT] was like too easy a target and it's also from states that let's face it don't have that many Republicans in them. . . . It's really a vicious cycle. . . . it's going to be a massive tax cut for the country but it's going to be a big hit on one whole region of the country."[35] Republicans were also isolated in other high-SALT-deducting states, including California and Illinois. Of the twelve Republican representatives who voted against the TCJA in 2017, five were from New York, four from New Jersey, and two from California—the states with the first-, second-, and fourth-largest average SALT deductions, respectively. Not a single Republican senator represented one of the eight states that collectively accounted for more than 50 percent of all SALT deduction claims in 2016 (New York, New Jersey, Connecticut, California, Maryland, Oregon, Massachusetts, and Minnesota).

The change in congressional representation is part of a nationwide partisan realignment that has occurred in tandem with the rise of executive-centered partisanship. But Trump's sustained efforts to repeal the SALT deduction demonstrate that this development is not a natural extension of party polarization. Rather, it reflects the president's increasing rhetorical and administrative capabilities to target and reward specific constituencies of political interest. In the final days leading up to the 2018 congressional midterm elections, Republican leaders and President Trump appealed to voters by claiming that their policies helped communities that had supported the Republican Party in the last presidential election. Days before the 2018 midterms, Bill Haslam, Tennessee governor and chair of the Republican Governors Association, drove the point home on *Meet the Press*:

> You know, the new tax plan, you can no longer deduct your state and local taxes. And so states like Florida, like Tennessee, Texas, that don't have income taxes have all of a sudden become very happy hunting grounds for folks to go out and recruit, particularly out of some of the high states in the Northeast. We've seen that. Florida is on a boom. And if I was Florida, I would not want to turn that around.[36]

One week later, Rep. Adam Schiff (D-CA) articulated the Democrats' position: "This is a president who, more than any other, is punitive and I think we saw that in the tax cut by taking away state and local tax deductions. That was aimed at the blue states. Basically, he is only the president, I think in his view, of those who voted for him, the rest, he could care less."[37]

Haslam could have made the point that the cap on SALT deductions closed the gap between the proportion of income that the wealthiest and poorest

Americans paid. Schiff could have made a similar argument, especially given the Democratic Party's tendency to emphasize issues such as income inequality and greater government spending.[38] And, like previous administrations over the course of the twentieth century, the president could have emphasized SALT's implication for the breadth of the overall tax base—the general argument that economists levy against deductions overall—or the fact that the wealthiest Americans disproportionately accrue the SALT deduction's financial benefits.

But by 2017 the political fortunes of congressional Republicans were so tied to the success of the president that they were willing to forsake—rhetorically and practically—the constituencies that did not vote Republican in the last presidential contest. The logic undergirding the partisan rhetoric, and the explanation for why Trump was able to secure an important policy victory, owed decidedly to the confluence of forces that have privileged presidential partisanship. As a result, the president and his congressional allies chose to frame the issue in starkly partisan terms: SALT gave the president's opponents a tax break, subsidizing their high-tax and high-spending governments. Repealing SALT would be another notch on Trump's belt in making his opponents pay, and legislating in the people's interest would become another tool for advancing the president's own particular political goals.

THE FEDERAL JUDICIARY UNDER THE TRUMP ADMINISTRATION

Given the institutional developments we have described throughout this book, the consequences of executive-centered partisanship on president-Congress relations are not all that surprising, even if the political costs associated with it are greater than commonly thought. After all, the development of presidency-led parties was motivated, in part, by deep dissatisfaction over the institutional separation between Congress and the presidency that prevailed at the mid-twentieth century, which appeared to produce legislative gridlock, rampant clientelism, and unaccountable growth in the bureaucracy. From the intricacies of budget management to the glitz of the annual State of the Union address, the president did not so much usurp congressional authority so much as step in to meet the expectations thrust upon the office—including from those serving in Congress. To those who have grown up knowing only a Congress that is largely supplicant to presidential politics, the heightened levels of president-Congress agreement may simply seem normal and by design.

The courts, though, are different. Judges and justices are not elected, nor do they stand for reelection or reappointment. They are not supposed to reflect the naked partisan or political interests of the day or be implicated in the constitutional turf wars fought by elected officials. As Chief Justice John Roberts said during his Senate confirmation hearings in 2005, the job of a judge is like that of an umpire: "to call balls and strikes, and not to pitch or bat."[39] As Alexander Hamilton put it less colloquially, shorn of the power of the purse and sword, and limited to the exercising power only in matters pertaining to the cases brought before it, the judiciary is the "least dangerous branch"—its power depends on its exercise of impartial judgment. That impartiality, or the perception of it, justifies the judiciary's transcendent status; it endues the "cult of the robe," as the former Chief Justice William Rehnquist explained, and gives the American judiciary—one of the strongest in the world—the authority to declare acts of Congress unconstitutional or to tell the presidents that they cannot do whatever they want, even if they claim a mandate to do it.[40]

Has the judiciary, then, escaped the pathologies of executive-centered partisanship? Ostensibly, the partisan dynamics that fuel executive factionalism and legislative ennui are aroused by institutions subject to the "electoral connection." Insulated from the electoral process, judges and justices could still call balls and strikes impartially, even though presidential dominion has changed the rules of the game.

As its resistance to the White House's legal legerdemain in the wake of the 2020 election dramatically revealed, the judiciary, which now includes many Trump appointees, is not overawed by presidentialism. Nevertheless, Trump's presidency, marking the culmination of executive-centered partisanship, aggravated a legitimacy crisis that has tarnished the cult of the robe. Although the judiciary remains less vulnerable to the pathologies that have infected the administrative and legislative processes, hallmarks of executive-centered partisanship are present in judicial politics as well.

We begin with a basic question: Is the cult of the robe more myth than reality? If the Supreme Court's authority rests on its ability to present itself as a nonpartisan arbiter, it would seem that the public must view it on those terms. Even if the Supreme Court's jurisprudence is completely rational and logically consistent, that is not the source of its authority. The Supreme Court and lower

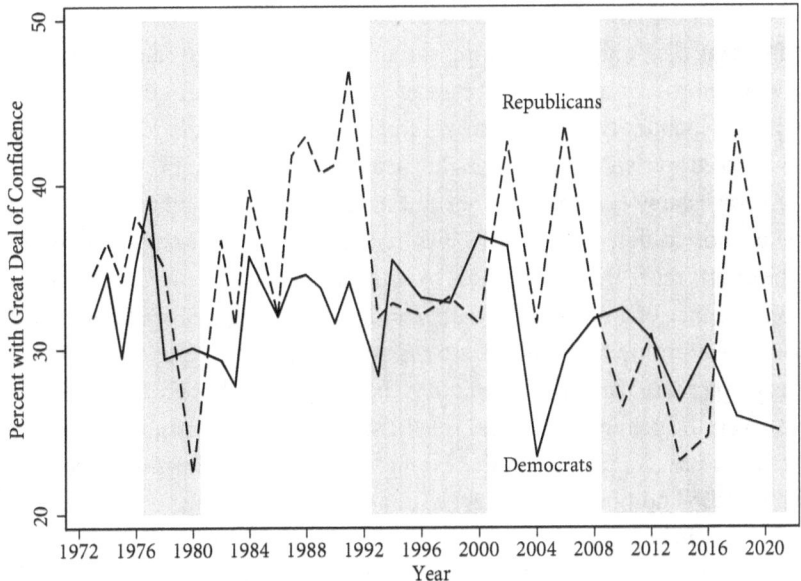

Figure 4.3. Percentage of self-identifying Republicans and Democrats who have a "great deal of confidence" in the federal judiciary from the early 1970s to the present. Democratic presidential administrations are shaded.

Source: General Social Survey, University of Chicago, and author calculations. *Credit:* Created by authors.

appellate and district courts are political in the sense that their legitimacy depends on public perceptions of the judiciary's nonpartisan nature. The more partisan Supreme Court justices and lower court judges appear, the less confidence Americans have in them, since they no longer live up to the lofty expectations of impartiality. Since the early 1970s, the General Social Survey at the University of Chicago has measured the degree of confidence Americans have in the federal judiciary and courts, in general. Considering how those attitudes manifest among self-identifying Republicans and Democrats, we can see how the public's perceptions of the courts have changed over time in figure 4.3.

It is true that the public is significantly more confident in the courts than in the other federal institutions (i.e., Congress and the presidency). While the proportion of Americans, on average, holding "a great deal of confidence" in the courts has hovered between 24 (2014) and 39 (1991) percent, this is substantially higher than the 12 percent of Americans, on average, who have had similar levels of confidence in Congress, or the 15 percent who expressed substantial confidence in the presidency. Much of this, we surmise, is a true reflection of the cult of the robe. Large numbers of Americans do buy into the notion that the judges are umpires—even if they get some calls wrong. And, so, while nowhere near 100 percent of Americans are particularly confident in the independence of the federal judiciary, it appears that the courts have weathered the crisis of institutional distrust better than the other branches.

Averages, however, elide important differences in the general population. One of those differences is partisanship. Republicans have tended to approve of the courts more than Democrats over the past sixty years, reflecting perhaps the emergence of a more conservative judiciary during this era. However, the courts' relationship to public opinion is not merely a matter of one party's loyalists being more trusting of the courts than the other. Rather, as we might expect given the president's central role in shaping political affairs, partisanship matters in judicial politics to the extent that confidence in the courts moves with the ebb and flow of presidential control. Democratic and Republican attitudes toward the judiciary change, depending not on what the courts are doing, necessarily, but on whomever sits on the other side of Pennsylvania Avenue in the White House. When Republicans hold the presidency, Republicans' confidence in the judiciary increases, while Democrats' confidence decreases. The reverse occurs when Democrats hold the presidency. And the shifting attitudes have become more dramatic over time, especially among Republican partisans who react to changes in presidential control to a much larger degree. At the start of Trump's presidency, for example, only one in four Republicans had a great deal of confidence in the courts; just two years later, positive attitudes nearly doubled, while Democratic views, which had grown during the Obama administration, fell. Tellingly, these partisan vacillations coincide with a secular trend toward declining confidence in the judiciary, particularly in the last twenty years as the shift between Democratic and Republican presidential administrations has become more frequent.

Clearly, not even the Supreme Court's authority is immune from the onset of presidential partisanship. Presidents, now the repository of party responsibility, cannot resist politicizing the judicial process. This politization routinely occurs during the course of presidential campaigns. Courts have never been off-limits during elections. Andrew Jackson's pioneering populism first showed how the democratization of the executive office inclined presidents to attack the independence of the judiciary.[41] But the courts face more regular political headwinds in contemporary politics, when not only judicial decisions but also the personal backgrounds and characters of justices are dragged into the muck and mire of presidential elections and nomination campaigns.

To be sure, some of this is reflective of the growing role that courts, pressured by the legal strategies of advocacy groups that carry on the cultural struggles unleashed by the sixties, have carved out in American society. Lincoln warned that allowing the courts to resolve issues of national importance like slavery would sacrifice self-government to the decrees of an "eminent tribunal." Today, the courts are regularly drawn into battles for the "nation's soul," where judges are expected to arbitrate deeply personal and polarizing issues like a transgender student's access to a restroom or a private employee's health care plan.[42] Yet the disrobing of the judiciary is also attributable to the growing dependence of Republicans and Democrats on presidential candidates and presidents to mobilize the party base, who are particularly animated by the high stakes of the country's "culture wars" and the important role that the federal judiciary plays in mediating those disputes. Most voters may still be motivated by bread-and-butter issues—the economy, defense, taxation—but a significant faction of each party is deeply engaged in the politics of the soul and attentive to how judicial politics, agitated by presidency-centered partisanship, has become the tip of the spear in the culture wars.[43]

The federal judiciary's legitimacy is thus challenged by growing presidentialism. So is its jurisprudence. Executive-centered partisanship has altered the institutional logic of judicial decision-making, both in structuring the actual composition of the courts through the nomination and confirmation process and through actual case law. Few moments are more contentious and closely followed by news media than when the Senate is asked to confirm a president's nomination to the Supreme Court. Just as Manichaean presidentialism has churned the legislative process, so it has polarized the appointment and confirmation of justices. Consequently, partisans have become more likely to play "constitutional hardball" in shaping the future of the courts.[44] No laws were broken when Republican Senate majority leader Mitch McConnell refused to hold confirmation hearings for President Obama's Supreme Court nominee following the unexpected death of Justice Antonin Scalia in February 2016. But the episode certainly pushed the bounds of what was expected—violated the norm that all presidents, regardless of party, have the chance to submit nominees to the Senate for consideration. If anything, we anticipate that these norms are respected out of pure self-interest; a Republican president, down the line, could find themselves in a similar situation (Trump did, with the death of Ruth Bader Ginsburg during an election year). Such episodes have revealed dramatically how much constitutional government depends not strictly on legal obligations but on norms—shared beliefs—that enable a complex system of checks and balances to work. Hardball politics emerges when these self-restraining imperatives no longer seem politically prudent.

Losing any sense of "forbearance" and "mutual toleration," as Steven Levitsky and Daniel Ziblatt have shown, hardball proceduralism is particularly corrosive when it involves the institutions that are supposed to judge the actual procedures.[45] The failure of a Republican Senate to confirm Merrick Garland—and that same body's hypocritical rush to judgment in confirming Justice Amy Coney Barrett—makes clear how the stakes of presidential elections and administration have become so high that constitutional norms are sacrificed in the service of partisan objectives. The winner-take-all politics of executive-centered partisanship, navigated masterfully by advocacy organizations like the Federalist Society, has further empowered the courts but at the cost of weakening the authority of judicial branch. The cult of the robe, after all, depends on a deeply rooted but fragile belief.

The same hardball tactics implicate the decisions the courts render, particularly as they relate to the limits of presidential power. In short, as presidents are increasingly motivated to push the bounds of permissible legal action, the courts are increasingly called on to enforce those bounds. And yet, failing to speak with one unified voice to set institutional guardrails, the courts are complicit in the growing ambiguity of presidential authority, particularly in policy areas that conservatives privilege in deploying administrative power, such as immigration enforcement and homeland security. Some commentators have been remarkably sanguine about the increasing politization of judicial decision-making. They point to the fact that on most major cases, the Supreme Court, as it has historically done, aligned with public opinion and delivered key losses to the Trump administration; the justices even ruled that Trump had to deliver his financial records to prosecutors and the House committee investigating his alleged fraudulent business practices.[46]

But Trump's effect on the Supreme Court cannot be gauged by the scorecard of a single term. Indeed, disappointed that a Court with three Trump appointees did not sanction his effort to overturn a free and fair election, the president turned legal defeats into base-pleasing recrimination as he cast aspersions and doubt on the Court's integrity. Confidence in the judiciary continued to fall, even as it sought to rein in the legal adventurism of the Trump administration. To the extent that the courts often rule in such a way as to reassert their judicial independence, and avoid taking center stage in electoral politics, presidential partisanship has proved to be an unshakable albatross.

Transforming the Presidency, One Judge and One Court Case at a Time

In running for office, Donald Trump promised to appoint antiabortion judges who would overturn *Roe v. Wade* to win over reluctant Christian right activists who were intrigued by his "Make America Great Again" pledge but fretted over his "personal failings."[47] Not since Nixon took direct aim at the Warren Court in 1968 for its "permissiveness" and its "sympathy for the past grievances of those who have become criminals" has a presidential campaign so directly staked its campaign on a promise to reshape the federal judiciary.[48]

Trump became the first presidential candidate to release a list of individuals he would appoint to the Supreme Court in May 2016, including potential candidates to replace Scalia, whose seat was kept vacant until after the election by Senate Republicans' refusal to even consider President Obama's nominee, Merrick Garland. None on the first list of eleven were nominated to the Supreme Court; however, Neil Gorsuch—Trump's first appointment—did appear on a longer list of twenty-one potential picks.[49] Crafted with the support of Republican leaders and two leading conservative interest groups—the Heritage Foundation and the Federalist Society—Trump's strategy to outsource potential nominees helped seal a partnership with a formidable network of conservative activists who played a critical role in the 2016 campaign and the development of White House causes and policies that appealed to the Republican base. While the Heritage Foundation and the Federalist Society had long been mainstays in traditional Republican Party politics—including claiming two former Republican attorneys general among their members—their influence for the most part was exercised out of public view. Trump gave them and evangelical Christian leaders unprecedented access and visibility, celebrating his alliance with movement organizations as evidence of his commitment to lead an all-out struggle to restore traditional American values.

Beyond the overt attempt to forge a primordial relationship with the Republican base, the plan to reshape the federal judiciary was joined to Trump's audacious deployment of executive power. The doctrine of a unitary executive has long been a pillar of the conservative legal movement's counteroffensive against the liberal state. Ironically, as we discussed previously, these conservatives had a more expansive view of presidential power than did Franklin Roosevelt—the president whom opponents of the liberal state had once disdained. Starting with the Reagan administration, the conservative legal movement developed the ideological and organizational capacity to establish its constitutional interpretation of presidential powers as a core commitment of the Republican Party.[50] Reagan's attorney general Edwin Meese III—who sat on the board of the Federalist Society during Trump's presidency—argued for the widespread use of presidential signing statements, so that courts could interpret "presidential intent" alongside "legislative intent" when adjudicating institutional disputes. Or, as Meese's deputy attorney general, now Supreme Court justice, Samuel Alito, wrote in a memorandum to "make fuller use of the president's constitutionally assigned role in the process of enacting law":

> Since the President's approval is just as important as that of the House or Senate, it seems to follow that the President's understanding of the bill should be just as important as that of Congress. Yet in interpreting statutes, both courts and litigants (including lawyers in the Executive branch) invariably speak of "legislative" or "congressional" intent. Rarely if ever do courts or litigants inquire into the President's intent. Why is this so?[51]

By the time Trump campaigned for the presidency, not only was Alito fully ensconced on the Supreme Court but dozens of other judges were serving in the judiciary and applying such doctrine. Critics charge that unitary executive theory is not a constitutional doctrine but a pretense of originalism that justifies conservatives' deployment of unbridled executive power to advance their political objectives. Indeed, conservative legal scholars themselves debate the contours of the doctrine—whether it applies only to the president's control of the executive branch or, as Alito argued, also vested power in the president to disregard legal constraints. Nor have proponents of this doctrine settled the tension between the constitutional view that presidents have the republican responsibility to ensure competent administration against the vicissitudes of popular opinion and the normative position of democratic theory that elections and public opinion, not the other branches of government, should be relied on to hold the executive in check. As Jeremy Bailey has argued, the unitary executive is Janus-faced: under the doctrine, there is a need for two executives: "one chained to electoral accountability and one freed from it."[52]

We contend that the ambiguity of the unitary executive doctrine is inherent in movement conservatives' position that their objectives can no longer be served by rolling back the state. In the wake of the tumultuous sixties, Republican presidents and the party's base began to rally around their belief that liberalism had so corrupted the country's institutions that the national government has the responsibility to support "family values" (a view that permeates proposals to restrict abortion and LGBTQIA+ rights); to require work for social welfare programs; and to impose standards on secondary and elementary schools. From this perspective, the politics and legal theory animating modern conservativism give constitutional sanction to executive-centered partisanship—undermining the judiciary's claim to be an impartial guardian of the Constitution. Trump's alliance with the Federalist Society was therefore consistent with the position it has attained as a defender of conservative presidentialism, which he embraced with even more alacrity than his Republican predecessors. He saw more clearly than his rivals in the 2016 nomination contest the mobilizing potential and electoral possibilities of conservative statism, and how the Federalist Society's constitutionalism could bestow legitimacy on his own view of executive aggrandizement.

This partnership of convenience was critical to the remarkable imprint Trump had on the judiciary in four short years. Despite his occupying the White House for only a single term, Trump's impact on the courts is historically noteworthy (table 4.1). At the level of the Supreme Court, no single-termer of the modern presidential era has had such an influence on the membership of the high court. Of course, as a result of the constitutional hardball played during the 2016 presidential campaign season, Trump entered office with a vacancy to fill. But with the able support of Senate majority leader Mitch McConnell, his administration methodically filled positions in the lower courts as well. His appointments to the powerful courts of appeals approached and even surpassed levels of two-term presidents. Only Jimmy Carter appointed more appeals court judges during a single term.

Some of Trump's success in the lower courts was the result of a historically high number of vacancies at the end of the Obama administration, the result in no small measure of the same obstructionist tactics deployed by the Republican-controlled Senate that denied Obama's nomination of Merrick Garland.[53] The same determination of McConnell and the Republican Senate caucus to dominate judicial politics during Obama's second term helped secure for Trump a historically high nomination rate.[54] The percentage of Trump's

Table 4.1. Confirmed Nominations to the US Judiciary, by President

President	Supreme Court	Courts of Appeals	District Courts
Donald Trump	3	54	174
Barack Obama	2	49	268
George W. Bush	2	61	261
Bill Clinton	2	62	305
George H. W. Bush	2	37	148
Ronald Reagan	3	78	290
Jimmy Carter	0	56	203
Gerald Ford	1	12	50
Richard Nixon	4	45	182
Lyndon Johnson	2	41	125
John F. Kennedy	2	20	102
Dwight Eisenhower	5	45	127
Harry S. Truman	4	27	102

Source: United States Courts, Judgeship Appointments by President, 2022, accessed December 31, 2022, https://www.uscourts.gov/judges-judgeships/authorized-judgeships/judgeship-appointments-president#:~:text=Supreme%20Court%20justices%2C%20court%20of,as%20stated%20in%20the%20Constitution.

nominees confirmed by the Senate (92 percent, or fifty-four of the fifty-nine nominations) was surpassed only by that of Nixon, who saw all but one of his appointments to the federal courts of appeals confirmed. In contrast, nearly 20 percent of Obama's nominations failed, as did 30 percent of George W. Bush's and Bill Clinton's. The prevalence of insecure majorities in a fractured nation no doubt helped galvanize the White House and Senate to make hay while the sun shined—to fill as many nominations as possible in a short period of time.

The political hardball that characterized judicial politics during the Trump and Obama administrations also contributed to the growing legitimacy crisis confronting the judiciary. In 2016 and 2020, the Cooperative Congressional Election Study (CCES), which we analyzed in chapter 3, asked Democrats and Republicans about the two vacancies that emerged during the presidential campaign, following the deaths of Antonin Scalia in 2016 and Ruth Bader Ginsburg in 2020.

As table 4.2 illustrates, neither Republicans nor Democrats were consistent in their attitudes about the politics of confirming a justice to the Supreme Court during an election year (though it must be recognized that Scalia's death occurred much earlier in a campaign year than did Ginsburg's). Whereas close to 90 percent of Democrats favored the approval of Merrick Garland to the Supreme Court as the presidential campaign was going on, 80 percent said

Table 4.2. Partisan Attitudes toward Supreme Court Nominations in 2016 and 2020, CCES

	Democrats (%)	Republicans (%)	Trump Republicans (%)
2016: Approve the nomination of Merrick Garland to the Supreme Court	88.27	19.96	12.55
2020: Ruth Bader Ginsburg replacement selection should happen after new Senate and president are in place	80.54	8.68	3.46

Source: 2016, 2020 Cooperative Congressional Election Study.

that Trump should not have the same chance when it came to a vacancy during the 2020 presidential campaign. Republicans reacted similarly: nearly 80 percent opposed the nomination of Merrick Garland, whereas over 90 percent approved of Trump nominating a justice to replace Justice Ginsberg during the twilight of the 2020 campaign.

Harsh partisan opportunism is especially pronounced among those who strongly supported Donald Trump's presidency and voted for him in the primary (those we call "Trump Republicans" in table 4.2). Among all partisans, but especially Trump Republicans, we see a willingness to support the constitutional hardball tactics during the 2016 and 2020 campaigns. In fact, in 2020, a larger percentage of Republicans and Democrats held a partisan opinion on the question of Supreme Court nominees than even knew which party held power in the Senate or House of Representatives! About a third of self-identifying Democrats and Republicans either said they did not know who controlled the House or Senate, or incorrectly identified the party that controlled either chamber. But virtually no partisan refused to register an opinion on the all-important question of Supreme Court nominations.

The expression of opinions on institutional procedures is telling—symptomatic of the Trump administration's decision to make court politics a core part of its partisan strategy. Trump not only signaled his conservative bona fides by celebrating his list of Federalist Society judges but also raised the stakes of the 2016 presidential contest and galvanized Republican support for obstructing Obama's nominees to the judiciary. Throughout his presidency, Trump's success in reshaping the federal judiciary was widely celebrated or denounced as a significant achievement. Marc Thiessen, a noted conservative columnist for the *Washington Post*, touted Trump's judicial politics as his most important accomplishment in 2019; standing by Brett Kavanaugh through a tumultuous nomination contest was the best thing Trump did in 2018; rushing Justice Amy Coney Barrett's confirmation made the 2020 list at number 4.[55]

Trump's politicization of the courts went hand in hand with an attack on their independent authority, singling out judges and rulings with which he disagreed. Through his unmediated access to millions of Twitter followers (reposted countless times by mainstream media outlets), he directly attacked the idea of judicial legitimacy. The many prosecutions and investigations into his campaign and business during his term in office fueled the president's denigration of the criminal proceedings that also implicated key advisers and former members of his campaign: Roger Stone, Paul Manafort, Steve Bannon, and Michael Flynn, among others. Often drawing comparisons to how the alleged crimes of Hillary Clinton were handled, Republican attitudes toward the FBI increasingly soured during his administration; in 2018, just 49 percent of Republicans had a favorable opinion of the FBI (the same favorability rating as toward the IRS), compared with 77 percent of Democrats.

The disputes that aroused the most serious institutional combat between the White House and the courts came not over Trump's alleged nefarious business practices but with respect to legal challenges to his aggressive exercise of executive power. Trump's most controversial attack on judicial autonomy came in response to a November 2018 ruling that blocked his administration's new rules that would bar anyone crossing the US-Mexico border not through an official port of entry from receiving asylum. The president excoriated the ruling, issued by Judge Jon Tigar of the US Court of Appeals for the Ninth Circuit, which ordered the administration to accept asylum claims regardless of where migrants entered the country. He called the decision "a disgrace," attacked Tigar as "an Obama judge," and critiqued the Ninth Circuit as "really something we have to take a look at because it's not fair," adding, "That's not law. Every case that gets filed in the Ninth Circuit we get beaten." In a rare public rebuke, Chief Justice John Roberts insisted that the United States doesn't have "Obama judges or Trump judges, Bush judges or Clinton judges." We have, Roberts added, "an extraordinary group of dedicated judges doing their level best to do equal right to those appearing before them." The independent judiciary, he concluded, is "something we should all be thankful for." Trump did not back down. He took to Twitter to challenge Roberts's claim that the judiciary was impartial; it was infested with Obama judges, he insisted, who thwarted the policies of his administration that were necessary to protect "the safety of our country."[56]

This was a common refrain. Central to Trump's "law-and-order" campaign was a near-constant reference back to the idea that the courts unfairly prevented him from acting in the interest of homeland security. In a speech before police officers, Trump anticipated the possibility that his immigration policy might be resisted by the courts: "If these judges wanted to, in my opinion, help the court in terms of respect for the court, they'd do what they should be doing . . . courts seem to be so political, and it would be so great for our justice system if they would be able to read a statement and do what's right, and that has to do with the security of our country." Even John Yoo, a chief architect of the unitary executive during George W. Bush's administration, sounded frustrated with the president's persistent challenge to judicial independence: "I hate to see a president waste that kind of authority, which should only be deployed for our most important questions. . . . Trump is pressing the accelerator down to 120 miles per hour on every single issue. He will exhaust himself and exhaust his presidency."[57]

Although Trump's attack on the judges and court decisions posed a direct threat to the legitimacy of an independent judiciary, the question remains what effect his brand of law-and-order politics had on public policy and government action. Because judges and justices depend on the executive for enforcement, the reality is that courts are never fully "independent" of the president in exercising their judgments. They may proclaim their independence and attachment to the law, but as Alexander Hamilton's *Federalist* No. 78 sought to assure the opponents of the Constitution during the ratification contest who feared judicial imperialism, the court "must ultimately depend upon the aid of the executive arm even for the efficacy of its judgments."[58] Invariably, that institutional dependence drew the courts into the political process. As the resistance to Trump's asylum rule illustrates, the judiciary does not rubber-stamp executive orders. But prudence dictates that judges and justices calculate the political fallout of their actions when confronting presidential power. As William Howell argues, judges' "policy preference and legal doctrine come into play only when the possibility of executive defiance is low. Not once in the modern era have the courts overturned a president who enjoys broad-based support from Congress, interest groups, and the public. Surely, though, there have been occasions when judges, owing to ideological precommitments or legal philosophies, would have liked to."[59]

At first glance, Trump's relationship to the judiciary seems to fit this description. Never backed by an approval rating above 50 percent, his executive audacity, which aroused bitter opposition, emboldened the courts. An analysis of his "win rate" before the Supreme Court by Lee Epstein and Eric Posner shows that compared with his predecessors, Trump not only lost the majority of cases to which he was a party (he won only 47 percent of cases) but lost more than any other president in modern political history (since FDR).[60] Looking at cases argued throughout the judiciary, specifically related to the president's administrative powers, the Institute for Policy Integrity found that Trump lost 192 of the 246 legal challenges brought against the administration (78 percent).[61]

Of course, a simple count of judicial actions for or against Trump risks conflating the challenges as equal. Many of the claims brought against the Trump administration were quite narrow. Our review of the ten most significant questions brought before the court paints a somewhat more mixed picture for the president-court relations during the Trump administration (table 4.3). Of these ten, which were among the most high-profile and potentially disruptive challenges to existing law, Trump lost six. He prevailed in his attempts to institute a "Muslim ban," although it was subject to significant delay and revision. However, on several of its most highly charged administrative actions—changing reapportionment to discount noncitizens, moving federal moneys to build a border wall, restricting legal mandates under the Affordable Care Act—the Trump administration prevailed. Indeed, in a case involving the president's control over a federal agency structurally protected from direct political direction, the court issued a strong defense of the unitary executive doctrine.

At the start of his administration, Trump had gone head-to-head with the director of the Consumer Financial and Protection Bureau (CFPB)—the brainchild of Senator Elizabeth Warren—which was created in pursuance of the Dodd-Frank Act (2010), enacted in response to the Great Recession to prevent, "unfair, deceptive, fraudulent" business practices. Determined to exert control over the CFPB's aggressive regulatory measures against lenders it targeted for predatory and discriminatory practices, the Trump administration pressured Obama's choice to head the agency, Richard Condray, to resign, obviating the Dodd-Frank proviso that the CFPB director was appointed to a five-year term and could not be dismissed without cause, defined as "inefficiency, neglect of duty or malfeasance." Eventually a lawsuit brought by a law firm that challenged the CFPB's investigation of its debt relief services on the grounds that the director who originally sanctioned the investigation was unconstitutionally insulated from presidential control reached the Supreme Court. In a 5-to-4 decision, Chief Justice Roberts's opinion for the majority

Table 4.3. Major Questions of Presidential Powers Adjudicated during Trump Administration

Case	Question	Holding
Trump v. Hawaii (2018)	Does the president have the authority to deny entry to foreign nationals and unilaterally suspend and revise refugee processing procedures?	5–4 for Trump
Department of Commerce v. New York (2019)	Did the secretary of commerce violate the law when reinstating a question asking about citizenship on the 2020 US census?	9–0 against Trump
Maine Community Health Options v. United States (2020)	Must the Trump administration reimburse insurance companies that lost money while following legal requirements of the Affordable Care Act?	8–1 against Trump
Department of Homeland Security v. Regents of University of California (2020)	Was the decision to end the Deferred Action for Childhood Arrivals (DACA) policy "arbitrary and capricious"?	5–4 against Trump
Seila Law LLC v. Consumer Financial Protection Bureau (2020)	Did Congress unconstitutionally vest executive power in an independent agency with a single director, with legal protection from presidential removal?	5–4 for Trump
Little Sisters v. Pennsylvania (2020)	Did the Department of Health and Human Service's rules expanding the "moral" exemption to contraceptive care requirements violate the Administrative Procedures Act?	7–2 for Trump
Trump v. Vance (2020)	Must a sitting president comply with a subpoena over an issue, which the president claims violates executive privilege?	7–2 against Trump
Trump v. Sierra Club (2020)	Did the president act lawfully when diverting $2.5 billion in military funds for a wall along the U.S.-Mexico border?	Injunction against Trump lifted

continued

Table 4.3. (continued)

Case	Question	Holding
Trump v. New York (2020)	Can states and localities sue the president challenging his proposal to exclude noncitizens in reapportioning seats for the US House of Representatives?	6–3 for Trump
Trump v. Committee on Ways and Means (2022)	Must Trump comply with an order from the US House of Representatives to disclose his tax records?	Per curiam against Trump

declared that the unusual autonomy of CFBP's director violated the separation of powers. The decision stopped short of declaring the agency and its mission unconstitutional, disappointing some conservatives, but ruled that its director "must be removable by the president at will." The Roberts Court's decision enabled the Trump White House to curb an important agency's enforcement powers and, more broadly, established an important precedent that enhanced the president's control over regulatory politics.[62]

Even in cases that ostensibly curbed presidential aggrandizement, the Supreme Court staked out some important caveats to its curtailment of executive powers. The court proscribed the Trump administration's unbounded claims of executive privilege in adjudicating disputes over congressional investigations, but it remains unclear whether these precedents will have meaningful constraint over policymaking; the rationales for the subpoenas against Trump all dealt with personal and business matters, not presidential policy. In two of the most significant decisions against Trump's administrative actions, the court confined its rulings to narrow procedural issues, leaving untouched the authority of a president to act unilaterally in a given policy area. For example, the court actually agreed with the Trump administration's interpretation of the law granting the secretary of commerce the ability to unilaterally add a citizenship question to the census; it took issue with the way in which the administration rationalized its decision. Likewise, the court did not say that Trump could not rescind DACA, which provided deportation relief to the Dreamers (see chapter 3); the opinion said that the administration could not give one rationale for doing so and then change its reasoning later on. Even though it labeled the president's administrative action as "arbitrary and capricious," the court tacitly recognized the president's authority to unilaterally terminate the policy, so long as, in the future, it provided the rationale to do so at the time of repeal.[63]

In effect, the justices offered the administration—or future administrations—a legal road map for repealing DACA, which the Trump administration soon embraced in the middle of his reelection campaign.[64] If Trump had had better administrative lawyers, the outcome would look very different.

Trump's relationship with the judiciary is more than the sum of court decisions—as important as those specific instances are to the development and stability of American law. At the end of the day, those decisions only have force because they are viewed as legitimate constraints on presidents' actions. Trump did not act in violation of any of the decisions against him, but his political response to such decisions challenged the judiciary as an ultimate authority that upheld the rule of law.

The Trump White House's all-out fight to add a citizenship question to census forms shows how, even in losing a legal battle, Trump succeeded politically. It is another example of how policy battles that are often dismissed as "too wonky" and "inside baseball" were red meat for the president's base. The White House lost this fight in the Supreme Court, when Chief Justice Roberts ruled against its effort to weaponize the census. Nonetheless, the contretemps over the citizenship question allowed the president to cast himself as a strong leader, willing to shake things up in defense of the "silent majority."[65] The battle over the census added fuel to his boast that only a real conservative could reshape the judiciary (his appointees voted "right").

True to the dynamics of executive-centered partisanship, Trump responded by placing two new political appointees at the head of the Census Bureau, just as operations resumed from the COVID-19 pandemic.[66] Having reinforced the agency with political allies, the president signed a memo, issued in July 2020, stating that it would be the "policy of the United States to exclude from the apportionment base aliens who are not in a lawful immigration status under the Immigration and Nationality Act." This provocative move to exclude undocumented immigrants from the census was unprecedented, and it seemed to contradict the Constitution's directive that the decennial exercise count all "persons" living in the United States.[67] Like Trump's effort to include a citizenship question on census forms, this order was challenged by a flurry of lawsuits. This time, however, the administration won a reprieve. The Supreme Court, now fortified by six conservative justices, chose not to rule on the order, arguing that it was "premature" to resolve a case that "was riddled with contingencies and speculation." As the unsigned opinion, which legal experts speculated was authored by Roberts, concluded, "Right now . . . we don't know what the president is going to do. We don't know how many aliens will be excluded. We don't know what the effect will be on apportionment." So why, he asked, aren't we "better advised" to wait until we have that information?[68]

The court waited through the 2020 election. The constitutionality of Trump's partisan administration of the census, like many other legal tests that were wending through the courts, became moot when the Biden administration rescinded Trump's order soon after the new president took office. Had Trump won reelection, the court would have been pulled deeper into a partisan fight stoked by Trump's nativist appeals to his base.

PRESIDENTIAL FEDERALISM UNDER TRUMP

The creation of the American presidency—celebrated as the first republican executive—reflected an important development in constitutional thought and practice, and the attempt to balance the unity and energy of the executive office with a system of separated and divided powers has animated American politics ever since. But, arguably, the most innovative invention that emerged from the Constitutional Convention was federalism—an unprecedented effort to combine one and many communities, to achieve the security of a large republic while harnessing the promise of self-government that depends on empowering local decision-making.[69] In overcoming this "dilemma of scale," not only would the president's powers be constrained by the Congress and the courts but the executive power would also compete with institutions that represented different geographic polities that made up the federal union: the states, exalted by Hamilton as the "sentinels over the persons employed in every department of the national administration."[70]

The original Constitution also embedded state and local influence into the national institutions, especially the Senate, elected by state legislatures and composed of two representatives from each state, regardless of its population. Contrary to the claim of unitary executive theorists, the Senate was vested with legal and administrative powers that defied the president's complete control over the executive branch: it would try presidents indicted by the House for impeachable offenses, confirm presidential nominations to the courts and the executive branch, and ratify treaties. Tellingly, these administrative responsibilities were not lodged in the House, which is more reflective of national majorities. Instead, they were placed in the Senate, which "would derive its powers from the States as political and coequal societies."[71] The Electoral College, as we learned dramatically in the 2000 and 2016 elections, adds a federal ingredient to the presidential selection process, balancing popular support and a broad distribution of geographic representation. Although we often identify the president as the national office, executive power is in no small measure tied to the impulses and incentives of American federalism.

Consequently, as the president took on more responsibility for conducting the nation's partisan and administrative affairs, so too did the modern executive become more deeply embroiled in the politics that negotiates federal and state authority. Leveraging the fact that nearly 20 percent of congressionally appropriated funds are ultimately funneled through state and local governments, a growing body of evidence shows how presidents redirect grants and make appropriations decisions favorable to specific states.[72] Presidents increasingly negotiate, and sometimes command, state and local leaders to enact policies that reflect the president's priorities.[73] Increasingly, since the 1980s, presidents have issued waivers to certain provisions of the law, so that states might adapt federal programs that serve the administration's overarching objectives.[74] Governors loom large in presidential federalism, participating in national partisan politics as partners or opponents of the incumbent administration.

Although presidential federalism is sometimes celebrated as a check on the mischiefs of a polarized capital,[75] the states have become deeply implicated in executive-centered partisanship. Federalism persists; the states remain central to national administration. Yet the enduring structure of federalism has been significantly altered by presidential partisanship. In spite of the way the Senate and the Electoral College inject a measure of federalism into the presidency, the emergence of the modern executive and the leading role it has played since the 1960s in reshaping partisan politics have brought into full view the inherent tension between the national and state communities. The president—the only constitutional office elected by the whole country—is centralizing and uniform; the states are decentralizing and diverse. As Martha Derthick warns:

> The upshot is that the electorate can have no idea who is in charge, and is caused either to cease caring . . . or, if it dares to care, to become disillusioned when the president, upon whom its expectations innocently focus, fails to deliver, as fail he must in respect to most domestic matters. Presidential candidates cam-

paign as if they were to be the national superintendent of schools, while local superintendents, if they are prudent, will keep for ready reference a handbook of law and education, in which many Supreme Court decisions are entered.[76]

As the modern executive has staked out a greater claim to policymaking authority, the states have been at the vanguard of challenging presidential policy. But far from reflecting a principled or pragmatic defense of state and local differences, contemporary federalism is roiled by polarizing dynamics of executive-centered partisanship. Perhaps no evidence to this point is clearer than the increasing role that state attorneys general (AGs) play in challenging federal policy. These trends, scrupulously documented by Paul Nolette and presented in table 4.4, show not only that state AGs have become more likely to sue the federal government (a reflection of policy nationalization and presidential unilateralism) but that this litigation is also especially partisan. Most state AG lawsuits come from the opposing party of the presidency. As Nolette and Colin Provost wrote during the Trump presidency, "AGs' conflicts with the federal government intensified sharply during Trump's first year." Even in comparison with the George W. Bush and Obama presidencies—both of which featured considerable intergovernmental conflict originating with the AGs—the scope of AG activism has been "more frequent, addressed a broader range of issues, and emerged far earlier in the president's term in office.... [Moreover], this federal-state conflict has been overwhelmingly partisan, continuing trends emerging in the second half of Obama's presidency."[77] During the Obama administration, then Texas attorney general Greg Abbott used to boast that his job boiled down to this: "I go into the office, I sue the federal government."[78] During Trump's tenure, California and New York's AGs could say the same thing.

State litigation is not merely a road to upward political mobility for ambitious attorneys general—although many, such as Greg Abbott, have deployed their notoriety to ascend to the position of governor. With the nation sharply divided between red and blue states, AGs believe they are obligated to protect their home turf—to take advantage of the special claim states have under federal law to protect the rights of their citizens and to achieve standing in suits against the federal government when few other parties can. In the ten cases reviewed in table 4.3, states or state-supported organizations were party to six; sometimes they won, and sometimes they lost.

Table 4.4. Number of Multistate Lawsuits against Federal Government from States, 1981–2021

President	Number of Lawsuits from States	Number of Opposition Party Lawsuits (%)
Donald Trump	160	155
Barack Obama	80	58
George W. Bush	76	38
Bill Clinton	42	1
George H. W. Bush	20	9
Ronald Reagan	30	10

Source: State Litigation and AG Activity Database, "Multistate Lawsuits vs. the Federal Government—Totals," https://attorneysgeneral.org/multistate-lawsuits-vs-the-federal-government/statistics-and-visualizations-multistate-litigation-vs-the-federal-government/.

Regardless of the outcomes of these suits, state governors and AGs benefit from presidential partisanship—both in opposing a president and in securing policy victories from a sympathetic one. Some of the most significant policy changes achieved by the Trump administration took place through the complex and largely hidden terrain of intergovernmental relations.[79] But, as Frank Thompson, Kenneth Wong, and Barry Rabe summarize in their account of the Trump presidency, while "Trump has pushed the envelope of executive action to unprecedented levels in the annals of the administrative presidency . . . our analysis also suggests the limits to executive action as a vehicle for policy transformation."[80] Whether presidential federalism benefits or antagonizes the incumbent administration, it deeply engages states in national partisanship that has become untethered from distinctive state and local concerns.

Glass Half-Full or Glass Half-Empty?

Federalism is, by its nature, chaotic.[81] And evaluating Trump's legacy through a federal lens offers contradictory evidence. On the one hand, state and local governments retained a large degree of constitutional authority to govern as they see fit—often in direct opposition to the Trump administration. For instance, after Trump pulled the United States out of the Paris Climate Accords, the US Conference of Mayors launched a nationwide effort to keep every major municipality committed to its goals—with great success. When Trump announced his Muslim ban, states—notably, Hawaii and Washington—drew on their unique constitutional authority for safeguarding citizen rights to claim standing in their challenge to the administration. And despite having a clear policy in support of school choice and market-oriented education reforms, state and local education officials continued to resist federal sticks and carrots that would completely commodify traditional public schools.

On the other hand, while many subnational governments—particularly those led by Democratic elected officials—rediscovered a sense of independence, they were not necessarily acting independently of national politics. The venue of conflict moved to the statehouses in many instances, but the epicenter of politics was still the White House. When thousands of localities declared themselves "sanctuary cities" in response to Trump's immigration policies, not only did the federal government seek to withhold federal funds but state governments led by Republican leaders restricted the powers of cities, which are, after all, functionally and legally dependent on state governments. The rescission of the Obama-era Clean Power Plan, as with the SALT deductions described earlier, was clearly framed in terms of red state and blue state estrangement; states dependent on oil, natural gas, and coal experienced a financial boom, while states transitioning to renewable energy lost. California was an especially apt target for federal litigation and regulatory enforcement: the Trump administration sued the state after it adopted statewide "sanctuary" policies; it declined to extend California's waiver for adopting its own emissions standards; it challenged California's ability to negotiate over how federal lands within the state were managed; and Trump, a climate change denier, even threatened to withhold federal funding for disaster relief as historically devastating wildfires ripped through the state. "You gotta clean your floors, you gotta clean your forests," he bellowed at an election rally. "Maybe we're just going to have to make them pay for it because they don't listen to us."[82]

This muddled picture is nothing new; indeed, "situational constitutionalism," as J. Richard Piper has argued, is endemic to the modern presidency.[83] Trump lambasted President Obama's "major power grabs of authority," particularly as they related to Obama's intergovernmental policymaking.[84] Once ensconced in power, however, Trump seized the opportunities and risks of presidential federalism with even more fervor than did his predecessor.

Early in Trump's presidency, Republicans in Congress struggled to produce an alternative that would "repeal and replace" the Affordable Care Act. Obamacare, as it aptly came to be called in the age of presidency-centered partisanship, was a national policy, yet it was built atop decades of painstaking negotiation between state and federal actors over the structure of Medicaid—a jointly funded and state-administered program for insuring adults making below a national income threshold. Overlooked amid the botched effort to repeal and replace Obamacare—the conservative objective that most united the strategic vision of the White House and congressional Republicans—is the fact that on his first day in office Trump issued an executive order that instructed federal officials to ease regulations associated with the Affordable Care Act by directing agencies "to waive, defer, grant exemptions from or delay the implementation of any provision or requirement of the Act that would impose a fiscal burden."[85] The early efforts of the Trump administration to repeal and *replace* Obamacare—the signature legislative achievement of his predecessor—stalled in the Congress largely because Republicans could not reach a consensus about what health care policies should supplant it. But this only led the Trump White House to double down on an administrative strategy.

Having failed to replace Obamacare through the legislative process, Trump turned to partisan administration, which had become closely intertwined with federalism. Seeking to transform health care through executive action, the White House encouraged states to recast the most progressive feature of the Affordable Care Act: the extension of Medicaid benefits to those whose income was below 138 percent of the poverty level. Almost one year after taking office, the director of the Centers for Medicare and Medicaid Services (CMS), Seema Verma, who had worked with then governor Mike Pence to impose premiums on Medicaid recipients in Indiana, sent a guidance letter to every state Medicaid director informing them of the opportunity to attain a Section 115 waiver to pursue a new demonstration project. Waivers have always been a tool available to federal administrators, and they are authorized by the original 1962 law as an administrative device that can reduce costs, increase state-level innovation, and give states added flexibility to meet demands particular to their community.[86] But discretion can be an invitation to partisan politics; since the 1980s, waivers have increasingly had less to do with the "apolitical" differences between states, such as population size or bureaucratic structure, and more to do with partisanship and ideology.[87]

According to CMS guidelines, states could rescind the Medicaid benefits of able-bodied adults if they were not seeking work or demonstrating other forms of "community engagement." In redefining the eligible population of beneficiaries, the guidance letter promised, or threatened, the most significant change to the program since the legislative expansion of benefits under the Affordable

Care Act. The press and pundits viewed the Republicans' failure to repeal and replace Obamacare as a devastating defeat. But with a waiver from CMS, state officials tried to remake health care for the poor into a more conservative program—to remake the most redistributive features of Obamacare through administrative fiat. Within a day of issuing guidance standards, CMS approved Kentucky's plan to impose work requirements and remove ninety-five thousand state residents from Medicaid rolls, saving an estimated $2 billion over the course of five years.[88]

Although the Affordable Care Act required states to expand Medicaid, lest they lose federal funding for the program, Chief Justice John Roberts's majority opinion in *NCIB v. Sebelius* declared such a mandate too draconian and ruled that states could decide whether or not to expand Medicaid eligibility, without risk of losing general funding. Although many predicted that the Trump administration's waivers would encourage states that had initially declined to adopt new federal standards to accept funds that could be limited to the "deserving poor," just one state legislature decided to expand Medicaid, knowing that it could use a Section 115 waiver to curtail benefits: Virginia. By the end of the Trump administration, thirteen states had received federal approval to adopt work requirements, although due to changes in state administrations, court orders, and the COVID-19 pandemic, only Ohio and Wisconsin, which never accepted expanded Medicaid benefits, successfully adopted the new rules. Nine other states had applied but failed to receive approval for similar work requirement waivers.[89]

Rather than reinventing Medicaid expansion, therefore, the Trump administration's brazen attempt to weaponize Section 115 waivers aroused a strong countermobilization that galvanized public opposition in several states. Linking Medicaid to reciprocal responsibility was a key issue in Kentucky and Virginia gubernatorial campaigns, contributing to the election of Democratic governors in 2019, both of whom quickly withdrew the work requirements from their state programs. Even in some conservative states that remained under Republican control, the broad appeal of enhancing health care benefits led to ballot initiatives in six states that approved Medicaid expansion without work requirements: Idaho, Maine, Missouri, Nebraska, Oklahoma, and Utah (South Dakota would approve Medicaid expansion in a public referendum after Trump left office in 2022). Once in power, the Biden administration withdrew Section 115 work requirements in those states where waiver applications were still pending. Executive-centered partisanship thus transformed the ongoing struggles over Obamacare's Medicaid program into a battle to command the health care bureaucracy, with governors and state legislatures manning the front lines.

Partisan administration also agitated what has become a Manichaean battle over education policy. Although Congress enacted No Child Left Behind—a leading priority of the George W. Bush administration—in 2002 with bipartisan support, this consensus soon erupted into a battle over how to administer the controls the legislation imposed on elementary and secondary education. The Obama administration capitalized on the broad acts of discretion given to the Department of Education and though a combination of waivers, bureaucratic regulations, and an innovative grant program—"Race to the Top"—redefined the federal approach to education policymaking with virtually no consultation with Congress. Congress enacted the Every Student Succeeds Act in 2015 to ameliorate the efforts by both the Bush and the Obama administration to force national policies pertaining to student and teacher accountability on the states. Yet even with the Congress's effort to restore discretion to the states, a national partisan battle continued into the early days of the Trump administration over what objectives these unprecedented federal government interventions in public education should serve.[90]

Trump's controversial choice to head the Department of Education, Betsy DeVos, had long been an advocate of local discretion; but once ensconced in her new position, she began to pursue an aggressive federal policy that stressed the "privatization" of public schools, most notably by expanding charter schools and vouchers, albeit with regulatory and financial support from the Department of Education.[91] She thus weakened the authority of some department divisions, while retooling and empowering others. Not surprisingly, Education Department's Office of Civil Rights has lost much of the independent regulatory authority it built for itself over the last decade. Trump issued an executive order in April that called for a review of the department's regulations and guidance documents; four months later, DeVos rescinded the Obama-era "dear colleague letter" that universities and colleges used to adjudicate Title IX complaints. While DeVos curbed the authority of the Office of Civil Rights, she used the department's student loan division to support for-profit colleges and universities and to protect student loan providers. By rewriting the gainful employment regulations and contracting with private collection agencies to more aggressively recoup student loan debt, the department was not weakened; rather, it was retooled to provide state support for market-driven education providers. The commitment to "privatize" public education motivated the Trump administration's proposal, announced in June 2018, to merge the Department of Education and the Department of Labor and to create a new Department of Education and the Workforce. The Education Department's mandate to enforce federal civil rights in schools would be further diminished if such a plan was implemented, and DeVos's objective to treat schools as places that train future workers embellished.

Despite its clearly national (even global) orientation, environmental policymaking is another area where the Trump administration revealed how, under the dynamics of executive-centered partisanship, federalism offers ample opportunity for presidents to mobilize the base, shift policy in a partisan direction, and centralize political decision-making in the White House.

Trump had a clear environmental agenda, described by one leading set of policy scholars as a "search and destroy" mission, with a particular aim on Obama-era regulations.[92] Consequently, there was no consistent federalism agenda. When Trump officials could pursue their environmental goals by constraining or preempting state law, they did so; when states that were friendly to the deregulatory agenda Trump pursued requested greater flexibility, they received it. The White House's relationship to the states, as with education and health care policy, reflected presidential prerogatives. On the environmental front, too, partisan administration brought limited policy gains as a result of legal battles and progressive states like California having considerable policymaking capacity and experience in meeting environmental goals. However, presidential federalism, animated by the White House's partisan objectives, is often more about politics than it is about concrete policy achievements. Fighting the good fight against the "deep state" is at least as important to the president's partisan base as concrete results.

Trump signaled as much when he appointed Oklahoma's attorney general, Scott Pruitt, to lead to the Environmental Protection Agency (EPA) soon after taking office. During the Obama administration, Pruitt had garnered a national reputation for suing the federal government more than a dozen times, especially over its environmental agenda, which included the controversial Clean Power Plan. Far from espousing any principled understanding of a reformed federal-state cooperative relationship, Pruitt personified executive-centered partisanship's winner-take-all mentality—a national strategy that obviates the political reality that the states vary widely in their climate goals and production of energy.

This reality was most clearly confronted in California, which has developed some of the world's most aggressive regulations to reduce carbon emissions. Still, California is not its own country; it has adopted its environmental agenda within a federal framework where it must negotiate with national officials, including the director of the EPA. Pruitt's crusade for states' rights disappeared once he settled into power. Three months into Trump's presidency, the EPA, along with the National Highway and Transportation Safety Administration, announced that it was reviewing a nearly fifty-year-old waiver California had long depended on to set its own emissions standards for vehicles sold within the state. It allowed California to set regulations for fuel use above the federal Corporate Average Fuel Economy (CAFE) standards; moreover, the federal government had often adjusted its own CAFE standards to meet California's in order to maintain regulatory unity across the country.

The Trump administration's challenge to California's vanguard position was more than a dispute over the importance of maintaining uniform regulatory standards; the withdrawal of the state's CAFE waiver was an important battle in the White House's partisan campaign to redeploy national administrative power. Given California's size, the state's emissions standards were highly influential on automobile manufacturers' production plans for the entire US market; even Canada had adopted California's standards so as to not risk closing off access to American automobile manufacturers. The state's waiver, in short, had widespread consequences for the development of more stringent fuel emissions in the country, and its removal drew intense scrutiny from industry and interest groups. Four of the country's leading automobile manufactures—Ford, Volkswagen, BMW, and Honda—ultimately negotiated a separate arrangement with California during the intergovernmental feud, even though the state's proposed regulations were more arduous than the ones proposed by the Trump administration.

Flexing its muscles in national politics, California led a coalition of states, amounting to nearly 40 percent of the domestic car market, against the Trump administration. Escalating the conflict, a Republican-backed multistate lawsuit sued California, arguing that its internal market regulations were unconstitutionally swayed by elected officials outside their borders. As the lawsuits worked their way through the judiciary, both sides in the intergovernmental feud stoked their bases, providing supporters and opponents of the president ample fodder for fundraising emails, TV spots, and debate rhetoric. In the end, the Supreme Court successfully waited out the clock. Trump left office, the final rule changes that would have officially rescinded California's waiver were withdrawn by the Biden administration, and another chapter of presidential federalism—marked by dueling administrative action—began.

At the end of four contentious years of provocative executive-centered partisanship, federal-state relations remained a flash point for American tribalism. Proponents of unitary executive theory might argue the Trump administration's attempt to repurpose Medicaid was justified, since repealing Obamacare was a salient 2016 campaign promise; however, seeking to do so through waivers, guidance documents, and litigation may mask from rank-and-file citizens how work requirements would affect health care—and who would be held accountable for such reforms. Moreover, the pursuit of "reform" by administrative fiat fosters a highly charged partisan politics that defies the diversity of the country and undermines the rule of law. In many cases, the federal courts—and sometimes citizens themselves at the ballot box—thwarted Section 115's march through the states. Yet, waivers as a tool for policymaking remain on the books, ready for the next presidential administration to leverage—likely after reviewing the administrative flies in the ointment that limited Trump's partisan ambitions. The Biden administration turned to guidance documents with equal enthusiasm. And policies in one state are increasingly determined by lawsuits brought by attorneys general from across the country. Though executive-centered partisanship may sometimes be a blunt instrument to bring about policy change—and it is the case that very few Americans were actually affected by work requirements—presidential federalism in a polarized nation has profound constitutional consequences.

Far from diminishing presidential power, the sharp divide between red and blue America has allowed the executive to exploit the states as proxies in advancing partisan objectives. The result is an intractable, national conflict that threatens to dismantle the compound republic. The current dynamics of executive-centered partisanship make it likely that "no matter what their preferences about intergovernmental relations, presidents have policy goals, political needs, and obligations of office that drive them to employ—and usually to extend—the powers of the federal government."[93] Presidential federalism does not strengthen the institutions that sustain America's federal republic; it corrodes them.

CONCLUSION: DID THE CONSTITUTION HOLD?

The displacement of party politics by executive administration has not made Congress, the courts, or the states inconsequential. Rather, as Democrats and Republicans have come to rely on the White House to fulfill their collective goals, they have ceded greater authority to the presidency. In an era marked by vigorous party competition at the national and state levels, divided government, and tribal struggles to control the judiciary, Trump's influence on the course of American politics was pervasive—the outgrowth of multiple institutional and cultural developments that have transformed the operation and logic of America's constitutional structure. Consequently, with partisan loyalties largely displacing institutional attachments, Congress, the courts, and even the states have for the most part provided tepid resistance to the onward march of presidency-centered partisanship.

And yet, there have been some signs of life in the "Madisonian system." The courts did slow the provocative refugee order; states were at the forefront of multiple legal challenges that reined in presidential excesses; and in response to the ongoing scandal over Russian interference in the 2016 elections, Congress passed tough sanctions on Putin and his allies, over Trump's objections. Indeed, it is likely that Trump only signed the bill to avoid the embarrassment of a veto override, as it was passed with a bipartisan, veto-proof majority. Moreover, the measure, which imposed a waiting period of thirty days on the White House before it could renegotiate any sanctions, expressed the deep skepticism among lawmakers in both parties about Trump's "bromance" with Putin. In particular, the legislature's unusual incursion into the president's authority in national security seemed like an effort to prevent Trump from overlooking the Kremlin's 2014 annexation of Crimea, sustained military intervention in Ukraine, and its meddling in American elections.

That the Russian government's retaliation—seizing two American diplomatic properties and ordering the United States to reduce its embassy staff members in Russia by 755 people—occurred before Trump signed the law might have signaled Putin's intention to target Congress rather than the White House. Indeed, although Trump reluctantly signed the legislation, his approval came with an important caveat—a signing statement that judged those parts of the law that proscribed his discretion to make deals with a foreign nation unconstitutional.[94] His executive assertion had little effect in the face of near-unanimous congressional opposition, but it did signal a growing schism between the Republican establishment and the Trump White House in the shadow of a deteriorating relationship with an authoritarian regime and the growing precarity of American influence overseas more broadly.

Nevertheless, Trump remained undeterred, betting that in the face of polarizing controversies, partisans in Congress would remain steadfastly devoted to the president—even in the face of clear deceit and wrongdoing. To be sure, Trump had engaged in aberrant behavior since the start of his administration. The president's interference with independent counsel investigations, his refusal to comply with congressional subpoenas, and his condemnation of the press as "the enemy of the people" posed unprecedented dangers to the norms and institutions of liberal democracy. His actions continuously tried the patience and loyalty of his fellow partisans. But confident that his primordial connection to the GOP base would keep wavering Republicans in line and frustrated by divided government, Trump's executive indiscretions became bolder after the midterms. Growing audacity led to a swarm of controversy and partisan recrimination that erupted in the fall of 2019, after a leaked whistleblower complaint alleged that the president had made the release of American military assistance conditional on Ukraine opening an investigation on his leading political opponent, former vice president Joe Biden.

Trump won his bet. As news broke that the president had blocked $400 million in congressionally appropriated aid, the extraordinary events, resulting in the House voting to impeach the president, fit a pattern now endemic to executive-centered partisanship. The president and his allies denounced the impeachment proceedings as a partisan "witch hunt"; Democrats closed ranks and relentlessly pursued the impeachment and trial of the president with virtually no support from Republicans. Many might have hoped that the calm presentation of facts and hours of deposition by respected foreign service officers might have persuaded at least a few minds. But, as it turned out, the drama peaked during a showdown vote in the Senate on whether to permit witnesses. Just two Republicans broke party lines: Susan Collins and Mitt Romney. Only Romney braved the threats of severe retribution to cast a guilty ballot—the first senator in history to vote to convict a president of his or her own party.

The raw factionalism of Trump's first impeachment reveals how the transformation of the party system has severely weakened the ability of Congress to hold the president accountable for abuses of power. The American party system was formed during the first four decades of the nineteenth century to restrain presidential power. But over the course of the twentieth and twenty-first centuries, partisanship has been weaponized in personalized political wars President Trump seemed to relish.

The partisan fury of the Trump impeachment was not in itself irregular. As Alexander Hamilton warned in *Federalist* No. 65, "[Impeachment] will seldom fail to agitate the passions of the whole community . . . [it] will enlist all their animosities, partialities, influence and interest on one side or on the other; and in such cases there will always be the greatest danger that the decision will be regulated more by the comparative strength of parties, than by the real demonstrations of innocence or guilt."[95] The impeachment of Andrew Johnson and Bill Clinton seriously agitated the nation. Even Nixon's reckoning was a highly partisan affair until a "smoking gun" was discovered on a White House tape.[96] Yet, Hamilton could not have envisioned how the fusion of presidential power and ritualized partisan combat would make the public, and its representatives, recklessly coarse to constitutional norms.

Indeed, the expansion of presidential prerogatives is a direct consequence of the political developments that have given rise to executive-centered partisanship. Trump and his Republican allies defended his machinations by invoking the progressive conceit—embraced by conservatives in the wake of the polarizing conflicts of the sixties—that the president embodies the national interest. The mystique of presidentialism led Congress to delegate immense power to the executive, with little oversight, further conflating the president's personal or partisan interest with the national interest. Trump deployed the powers of the modern executive office with more impunity than his predecessors, but his attempt to coerce a quid pro quo deal from an American ally exploited precedents set by Congress and the courts, which emboldened presidents to carry out a vast array of policies unilaterally, to withhold appropriated funds, to undertake major foreign policy initiatives secretly, and to direct intelligence and law enforcement agencies to do the president's bidding. Few defenders of the separation of powers will find consolation in the fact that the public, let alone members of Congress, was only aware of Trump's Ukrainian actions because of a single whistleblower and the decision of Michael Atkinson—inspector general of the intelligence community—to flout his White House superiors and take the report to the House Intelligence Committee.

This is not to suggest that a different president would have behaved exactly as Trump did in dealing with an important Eastern European ally, let alone that phone call with the Ukrainian president Volodymyr Zelenskyy. But it is clear that Trump's usurpations were abetted by the subordination of institutional loyalties to partisan allegiances. In a political environment where the political fate of Democrats and Republicans depends on the fortunes of each respective party's president, achieving bipartisan support for holding the White House accountable was doomed from the start. Given how deeply executive-centered partisanship is now rooted in American democracy, it is hardly surprising that reactions to the president's behavior fell along predictable party lines and counterarguments from both sides fell on deaf ears. In the never-ending campaign season, Republican senators stoked the president's base with "deep state" conspiracy theories promoted by Fox News and conservative talk radio. Determined not to let a good business opportunity go to waste, Trump's campaign used the impeachment proceedings to motivate Republicans to open their pocketbooks. Ads poured out of the Republican National Committee designed to fire up the president's "most LOYAL supporters." Certain fundraising ads even permitted donors to jointly contribute to the accounts of Republican nominees in districts targeting vulnerable House Democrats who had voted to impeach the president.[97] During the last quarter of 2019, as the impeachment followed its predictable course, the president's campaign hauled in more than $46 million, including contributions from six hundred thousand new donors, exceeding any previous record.[98] On the eve of the House's vote to impeach the first US president running for reelection, Trump's campaign manager celebrated the president's good political fortune: "That has put money in our bank. It has added volunteers to our field program. It's filled up the rallies easier."[99]

In an earlier era, Nixon's pioneering and corrupt advance of executive-centered partisanship resulted in efforts to restore the "guardrails" of liberal democracy. One might have hoped that the Trump impeachment episode and its aftermath, which saw the White House take retribution against career diplomats and civil servants who testified in the impeachment investigation, might have resulted in a renewed effort to restore constitutional norms and institutional constraints. But since the first impeachment trial, efforts to reform the presidency have stalled. Rather than triggering a revival of liberal norms and institutions, Trump's capture of the Republican Party—and the perception of Democrats that they would have to fight fire with fire when their party regained the White House—have further encouraged leaders to scorn the restraints that are a vital ingredient of constitutional government. Trump's misdeeds have been personalized, and the institutional pathologies we describe throughout this chapter have been dismissed by some scholars and pundits as idiosyncratic. But those who would seek to restore institutional restraints must face the imposing obstacle of a government that for years has sacrificed responsible leadership to aggressive and resolute partisan administration. Trump alone is not to blame, even as his personality colored the constitutional crisis that played out during his time in office. The Constitution held, but it would face its biggest test during the spring of 2020, as a global pandemic engulfed the country in a political crisis not seen since the Great Depression.

5. The Presidency in Crisis
COVID-19, Racial Justice, and the 2020 Presidential Election

The rise of the modern executive, especially in a political culture that proscribes centralized power, is inextricably connected to American war-making and domestic emergencies. Unlike some other republican charters, the US Constitution does not have formal provisions that establish prerogative executive power in times of emergency.[1] However, crises have created opportunities for presidents to cut through the normal working arrangements of American politics. The central role of the presidency as a vanguard of institutional change has long been noted by scholars; furthermore, territorial expansion, globalization, and the nationalization of American political culture have encouraged the consolidation of an executive-centered state. The imperative to act—especially when confronted with the existential possibility of the state's destruction—leads to creative extensions of existing administrative power and social policy.[2] As soon-to-be president John F. Kennedy said at the height of the all-consuming Cold War, "Effort and courage are not enough without purpose and direction."[3]

No matter who was president in 2020, their administration would have confronted some of the most profound challenges the United States has faced in its history. What already promised to be a disruptive year with a looming presidential election in a deeply divided country was pushed to the precipice when news of a highly contagious virus from China sent Americans into lockdown and social disarray in March. As COVID-19 plunged the economy into a deep recession and overwhelmed the public health system, the nation was further tested on May 25 when the murder of George Floyd at the hands of a police officer in Minneapolis ignited a wave of protests and civil unrest across the country, reigniting debates on racial justice, police brutality, and the need for systemic change. These crises aroused a deeply divisive presidential campaign that reverberated through contests up and down the ballot. Already intractably divided, America's raw partisan polarization was exacerbated by these converging crises, as deep divisions along racial, ideological, and socioeconomic lines erupted. Moreover, the pandemic posed daunting challenges to conventional voting methods in the shadow of a yearslong campaign orchestrated by Donald Trump to discredit the legitimacy, safety, and fairness of the American electoral system. Amid this turmoil, the nation faced a crucial test of its democratic resilience, as the election process was strained by disinformation campaigns, claims of voter fraud, and heightened political rhetoric stressing that the "soul of America" was at stake.

Many scholars and pundits speculated that a deadly pandemic and racial reckoning might transcend the partisan combat that sharply divided the nation. As James Grossman, executive director of the American Historical Association, waxed hopefully, "You look at the Great Depression and how Roosevelt made a concerted effort to unite the country—the fireside chats, the New Deal. That is the instinctive reaction of almost every president in crisis. Even if you don't succeed, you try to convince people that they're all in this together."[4] From this perspective, Donald Trump, who sustained his commitment to executive-centered partisanship during the pandemic, therefore seemed exceptionally abnormal. While we agree that a different president would have likely done much more to buttress faith in public health experts and at least attempt to offer more unifying leadership, we nevertheless think that solely focusing on Trump's idiosyncrasies deflects attention from institutional developments that have created an ongoing political crisis in the United States. The events of 2020 underscore the urgency of addressing the underlying issues driving executive-centered partisanship and the growing fractures within American society.

As we document throughout this chapter, the coronavirus pandemic, deepened by a dramatic struggle for racial justice, allows us to view the underlying factors that sustain presidential partisanship in full relief. We see similar patterns of party leadership and the irrelevance of the mythical median voter that we documented in chapter 2. We confirm much of what we described in chapter 3 on the partisan tactic of presidential unilateralism because Trump's boldest administrative actions carried out in the name of making America great again were pursued under the cover of a global pandemic—subordinating public health measures to partisan and personal objectives. Moreover, Trump's administrative audacity during converging public health, economic, and civil rights crises intensified his administration's assault on the institutional capacity of Congress, the courts, and the states that we detailed in chapter 4. Consequently, the Trump administration's response to the COVID-19 pandemic—and its broader consequences for social protest and the presidential election—allows for a synoptic analysis of the developments we have discussed throughout this book.

The trials of a "wartime footing" that so often accompany national crises have, from George Washington's days, tested the resilience of our constitutional system. Yet, the Trump administration's "wartime" presidency during the pandemic might have posed the most serious challenge to the system of divided and separate powers. Trump's primordial bond with his most ardent followers compelled his partisan allies in Congress and the states to endorse his wayward approach to crisis management. While much of the public and scholarly attention to a raging pandemic has focused on governmental failure—evidenced, chiefly, by the inability to "flatten the curve" or fully reopen the economy by the time most experts once thought possible—we highlight the administration's determined pursuit of partisan objectives. Other presidents would have responded differently, perhaps with greater success in stemming the virus's spread. Trump's approach was nonetheless a purposeful pursuit of "America First" objectives: a crackdown on legal and undocumented immigration; a campaign of "law and order" to quell civil rights demonstrations; and deconstruction of the "deep state." No decision made or not made escaped the partisan lens through which seemingly every presidential decision is now subject. Although Republican tacticians and public servants grew increasingly concerned over the president's waning support in pivotal battleground territories, they scarcely opposed his contentious actions amid the pandemic and the protests against police brutality. The evidence we gather in this chapter shows that, contrary to popular belief, the Trump administration's approach to the year of crises should not be understood merely as an episode of executive mismanagement; rather, it entailed a tactical redeployment of national administrative power to achieve partisan goals within a party system increasingly reliant on executive power.

Trump's final year in office thus reveals how executive-centered partisanship makes American presidents less likely to provide unifying leadership during crises or to face political consequences for their failure to do so. Although it is unlikely that Barack Obama or Joe Biden (or any Republican who ran against Trump in 2016) would have governed the same way, we doubt that the current context of American politics leaves room for the unifying leadership national emergencies demand. Certainly, President Joe Biden's leadership during the tail end of the COVID-19 pandemic was less overtly partisan than Trump's—his temperament and leadership style are much more attentive to "neutral competence" and collective party responsibility. Nevertheless, from the early days of his presidency, Biden, too, struggled to escape from the cultural and institutional forces that have embedded executive-centered partisanship in American democracy. Despite claims to the contrary, Biden's early performance in office, especially with respect to the COVID-19 crisis, reinforced the essential features of presidential partisanship.[5] In part, Biden's travails should be understood as a sign of Trump's enduring influence—evidence of how he brought partisan administration to a dangerous culmination, fanning, rather than dousing, the flames of social discord at a time when the presidency faced national crises of the highest order.

At the end of this chapter, we consider how Trump's harsh partisanship during the final months of his presidency seems to have escaped the judgment of history. Instead of subjecting his party to the "blue wave" many Democrats hoped for, Trump's polarizing leadership agitated a highly mobilized and fiercely contested election that reinforced his spell on the Republican Party and rendered more intransigent the divide between red and blue America. Despite his failed reelection campaign, Trump reigned over his party and reveled in the adulation of its base supporters. His enduring relevance suggests how the American state offers modern presidents not only the opportunity to strengthen their commitment to partisan tactics under the cover of national emergencies but also the power to do so without the traditional constraints of party, Congress, and the states.

ATTACKING THE DEEP STATE: DENIGRATING EXPERTISE FOR POLITICAL GAIN

For liberals and conservatives alike, the grandeur of an energetic executive has been forged during the country's most perilous, unpredictable moments in history. The long history of American wars and domestic emergencies, often perceived as morally equivalent to wars, has shaped much of modern government. And with the consolidation of modern executive power, what was once episodic has become a routine feature of political life in the United States. Two centuries of territorial expansion, globalization, and the nationalization of American political culture have raised the stakes of presidential decision-making, producing flash points and episodic travails that have nurtured the development of an executive-centered state. The need to act—particularly when faced with the potential annihilation of the state—gives rise to inventive expansions of existing administrative power and social policy.

During significant periods of hostility, political conflict is redefined, with wartime presidents taking center stage in shaping new or emergent expectations for governing authority. As David Mayhew notes, wars "seem to be capable of generating a whole new political universe."[6] Overwhelming emergencies create opportunities for presidents to act unilaterally, allowing for political outcomes in foreign and domestic policy that would be largely unimaginable without the nationalizing and centralizing tendencies of national crises.[7] And as John Lapinski highlights, "Crises often delegitimize existing government policies that are directly and, in some cases, indirectly linked to the event."[8] Although Congress and the courts do not disappear during prolonged states of crisis or war, "modern presidents are undoubtedly the preeminent actors."[9]

Frequently, war and crisis are studied as they relate to the evolution of foreign policy institutions within the presidency, such as the National Security Council. However, the distinction between foreign and domestic crises is not so easy to discern. Emergency powers used to stem a foreign threat often bleed into domestic responsibilities and expectations that bestow plenary executive power at home and abroad. It is the president, after all, who is responsible for the nation as a whole. But the contemporary executive, dependent on loyal partisans, is not an institution that works on behalf of the "whole people" or rallies the country to tackle national crises through enduring reforms. Even in the work of administering less politically charged programs, such as disaster funding or decisions to close military bases, the modern presidency is electorally motivated and often acts to serve its core constituency.[10] What does crisis leadership look like with the rise of an executive-centered partisanship, with presidents representing their party's most loyal followers?

Table 5.1 offers some answers. Using the same classification scheme that we developed in chapter 2, we consider how Trump Republicans, non-Trump Republicans, and Americans in general viewed the government's response to the COVID-19 pandemic, drawing on an extensive set of questions from the 2020 American National Elections Studies (ANES). In general, among all Americans, satisfaction with governing officials was deeply split. No government—federal, state, or local—had strong approval, but when it did, it was concentrated among partisan factions. Only Trump Republicans, for example, held favorable attitudes toward the federal government or Trump's leadership. Americans, on average, and non-Trump Republicans were largely dissatisfied

Table 5.1. Approval Ratings of Elected Officials, 2020 ANES

	All Americans (%)	Non-Trump Republicans (%)	Trump Republicans (%)
Strongly approve the way President Donald Trump has handled the coronavirus, or COVID-19, pandemic.	25.24	10.10	72.43
Strongly approve the way Democratic governor has handled the coronavirus, or COVID-19, pandemic.	38.30	26.13	24.24
Strongly approve the way Republican governor has handled the coronavirus, or COVID-19, pandemic.	37.79	35.80	44.10
Strongly approve the way your local government has handled the coronavirus, or COVID-19, pandemic.	38.58	33.61	39.31
The federal government's response to the COVID-19 outbreak earlier this year was about right.	33.48	35.13	76.86

Note: Data are weighted; the unweighted sample includes 8,200 individuals, including nonvoters, who were asked the policy questions. Among those, the unweighted sample included 2,329 Republicans who we identified as Trump Republicans and 1,147 Republicans who had some degree of reservation about the president. To be sure, just 571 of those Republicans, or 16 percent, disapproved of Trump's performance in office.

with Trump's management of COVID-19. And while state governors—Democrat and Republican—largely had higher evaluations than the president, partisanship still informed the negative evaluations toward Democratic governors and the more favorable reactions to Republican governors. Among Republicans, however, no person was more popular than their leader—President Trump.

Further evidence shows that the partisan reaction to Trump was more than what political psychologists call "expressive responding"—that is, professing to believe something that they do not really believe to show support for their party's leaders or hostility toward their political enemies' leaders.[11] Trump's most loyal supporters simply saw a different pandemic than the average American. Their strong approval of President Trump reflected significant differences with the general public and non-Trump Republicans with respect to the severity of the COVID-19 pandemic and the appropriate public health measures that were necessary to ameliorate it.

Our task is not to judge which political tribe saw things correctly but to take note of the profound challenge created by a presidential system that is rooted in the presumption that the modern executive could be a transcendent leader in an era of deep partisan conflict, in which even the very idea of an "emergency" can be politically contested. While clear majorities of Americans disagreed with the idea that public health controls in 2020 were too strict, nearly a majority of Trump Republicans agreed. While a plurality of Americans (42.67 percent) thought public health authorities got it right, the loudest opponents to the measures were Trump loyalists; just 12 percent of Trump Republicans thought the measures were not strict enough. The same pattern holds when asking about how important it was for science to inform public health decisions. Most Americans responded "extremely important"; even a sizable plurality of non-Trump Republicans supported that idea. But among Trump Republicans, just one in five were willing to support scientifically informed government decision-making. Trump Republicans were far more likely to look to their charismatic leader for answers to questions pertaining to the origins and hazards of COVID-19. Evidence did, in fact, eventually emerge suggesting that the virus might have originated from a Chinese lab. Whatever the source of the pandemic, our evidence highlights how partisanship—particularly presidential partisanship—structured beliefs. For example, only Trump Republicans supported the unsubstantiated idea that the antimalarial drug hydroxychloroquine was a safe and effective treatment for COVID-19—a position touted by Trump since the early days of the pandemic, as governments around the world struggled to find, produce, and distribute lifesaving drugs (table 5.2).

These survey results from October 2020 reflect several months of partisan conflict over how to manage the COVID-19 crisis. A defining aspect of Trump's response to the pandemic was his public refusal to accept and validate public health experts' recommendations on lockdowns and masks; instead, he aligned the White House with governors and activists in red states who resisted a scientific approach to the crisis. The day his administration declared COVID-19 a national emergency (Friday, March 13), President Trump emphasized that the American response would be shaped and guided by as little direct government intervention as possible. His administration's approach would be tied to making America great by supporting big business. Gathering CEOs from some of the country's largest companies, including Walmart, Target, and Walgreens, Trump announced that corporate America and the private sector would lead the public health response: offering parking lots for testing,

Table 5.2. Attitudes toward COVID-19 and Government Actions, 2020 ANES

	All Americans (%)	Non-Trump Republicans (%)	Trump Republicans (%)
Do you think the limits your state placed on public activity because of the COVID-19 pandemic were too strict? [Yes]	22.11	25.11	48.53
In general, how important should science be for making government decisions about COVID-19? [Extremely important]	50.22	39.01	19.51
The novel coronavirus (COVID-19) was developed intentionally in a lab. [Agree]	49.64	47.13	76.42
There is clear scientific evidence that the antimalarial drug hydroxychloroquine is a safe and effective treatment for COVID-19. [Agree]	25.87	26.29	52.78

Note: Data are weighted; the unweighted sample includes 8,200 individuals, including nonvoters—who were asked the policy questions. Among those, the unweighted sample included 2,329 Republicans who we identified as Trump Republicans and 1,147 Republicans who had some degree of reservation about the president. To be sure, just 571 of those Republicans, or 16 percent, disapproved of Trump's performance in office.

developing new websites for resource location, and creating viral tests. Few of these initiatives succeeded, and state and local public authorities soon had to rush to create solutions of their own. Still, the president wanted to send a message, and the markets responded in kind; the Dow Jones Industrial Average rose a record-breaking 9.4 percentage points that day.

All this is to show that, for Trump and his Republican backers, the most significant threat facing the country with the spread of COVID-19 was financial. Of course, some deep concern about the economy was warranted: business shutdowns, unemployment, and the pandemic's disproportionate toll on low-income earners were important factors to be considered in weighing the benefits and costs of public health measures. Scholars—including some on the left—are increasingly attentive to the fact these measures widened material inequality.[12] But even during those rare moments when he acknowledged the dangers of the pandemic, President Trump consistently downplayed public health experts' grave warnings about potential surges in cases if the national government and states did not remain vigilant. Instead of discussing trade-offs, Trump sought to take political advantage of the pandemic. His approach was fueled by divisive rhetoric and actions. Even as a second coronavirus wave (or a continuation of the first) peaked, the president remained steadfast in opposing national calls for a mask mandate or clarifying reopening guidance for state and local governments. Masks, which do not carry an economic burden or cost, became the symbolic political flash point for the partisan conflict Trump exploited. Political psychologists were baffled by surveys showing conservatives, who previously demonstrated greater fear of communicable diseases crossing borders (focusing on "purity"), such as the Ebola outbreak during the Obama administration, supported the president's politically motivated and medically reckless call for a return to normalcy. As the *New York Times* columnist Thomas Edsall wrote, "The pandemic has become another example of Trump's mastery over his most loyal subjects, his ability to manipulate them into violating their own instincts. It is this power over a substantial bloc of the electorate that has put him in the White House—and continues to make him so dangerous."[13]

No less dangerous was Trump's shameless promotion of COVID-19 treatments and vaccines for which there was no scientific evidence of effectiveness. The president's endorsement of these false remedies was a striking example of a right-wing populist's direct challenge to the credibility of public health experts who, he feared, threatened the economy and his reelection prospects. The White House pressured the Food and Drug Administration (FDA) to grant emergency use authorization for hydroxychloroquine, even announcing the president was taking it himself to protect against COVID-19. When the agency reversed course, citing evidence of serious side effects such as heart problems, Trump was predictably accused of putting politics ahead of science.

Undeterred, the White House continued to exert pressure on the Centers for Disease Control and Prevention (CDC) and the FDA to limit testing and to fast-track questionable therapeutics and potential cures. The CDC faced criticism from numerous medical and public health groups and infectious disease experts for suddenly altering its testing guidelines, no longer recommending testing for asymptomatic individuals even if they had had contact with an infected person. This change aligned with the president's desire to reduce testing and shift focus away from surging case numbers in states that had begun reopening their economies. At a June campaign rally, Trump revealed the election strategy: "When you do testing to that extent you're going to find more people, you're going to find cases," Trump said. "So I said to my people,

'Slow the testing down, please.' They test and they test. We got tests for people who don't know what's going on." On the eve of the Republican National Convention in late August, Trump also praised the emergency authorization for convalescent plasma as a "very historic breakthrough," a statement initially supported by the FDA commissioner Stephen Hahn. After scientists and public health experts vehemently dismissed this as a gross exaggeration, Hahn was forced to apologize for his claim that thirty-five of one hundred people with COVID-19 "would have been saved because of the administration of plasma." Hahn's attempt to regain professional respect by assuring that he and FDA experts would not be pressured into approving a vaccine before its efficacy was proved through clinical trials elicited a critical tweet from the president. The FDA, Trump alleged, was trying to sandbag his election prospects by slowing progress on COVID-19 treatments and vaccines until after November 3, Election Day.[14]

Trump's populist commitment to find a rapid cure for the pandemic did animate the most effective initiative of his response to the coronavirus: Operation Warp Speed, which was launched in May 2020. The US government, trying to defy the timelines that have governed the development of vaccines for decades, awarded almost $11 billion to seven different companies to develop vaccines, three of which—Moderna, AstraZeneca, and Pfizer—were in late-stage trials only five months later. Prior to the launching of this initiative, there was already a unit within the Department of Health and Human Services whose responsibility was to give money to companies that were developing vaccines. Operation Warp Speed got more companies involved on a much greater scale. More novel, however, was the way the Trump administration approached manufacturing. Normally, a pharmaceutical company would not be willing to start to mass-produce its vaccine until the lengthy clinical trial period showed enough evidence to warrant FDA approval. To obviate this risk, the federal government paid companies to start mass-producing millions of doses of their vaccine before they knew that it was safe and effective. To further speed the manufacture and distribution of a vaccine, the White House enlisted the Department of Defense, which has much experience in logistics, to distribute quickly a vast number of materials, whether for clinical trials, for manufacturing, or to vaccinate millions of Americans.[15]

Although Operation Warp Speed showed promise by the end of the summer, the White House's partisan approach to the pandemic and the political pressure it imposed on the FDA and CDC aroused skepticism that it would deliver a safe vaccine that would immunize the nation by, as promised, the end of 2020. A letter from Dr. Robert Redfield, director of the CDC, to the nation's governors with an urgent request did little to disconfirm the idea that the single overriding objective of Trump's White House was not tied to his reelection. As he explained, the Trump administration wanted states to do everything in their power to eliminate hurdles for vaccine distribution sites and to be operational by November 1—even without a vaccine. "The normal time required to obtain these permits presents a significant barrier to the success of this urgent public health program," Redfield wrote. Setting a deadline that would offer the first vaccines to Americans just days before the presidential election caused concern that the Trump administration was subordinating science to politics—especially when public health experts warned that the target date did not account for the time it would take pharmaceutical companies to complete the final demanding phase of clinical trials. Public messaging reinforced these concerns. At the Republican National Convention that convened soon thereafter, President Trump, Vice President Mike Pence, and the president's daughter Ivanka all celebrated the vaccine as the "miracle" Trump had wishfully anticipated at the outset of the crisis, and they flirted with the idea that the vaccine would be available just in time for Election Day.[16]

As with mask requirements and the trade-offs between public health measures and the economy, attitudes toward the "miracle" vaccine were heavily influenced by partisanship. The White House's relentless political pressure on government health experts, which threatened to undermine the integrity of the FDA's drug approval process, poisoned the public's faith in a vaccine. In late July, for instance, a poll by Yahoo News and YouGov indicated that only 42 percent of Americans planned on getting the vaccine—down 13 points from May. Not only did Republicans question the need for and/or the safety of the vaccine, but public skepticism was also pronounced among Democrats, generally far more willing to accept medical advances, whose confidence in public health measures soured amid their antipathy to Trump's charged partisan response to the public health crisis. Leading Democrats confirmed this skepticism; both Joe Biden and Kamala Harris publicly questioned whether any vaccine approved by the Trump White House would be safe.[17] At the start of the pandemic, 70 percent of Democrats said they would take the vaccine; after three months of partisan jousting, barely half agreed.[18]

THE "WARTIME PRESIDENT" AND INSTITUTIONAL COMBAT

It is often the case that national disasters bring the country together, and for a few weeks at the start of the pandemic, it seemed as if COVID-19 might do just that. Although it was clear from the outset that the Trump administration was more concerned with the economic fallout of the disaster, there were moments in March and April 2020 when it was also apparent that Trump recognized the political stakes (or opportunities); indeed, he quickly declared himself a "wartime president."[19] Congress also seemed determined to meet the crisis head-on when Democrats and Republicans collaborated to quickly roll out three relief bills. The most ambitious of these measures, the Coronavirus Aid, Relief, and Economic Security Act (CARES Act), was the largest economic stimulus package in American history. Seeking to take full political advantage of this sudden burst of bipartisanship, Trump placed his printed signature on the stimulus checks that distributed direct aid to tens of millions of people, the first time in history that an American president's name was displayed on a disbursement check from the Internal Revenue Service.[20]

But these early signs of bipartisanship were severely tested by the partisan warfare that Trump relished and that executive-centered partisanship encourages. Trump was a wartime president, but as time went on, it increasingly became clear that his was a war that targeted anyone who dissented from his administration's COVID-19 policies. Not only did public health experts suffer his wrath but the nation's governors and mayors—whose involvement was necessary for a coordinated response—were often derided as adversaries, not partners. Congress, for the most part, remained sidelined, as the nation's executive officers and their administrative counterparts struggled to maintain independence in the face of aggressive presidentialism.

Most analysis of the Trump administration's response to COVID-19 has focused on the president's combative management and the resistance he encouraged to public health measures.[21] However, this emphasis on national politics deflects attention from the important role that the states played as first responders to the pandemic. No matter who was president in March 2020, the country's response to the pandemic would have required enlisting governors and local officials in any coordinated response. There are constitutional and administrative limits on what the federal government could accomplish in terms of a rapid and comprehensive response to a public health emergency. The states, in contrast, were already deeply involved in regulating and establishing public health systems. During previous crises, states and municipalities had worked in tandem with federal officials to produce a national response. However, America's federal democracy was sorely tested during the COVID-19 crisis by the deep partisan divisions that roiled American politics, which were further aggravated by the White House's presidential partisanship and persistent efforts to mobilize its supporters in red states against strong public health measures.[22] With the subordination of party organizations to the White House, states did not tailor their response to local conditions but rather to the electoral calculations of President Trump. The maps of red and blue states, which had traditionally been useful heuristics for making sense of electoral returns, quickly became guides to the partisan battles over the worst public health crisis in over a century that were playing out throughout the country.

There were some moments that revealed the enduring strength of America's unique federal structure. In the early days of the pandemic, states entered into regional agreements with one another to collaborate on common reopening criteria.[23] New York, New Jersey, and Connecticut governors worked together on initial "shelter in place" rules.[24] Moreover, without clear directives from the CDC, state health officials took center stage, with support from state legislatures that approved new license reciprocation and waiver rules that allowed doctors to traverse the country as the virus surged in some places and waned in others. After the coronavirus began to taper off in his state, Washington's governor returned critical ventilators to the national stockpile for use in New York and other states hit hardest by the COVID-19 outbreak in the early stages of the crisis.[25] Some of this collaboration in the absence of a strong federal response showed how a decentralized government could fill the void on the front lines. "Maybe federalism works best in crisis times when there is a high premium on promptness, local knowledge, and adaptation," the constitutional law scholar Michael Greve suggested. "And maybe the confidence that the public has placed in state and local institutions will endure."[26]

Yet President Trump was not comfortable with the states at the vanguard. He did not seek to preempt state-led collaboration on decisions about how long shutdowns would last; however, he claimed, falsely, that he had "absolute power" to command a national war against the pandemic.[27] At the same time, the states found it difficult to respond adequately to a raging pandemic in the absence of purposeful executive leadership. They struggled to find necessary personal protective equipment (PPE) and ventilators while the president—focusing like a laser on the cratering of the economy—avoided any responsibility for coordinating, let alone exercising, absolute power over state efforts. For a time, he told states that they should "try getting medical supplies themselves"; after all, he insisted, the federal government was not a "shipping clerk."[28] In truth, the federal government was a willing shipping clerk in responding to the requests for medical supplies of some states, notably Florida, led by Republican governor Ron DeSantis. Even as Northeastern states like New York had trouble finding PPE and ventilators for its overwhelmed hospitals, Florida received 100 percent of its first two requests to the federal emergency stockpile, with both the president and DeSantis touting their strong relationship. During a phone call between the two, DeSantis complained about people with the coronavirus traveling from New York to Florida. Minutes later, Trump publicly said he was considering a quarantine for New York, New Jersey, and Connecticut. He ultimately decided against taking such drastic action, but the rapid White House response to Governor DeSantis's fear of a coronavirus infestation from a blue state sent a strident partisan message. As one White House official anonymously told the *Washington Post*, "The president knows Florida is so important for his reelection, so when DeSantis says that, it means a lot.... He pays close attention to what Florida wants."[29]

Trump's crisis "leadership," with a never-failing eye on reelection, was frequently more performative than programmatic. The president held more than ninety conference calls with state, local, and tribal leaders in the first three months of the pandemic. Many of those participants were quick to point out that the president seldom used the high-profile meetings to clarify federal guidance or to solicit an exchange of ideas; rather, he viewed them as an opportunity to shift blame to the states and call out specific governors for their alleged mismanagement.[30] Most calls ended with governors relying on back channels to reach Vice President Pence, who, according to press reports, was more sympathetic to the coordination struggles confronting the governors. Although the partisan bouts between the president and governors were largely rhetorical, there is evidence that they spilled into administrative decisions. Seeking to curtail the efficacy of the Pence-led back channel, Trump admitted during a press conference that he had directly intervened at least once, telling Pence, "When they're not appreciative to me, they're not appreciative to the Army Corps, they're not appreciative to FEMA, it's not right... don't call the governor of Washington. You're wasting your time with him. Don't call the woman [Governor Gretchen Whitmer] in Michigan."[31]

With trillions of dollars and the lives of Americans at stake, the president thus escalated his long-standing confrontation with Democratic governors and mayors into a full-throated attack on the communities they represented. Before the virus had begun to spread noticeably in rural, less densely populated counties, the administration was adamant that the most affected states—most of which had Democratic governors—would be left to manage the virus on their own. Republican leaders in the states and localities enlisted in Trump's partisan tactics; most GOP governors and congressional members fixed a jaundiced eye on any "bailout" for "blue states." As thousands died across the country, the president tweeted, "Why should the people and taxpayers of America be bailing out poorly run states (like Illinois, as example) and cities, in all cases Democrat run and managed."[32]

The emergency measures some governors imposed to "stop the spread" were among the most intrusive and controversial ever employed by an American government outside of wartime. Predictability, they aroused deep skepticism and concern. However, rarely did controversy lead to serious deliberation about how public health regulations, though understandable given the lethal spread of the coronavirus, aroused legitimate concerns—about growing inequality, increasing deaths of despair, and childhood learning loss. Rather, pandemic politics was subsumed by executive-centered partisanship. Presidentialism, so militantly practiced by Trump, transformed a national war against a deadly pandemic into a Manichaean struggle. As had been his penchant since he and Melania rode down the escalator in Trump Tower to launch his presidential campaign, Trump painted a complex policy debate as an existential struggle between winners and losers, tyrants and victims, overreaching blue states and virtuous, freedom-loving red states.

The danger of the president's strategy was vividly illustrated on April 15, 2020, as a group of protesters, many of them wearing MAGA hats and brandishing menacing firearms, assembled outside the Michigan statehouse in Lansing and demanded an end to the policy declared by the state's Democratic governor, Gretchen Whitmer, that locked down the state's schools and businesses. Smaller demonstrations were mounted in Virginia and Minnesota. The movement spread rapidly across the country. By the weekend, rallies were being held in six other states, most of them led by Democratic governors, but also including Republican-led Texas and Maryland, where the governors had been cautious in their commitment to open the economy. Governor Larry Hogan of Maryland, a rare moderate in the Republican Party, had been especially harsh in his criticisms of the administration's failure to provide fiscal support to the states.

The resemblance to the Tea Party demonstrations that had erupted during Barack Obama's first term was not coincidental. Among those fighting the orders were FreedomWorks and the Tea Party Patriots, both of which had played pivotal roles in the beginning of Tea Party protests starting more than a decade earlier. These national conservative organizations quietly worked to organize protests and to apply political and legal pressure to overturn local and state orders intended to stop the spread of the coronavirus. The conflicts they agitated emerged as a galvanizing cause for Trump's base and others on the political right. Conservative organizers saw an opportunity to unify social conservatives, who viewed the orders as targeting religious groups; fiscal conservatives who decried the economic devastation wrought by the restrictions on businesses; and civil libertarians who contended that the restrictions infringed on constitutional rights.[33] Embodying the ties between presidential prerogative, grassroots mobilization, and party conflict that define executive-centered partisanship, President Trump seized the mantle of these demonstrations and placed himself at the vanguard of this revolt against blue states. He grabbed the attention of the media by strongly endorsing the protests, which took direct action against rules that subscribed to his own administration's CDC guidelines for restarting the economy:

> "LIBERATE MICHIGAN!," the president tweeted on Friday, April 17.
> "LIBERATE MINNESOTA!"
> "LIBERATE VIRGINIA," he concluded, adding that the protesters should also "save your great 2nd Amendment. It is under siege!"[34]

This call to arms seemed even more incendiary in early October, when the Federal Bureau of Investigation foiled a plot by antigovernment vigilantes to kidnap Governor Whitmer and try her for treason. Although there was no evidence that the planned insurrection was inspired by the president's rallying cry, Whitmer and other Democrats warned that the president's rhetoric had helped spark the alleged plot and the vicious attacks against her on social media.

The plot to capture Whitmer was the most extraordinary extension of Trump's bellicosity; however, presidential partisanship also embroiled the statehouses in less dramatic but consequential conflicts. Republican governors, with a few notable exceptions, were the foot soldiers in the White House's campaign to downplay the severity of the public health crisis; they joined Trump's determined effort to shift the narrative from the coronavirus to the economy. It would collapse save for Donald Trump's resolute stand against the Democrats and their "deep state" allies.[35] Loyal partisans who occupied the governors' mansions in red states followed the president's party leadership at nearly every turn: refusing to issue mask mandates (Georgia governor Brian Kemp even sued "Democratic-led" Atlanta after the city imposed one), reopening restaurants and bars in advance of CDC recommendations, and adopting the president's general attitude that the virus's threat was overstated and distant.[36] As the virus continued to rage into the autumn, the single largest factor that determined whether a school district reopened in person was that district's vote share for President Trump in 2016, not the number of cases in the community or its potential risk for community spread.[37]

Presidents have previously sought to circumvent the institutional roadblocks posed by divided partisan realms, both by exercising a mix of emergency powers over constituent governments and by using the office's prestige and public position to nurture cooperative relationships with the leaders of state, local, and tribal governments. Instead, Trump followed the script of executive-centered partisanship, leveraging federalism not for cooperative purposes but as an opportunity to shift blame to, and even punish, states that strayed from his preferred messaging.[38] Although the coronavirus did not discriminate between red and blue states, the president used the state-led, patchwork response to the public health crisis to exacerbate partisan divisions in the months preceding the 2020 election. Although there are legitimate differences between the states that may distinguish various governments' responses to a public health emergency, including disparate economic effects, the president's partisan rhetoric and the politicization of administrative processes defied efforts to negotiate trade-offs between the economy and public health. Following a partisan strategy, Trump exploited the separation of government powers to demonize Democratic governors, whom he insisted were the real danger to Americans.

UNDER THE COVER OF AN EMERGENCY: SECURING POLICY GOALS UNILATERALLY

As presidents have assumed the mantle of partisan leadership and as partisans increasingly owe their political fortunes to the president's personal success, it has become more difficult to separate national goals from the president's goals. In fusing the institutional interest of the presidency with the "public interest," emergencies offer even greater opportunity for presidents to justify partisan objectives as national imperatives. The informal and formal mechanisms that provide a modicum of accountability during normal times—scrutiny from the press, congressional reporting and oversight, full and unabridged hearings before the courts—are stunted by new and unpredictable protocols of emergency management. Newspaper headlines obsessively cover the crisis with bold, above-the-fold headlines; far less attention is paid to the administrative politics churning departments and agencies. Congress is also consumed by the exigencies of the emergency at hand—shifting to an unusually high gear to enact ameliorative legislation.

As noted, bipartisan majorities approved a huge aid package in March with bipartisan support: the CARES Act. However, bipartisan unity was short-lived; the political process grew more fractious as Congress spent months negotiating additional pandemic relief bills. Republicans in Congress ultimately agreed to the president's demand for another round of stimulus checks, albeit for less support than Trump demanded. Preoccupied by his attempts to "stop the steal" by the time the relief bill came to his desk, Trump wanted the checks increased from $600 to $2,000, hoping perhaps a second round of large payouts to the American people would increase support for his efforts to overturn a free and fair election. Although he backed off his threat to veto the legislation, which also included a government funding bill to avert a shutdown, Trump made clear that he would continue to press his populist America First message on the Republican Party. Scolding congressional Republicans for not being willing to enact more generous relief, he reminded them that the war against COVID-19 was a global struggle. "Remember," he bellowed, "it was China's fault!"[39]

As the media shined a light on the president's assault on public experts and members of Congress who resisted his brand of right-wing populism, the Trump administration focused like a laser on administrative politics—using the cover of the pandemic to gain momentum in its war against the bureaucracy. Throughout Trump's term, his administration pushed the bounds of legal appointments to serve as agency heads, with a record number of Senate-confirmed positions being filled by "acting" heads. In late 2020, the administration's political appointees leveraged their temporary positions to gain permanent employment in the agencies they once oversaw. While the conversion, or "burrowing," of political appointees to permanent civil service positions is a Democratic and Republican tradition—especially before a presidential transition—the Trump administration went to new lengths to permanently shift the composition of the federal bureaucracy.[40]

Not only did the politically appointed head of Trump's Office of Personnel Management stonewall an investigation by that agency's Inspector General (IG) into increased burrowing, but the administration also reaped its reward after systematically dismantling the IG system. The Trump administration had undermined oversight bodies since the president's first days in office, blatantly flouting norms and violating ethics laws; however, it chose to launch an unprecedented attack against IGs in the middle of the pandemic.[41] Much attention focused on the president's firing of high-profile IGs, including Michael Atkinson, who shared the initial whistleblower complaint that led to the president's first impeachment. More consequential, in all likelihood, was the fact that the president had hollowed out IG offices in sixteen federal agencies and departments by attrition, including those charged with overseeing the massive government spending in response to COVID-19.[42]

In escalating the attack on the deep state while the media and public were preoccupied by a rampaging pandemic, the Trump presidency extended the logic of the unitary executive doctrine to its limit. Throughout the pandemic, the Trump administration lambasted the perceived obstruction and dissent from career civil servants, especially long-serving members of the Senior Executive Service—the front line of the deep state. Just days before the election, the White House released a little-noticed but massive change to the classification of civil servants in "policymaking" roles. Claiming existing legislative authority reaching back to the Executive Reorganization Act of 1939, the Trump administration, with the stroke of a pen, created a new classification of federal employee—Schedule F—and mandated that a preliminary review of eligible positions be completed by January 19, 2021, the day before Biden's inauguration. Under the rule change, any presidential administration could terminate someone in the new Schedule F classification without following standard due process requirements, even if they were hired in positions that would have been covered by merit-based protections. Depending on how far-reaching the initial reclassification went, and the procedures established for reclassification, this order could have subjected hundreds, or possibly thousands, of "policymakers"—from agency heads such as Anthony Fauci to potentially lower-level careerists who had openly spoken out against a White House decision—to political retribution.[43]

Just as the creation of Schedule F civil servants represented a logical extension of a months-long war with civil servants during the pandemic, so, too, did the Trump administration escalate the intergovernmental conflict with various states. Democratic governors' alleged incompetence became a justification for the central government to take preemptive action, especially as it related to a crackdown on unauthorized immigrants. In truth, the coronavirus was merely a pretext that the White House used to curtail immigration throughout 2020. In March, Chad Wolf, the acting secretary of homeland security, warned that undocumented immigrants were spreading the virus to Customs and Border Protection (CBP) agents, and such a risk justified the need to rapidly deport all migrants—including asylum seekers and children—without hearing or due process.[44] Trump then used Title 42 authority to enact the policy, which would, over the course of three years, export 2.8 million migrants at the US-Mexico border without any hearing for asylum.[45] In June, the president extended a near-total ban that the White House had first announced in April on entry into the United States by immigrants seeking "green cards" for permanent residency. The newly expanded version of the policy also severely restricted temporary work visas, including for highly skilled workers, such as doctors and nurses.[46] Moreover, as the school year approached, the administration also announced that only international students studying for classes in person would be granted a visa. After a strong backlash from university leaders, the revised policy was limited to new students enrolling in universities that offered only remote classes.[47]

From the earliest days of the Trump administration, the president's White House adviser on immigration policy, Stephen Miller, who had close ties to anti-immigration organizations, had tried repeatedly, without success, to use an obscure law to protect the nation from disease overseas as a justification to tighten borders. In imposing restrictions under the cover of the pandemic, he relied not only on the public health authority but also on Section 221(f) of the Immigration and Nationality Act, which grants sweeping power to the executive, but under circumstances that set a high legal bar for its use. Miller took advantage of the pandemic to pursue policy goals, such as finding a way to quickly deport children who had traveled to the United States without a parent or guardian, while violating the substantial due process requirements designed to ensure that deportation would not place them in harm's way.[48] Even as the coronavirus threatened the Trump administration's agenda, the White House remained focused on its task—indeed, armed with emergency powers the pandemic bestowed, it sought to double down on its policy priorities.

Besides imposing draconian restrictions on immigration, the other major objective of the MAGA program was to protect the US economy and workers against unfair trade deals, especially the disadvantages of economic relations with China. In the tariffs that the Trump administration leveraged against China and its renegotiation of the North American Free Trade Agreement accord, the White House had one principal objective: "an aggressive agenda of increasingly squeezing China out of global supply chains while pressing for structural change in Beijing."[49] However, the pandemic opened a new front in the president's aggression; COVID-19 prompted the White House to turn retaliatory measures against China for withholding information about the coronavirus into a provocative and polarizing campaign. The Trump administration and its Republican allies in Congress explored drastic measures, including the elimination of China's sovereign immunity, which would allow the US government or victims to sue for damages.[50] Seeking to absolve his administration of any responsibility for the devastation the pandemic wrought on public health and the economy, Trump and his political aides routinely described the "plague" in racist and stigmatizing terms, calling it the "Wuhan virus," the "China virus," and, most egregiously, the "Kung flu."

Most Americans agreed with the president that China had mishandled the initial outbreak and subsequent spread of the virus. A Pew Research Center poll taken in late July showed that 73 percent of US adults said they had an unfavorable view of China, an increase of 26 percentage points since 2018 and a seven-point increase since March, when COVID-19 hit the country like a gale force. However, Republicans, echoing the visceral attacks of the president, were far more likely than Democrats to blame China for the global spread of the virus: 78 percent of Republicans held China responsible, while only 38 percent of Democrats did so.[51] Scholars and pundits worried that the partisan and racist attacks on China precluded conventional diplomatic efforts to ease tensions. "I think we're in a dangerous and precipitous spiral downward, not without cause, but without the proper diplomatic skills to arrest it," warned Orville Schell, director of the Center on U.S.-China Relations at the Asia Society. The severity of the confrontation, he said, "has jumped the wall from specific and solvable challenges to a clash of systems and values."[52]

This clash over worldviews showed that partisan conflicts over state power during a crisis do not just involve administrative decrees that can be—and in some matters were—easily reversed by a new administration. The control of state power is not consequential only for the precedents it creates. Rather, it leaves a lasting imprint on the fabric of American society and the public conscience because state power centers on profound questions of identity and belonging. Asian Americans feared that Trump's demonization of China might irreparably damage their status in the country. As the coronavirus spread across the globe in February 2020, the World Health Organization urged people to avoid terms like "Wuhan virus" or "Chinese virus," concerned that it could instigate a backlash against Asians. President Trump's failure to take that advice had immediate repercussions. On March 16, 2020, he first tweeted the phrase "Chinese virus." That single tweet, researchers later found, fueled exactly the kind of backlash the World Health Organization had feared: it was followed by an avalanche of tweets using the hashtag #chinesevirus, among other anti-Asian phrases. Not only did more people use the #chinesevirus hashtag days after Trump's tweet, but those who did were more likely to include other anti-Asian hashtags in their tweets, according to a peer-reviewed study published by the *American Journal of Public Health*. Also well documented was the wave of racist attacks and threats against Asian Americans, which some advocates blamed on Trump's persistent anti-Chinese rhetoric against the pandemic.[53]

The lasting consequences of these policy changes outlived the pandemic. President Biden struggled to rescind the Title 42 policy, facing both political and legal obstacles to dealing with the backlog and the growing number of unauthorized border crossings. International student enrollment did not immediately rebound, even as universities in Canada saw increased interest from overseas.[54] The enduring importance of Trump's unilateralism revealed the importance of his attack on the deep state. Although attacks against the bureaucracy did not begin with Trump, he escalated them to the point where the bedrock qualities of public service—public trust, neutrality, a competent and functional workforce—could no longer be taken for granted. As Donald Moynihan wrote of Trump's potential imprint on the civil service, "A dysfunctional bureaucracy lacking basic professional autonomy is less able to deliver upon the promises of democracy and gives people less reason to have faith in collective action, even as they expect more from government."[55] A second Trump term will further diminish the protections afforded by an energetic and competent federal bureaucracy; nevertheless, presidential conflicts with the civil service are an endemic symptom of executive-centered partisanship. In the final analysis, the pandemic showcased how state power, wielded in a partisan manner, could exacerbate existing divisions and raise fundamental questions of identity and belonging, ultimately undermining the nation's unity in the face of a crisis.

A NATION DIVIDED: PRESIDENTIAL LEADERSHIP AND RACIAL JUSTICE

Presidents have often struggled to provide moral clarity during periods of social unrest and protest. And yet, while often marked by public and epic clashes, presidents have sometimes found some common ground with social movements.[56] As Bruce Miroff has argued, for most of the twentieth century, presidents increasingly sought to find a "symbolic balance point" where they could champion the goals of social movements to a limited extent all the while maintaining a "special commitment to law, order, and the general good."[57]

In the summer of 2020, all pretensions toward some "balance point" were thrown out the window. Just as the Trump administration eagerly sought to politicize nearly every aspect of the coronavirus pandemic for electoral advantage, so the White House sought to capitalize on the social unrest that followed the murder of George Floyd, deploying state power against civil rights protesters and making the visible and dramatic displays of "law and order" central to the president's reelection bid. Trump's response to the pandemic continued the strategy of executive-centered partisanship that had shaped his first three years in office, but the fusion of executive prerogative and partisanship became especially combustible as he claimed emergency powers to confront the protests that broke out throughout the country—from large urban areas to small towns and rural areas.[58] The Black Lives Matter (BLM) protests were not simply a distraction from the public health crisis. Most people reported they had gone to protests because they believed in racial justice and supported the BLM movement; however, for many, particularly those who had never before turned out for a BLM protest, what pushed them into the streets was being harmed financially by the pandemic. The pandemic thus helped fuel what scholars considered the broadest and most sustained social movement in US history.[59]

Data from the 2020 ANES confirms those broader attitudes in support of the BLM movement, even months after the height of the protests. As shown in Table 5.3, a majority of Americans agreed both with the idea that police officers are likely to use force more often than they should and with the idea that they are systematically more likely to treat whites better than Blacks. On average,

Table 5.3. Attitudes toward Law-and-Order Issues, 2020 ANES

	All Americans (%)	Non-Trump Republicans (%)	Trump Republicans (%)
Police officers use more force than necessary. [Never or rarely]	42.43	55.97	73.41
In general, the police treat whites better than Blacks. [Agree]	62.64	59.03	28.34
Most important to use all available force to maintain law and order, no matter what results. [Agree]	18.18	11.70	47.82
During the past few months, would you say that most of the actions taken by protesters to get the things they want have been mostly violent? [Agree]	32.90	32.51	68.39

Note: Data are weighted; the unweighted sample includes 8,200 individuals, including nonvoters, who were asked the policy questions. Among those, the unweighted sample included 2,329 Republicans who we identified as Trump Republicans and 1,147 Republicans who had some degree of reservation about the president. To be sure, just 571 of those Republicans, or 16 percent, disapproved of Trump's performance in office.

only a third of Americans said that the protests in support of BLM were mostly violent. And, when asked to indicate on a seven-point scale whether it was important to "use all available force to maintain law and order, no matter what results," just one in five Americans answered in the most extreme, unequivocal terms.

But as with the pandemic, those in Trump's base saw a different America. Instead of protest, they saw riots; instead of systemic injustice, the president and his allies only saw "some bad apples"; where a majority of Americans were willing to seize the moment and utter the words "Black lives matter," Trump labeled the phrase a "symbol of hate."[60] Even more than with his other overtures to his base, Trump's commitment to "law-and-order" policy was a clear and direct attempt to govern on behalf of a small minority of loyal partisans who were far outside the mainstream of American politics. And while not every Trump supporter denied the existence of systemic racism in policing, or unquestioningly endorsed the president's hard-nosed tactics to quell dissent, it is clear that his most "loyal customers" were the only constituency that mattered in Trump's decision-making.

Defying the broad sympathy for the protests against racial injustice, Trump rallied his base against the BLM demonstrations, echoing Richard Nixon's refrain that "law and order" was the "first civil right of every American." Trump chose this moment of national reckoning over racial justice to declare himself "your president of law and order"—praising most law enforcement officers as "great people" and threatening to treat the protesters, who were portrayed as "terrorists," with overwhelming and "dominating" force. Trump believed, as Nixon did at the birth of a new Republican Party, that a "silent majority" supported his commitment to "traditional values." Living not just in rural and exurban areas, but also in working-class suburbs like Macomb County outside of Detroit, these voters and potential voters, even if disgusted by police violence, were not joining the protests.[61] As the 2016 election showed, these communities were critical for President Trump's Electoral College strategy, and he would have to rely on these disproportionately powerful counties once more in 2020.

Black Lives Matter and the civil rights demonstrations across the country in the summer of 2020 had a tangential relationship to the state's response to COVID-19; however, the use of the federal tactical units was part of the Trump administration's effort to control BLM protests nationwide, embellishing his claim that state and local Democratic leaders were incapable of governing, and deflecting attention from his disruptive management of the COVID-19 crisis. When resisted by Secretary of Defense Mark Espers, Trump abandoned his threat to invoke the Insurrection Act, a law passed in 1807 that empowers presidents to deploy military and federalized National Guard troops within the United States to suppress civil disorder, insurrection, and rebellion. But employing various statutes that authorized the federal government to prosecute trespassing and vandalizing of federal and state memorials, the administration sent federal authorities into Portland, Oregon; Washington, DC; and other cities to quell demonstrations.[62] Relying primarily on the Department of Homeland Security (DHS), which he had deployed to crack down on border crossings from Central America in 2018 and 2019, Trump crafted the image of a strongman willing to dominate protesters—an incursion that confounded most participants in the BLM demonstrations, who were peaceful, and those agitators at the margins of the movement, who took advantage of the unrest to burn and loot property.

Like the Trump White House's joining of executive prerogative and partisanship in matters of immigration, this aggressive protection of the homeland from so-called domestic terrorists in American cities was closely tied to the president's reelection.[63] In the absence of department leaders who could win Senate confirmation, Trump filled key positions in the DHS with partisan figures, such as Acting Director Chad Wolf, CBP commissioner Mark Morgan, and Ken Cuccinelli, christened with the political double-speak title of the "senior official performing the duties of the deputy secretary." All three made regular appearances on Fox News, defending Trump as a strong leader who stood his ground against the chaos fomented by domestic violence and weak Democratic leadership.[64]

Under this institutionally vapid system, with little oversight from Congress or the judiciary, federal agents assumed broad authority to enforce federal laws—for example, to protect a federal courthouse under siege in Portland, Oregon—even against the wishes of local authorities. However, DHS forces, redeployed from the crackdown on immigration, seemed to cross that line as they roamed American cities, intruding on local policing. Just as problematic, relying on CBP and Immigration and Customs Enforcement (ICE) agents who are accustomed to operating at airports and border crossings, where they are generally subject to fewer constraints than ordinary police officers, the Trump White House used a strategy that was as likely to aggravate as to subdue BLM protesters. The fact that many of those officers were not accustomed to dealing with urban unrest, critics charged, was a further indictment of the White House's strategy.[65]

The White House and the Department of Justice also deliberately targeted BLM protests—and seized authority from state and local law enforcement—with heavy-handed criminal prosecutions. In contrast with the way the government handled the COVID-19 protests against local government shutdowns and mask mandates, President Trump and Attorney General William Barr issued directives to press federal charges against BLM protesters. A study conducted by Creating Law Enforcement Accountability and Responsibility, a legal advocacy clinic associated with the City University of New York School of Law, found that in 92.6 percent of the criminal cases analyzed, there were equivalent state-level charges that could have been brought against defendants. Among those cases, 88 percent of the federal criminal charges carried more severe potential sentences than the equivalent state criminal charges for the same or similar conduct. Trump and Barr used these arrests and prosecutions, the report argued, to justify their rhetoric that the protesters were radical and violent agitators.[66]

In an episode that came to define Trump's epic clash with those protesting police brutality, federal law enforcement using tear gas, pepper spray capsules, rubber bullets, and flash bombs removed peaceful BLM protesters from Washington's Lafayette Park. They did so with the enthusiastic approval of President Trump, who moments earlier delivered Rose Garden remarks in which he declared himself "your president of law and order" and demanded that governors use police and National Guard units to "dominate the streets." Trump then strode through the park to the historic St. John's Church—flanked by family members, administration officials, and camera crews—where he held up a Bible and said, "We have the greatest country in the world. Keep it nice and safe." Having accomplished his purpose, Trump headed back to the White House—boasting on Twitter the next morning: "Many arrests. Great job done by all. Overwhelming force. Dominance." By Tuesday afternoon, however, the crowds were back and even bigger.[67]

The battle of Lafayette Square, not surprisingly, also divided religious leaders. Clergy of established churches, including Bishop Mariann Edgar Budde of the Episcopal Diocese of Washington, who was not consulted beforehand, were outraged over the use of an iconic religious site as a political backdrop to boast of squelching protests against racism. But the president's evangelical base was ecstatic over his counterdemonstration. As Robert Jeffrees, a Dallas megachurch pastor, told the *Atlantic*, he thought the moment was "completely appropriate." "By holding up the Bible," he added, "[the president] was showing us that it teaches that, yes, God hates racism, it's despicable—but God also hates lawlessness."[68]

Embarrassing revelations soon surfaced that exposed just how reckless the polarizing federal surge to repress demonstrations in Washington had been. Disgruntled DHS officials revealed that the Trump administration flew immigrant detainees to Virginia, and circumvented restrictions on the use of charter flights for employee travel, to facilitate the rapid deployment of DHS tactical teams in Lafayette Square. Immigration and Customs Enforcement officials said the agency moved the detainees on "ICE Air" charter flights to avoid overcrowding at detention facilities in Arizona and Florida, a precaution they said was taken because of the pandemic. But a DHS security official with direct knowledge of the operation, and a former ICE official who had learned about it from other personnel, said the primary reason for the transfers on June 2 was to skirt rules that bar ICE employees from traveling on the charter flights unless detainees are also aboard. Statistics from ICE confirmed that the facilities the detainees came from were not near capacity on June 1, when the transfers were arranged. After the transfers, dozens of the new arrivals tested positive for the coronavirus, fueling an outbreak in the Farmville, Virginia, immigration jail that infected more than three hundred inmates, one of whom died.[69] The Trump administration was willing to use such dangerous and questionable methods to redeploy ICE units to shift attention from the pandemic—which reflected so badly on the White House—to law and order, a theme that rallied the Republican base.

CONCLUSION: LEGACIES OF EMERGENCY GOVERNANCE

Emergencies are exceptional moments, but although episodic and unique, they can help clarify the nature of power in a regime. The Trump administration's final year in office makes clear that the contemporary presidency does not function for the benefit of the "whole people" or unite the nation in addressing national crises through lasting reforms. As noted, our argument is not that a different president would have managed the twin crises of a pandemic and racial reckoning the same way. In fact, the phenomenon of executive-centered partisanship predicts quite the opposite. Presidents govern with an eye toward satisfying core constituencies. As a result, their desire to offer transcendent and unifying leadership is severely hamstrung by the constraints and incentives that fuel modern presidentialism.

Looking beyond Trump, it is clear that the demands of party leadership also made it difficult, if not impractical, for President Biden to "reach across the aisle" as he took over the task of managing an ongoing pandemic in January 2021. Although Biden pledged to "stop the shouting, and lower the temperature," he learned the hard lesson that Democrats, no less than Republicans, depend on presidents to advance their party's objectives. Like his predecessors who have promised to be uniters, not dividers, Biden's campaign commitment gave way to personal ambitions and the powerful forces that divide red and blue America. From the start of his tempestuous first year, he embraced the combustible combination of executive prerogative and partisanship that defined Trump's administration. Especially with respect to COVID-19, Biden exercised the powers of the modern executive office forcefully and in defiance of his stated commitment to respect and rebuild interbranch and intergovernmental partnerships that were further eroded during his predecessor's term.[70]

Nor is this style of politicking unique to episodic crises; indeed crises—real and fabricated—are now more routine. Even when managing less politically contentious programs, like disaster funding, the modern presidency is driven by electoral motives and often caters to its core constituency. Contemporary presidents are more apt to use the language of an emergency or crisis to legitimize their bending the rules. During emergencies, well-coordinated and highly determined factions within a single party can exploit the institution to implement unpopular and divisive strategies. Furthermore, the dependence on unilateral administrative actions to promote party goals—dubiously justified in the guise of the "national interest"—further weakens legislative institutions during times of crisis. In a country divided by profound cultural chasms, such presidential unilateralism incites fundamental disputes over whether a crisis even exists.

Although we have emphasized the policy consequences of this institutional imbalance, high-stakes battles over domestic and international policy are now inseparable from constitutional hardball that challenges the resilience of liberal democracy. Under the operating assumptions built into the US Constitution, Donald Trump's mishandling of the gravest national crisis since the Great Depression should have destined him to share the fate of "a late regime affiliate"—such as Herbert Hoover or Jimmy Carter—and led to a harsh political reckoning: "the ultimate repudiation of a defunct conservative political order and the ascent of a new progressive regime."[71]

Just what price did Donald Trump's crisis management exact? On the one hand, he lost his reelection bid. To the relief of many scholars and pundits, the Constitution appeared to hold. Having failed to gain the trust of a large part of the country and failing to produce a winning coalition, he was booted from office, resorting, as we will discuss in the conclusion to this book, to an unsuccessful and unprecedented effort to prevent a peaceful transfer of power. On the other hand, it is hard to walk away from 2020 believing that the institutions and public officials, standing like Horatius at the bridge, could thwart Trump and the movement he leads a second time. Trump, as we have repeatedly insisted, is not a cult of personality—a one-off. After all, Republicans did better down ballot than most preelection surveys predicted; they gained eleven seats in the House and maintained control of most state legislatures. Moreover, Trump's term in office enabled Republicans to solidify a conservative majority on the courts. As a result, his successor, Joe Biden, came into office having to navigate public health and economic crises with a bare majority in the Senate, statehouses and governors more deeply divided than Congress, and a judiciary in which 28 percent of all sitting judges were appointed by Trump, including three new justices on the US Supreme Court. Trump himself, as he would repeatedly claim in an effort to sow doubt about the election, won 11.2 million more votes than he did in 2016; the 2020 race saw 66 percent of eligible US citizens turn out to vote—a highwater mark not broken since the reelection of William McKinley in 1900.

Accountability was thus quite limited for Trump, especially when compared with previous presidents who failed to reckon with a national crisis. Even in defeat, Trump saw his brand of conservative nationalism and MAGA Republicanism not only endure but thrive. With Trump and his movement unyielding, the 2020 election left an indelible scar on American democracy. Despite overwhelming evidence and over sixty court rulings that showed Trump's claims of a stolen election to be a fabrication, the "Big Lie" lived on, shaping primary contests in 2022 and becoming a litmus test for GOP hopefuls in 2024. A considerable portion of Trump's supporters continue to believe in the canard that the 2020 election was fraudulent. As Gary Jacobson documented in early 2023, "Overall support for the big lie has averaged 71 percent among Republicans, 76 percent among Trump voters, with only modest declines in the ranks of believers after the invasion and trashing of the Capitol on 6 January 2021, and again after the first round of House hearings on that event in the summer of 2022."[72]

The consequences of this widespread falsehood thus extended far beyond the 2020 election, continuing to animate the Republican Party's leadership, candidates, and base and enduring into the 2024 presidential campaign. The persistence of the Big Lie deeply entrenched partisan divisions in America, with statehouses and governors becoming increasingly polarized around the myth of electoral fraud. Republican governors have made the prosecution of ballot "security" a central concern, even though there is scant evidence of election fraud; hoping to stand as an alternative to Trump as the 2024 Republican nominee, Florida governor Ron DeSantis created an "election police force" and worked with the state legislature to further restrict the use of ballot drop boxes and voting by mail.[73] This toxic political environment made it increasingly difficult for Biden's administration to address pressing issues such as the public health and economic crises facing the nation. With three-fourths of the opposition denying he is the legitimately elected president of the United States, creating a broad basis of support is a chimera.

Many of the specific claims made by Trump and his operatives were rooted in the contingency plans states and municipalities made to carry out the presidential election in the midst of a deadly pandemic; the death toll was on the rise in November 2020 and would soon reach its all-time high two months later. But Trump's specific claims of voter fraud through mail-in ballots or early voting were a coda to his yearlong attempt to sow doubt about the fairness of American elections. In 2016, he refused to state that he would concede the election, and one of his first acts as president was to create the Presidential Advisory Commission on Election Integrity after claiming, without evidence, that his failure to win the popular vote was the result of three to five million unauthorized immigrants voting for Hillary Clinton. No evidence from this commission ever supported the president's claims.

The intertwining of executive prerogative, movement politics, and partisanship defied efforts to identify any sense of the public interest in the face of the direst political circumstance since the Great Depression. Reflecting on that crisis, however, it seems unlikely that even a more inclusive leader could have forged a new majority coalition. With over a million lives lost, we walk away with a humbling lesson that in order to strengthen the resilience of American democracy, we must confront the deeply rooted pathologies that enabled a dangerous, charismatic leader to command his party and half the nation at a political moment that cried out for transcendent leadership.

Conclusion: The Future of the American Presidency

Most books about presidents and their presidencies have a neat and tidy ending. Forty-four times, since 1797, presidents have willingly, and without much fanfare, simply left the office. In nearly half those instances—twenty-one times—they handed power over to a partisan rival. Except for the 1860 election, which precipitated the Civil War, the peaceful transfer of power from one presidential administration to the next has been a celebrated ritual in American politics.

The chaos and violence of January 6, 2021, violated a revered precedent at the heart of a representative constitutional government; it did not end Donald Trump's influence on American politics. The former president may have left office, but his spell over the Republican Party continued. He still dominated the news cycle, receiving more attention as a disgruntled former president than the occupant of the White House; and he and the MAGA Republicans, who maintained a primordial relationship with their charismatic leader, perpetuated the "Big Lie" that Joe Biden and the Democrats stole the 2020 election. As we learned soon after completing this book, Trump's appeal went beyond his movement. With a decisive triumph, which saw Trump improve his margin of victory in every state from 2020 to 2024, he will return to the White House on January 20, 2025. The story we tell in this volume of his first term and its mercurial aftermath, we believe, offers more than a few clues about how act 2 of the Trump presidency will turn out.

In a presidency marked by many "firsts," Trump continued to tally them up after he left the White House: the first to be impeached and run for reelection; the first to be impeached twice, once after losing an election; the first president never to have received above 50 percent on Gallup's presidential approval tracker; the first former president to be indicted by a criminal grand jury. Indeed, trying to predict the future of the American presidency as Trump eagerly returns to the White House is like trying to predict what a Donald Trump presidency would have looked like on the afternoon he made his fateful descent down the escalator in Trump Tower.

However, as we have argued throughout this book, for all the precedents shattered by his presidency, Trump also fits a pattern. Focusing on all his eccentricities and scandals—while important—neglects the larger developmental processes that shaped the first term of his presidency, and which will continue to shape the incentives and behavior of future American presidents. Although there may never be another president exactly like Trump, the patterns of executive-centered partisanship highlighted throughout previous chapters remained highly salient during Trump's post-presidency and that of his successor, Joe Biden. Having brought long-standing trends that have braided executive prerogative and partisanship to a culmination, Trump has left an indelible mark on the modern presidency and political parties. Now that he has been granted another term as president, it will be all the more difficult, if not impractical, for America to come home again.

Indeed, Trump will simply pick up where he left off. In preparation for a potential return to the White House, Trump clearly spelled out his plans, promising to resurrect his Schedule F appointment scheme that would allow him to reclassify and fire civil servants; to reorganize the executive branch to bring independent regulatory agencies under the control of the White House; and to restart the practice—declared illegal during the Nixon administration—of impounding funds for programs and grants to which he objects. Even if Trump is not successful in some of his boldest plans, such as the reclassification of prominent senior executives, one conclusion Trump and his allies took from his four years in office is that they must better insulate the White House from traditional conservative organizations, which filled the ranks of the administration, but whose allegiances were sometimes tenuous. Indeed, although Trump's relationship with the Federalist Society was historically noteworthy and consequential for his reshaping of the federal judiciary, it was also the source of some internal resistance to Trump's most legally dubious plans. He and his closest political allies most resented the White House and Justice Department legal officials who repelled his attempts to overturn the 2020 presidential election. But as the *New York Times* reported in November 2023, senior advisers to the Trump campaign were replacing the lists of lawyers once handed to them with new ones of their own creation, composed of a "different type of lawyer committed to his 'America First' ideology and willing to endure the personal and professional risks of association with Trump."[1]

The plan to further strengthen the presidency is not envisioned as an end in itself. In anticipation of Trump's return to power, the Heritage Foundation released a nearly nine-hundred-page report, *A Mandate for Leadership*, with many former Trump officials among its contributors, detailing on an agency-by-agency level the plan to further consolidate governmental power and redeploy it for conservative ends. The explicit theme that "personnel is policy" reverberates throughout the document. Amid mainstream reforms to economize government and trim waste are provocative proposals to would whet the sword of executive power to advance partisan objectives: "break up" the Oceanic and Atmospheric Administration because it is a "colossal operation that has become one of the main drivers of the climate change alarm industry and, as such, is harmful to future U.S. prosperity"; install a "pro-life task force" within the office of the secretary of the Department of Health and Human Services to find ways to "use their authority to promote the life and health of women and their unborn children"; and find "committed political appointees and like-minded career employees" to "command and control" US Census Bureau operations and "align the Census Bureau's mission with conservative principles." An especially important mission of this enhanced conservative state will be to resuscitate efforts during Trump's presidency to impose draconian restrictions on immigration. The chapter on homeland security, written by former Trump official Ken Cuccinelli, calls for a new cabinet-level "border and immigration agency," which would contain more than "100,000 employees, making it the third largest department measured by manpower" (eclipsed by Defense and Veterans Affairs).[2] Although he dismissed these plans as "ridiculous and abysmal" during the 2024 presidential campaign, after claiming victory several of the report's authors were nominated to prime positions in Trump's administration: Russell Vought as director of the vastly important Office of Management and Budget, Tom Homan as "border czar; and Stephen Miller as deputy chief of policy inside the Executive Office of the President.[3]

While many Trump critics dismiss him as an unstable narcissist, Trump—spurred on by his most ardent supporters—is dedicated to consolidating a conservative state that has been forged in fits and starts since the Nixon administration. His attempt to retake power is joined to the mission of translating this programmatic ambition into transformative institutional and policy change. As one former staffer summarized, "The president's plan should be to fundamentally reorient the federal government in a way that hasn't been done since F.D.R.'s New Deal."[4] Although this may sound fantastical, it is sobering to contemplate that by the end of his second term, Trump will have loomed over American life for as long as Roosevelt's dozen years in the White House.[5]

The development of executive-centered partisanship in the decades prior to Trump's ascension to the White House may abet his ambition. But the experiences laid bare during his presidency and its tumultuous aftermath raise the fundamental and troubling question of whether presidentialism has overwhelmed the Madisonian system of checks and balances. Since the late 1960s, both Democrats and Republicans have depended on presidents to pronounce party doctrine, raise funds, mobilize base supporters, and advance party programs. The advance of presidency-centered parties corroded constitutional norms and institutions, weakened party organizations and party leaders that served as gatekeepers of collective party responsibility, and cultivated a winner-take-all politics that intractably divides red and blue America. These developments, combined with fundamental cultural and economic conflicts, created a tribal politics that enabled an iconoclastic reality TV star to set ablaze combustible political conditions that were more than half a century in the making. His presidency exposed sores on the body politic that will be difficult to heal, especially since Democrats, traumatized by Trump's assault on norms and institutions, are tempted to fight fire with fire—to counter Trump and the MAGA movement with their own brand of constitutional hardball. Public officials willing to "think institutionally" are an endangered political species.[6]

Consequently, Trump's bombastic presidency and his desperate, nefarious plot to hold on to power have led many scholars to question the resilience of American democracy. At one time, comparative politics scholars, most notably the eminent Juan Linz, argued that the United States had somehow escaped the tendency of presidential systems to backslide into authoritarian regimes.[7] Thirty years before the 2020 presidential election, Linz wrote a classic piece, "The Perils of Presidentialism," in which he argued that parliamentary systems, governed by cabinets with a collective sense of responsibility, tended to constrain executive power and cultivate compromise between competing factions within and between parties. Presidential systems, in contrast, were more likely to degenerate into a plebiscitary politics—fertile ground for a "strongman personality," presuming to represent "the People," who treated legislatures and the rule of law with contempt. Rather than encourage compromise, presidential systems created winner-take-all politics and promoted policies that sharply divided nations.

Linz's analysis of the dangers inherent in presidential systems was informed by conflicts between presidents and legislatures that had preceded military coups in Chile, Brazil, and other Latin American countries, leading to brutal dictatorships. But the United States, with its venerable presidential system and tradition of constitutional government, long posed an empirical anomaly for Linz and other scholars who viewed presidential systems as antithetical to the sort of collective responsibility and compromises that parliamentary governments cultivated. America's exceptional history of presidentialism, Linz emphasized, was not, as most scholars and commenters had assumed, a result of its Madisonian system of check and balances. Rather, Linz attributed the resilience of American democracy to two societal factors: public opinion, which he viewed as "overwhelmingly moderate," and, relatedly, "the uniquely diffuse character of American political parties," which staged partisan conflict within a "moderate consensus."[8]

Trump's presidency revealed that the conditions that sustained democratic stability in the United States were forlorn; in truth, even as Linz was writing, the era of "catchall" and decentralized parties was coming to an end. The rise of Donald Trump, a poster child for Linz's fear of presidentialism, was a symptom of long-term trends that united executive prerogative and partisanship, which denigrated parties as collective organizations with a past and a future and exposed the polity to factional leaders who viewed themselves, as Theodore Roosevelt put it in an alluring and mischievous phrase, "the steward of the public welfare."[9]

Linz's analysis raises important questions about the growing tension between American presidentialism, no longer an outlier, and the Madisonian system. Emphasizing the tendency of presidential regimes to degenerate into "explosive social and political strife," Linz also notes that, paradoxically, one of the "oft-cited advantages of presidentialism is its provision for the stability of the executive." Unlike prime ministers, who are subject to votes of no confidence, presidents usually serve for fixed terms and can be removed only by impeachment, "a very uncertain and time-consuming process, especially compared with the simple parliamentary vote of no confidence." But this stability is bought at the price of "rigidity." Flexibility in the face of changing conditions is not presidentialism's strong suit; moreover, attempting to dislodge a president who has lost the confidence of his party or the people is extremely difficult. It might lead, Linz warns, the incumbent's supporters to "feel cheated" and to rally behind their leader. Such impasses are extremely dangerous, Linz concludes, often leading to resolution by nondemocratic institutions—like the courts or, in the worst case, the military: "What in a parliamentary system would be a government crisis can become a full-blown regime crisis in a presidential system."[10]

Rigidity is not the first word that comes to mind when reflecting on the Trump presidency. The day-to-day machinations that made headlines—from the president tweeting that transgender individuals could not serve in the military, to First Lady Melania's cryptic jacket message during a visit to the southern border ("I really don't care, Du You?")—leave the impression of an undisciplined and unpredictable presidency. As we have acknowledged throughout this book, it is tempting to explain these vicissitudes as resulting from the idiosyncrasies of the First Family. However, the president tweeting out a major change in military policy and the First Lady expressing contempt for the media's criticism of the White House as she visits a major site of her husband's provocative child separation immigration initiative are both indicative of the Trump administration's persistent disregard for the core institutions and norms of representative constitutional government. As the discussion of the first impeachment episode in chapter 5 showed, whenever the press, the bureaucracy, or Congress attempted to hold the president accountable for his subversive behavior, the base predictably rallied to his defense, a foreboding warning of the coordinated effort to mobilize a movement in 2020 to overturn a free and fair election.

Linz's warning about the pathological rigidity of presidential systems is perhaps best illustrated in the United States by the way executive-centered partisanship has been woven into the fabric of American democracy. Just as Trump captured the Republican Party, so its loyalists in Congress, the states, and advocacy groups were dependent on the president to advance their objectives. Symptomatic of presidential partisanship, the Republican Party has been unwilling to hold Trump accountable for his transgressions, distance itself from his MAGA acolytes in elections or public office, offer a *party* platform that distinguishes the party as a collective organization, or expand the Trump base beyond a faction that can win a majority of the Electoral College but not the popular vote. Trump did win the popular vote in 2024, but his margin over his Democratic opponent, Vice President Kamala Harris—49.3 to 48.3—was one of the smallest margins ever in a presidential race. And it did not include a majority of American voters.

Although their party is more diverse, the Democrats also have been ensnared by the wiles of executive-centered partisanship. An inclusive leader with pragmatic instincts, President Joe Biden—once a strong proponent of congressional prerogatives—proclaimed during the 2020 election campaign, "I am the Democratic Party."[11] Biden lacks Trump's primordial relationship with his party's base supporters; nevertheless, recognizing how contemporary partisanship is animated by the relationship between the White House and advocacy groups, Biden, often at the urging of his legislative brethren, has acted unilaterally when Congress would not act, to redeem campaign pledges to the social activists who have filled the vacuum left by the hollowing out of party organizations. Even though most Democratic loyalists would have preferred that President Biden—the oldest president in American history—not run for reelection, he lacked a serious challenger during the primary campaign. Indeed, in an unprecedented intrusion on the presidential selection process, the president pressured the Democratic National Committee to reorder the primary schedule so that South Carolina, a critical state in his surge to the nomination in 2020, would replace New Hampshire as the first Democratic primary contest. The new primary schedule also moves other states that gave Biden a boost in 2020, such as Georgia and Michigan, toward the front of the nominating contest, thereby nearly eliminating any path for a potential Democratic primary challenge ahead of 2024 by elevating states that represent the president's base of support.[12] His disastrous debate performance against Trump in late June, which belatedly forced him to give way to Vice President Harris, hardly contradicted the hard truth that neither Democrats nor Republicans have the institutional capacity to cultivate a collective sense of partisanship—as Martin Van Buren put it, to "transform personal preference into party principle."[13]

In an intractably divided nation, both parties seem bound to a ritual tribalism that combines presidential prerogative, social activism, and high-stakes struggles over domestic and foreign policy. As presidentialism has come to dominate American politics, we have witnessed what Linz feared most: the inability of "leaders to govern, to inspire trust, to respect the limits of their power, and to reach an adequate degree of consensus." Echoing Van Buren, Linz warns, "Heavy reliance on the personal qualities of a political leader—on the virtue of a statesman, if you will—is a risky course."[14]

STUCK IN THE AGE OF TRUMP: CONSERVATIVISM AND TRUMPISM

Donald Trump's presidency was transformative not just for the conservative movement but for the nation. The conservatism that currently roils American politics can be a "rigid doctrine," but not in the classical sense of conserving first principles. In the decades leading up to Trump's nomination, the Republican Party's commitment to traditional conservative tenets—free-market capitalism, limited government, individual liberties, and an overarching commitment to constitutional norms and institutions—was severely challenged by the antinomian movement politics loosed by the sixties. The primary motivation of conservative politics was no longer to conserve but to "make America great again"—a slogan first used during Ronald Reagan's 1980 campaign—which presupposed the expansion of government power. Trump's outsize influence on the Republican Party was vivid testament to the joining of conservatism and national administrative power.

Big-government conservatism did not begin with Trump; as we have noted in chapter 1, it originated with Richard Nixon's discovery that the modern executive, ideologically, could be a doubled-edged sword that could cut in a conservative direction as well as a liberal one. But Trump's rhetoric and policies brought to full realization the Republican Party's embrace of a national conservatism, dedicated to protective tariffs, border security, law and order, the renewal of "traditional" values, and an "America First" foreign policy that eschewed multinational alliances. Though this program alienated Never Trumpers, especially in its rejection of free trade and the ideal of America as a city on a hill, it rallied the Republican base that embraced Trump's populist rhetoric and policies—his populist view that "a small group in our nation's capital has reaped the rewards of government, while the people have borne the cost."[15] Right-wing populism appealed especially to the white working class, which had been abandoning the Democratic Party since the late 1960s over cultural issues, driven by the perception that establishment Democrats are more prone to prioritize identity politics and multiculturalism over the traditional economic concerns that once formed the backbone of their alliance. Trump's attack on globalism and his promise to restore manufacturing jobs that once gave the American worker access to the middle class added an economic dimension to the culture wars that had divided the country for over half a century.

The rout of the rear guard of establishment Republicans and the hegemony of Trumpism have not just remade what it means to be a conservative in the United States; they have also transformed the GOP into a decidedly right-wing organization that resists—rigidly—social and demographic changes in a country that promises, or portends, the emergence of what Jesse Jackson once called a "rainbow coalition": young people, minorities, the LGBTQIA+ community, and educated white professionals. Presidentialism and the diminishment of the Republican Party as a collective organization that can resist the allure of executive-centered partisanship have made it possible for a demagogic leader to advance a winner-take-all politics that has made conservatism a harsh and uncompromising force—one that champions a New Right coalition of blue-collar, religiously devout, and nonurban whites who expect the national and state governments to take positive action to thwart social change they fear is turning the United States into a country to which they no longer feel an allegiance.

Trump's departure from conventional political decorum, his direct confrontations with the mainstream media, and his provocative—politically incorrect—language gave voice to these sentiments of discontent and cultivated a devoted following. His "most loyal customers" have followed him through thick and thin. Controversies such as Russian collusion, pressuring Ukraine to investigate a political rival, forming alliances with white supremacist groups, and even machinations to prevent a peaceful transfer of power were dismissed as "witch hunts" and "fake news." Trump's very iconoclasm only seemed to strengthen the bond between him and the Republican base. Just as they viewed themselves as victims of a liberal establishment that dismissed them as relics of the past, so Trump played the victim—of journalists who were the "enemies of the people" and urban elites who scorned his MAGA movement as a "basket of deplorables," a phrase used by Hillary Clinton during the 2016 campaign. Consequently, Trump is not merely a one-off, representing a cult of personality. By remaking the Republican Party, he has assured that Trumpism will endure; in Max Weber's terms, his "charisma" has been "routinized."[16]

Perhaps the most perilous consequence of presidentialism is the confounding of the national and factional interests. With its steadfast emphasis on immigration enforcement, economic protectionism, and neo-isolationism, Trumpism does not have anywhere near majority support in the United States. Trump's America First insistence superseded global cooperation, free trade, and multilateral military alliances—all pillars of the postwar conservative establishment that have a solid institutional basis and continue to have strong public support. Similarly, although the surge of immigration during the Biden administration rallied Trump's 2024 supporters around the nativist banner of "mass deportation," a majority of Americans still favor the more welcoming immigration policy that Ronald Reagan and George W. Bush supported over the harsh policies the Trump administration pursued.[17] Yet the marginalization of traditional conservatism in favor of Trump's brand of right-wing populism shows no signs of abating. Indeed, no candidate who ran for the Republican nomination in 2024 seriously challenged the Make America Great Again program. The variety of Republicans who sought to challenge him for the nomination sought to champion Trumpism without Trump, an ultimately unsuccessful endeavor.

While some policy disputes—particularly over free trade and support for Ukraine—may linger and roil the second Trump administration, debates over Trumpism are over. Trumpism has been institutionalized—Trump leveraged his relationship with the party's base to gain control of the Republican congressional caucuses, the Republican National Committee, and state parties. Consequently, the traditional gatekeepers of collective responsibility have been replaced by MAGA Republicans, who showed little interest in holding Trump accountable for his indiscretions, even after he left the White House in disgrace.

It seemed, for a time, that in the immediate aftermath of the January 6 Capitol riot Trump had finally crossed a red line that would end his spell over the party. At one point in American political development, this would have been foreordained. The traditional, decentralized party system, composed of competing factions and institutionally invested in representing as broad a swath of the electorate as possible, might have held such a charismatic leader accountable.[18] To be sure, remnants of that former collective partisan responsibility did surface. Cue Mitch McConnell, the Republican majority leader of the Senate, in the immediate aftermath of January 6: "There's no question—none—that President Trump is practically and morally responsible for provoking the events of the day." It was, he continued, "a disgraceful, disgraceful dereliction of duty."[19] Kevin McCarthy, House minority leader, who would become Speaker of the House after the 2022 elections, echoed these words: "Let me be clear: Last week's violent attack on the Capitol was undemocratic, un-American and criminal. . . . And make no mistake: Those who are responsible for Wednesday's chaos will be brought to justice. . . . The president bears responsibility for Wednesday's attack on Congress by mob rioters."[20] Lindsey Graham, an institutionally minded senator who once had close ties to the late John McCain, had made peace with the president after he won the 2016 election, becoming an important ally. But he now appeared ready to break that alliance, stating: "The President needs to understand that his actions were the problem, not the solution, that the rally yesterday was unseemly, it got out of hand."[21]

Almost overnight, however, Trump's dominance of the Republican Party—executive-centered partisanship—returned to form. The Republican "establishment," feeling the pressure of Trump's unwavering loyalists, reversed course in a few days. As the Democratic majority in the House closed ranks to begin an impeachment investigation into the president's role in the January 6 attacks (separate from the House Select Committee that would investigate the January 6 attack on the Capitol when the new Congress convened in 2021), most Republicans lost their appetite for holding the former president accountable. Fearing they would be "primaried" if they did not support the former president, they surrendered to a small minority of Americans who would show up on primary day. McConnell and McCarthy shifted blame to House Speaker Nancy Pelosi and Democrats, citing their failure to investigate how the Capitol was left unsecured on their watch. Backbenchers in the House were even more eager to prove their allegiance to Trump. Just ten Republicans voted to impeach him for inciting the Capitol insurrection, dismissing the impeachment inquiry as a partisan tactic. Senate Republicans were not quite as loyal: seven broke with party leadership and voted to convict Trump. Those Republicans who voted to impeach or convict Trump risked their political careers in vain; their principled stand failed to stop the momentum within the Republican ranks to stage a strident denial of the former president's unprecedented plot to prevent a peaceful transfer of power.

Instead of holding Trump accountable for his actions, most Republicans in the Senate and House began to concoct a story that January 6 was not even all that momentous. Though the president's rhetoric was incendiary—"Fight like hell" and "When you catch somebody in a fraud, you're allowed to go by very different rules"—they insisted that these words did not cause an attack on the Capitol; it was merely a peaceful demonstration. Some Republicans went so far as to claim that the rioters who smashed windows, broke down doors, and attacked police looked like they were participating in a "normal tourist visit."[22] As part of this narrative, the death of one rioter who tried to break into the room where members of Congress sought sanctuary—Ashli Babbitt—was an "execution." She, not the Capitol Police, many of whom were badly hurt and some of whom died or committed suicide in the wake of the standoff, was a martyr in the January 6 protest. As Rep. Jody Hice (R-GA) told reporters, "It was Trump supporters who lost their lives that day, not Trump supporters who were taking the lives of others."[23] Weeks after his election as Speaker, McCarthy completely changed his tune, using the privilege of his office to support

Republicans' pro-Trump revisionism. He turned over thousands of hours of Capitol security footage to then Fox News host Tucker Carlson, who wove together a highly edited version of events that purportedly showed that Trump's supporters posed no real threat to the nation's top leaders that day. "These were not insurrectionists. They were sightseers," Carlson said as the footage rolled.[24]

Those who dissented from the Trump apologists paid a heavy price. In early May, the Republican caucus stripped Liz Cheney of her number-three leadership post. It was not the first time the caucus had come after Cheney; supported by McCarthy, she had survived a vote to remove her from leadership in February, shortly after the January 6 attacks and after she cast a vote to impeach Trump. But the way the Republican base denied the results of the 2020 election and insisted that the January 6 riots were a peaceful protest kept the hope of Trump's future as the leader of the GOP alive. Trump won, they insisted, and he and his followers were expressing righteous indignation on January 6 against the widespread fraud that enabled Joe Biden and the Democrats to steal the election. As Trump's dominance over the Republican Party endured, Cheney was no longer able to ward off attacks from the former president's congressional allies. McCarthy, eyeing the Speakership and recognizing that the prize he had long coveted could not be won without the support of MAGA Republicans, left Representative Cheney in the lurch. Further scorned for her willingness to serve as the cochair of the House Select Committee to Investigate the January 6th Attack on the United States Capitol, Cheney lost a primary challenge in a landslide to a pro-Trump Republican in Wyoming, after the RNC funded her challenger and Trump's children toured the state campaigning against her.[25]

Cheney may have been the most visible target of the new Republican orthodoxy, but she was just one of many victims whose political fate was sealed by Trump's capture of the Grand Old Party. Trump's handpicked nominee to run the RNC during his time in office, Ronna McDaniel, won a hard-fought reelection campaign to serve through the 2024 presidential race. With the former president's backing, she won by a margin of 111 to 51 ballots, despite presiding over the national party organization during Trump's failed reelection campaign and the disappointing results in the 2022 midterm elections.[26] McDaniel's resilience owed to her loyalty to Donald Trump. In 2022, the RNC, at McDaniel's direction, censured Cheney and Adam Kinzinger (R-IL)—the other Republican who agreed to serve on the House Select Committee to investigate the events of January 6.

The events of January 6, the RNC insisted, were "ordinary citizens engaged in legitimate political discourse."[27] Representative Kinzinger chose not to run for reelection rather than face a primary challenge. The RNC thus confirmed Trump's remarkable sway over the Republican Party as a former president—abetted by the belief that his visceral relationship with the base could be leveraged to win back the White House in 2024. Despite her unwavering belief in electoral fraud, McDaniel's loyalty to the former president was severely compromised in the eyes of Trump supporters when the RNC tried to remain neutral during the 2024 primary contests. Once Trump vanquished the final challenger standing—the former governor of South Carolina and his first ambassador to the United Nations, Nikki Haley—and he became the presumptive nominee, McDaniel resigned. She was quickly replaced by Michael Whatley, who as chair of North Carolina's Republican Party led the effort to censure Richard Burr (R-NC) for his impeachment conviction vote and, more provocatively, was complicit in Trump's efforts to overturn the vote in Georgia. Completing his personal domination of the RNC, Trump named Lara Trump, his daughter-in-law, as the cochair of the committee.

Trump's sway over the party machinery was not limited to the RNC. The former president mobilized his movement to deepen his imprint on the Republican Party at the state and local levels. The methodical work to remake the Republican Party in the statehouses and the state GOP organizations, as we detail in chapter 2, began during Trump's presidency. These efforts continued with the same urgency after Trump left the White House. The Big Lie became the rallying cry of Republican state politics. Even in "blue" and "bluing" states, where one would think electoral incentives called for moving the party closer to the median voter, state GOP officials, pressured by Trump and his MAGA loyalists, doubled down on election denialism and right-wing populism. The Hawaiian Republican Party blurted out tweets defending conspiracy theorists who deny the Holocaust; the Oregon state party censured Republicans who voted to impeach Trump, claiming "there is growing evidence that the violence at the Capitol was a 'false flag' operation designed to discredit President Trump;"[28] and the Arizona state GOP censured Governor Doug Ducey, former US senator Jeff Flake, and Cindy McCain, the wife of the former Republican presidential candidate John McCain, for not being sufficiently loyal to Trump.[29]

Many of these actions were symbolic, but they showed that the party's foot soldiers were determined to enforce loyalty to Trump—a resolve that had an important effect on nomination contests during the midterm elections.

Although the loudest proponents of Trump's election fables failed to win statewide elections in 2022, denialists captured the chairs of several state party organizations, solidifying a trend that began at the direction of Trump's White House. Trump loyalists seized the levers of power in Colorado, Kansas, Georgia, Michigan, and Massachusetts.[30] These loyalists would have an important influence on the 2024 nomination contest. Most of the delegate-selection rules for the Democratic Party are standardized across states; however, Republican state party officials still enjoy broad discretion to tailor the rules. Trump's 2024 campaign was just as attuned to an inside strategy: previously an outsider, he now invited these new state officials to Mar-a-Lago, met with them whenever he traveled to their bailiwicks, and engineered rule changes on a state-by-state basis to re-create the appearance of a party in lockstep with Trump.[31] This strategy paid off handsomely in 2020, when just one delegate opposed Trump at the Republican National Convention—a lone wolf from Iowa who pledged support for former Massachusetts governor Bill Weld.[32] It was even more effective in 2024, when the former president and his political allies dominated the field of contenders of substantial figures that, besides Haley, included former vice president Mike Pence, Florida governor Ron DeSantis, and South Carolina senator Tim Scott.

Trump's hegemony cannot be understood without recognizing the importance of his takeover of the party apparatus—and the long-term attenuation of the national and state party organizations that made them vulnerable to the White House's predatory practices. Polls taken in early 2023 indicated that only a third of Republican primary voters fell into the "always Trump" faction of the party.[33] Yet given delegate selection rule changes, the importance of conservative media voices, and Trump's influence on the base, no other Republican candidate for the 2024 presidential nomination was able to gain traction in the early months of the campaign. Trump did not even feel compelled to attend the debates hosted by the RNC! Most of Trump's opponents, fearful of alienating the rabid, minority faction of his supporters, refused to take on the former president directly. Even the former vice president, Mike Pence, the target of Trump's wrath for his refusal to stop the certification of Joe Biden's election, demurred—believing that as a loyal partner in the pursuit of the former president's MAGA program, he was the rightful heir to Trump's throne. Pence's strategy seemed doomed from the start, however, given that the GOP base was unwilling to separate loyalty to Trump from loyalty to Trumpism. Governor Ron DeSantis, who claimed to have advanced MAGA policies in Florida while winning a landslide reelection, seemed better suited to threaten Trump's front-runner status. DeSantis captured national headlines with his political attacks against "wokism" and the "woke"—be they academics, DEI officers, transgender athletes, or Walt Disney World. However, he seemed awkward when practicing the right-wing populism that Trump mastered, leaving him flailing in the early going and eventually losing his status as the best MAGA alternative to Trump.

Nikki Haley gained an enthusiastic following among the forlorn establishment wing of her party and independents, but by refusing to distance herself from the MAGA movement—making it clear she was not a member of the "resistance"—the former ambassador failed to articulate a vision for a new generation of conservatives she presumed to lead. After suffering a landslide defeat to Trump in her home state and absorbing overwhelming losses in the Super Tuesday primaries, Haley ended her presidential campaign. Even as she initially refused to endorse Trump, Haley offered little hope or inspiration for her followers who yearned for a Republican Party that was not beholden to Trumpism.[34]

As Linz's analysis reminds us, the personalization of politics is endemic to presidential systems with zero-sum elections and fixed terms. Presidentialism creates the perception, which can readily become the reality, of a deeply divided electorate, mobilized around the personas of two candidates. The Capitol riot that Trump and ultraright groups summoned eerily resembles democratic backsliding in other presidential systems. A recent case in point is the 2022 presidential election in Brazil, when thousands of supporters of the losing candidate, President Jair Bolsonaro, a friend to and supporter of Trump's brand of right-wing populism, stormed and ransacked the presidential palace, congress, and Supreme Court, hoping to overturn the election won by his left-wing opponent, Luiz Inácio Lula da Silva, by more than two million votes. It may be a sad commentary on the current state of American democracy that, unlike Trump, Bolsonaro was held accountable for falsely claiming that the electronic ballots used were vulnerable to hacking and fraud. In July 2023, the Brazilian Supreme Court, by a 5-to-2 vote, banned the former president from running for office for eight years.[35] Perhaps Brazil, not the United States, suggested Omar Encarnacion, a scholar who has studied both systems, "can provide a model on how to fight new anti-democratic threats."[36]

Throughout American history, decentralized party organizations have prevented the parties' images from calcifying into a cult of personality. But the forces Trump commands confirm just how weak these centrifugal forces have become—how presidency-centered partisanship has greatly diminished the intraparty factionalism that once constrained the personalization of partisanship. Trump's reelection seemed to solve the conundrum vexing conservative leaders as to whether Trump's foibles—his two impeachments, election denialism, personal excesses—were so egregious as to prevent him from securing a popular mandate in presidential elections. In 2024, Trump won a near majority of the popular vote and made deep inroads among traditional Democratic voters: Latinos, Black men, and union members. Still, Republicans must grapple with the question of whether Trump's brand of right-wing populism is inextricably tied to Trump's persona or a potential rallying cry for a new right-wing movement that has redefined Republican conservatism. Consequently, a key question that influenced the early going of the 2024 Republican presidential primary contest, which Trump dominated, and hovered over the lead-up to his second term, is whether anyone but Trump could capture the Trump "movement."

The relationship between presidents and social movements has long been a critical dimension of change in American politics.[37] However, prior to Trump's presidency this top-down, bottom-up alliance had been uneasy—a complicated "mating dance." In contrast, Trump has styled himself as a movement leader, seeking to defy the strategic distance that reform presidents such as Lyndon Johnson and Ronald Reagan had thought necessary to maintain in order to forge a majority coalition. Influential conservative social movements, most notably the Christian Right, which Reagan enlisted into the Republican Party, have responded in kind, supporting Trump even through the travails of impeachments and indictments. Their courtship with Trump, which has been far more requited than the relationship the Christian Right formed with Reagan, reveals that social activists no longer aspire to be a faction of a conservative coalition; rather, the Republican Party must be transformed into a movement. In making Trump their cause, however, social activists risk sacrificing their principles to the wiles of a clever demagogue.

ARRESTED BY GRIDLOCK: THE HIGH STAKES OF NATIONAL ADMINISTRATIVE ACTION

Trump and Trumpism have remade conservatism in Republican Party politics. But the culmination of executive-centered partisanship during the Trump administration also has implicated the Democratic Party—with significant consequences for the Biden administration. Presidency-centered politics is the driving force of the American party *system*, and although Trump and Biden could not be more different in their personalities and leadership styles, presidentialism has made its mark on both parties. Trump's provocative leadership style and machinations to overturn the results of a free and fair election aroused all the most dangerous tendencies of presidential partisanship, making the sharp divisions between red and blue America even more intractable. As President Biden discovered after ascending to the White House, presidentialism is so deeply embedded in American politics that even a pragmatic politician, determined to reach across the aisle, will be whipsawed between the movement wings of his own and the opposition party, rendering the task of unifying the country seemingly impractical.

Before the maturation of executive-centered partisanship, party organizations displayed at least some commitment to collective responsibility in campaigning and governing, adapted party principles and policies to changes in the electorate and political environment, and added an important ingredient of pragmatism that moderated the winner-take-all politics of presidentialism. Presidentialism, unfiltered by vital party organizations, exposes representative democracies to the hazards that Linz fears: "Winners and losers are sharply defined for the entire period of the presidential mandate. There is no hope for shifts in alliances, expansion of the government's base of support through national-unity or emergency grand coalitions, [or] new elections in response to major new events."[38]

During Trump's tenure, the pathological "rigidity" of presidency-centered politics widened the distinct worlds that Democrats and Republicans now occupy, while opportunities for bipartisan agreements were sacrificed to the performative politics that the former TV star relished. Constant controversy and two impeachment episodes led to recriminations that encouraged Democrats and Republicans to view their opponents as existential threats to their way of life and eroded trust in the national government, including, as we have noted, the Supreme Court, the media, and election officials.

Biden thus inherited a fractured nation, engaged, as he emphasized during the 2020 campaign, in a battle for the country's soul. His hope to resolve that struggle by somehow soothing the nation's soul was made more elusive by the refusal of Trump and his followers to accept him as a legitimate president. Presidentialism, shorn of mediating institutions, entraps incoming presidents in a seemingly insoluble dilemma. On one hand, they must consider whether attempts to reconcile with their recent adversaries might weaken their attachment to the party's base. This was clearly a concern for Biden, who came into office pledging unity and reconciliation but faced intense pressure from progressive factions within his own party to pursue their causes and programs. On the other hand, new presidents must grapple with the possibility, which has grown more likely since the 1980s, that the opposition will refuse to reciprocate any peace offerings, leaving them politically isolated. Public rejection of an extended olive branch is likely to harden positions on both sides, leading to heightened, rather than diminished, hostility and polarization.

We saw this play out in the early days of Biden's presidency, when bipartisan overtures were often spurned and the polarization inherited from Trump's four years in the White House persisted. At the same time, President Biden's attempts at bipartisan outreach collided with the demands of his own Democratic base, even as crises like the ongoing COVID-19 pandemic demanded a united front. While Biden made considerable efforts to restore trust, the scars left by the Trump presidency, his ubiquitous presence in the aftermath of the strange denouement of the 2020 election, the all-consuming divide between Republican and Democratic loyalists, the high-stakes political maneuvering in the nation's capital and states about how to manage a global pandemic and the economic disruption it caused, and the powerful demands for a racial reckoning in the aftermath of the George Floyd killing underscored the imposing obstacles to the White House rallying unified national action. That Biden, a pragmatic centrist, has suffered the same low public approval ratings as his provocative predecessor suggests how the presidency itself has become a polarizing force in American politics. The combustible combination of political alienation and the rigidity that teed up a replay of the 2020 contest that a large majority of Democrats and Republicans wanted to avoid testifies to how the perils of presidentialism are undermining the foundation of the modern presidency and the elusive, exalted hope of its architects that it could become the steward of the public welfare.

It would be a mistake to assume that Biden is merely the victim of America's ongoing "cold civil war." Although he captured the Democratic nomination by positioning himself as the ballast that would keep his party from veering too far to the left, he nonetheless contributed to the partisan wars he sought to avoid. Despite Biden's personal inclinations, the political incentives of executive-centered partisanship encouraged him to sustain presidential dominion. His very attempt to declare independence from the progressive wing of his party in the first presidential debate—denying Trump's charge that the Democrats supported Medicare for All—led to Biden's boast, "I am the Democratic Party right now." Such a self-aggrandizing utterance in the service of pragmatism—unusual for the generally self-effacing former vice president—unwittingly gave voice to a powerful feature of contemporary American politics that not even Biden can avoid: presidents are the repository of party responsibility.

Despite his debate pledge, once in office, Biden soon learned that the demands of executive-centered partisanship made it impossible to distance himself from the activists in his party—and to fend off the relentless attacks from congressional Republicans. He pledged to "stop the shouting and lower the temperature." However, the fierce partisanship that plagued his first two years in office taught him a hard lesson—first acknowledged on Twitter, no less, as governors in red states thwarted his efforts to control a pandemic. "Republicans just have to let us do our job," he tweeted. "Just get out of the way."[39] Like many of his predecessors, including Barack Obama, who promised to be uniters, not dividers, Biden's campaign commitment to be a transcendent leader quickly gave way to personal ambitions and the powerful forces that push presidents to collaborate with the partisan base.

Every president since Franklin Roosevelt has considered the first hundred days of the administration as a critical testing ground. Staring down the polarization that resisted entreaties for national unity and his party's very small majorities in the House and the Senate, Biden sought from his first day in office to fulfill the pledge of his 2020 campaign to advance a second New Deal. In the final days of the campaign, he traveled to Warm Springs, Georgia, a place where Roosevelt went to use the therapeutic waters to rebuild himself from the ravages of polio. There, Biden promised to govern as "an American President"—"to restore our soul and save our country." At the same time, the Democratic candidate insisted that curing the pathologies that afflicted America—an "insidious virus, economic anguish, and systemic discrimination"—required a program no less ambitious than the New Deal, one that did more to divide than to unite the parties.[40]

Although Biden's race for the White House often promised a return to normalcy, he and the progressive Democrats, who dominated the congressional caucus, following the script of executive-centered partisanship, acted as though they had won a mandate to pursue a transformative program requiring massive new spending. Indeed, Biden's dreams of a second New Deal came with a $6 trillion price tag, which surpassed the most audacious mandates presidents have claimed in the past and bore little resemblance to his competing commitment "to bring the Republicans and Democrats together, and deliver economic relief for working families, and schools, and businesses."[41] Bill Clinton's budgetary proposals come closest to Biden's program, with his 1993 requests totaling $2.6 trillion in new spending. Obama's 2009 spending requests during the Great Recession, which came in at just $937 billion, paled in comparison to Biden's. Even in comparison to FDR's $67 billion request ($1.4 trillion, adjusted for inflation), Biden's programmatic demands were historically unprecedented and one-sided.

Despite narrow majorities, Biden—the seasoned Senate operator—got much of what he wanted. Determined to do something dramatic during his first hundred days, Biden persuaded congressional Democrats to rush through the $1.9 trillion American Rescue Plan—on a strict party-line vote, enacted as a reconciliation bill to circumvent a Senate filibuster. Later in the year, he pushed through a bipartisan infrastructure bill—the $1.5 trillion Infrastructure Investment and Jobs Act, which garnered thirteen Republican votes in the House and nineteen in the Senate, surpassing the sixty-vote threshold now routinely needed to get regular legislation through the upper congressional chamber. The final bipartisan infrastructure package represented a significant compromise, a slimmed-down version of the president's much more ambitious proposal to fund "human infrastructure"—a third of the original proposal dealt with subsidies for in-home care and tax credits for affordable housing. Biden was willing to accept these concessions to prove his bipartisan bona fides. As Mike Donilon, a senior adviser to Biden, said after the infrastructure bill was passed, the White House thought it "was important partly just to have a bipartisan agreement that in and of itself had meaning."[42] Nevertheless, not wanting to stray too far from his base, the president, relying once more on a reconciliation measure, secured another $900 billion in funds in 2022 when Congress, on a strict party-line vote, passed the Inflation Reduction Act, which included some substantial tax incentives to encourage alternative sources of energy.

Two aspects of the legislative process during the first two years of the Biden administration are noteworthy for how they reflected presidential partisanship. First, with the partial exception of the infrastructure bill, spending was dedicated to Democratic priorities—reflected in the enactment of progressive measures strictly along party lines. Second, and no less telling, is that the new budgetary initiatives omitted key priorities that were championed by the progressive wing of the party: a minimum wage increase, substantial spending to combat child poverty, and a program to shore up affordable housing.

Biden thus bet his presidency, and the future of the Democratic Party, on a *presidential* program—dubbed Bidenomics by the press—a plan that, for the time, obviated the most polarizing policies demanded by his left flank. Along with the bipartisan Chips and Science Act of 2022, which invested a significant amount of money in enhancing the semiconductor industry in the United States, Biden's economic program sought to thread the needle between globalization, which recent Democratic administrations had embraced, and Trump's right-wing nationalism. It emphasized job programs and place-based reform that promised to incentivize high-tech and alternative energy businesses to increase their domestic production and to expand opportunities in rural areas and small towns, which have abandoned the Democratic Party in droves. Yet the White House's partisan administration tilted the bipartisan Chips Act toward the progressive wing of the Democratic Party: conservatives' support for the bill dissipated as the Biden administration required that beneficiaries of the law provide workplace day care, an important priority of progressive activists and officeholders. Just as Barack Obama warmed to the labeling of his slightly left-of-center health care program as Obamacare, so Biden eventually took ownership of his economic policies. "I don't go around beating my chest. . . . [But] the press started calling it Bidenomics," he told reporters. When asked if his forbearance meant he disliked the term, Biden responded, "No, I like it. It's fine. Yeah, it's fine. Because it is my policy."[43]

Since the 1960s, Democrats and Republican have tied their electoral fortunes to the White House, with those in control of the presidency investing their hope in the incumbent and those in opposition heaping scorn and derision on the leader of their political opponents. Donald Trump's presidency, which aroused fierce loyalty and incurred hostile opposition, appeared to be a high-water mark of the polarizing potential of presidentialism. Like Trump, Biden enjoyed unified government during his first two years; like Trump, Biden also sought to capitalize on Congress's suppliance to executive-centered partisanship. In fact, Biden was far more successful than Trump in getting legislation passed, despite having smaller majorities. For example, Trump was unable to push an infrastructure deal through Congress. In doing so, however, Biden capitalized on billions of unused COVID-19 moneys that bipartisan majorities had allocated during a time of extreme duress and uncertainty.

The infrastructure legislation authorized additional flexibility for unspent COVID relief funds by states and localities—empowering communities to use pandemic relief for other purposes. Favorable circumstances, therefore, may explain as much of Biden's success in getting an infrastructure bill through Congress as his legislative acumen. Yet, Biden's adroit use of the levers of presidency-centered partisanship was also important, resulting in an impressive legislative record. Nevertheless, the enactment of four major pieces of legislation, two of which had enough Republican support to avoid filibusters, won him little public favor. The president's approval rating for the first two years in office averaged 44 percent. Even before the 2024 campaign heated up, the president had become the target of a crude rallying cry: "Let's go, Brandon!" (a conservative code for a vulgar slogan, "F— Joe Biden).

Some of this anger was a reaction to Biden's executive actions, which responded to the demands of the progressive wing of his party. Just as Biden frustrated progressive Democrats in budgetary negotiations, so he attempted to secure some of their most sought-after objectives through executive action. He launched his presidency with a dramatic display of executive-centered partisanship. During his first hundred days in office, he signed more executive actions than any other president since Franklin Roosevelt. Not coincidentally, Biden's approval rating at the hundred-day mark had the largest gap between Democrats and Republicans of any recent president: 96 percent of Democrats approved of his performance, but just 11 percent of Republicans did so.[44] With historically thin majorities in both chambers of Congress, the cascade of executive orders, memorandums, and other administrative actions demonstrated how intent the president was to address many of the immediate concerns of his most progressive partisan allies. About half of Biden's actions reversed the most controversial policies of the Trump administration, with particular attention to undoing his predecessor's immigration legacy by halting border wall construction, pausing most deportations, rescinding travel and immigration restrictions on several Muslim-majority countries, and safeguarding DACA protections for children of immigrants. Biden's pro-immigration policies, reflecting the strong bonds he and President Obama had forged with immigration rights groups, continued for the first three years of his presidency and contributed to the largest surge of migrants to the United States since the great immigration boom of the late 1800s and early 1900s—a phenomenon that Trump and his followers eagerly drew attention to during the general election campaign.[45]

Not surprisingly, many of the president's early administrative initiatives also targeted the COVID-19 crisis. Biden began his presidency with calls for a nonpartisan approach to the pandemic. He promised better management that would restore faith in science and expertise—and develop policies based on a broad national consensus. This faith in neutral competence, however, was short-lived. By the end of his first summer in office, partisan disagreement and virus mutations diminished the administration's early optimism. Cross-sectional and survey evidence tell a straightforward story: Trump supporters were far more likely to refuse the jab; and Biden's appeals to expertise and science did little to close the vaccination gap between red and blue America.[46] Vaccination hesitancy and refusal are not unique to the United States; however, whereas America began 2021 as the leader in vaccination rates, by the end of Biden's first year in office it had fallen behind dozens of countries, even some with far fewer resources. More Americans died on Biden's watch than were lost during Trump's term of office—less a function of bad policy than of toxic politics. Tellingly, the United States was the last high-income country (among eleven countries typically included in the Commonwealth Fund's International Health Policy Survey) to fully vaccinate at least 60 percent of its population, taking almost a full year to do so. Although access to the vaccine was an important factor, the obstacle that affected the United States, perhaps more than any other nation, was profound political politicization and polarization.[47] In the face of this hazardous political struggle, Biden focused his partisan guns on Republican governors who refused to heed federal guidance on new mask mandates and vaccines. "I say to these governors, please help," Biden fumed. "But if you aren't going to help, at least get out of the way."[48]

President Biden thus came to the realization that his prospects for a successful presidency appeared to depend less on his ability to reach a vanishingly small political center than to mobilize his fellow partisans. With good reason, critics blamed the Trump administration for politicizing the COVID-19 crisis. Yet Biden did not just let government experts rule. As vaccination rates plateaued amid the rise of the Delta variant of the virus, the administration preempted the decision-making authority of its own CDC and FDA to roll out third doses (boosters) of the Pfizer and Moderna vaccines by the end of September 2021. It took that long for both the FDA and the CDC to convene panels to assess and approve each vaccine. Moreover, when the CDC panel limited its recommendation to adults over age sixty-five and those with underlying medical conditions, the agency's director, Rochelle Walensky—in an unusual move—overruled the recommendations, to align policy with the White House's earlier stated goal of including health care workers, teachers, and others whose jobs put them at risk.[49]

Biden placed the White House directly in the crosshairs of the COVID-19 party wars in issuing a controversial vaccine mandate in the fall of 2021. In September, a month after the White House press secretary declared that it was "not the role of the federal government" to issue mandates, the administration reversed course.[50] The Department of Labor's Occupational Safety and Health Administration (OSHA) announced that it would implement an emergency rule requiring vaccines or weekly testing on all businesses with one hundred or more employees.[51] Unlike other public health orders in most European countries and US municipalities, which required proof of vaccination to use certain public services, the Biden administration's rule risked the economic livelihood of those who refused to comply with the mandate. Most Americans approved of the vaccine mandates announced by the White House, which also included vaccinations for all federal workers and contractors, as well health care workers at Medicare and Medicaid health care settings. An Axios-Ipsos poll conducted soon after Biden issued the orders found that 60 percent of Americans favored requiring vaccinations for federal employees and business with more than a hundred employees; however, only 30 percent of Republicans supported the mandates, compared with 80 percent of Democrats and 60 percent of independents.[52]

Republicans in Congress immediately sought to exploit the controversy to mobilize their base and reach out to independent voters worried about the economy. But the states were ground zero for the struggle, with Republican governors refusing to get out of the way. More than two dozen Republican-led states immediately sued to stop the mandate applying to large employers. An additional ten states filed lawsuits against the mandate that applied to Medicare and Medicaid, arguing it would "exacerbate an alarming shortage of health care workers, particularly in rural communities, that has already reached a boiling point."[53] Although the vaccine mandates involved a variety of complicated legal issues, the central question revolved around a debate over whether OSHA, which is charged with protecting workplace safety rather than public health, could enforce a vaccine mandate.

The Supreme Court gave its answer in January 2022. In a 6-to-3 decision that sharply divided the conservative and liberal justices, the Court blocked the Biden administration from enforcing a vaccine-or-testing-mandate for large employers. The unsigned majority opinion stressed the novelty and sweep of the mandate issued by OSHA, insisting that Congress had not authorized the agency to enforce public health measures. The Biden administration did win a modest victory when the Court allowed the more limited mandate requiring health care workers at facilities receiving federal money to be vaccinated. This order, five of the justices ruled, including conservatives John Roberts and Brett Kavanaugh, involved the administration of two federal programs and, consequently, was legitimately within the province of the executive branch. This was some consolation to the White House and showed that there were some cracks in the staunch conservative bloc in overseeing presidential power to deal with a national emergency of the first order. However, the employer decision undercut one of Biden's most significant attempts to tame the virus and left the country with a patchwork of state laws and policies, largely leaving companies and businesses on their own.[54]

As we described in chapter 4, Trump's consolidation of a conservative Court raises questions about whether the judiciary can be relied on to arbitrate cases related to presidential power fairly or if, as its critics charge, it is emboldened to issue opinions that draw it into the vortex of intractable partisanship. Certainly, the Biden administration could argue that the threat of a deadly pandemic made the leap from workplace safety to public health reasonable. Yet several legal scholars, even some sympathetic to the order, warned, as Biden himself feared, that such a novel interpretation of administrative power, involving a large swath of the economy, required a congressional law that clearly authorized the president to take such action.[55]

In the end, the dynamics of executive-centered partisanship encouraged the Biden administration to overcome its stated reluctance to avoid solving the vaccine problem through administrative fiat. The vaccine mandates thus marked a turning point, which revealed that President Biden's promise to mount a unified effort to win the war against COVID-19 was not possible without a creative and constitutionally dubious expansion of executive power. This drew the judiciary, remade by Trump, into a bitter partisan contest. Ultimately, the 6-to-3 Supreme Court majority concluded, "This is no everyday exercise of federal power. It is instead a significant encroachment into the lives—and health—of a vast number of employees."[56]

As we have argued throughout this book, extraordinary executive power is no longer limited to emergencies; rather, executive aggrandizement has become a routine feature of American politics. Indeed, as the pandemic subsided,

Biden continued to rely on pandemic-era authority to fulfill progressive goals. Most significant was his decision to pursue a program of debt relief that he promised to address during the 2020 campaign—and that progressive activists had been pushing for since he was inaugurated. In a historic action, the White House announced a sweeping student debt relief program in August 2022: the cancelation of $10,000 of student debt for those with an annual income of up to $125,000 ($250,000 for couples); and up to $20,000 for low- and middle-income borrowers who previously received a Pell Grant, dedicated to financial aid for those in need. In addition, the Biden administration extended the moratorium set in place during the height of the pandemic on monthly student loan payments and interest through the rest of 2022. Social activists hoped for even more relief, but they were grateful that their pressure tactics had pushed the Biden administration to take action that would provide relief to forty-three million people—at a cost of some $350 billion to the federal government. Significantly, this measure was directed at two critical, but hitherto dissatisfied, constituencies of the Democratic base: young people and minorities.

Once again, a conservative Supreme Court majority, determined to block ambitious initiatives of the liberal administrative state, showed that presidentialism was not unbound. Chief Justice John Roberts, writing for the majority, said the law the administration relied on to justify its executive action—the Higher Education Relief Opportunities for Students Act of 2003, usually called the HEROES Act—did not authorize the Biden administration to cancel the debt. Echoing its decision in the vaccine mandate case, the majority claimed that actions of such economic and political importance must receive explicit congressional authorization. The Heroes Act, enacted after the terrorist attacks on September 11, 2001, gave the secretary of education the power to "waive or modify any statutory or regulatory provision" to protect borrowers affected by "a war or other military operation or national emergency." To extend this law to student debt relief seemed a stretch, Roberts argued, especially since the public health emergency had subsided.[57]

Although the Court, risking once again being drawn into the storm of the current party wars, blocked this action, centering so much emphasis on presidential politics and government dangerously undermines the foundations of American democracy. The politics of debt relief are indicative of trends during Trump's presidency that have been highlighted throughout this book: under the cover of an emergency, the president unilaterally enacted significant policy change, with no formal debate, with no role for representative officials, and with deeply polarizing consequences. Republicans were quick to pounce on reports that the $300 billion in additional costs would largely support high-income earners (since most student loan debt is held by higher-income individuals), and confined to just 13 percent of the adult population, all while inflation reached levels not seen since the 1970s.

Even though he lost the legal battle, Biden shored up his position as a president who tried everything in his power to deliver for an important constituency within the Democratic coalition—young, college-educated, largely urban voters. Yet Biden's effort at coalition management defied his hope to unify the country—to soothe the nation's soul in the face of Trump's never-ending provocations. Biden's partisan administration only further entrenched the divisions between red and blue America, underscoring the challenges of navigating the "perils of presidentialism" in a deeply divided society. A move that was hailed as a victory by progressive Democrats such as Senators Bernie Sanders and Elizabeth Warren, the White House's pursuit of debt relief is indicative of the inherent divisiveness of a presidential system that Linz warned against. In bypassing the complexities of the constitutional system of checks and balances, policy pursued by executive fiat deepens societal and partisan divisions. As much as this maneuver energized the Democratic base, it also alienated and inflamed the opposition, leading to further political polarization, and heightening the stakes of the next presidential election. Tellingly, in the wake of the Supreme Court rejecting his debt relief program, the Biden administration doubled down on partisan administration. Soon thereafter, the White House announced that it would liberalize the terms of federal loans granted under an income-driven repayment program. As a result, 804,000 borrowers had their loans canceled, erasing a total of $39 billion in debt. That comes on top of previous cancellations that had provided $66 billion in relief to 2.2 million borrowers—already more than any previous president.[58]

To this end, the Biden presidency, like that of Trump before him, offers insights into the potential hazards of a highly empowered presidency in an era of extreme political polarization—a time when the stakes of national administrative action are heightened, destabilizing, and seemingly inescapable. Whatever the arguments over whether debt relief was sound policy, Biden's actions on student loans highlighted the divisive potential of executive power in a socially and economically divided America. By unilaterally advancing debt forgiveness, the administration not only ignited debates over economic justice and responsibility but also underscored the presidency's capacity to drive policy that sharply delineates its coalition, thus deepening the factional divides within American politics. Millions of voters may not have known the intricacies of dozens of incremental eligibility changes, but Trump delivered a forceful rallying cry that Biden's actions were "vile" and "very, very unfair to the millions and millions of people who have paid their debt through hard work."[59] In this vein, it is little wonder why college-educated voters turned toward the Democratic Party with even greater force in 2024, while non-college-educated voters, including a large number of nonwhite, non-college-educated voters turned toward Trump. The reality of American politics is that the president is no longer a unifying figure but a factional leader wielding executive power to push through policies that cater to a personalized coalition. With Trump as the poster child for the hazards of presidentialism, his imprint on American politics has so institutionalized presidency-centered partisanship that even a pragmatic, often forbearing, politician like Joe Biden cannot escape the siren call of executive dominion.

THE ELUSIVENESS OF UNITY AND NATIONAL STEWARDSHIP

The persistence of presidentialism and the intractability of polarization does not mean that Biden's leadership is the mirror image of Trump's, or that the Democratic and Republican parties' contributions to the fracturing of America are equivalent. The "radicalization" of the Republican Party, which has led not just the base but also party leaders to apologize for violent rioters and to embrace conspiratorial tales about election fraud, poses a grave danger to American democracy. That is the most significant consequence of Trump's presidency.

Some of the criminal proceedings against Donald Trump are ongoing as we complete this volume; however, Trump's return to the White House and the Supreme Court's expansive ruling on presidential immunity—issued in July 2024—make it very unlikely that Trump will face further criminal probes at either the state or the federal level. Still, there are lessons in the drawn-out legal travails of a major partisan figure. It is noteworthy that Republican leaders and base supporters continued to support the former president even as the trials took place. And while it decried the excesses of Trump's presidentialism, an increasingly left-leaning Democratic Party never sought to redress the perils of presidentialism through institutional reform, as opposed to legal prosecution. Our fear remains that neither the indictments of Trump nor his incendiary campaign rhetoric is likely to arouse sustained opposition to the pathologies of presidentialism. Trump's recklessness is a glaring symptom of a political disease that afflicts both Republicans and Democrats. Criminal probes into a national leader's conduct were not just an effort to hold the former president accountable for denigrating the Constitution; these proceedings were also a stark warning that the guardrails that might have discouraged such behavior are enfeebled. In most other advanced representative democracies, such as France and Japan, when former heads of state have been convicted of crimes, it has come in the aftermath of rigorous legal investigations into leaders' abuse of the public trust to advance their own financial self-interests. Or, as noted, in the case of Brazil's former president Jair Bolsonaro, or Richard Nixon in the Watergate probes, efforts to corrupt constitutional norms or institutions have led to political exile.

But Trump's alleged crimes were different from criminal probes that have held corrupt public leaders accountable and resulted in strengthening or reforming constitutions. As a result of the Republican Party's association with Trump's machinations, and its loyalists' perception that law enforcement has been weaponized by Democrats and prosecutors, Trump's indictments posed a grave threat to America's constitutional republic. In the first indictment of a former president, issued by the Manhattan district attorney Alvin Bragg, an elected Democrat, Trump faced charges that he failed to disclose payments to Stormy Daniels, a porn star with whom Trump is rumored to have had an affair. As the indictment conceded, such payments were not illegal, and Trump's attempts to prevent Daniels from speaking were well known prior to the 2016 election. But the attempt to cover it up, according to Bragg, amounted to criminal conspiracy. Such unprecedented prosecutorial discretion was celebrated on the left as much as it was vilified on the right. Even some so-called Never Trumpers rushed to the president's side to support him in what they viewed as another partisan witch hunt against the former president. The night Trump first appeared in the Manhattan courtroom, his campaign broke its one-day fundraising record (first set on the night of his first impeachment) by hauling in over $4 million.

Nearly two months later, Trump was handed his second indictment, this time by a special counsel, Jack Smith, who was appointed by Attorney General

Merrick Garland to investigate Trump's mishandling of classified documents. Because this is generally adjudged a more serious charge, few of even the former president's most ardent allies defended him on the merits of the case. But more than Bragg's attempts to criminalize Trump, the federal indictment seemed to play more directly into the narrative that Trump had been building for years: the federal government cannot be trusted; Democrats play by a different set of rules; the "deep state" is out to get conservatives. The unprecedented nature of this indictment might have abetted Trump's victimhood. He made history as the first president to face federal criminal charges. He also became the first major party candidate facing federal charges to promise to continue running even if he was thrown in prison by the Justice Department of the incumbent president he was running against: Joe Biden.

It is not clear what Trump had to gain in keeping classified documents with him during his post-presidency and putting the country at risk by haphazardly storing them in easily accessible locations at his Florida resort, Mar-a-Lago. "The blame for this calamity rests solely on Mr. Trump and his childish impulse to keep mementos from his time in the Oval Office, no matter what the law says," the Republican strategist and former chief political adviser to President George W. Bush, Karl Rove, wrote.[60] Trump's efforts to suborn classified documents may have been puerile; however, his hoarding these materials may very well have put the country's national security in jeopardy. It is very troubling, therefore, that Trump's primary opponents offered tepid criticisms of the former president—more willing to endorse his unsubstantiated claims that this was clear-cut evidence that President Biden, who also had some classified documents in his possession (though far fewer, which he returned as soon as these items were discovered), was benefiting from a double standard in the enforcement of the Presidential Records Act.

As serious as the hush money and classified documents cases were, it was Trump's third indictment—the first that charged Trump with a crime during his presidency—that was most serious, and which cut to the matter of whether he posed an existential threat to American democracy.[61] Also brought by Special Counsel Jack Smith, this four-count indictment, relying heavily on evidence gathered by the Select House Committee to investigate the attack on the Capitol, charged Trump with employing the authority of government to overturn a free and fair election. To the surprise of many legal experts and pundits, the indictment did not charge the former president with launching an insurrection. Instead, staying away from the thorny issue of free speech, the indictment charged that Trump "exploited the disruption," using the riot to further his objective of stopping the certification of the election, including the "fake electors" scheme, and pressuring Vice President Pence to obstruct the final count of electors.[62] Despite the grave nature of the charges, which made the previous two crimes seem small by comparison, Republican loyalists and leaders, often without reading the indictment, parroted MAGA talking points: Trump was a victim, the charges were part of a partisan witch hunt, and Joe Biden's Justice Department was weaponized to undermine the campaign of the strongest Republican contender—the candidate who most threatened Biden's 2024 reelection campaign. A *New York Times* poll taken two weeks before Trump was charged showed that when asked their view of the former president's actions after the 2020 election, 72 percent of Republicans stated that he was "just exercising his right to contest the election."[63]

Despite all of the investigations, Trump's fate was decided in the court of public opinion. The legitimacy of the American legal system—a system Trump now heads again—seems to be the greatest casualty. The efforts of a special counsel, by no means a political hack, to hold Trump accountable to the rule of law more deeply implicated the Republican Party in Trump's personal recriminations and further aggravated conservatives' faith in the criminal justice system. At the same time, Joe Biden, saddled by the legal troubles of his son Hunter, struggled to assert his distance from the actions of his Justice Department—from the charge of Trump and his MAGA supporters, without evidence, that he ordered legal investigations of his most prominent political rival. After months of denying he would interfere with the administration of justice, the president issued a full and unconditional pardon for Hunter in December, waving aside years of legal trouble, including a federal conviction for illegally buying a gun and for tax evasion. Although the president insisted he still believed in the justice system, he acted because "raw politics had infected the process, and it led to a miscarriage of justice."[64] President Biden thus might have unwittingly abetted his political opponents' assault on the Justice Department, which they promised to intensify during Trump 2.0.

Although the current legal system is roiled by the slings and arrows of the right, it is important to recall that it suffered similar criticism from the left in 2016, when there was widespread outrage over then FBI director James Comey's decision to reopen the agency's investigation into Hillary Clinton's private email server just days before the election. Though she was not charged, Secretary Clinton lost critical momentum due to Comey's discretionary power, which very well might have cost her the election. Trumpian politics of resentment have bestowed bipartisan distrust on the country's law enforcement and electoral system. Playing the victim, he has left the country more deeply divided, unable even to agree on the foundational principle that no person—not even a president or former president—is above the law. Trump's is more than a personal trial; our democratic institutions, once a beacon of liberal democracy, are increasingly tarnished by presidentialism and the executive-centered partisanship it spawns.

America's exceptional experiment with presidentialism was not only a function of its catchall parties but also, as Linz emphasized, the "moderate" nature of public opinion. Teasing apart these two variables, however, is a fool's errand. Public opinion is a product of party messages, elite cues, and long-standing "brand" loyalties.[65] At the same time, parties play the game with the cards they are dealt—if society is polarized, then parties are sure to follow the votes. Presidentialism, however, animates the dangerous cycle of partisan and societal polarization. Presidentialism's influence on the interplay between public opinion and party politics was vividly on display during Trump's term in office and its chaotic aftermath. His administration leveraged harsh partisan messaging and stoked societal divisions to radicalize a fervent base of support. In doing so, Trump seized power and fulfilled many long-standing policy goals of the party's conservative base: the promotion of "traditional" values, a trade war with China, the disentangling of international alliances, a retreat from climate change initiatives, and a draconian immigration policy. After leaving office, Trump continued to champion this brand of national conservatism; however, increasingly, the advance of a more populist form of conservatism has been overshadowed by his election denialism—the Big Lie—and legal travails. The fact that endorsement of the Big Lie is now a litmus test for party leaders lends further evidence to the idea that the Grand Old Party is institutionally vapid—a victim of the primacy now placed on presidential reputation and legacy in the electoral prospects of both parties.

Prior to the emergence of executive-centered partisanship, parties, as collective and highly decentralized organizations, prevented the consolidation of power and authority in the hands of a single individual, forcing presidents to collaborate with Congress and the states and to seek a broad consensus that included a diverse array of interests. The consolidation of the modern executive office during the long tenure of Franklin Roosevelt embodied the hopes of progressive reformers who wanted to overcome the state and local orientation of the party system, which was suited to congressional primacy and poorly organized for progressive action on the part of the national government, and to establish a national executive-centered party, which would be more suitably organized for the expression of national purposes.[66]

Two of the most prominent scholars of the American presidency, William Howell and Terry Moe, echoing the refrain of reformers during the Progressive Era and New Deal, have defended executive power as a necessity to manage the extraordinary issues that are tearing at the fabric of America's civic culture: economic inequality, climate change, multiculturalism, immigration, and institutional racism. Only the presidency, they argue—the national office—has the capacity to serve the national interest. Witness, "There are no legislators on Mount Rushmore."[67] Congress, they claim, is inadequate to the pressing tasks our political and policy problems demand; a decentralized system privileges provincial interests that only the president can transcend. In truth, Howell and Moe argue, the United States has always needed strong presidential leadership to overcome the challenges posed by its large and diverse society and complicated constitutional structure. They acknowledge that unilateral executive action and carte blanche presidential control over the bureaucratic state are dangerous. But these threats cannot be ameliorated by restoring interbranch rivalry. Rather, Howell and Moe propose the remedy of giving the president more power over the legislative process—by extending the White House's authority to use fast-track authority, historically limited to trade policy, to all forms of legislation.

Giving presidents the incentive to engage more with the legislative process might check the current tendency to subordinate legislation to executive administration. Yet subjecting Congress to an up or down vote of presidential proposals might enlist the House and Senate in a winner-take-all politics that further weakens the prospects of forging majority coalitions in a large and diverse society. As the distinguished Congress scholar Frances Lee has written, "The Howell and Moe proposal for a universal fast track would not deny Congress the authority to pass judgment on the president's proposals. But what they envision—simple majority rule, up or down votes—is at odds with congressional practice. Perhaps presidents might aim to do what Congress currently does—assemble big bipartisan coalitions. But presidential administrations are not set up to succeed in doing this, even if they had incentive to do so."[68]

Thinking beyond proposals for reforming the function of the presidency, it is worth noting that the celebration of presidential greatness is a unique

American tradition: no other country has anything like a Mount Rushmore. For all the excesses of Trump's presidency, it reveals how exceptional presidential leadership—memorialized on a South Dakota mountain with larger-than-life carvings of George Washington, Thomas Jefferson, Abraham Lincoln, and Theodore Roosevelt—has now become a routine feature of American politics. Since Franklin Roosevelt, who came to office after the carving of Mount Rushmore was underway, all presidents, even seemingly forbearing ones like Jimmy Carter and Gerald Ford, have exercised extraordinary power.

Until Trump's ascendance to the White House, most presidents had not worn their ambition for grandeur on their sleeve. Trump unabashedly made known his wish to be on the mountaintop during the July 4 celebration that South Dakota governor Kristi Noem organized in 2020 at Mount Rushmore as the pandemic raged across the country. On the eve of this event, Trump tweeted out a picture of himself—an image that made him look as though he were the fifth presidential bust on the iconic monument. But the next day, rather than celebrate the principles of the Revolution that unite Americans—the rhetorical practice of those celebrated on Mount Rushmore—the president gave remarks laced with partisan ripostes that denigrated his political opponents as enemies of the republic—a charge that reverberated through the 2024 campaign:

> One of their political weapons is "Cancel Culture"—driving people from their jobs, shaming dissenters, and demanding total submission from anyone who disagrees. This is the very definition of totalitarianism, and it is completely alien to our culture and our values, and it has absolutely no place in the United States of America. (Applause.) This attack on our liberty, our magnificent liberty, must be stopped, and it will be stopped very quickly. We will expose this dangerous movement, protect our nation's children, end this radical assault, and preserve our beloved American way of life.[69]

The toxic atmosphere of Trump's presidency and its tumultuous aftermath has provoked the Democrats to respond in kind. Perhaps the signature speech of President Biden's presidency was given on September 1, 2022, remarks that raised the stakes of the approaching midterm election. Having despaired of soothing the raging tribalism of America, the president harshly attacked his political opponents in remarks delivered before the iconic facade of Independence Hall in Philadelphia, the site where the Declaration of Independence, justifying the Revolution, was signed. Biden, warning of the "radicalization" of the Republican Party, insisted that this was not a political speech, as the

Marine Guard in the backdrop was meant to symbolize. But it was a political speech meant to warn the American people that it was not just Donald Trump who threatened the foundations our republic—the Democratic candidate's message during the 2020 campaign—but also the MAGA Republicans he had bewitched:

> Now, I want to be very clear—very clear up front: Not every Republican, not even the majority of Republicans, are MAGA Republicans. Not every Republican embraces their extreme ideology.
>
> I know because I've been able to work with these mainstream Republicans.
>
> But there is no question that the Republican Party today is dominated, driven, and intimidated by Donald Trump and the MAGA Republicans, and that is a threat to this country.
>
> These are hard things.
>
> But I'm an American President—not the President of red America or blue America, but of all America.
>
> And I believe it is my duty—my duty to level with you, to tell the truth no matter how difficult, no matter how painful.
>
> And here, in my view, is what is true: MAGA Republicans do not respect the Constitution. They do not believe in the rule of law. They do not recognize the will of the people.[70]

Biden presumed to represent the nation; however, most Republicans, as well as independents, viewed his remarks as highly partisan—the angry words of a factional leader posing, with Marine Guard in tow, as the steward of the public welfare.

As we have acknowledged throughout this book, there was much truth to Biden's warning. Only one side has stormed the venerated halls of American democracy; we make no false equivalency. But to pretend these remarks were somehow above politics testifies to how presidentialism has displaced collective partisan debate and rendered conflict resolution a chimera. Trump's presidency and the fractured nation it left in its wake leave us with the uneasy conclusion that there will be no more presidents celebrated as worthy candidates for Mount Rushmore. It is fitting, perhaps, that there is not more room on that mountain, even as most modern presidents bask in the resplendence of the office. For the attempt to realize that promise of presidentialism, by placing greater faith in the presidency, will only bring us one step closer to constitutional peril.

Postscript

Donald Trump won a stunning victory in 2024. Despite the novel features of the campaign—an ex-president surviving two assassination attempts, an incumbent president forced to step aside for his vice president, felony charges leveled against the ex-president and the sitting president's son—Trump's successful tour of redemption likely ensures that he will renew the politics of disruption that gained momentum during his first term, with less resistance than he faced during his first four years as president. When he is inaugurated on January 20, 2025, Republicans will control the White House, the House, and the Senate; moreover, with Trump determined to hit the ground running after his reelection, his appointments and his plans to unravel civil service protections will surround him with loyalists who will advance the MAGA program and weaponize national administrative power to exact retribution from his political enemies, menacingly anointed during the campaign as "the enemies from within."

As Trump and his political supporters celebrated what they interpreted as a "massive mandate,"[1] political commentators of all political stripes breathlessly celebrated or fearfully conceded the arrival of a new political era. The triumph of a right-wing populist movement signaled an effective countermobilization against the political and economic changes of the past half century: free trade and the transition from an industrial to an information economy, the surge of immigration and massive demographic shifts, the growing inequality between metropolitan and rural areas of the country, and gender politics that challenged the traditional status of men and conventional sexual identities.[2]

Of course, that new political era began years earlier, despite the travails, missteps, and unexpected "exogenous" forces roiling Trump's first administration. Nevertheless, Trump's reelection confirms, more resoundingly than we might have expected, that his sway over the Republican Party and American politics is not the triumph of a cult of personality; rather, it brought the systemic developments that have remade the American political landscape over the past half century into stark reality. It marked a new stage in the ongoing struggle between progressives and conservatives—between the coalition of the ascendant (the scattered but potentially powerful alliance of young people, minorities, the LGBTQ+ community, and educated professionals that animated

Barack Obama's presidency) and the coalition of restoration (composed of blue-collar, religiously devout, and nonurban whites, forged during Trump's campaigns and presidency). In 2016, Trump made substantial gains among voters without college degrees; since then, he has shaken the new progressive coalition, increasing support among Black, Hispanic, Asian American, and young working-class voters.

Consequently, the culture wars that the tumultuous sixties unleashed have become intertwined with economic issues, significantly advancing, if not bringing to a culmination, a partisan realignment that has transformed the class conflict that agitated the New Deal political order into an educational divide. Democrats now depend on the support of the former Republican base of college-educated professionals, while Republicans presume to replace the Democrats as the party of the working class, even as the president-elect forms a close alliance with the richest man in the world, Elon Musk. Until the 2024 election, Democrats had reason to believe that demographics were destiny—their view that a majority of minorities, supported by cultural and political elites, could coalesce around issues such as immigration, criminal justice, and LGBTQ+ rights. This faith in a multiracial and sexually liberated future persuaded many progressives that right-wing populism was sustained by "constitutional gerrymandering"—the Electoral College, the Senate, and the courts. Kamala Harris's campaign epitomized those concerns, rallying around a message to "save democracy" and seeking refuge as "institutionalists"—a message congenial to the Democratic Party's core base of well-educated and credentialed elites, despite the fact that a majority of American voters in 2024 indicated that they believed Trump, not Harris, was the most likely to preserve America's constitutional experiment.[3] Time will tell how committed Trump is to his core policy messages and his growing constituency. At the very least, though, his victories in the Electoral College and the popular vote shattered the left's faith that inevitable forces privileged a changing, more educated, and more diverse America. The idea that the MAGA movement would wither away due to old age or rural depopulation was fully discredited with Trump's reelection.

The Democrats' defense of institutions and optimism about the country's future might have been their undoing. To be sure, the Biden administration departed from the information age and global policies of the Clinton and Obama administrations. He pushed through Congress, sometimes with bipartisan support, place-based policies that joined progressive commitments such as addressing climate change to programs that promised to create good-paying jobs for those without a college degree in areas desolated by the shift from an industrial to a knowledge economy. However, "Bidenomics" did not sell well at the polls, partly because it did not address more immediate "kitchen table" issues, most notably high inflation and interest rates that squeezed middle- and working-class Americans. Just as important, Biden's economic program was ensnared by an executive-centered administrative state that seemed far removed from people's everyday lives and pushed funding out the door too slowly to ameliorate the economic stress that affected working-class families.[4] While communities waited for federal dollars to work through the grant-making process, the White House offered little consolation in the idea that inflation was merely "transitory" when not outright denying the fact that inflation ballooned during Biden's first year in office; given the delays and persistent inflation, the federal government actually spent *less* on infrastructure and transportation the last two years of the Biden administration than before passing the Bipartisan Infrastructure Law.[5] And a year after signing the Inflation Reduction Act into law, Biden even let slip that all the new spending had "less to do with inflation than it does providing alternatives to economic growth."[6]

Amid the anxieties most voters felt over rising prices and high interest rates, as well as porous borders and bellicosity in Ukraine and the Middle East, Joe Biden's aged and tempered leadership and the "politics of joy" that animated Kamala Harris's campaign fell short in the face of Trump's populist campaign that promised strong, if potentially dangerous, leadership. In effect, the MAGA movement's celebration of a strongman who would cut through the Gordian knot of an elite establishment was accepted by voters who had misgivings about Trump but believed he would "get things done." This judgment fell far short of a "massive mandate"; like previous presidents since the late 1960s, Trump's mandate is shrouded in factionalism that intractably divides the nation. The popular vote was very close, and GOP majorities in the House and Senate will be very narrow. However, the fervent pursuit of a mandate, no matter how tenuous, portends a second Trump presidency that will have more leeway than the first to attack the norms and institutions of liberal democracy, with the promise of fixing—or deconstructing—what many Americans had come to see as a rigged system.

Trump 2.0's antinomianism will agitate, as was the case in his first term, polarizing cultural issues. As important as the economy was to Trump's victory, he sought to mobilize his base with the poisonous exploitation of the cultural issues he has stressed since descending the escalator at Trump Tower in 2015: immigration, law and order, and "traditional" values. Trump, not Kamala Harris, appealed to the identity politics that has roiled the country since the late 1960s—a battle over the foundational question of who belongs to the American political community. Long the principal fault line of American politics, the cultural and economic changes of the past half century have made a struggle that once erupted episodically a routine feature of political life in the United States. There is no prospect that either the Democrats or the Republicans can escape identity politics, even as economic issues have increasingly been joined to, and further aggravated the conflict over, what it means to be an American. The Trump campaign's outlandish claims that Haitian immigrants in Springfield, Ohio, who were in the United States legally, were abducting and eating their neighbors' pets foretold just how craven Trump's sectarian nationalism might prove to be in a second term. The catchphrase "mass deportation now"—prominently displayed on signs at Trump's rallies—replaced "build the wall" as the rallying cry of the 2024 Republican campaign.

The immigration effect on Springfield, Ohio, suggests an opening that might have led to a fruitful debate between Democrats and Republicans over immigration—for example, an exchange highlighting the trade-offs between the economic and cultural benefits of immigration and the stress that porous borders might put on the schools and infrastructure of towns and cities in the United States. Yet the presidentialism that now dominates partisan conflict and public action in the United States transformed the potential for democratic debate and resolution—squelched by Trump's opposition to a bipartisan immigration reform bill hammered out in the early 2024—into a Manichaean struggle that invariably leads to dueling executive actions that undermine the rule of law and denigrate the system of checks and balances. Indeed, Trump's plans for his first day in office call not only for a draconian assault on immigration but also for a more comprehensive and audacious redeployment of administrative power: close the US-Mexico border; begin what Trump says will be "the largest deportation program in American history"; expedite permits for drilling and fracking; roll back environmental regulations; pardon people convicted of crimes related to the January 6, 2021, insurrection at the US Capitol; sign an executive order that would cut federal funding for any school "pushing critical race theory, transgender insanity and other inappropriate racial, sexual or political content onto the lives of our children"; roll back President Joe Biden's electric vehicle policies; and enact tariffs on goods coming in from Mexico, Canada, and China.[7]

It is far from certain that such a provocative beginning will lead to enduring policy change. These promises, as well as Trump's controversial nominations for key government positions, might very well lead to an overreach—one that leads to a backlash that reenergizes the Democratic Party and alienates Independents and Republicans at the margins of the MAGA movement. Yet the very pursuit of such a program by executive fiat—with a more suppliant party than the one that surrounded Trump in his first term—will place considerable stress on the norms and institutions of American constitutional government, already attenuated by the populist attack of institutions that has wended its way through the political system during the past half century.

The pledge to pardon the January 6 rioters and the threat to prosecute Liz Cheney, the vice chair of the committee that investigated the riot, on the trumped-up charge of "witness tampering," reveal that in spite of winning the 2024 election, Trump and the MAGA movement are determined to undermine the foundation of democratic representation: the peaceful transfer of power. Refusing even to accept victory graciously, he and his followers continue to perpetuate the "Big Lie" that the 2020 election was rigged and those who stormed the Capitol in an effort to overturn a free and fair election were participants in a "day of love"—for a demagogue who is infatuated with the possibilities of subverting republican government with an American version of authoritarian rule.[8]

Will the worst tendencies of a second Trump term arouse a vigilant and engaged citizenry that rededicates itself to representative democracy? Will the Democratic and Republican parties free themselves from the chains of presidentialism and restore a meaningful sense of collective partisan responsibility? Can conservatives and progressives carry on the never-ending struggle over who "We the People" are with a renewed faith in foundational civic values and political intuitions? These are the questions we raised at the beginning of the book. The events of the last year should elicit a clarion call for new safeguards that prevent presidents, as Hamilton feared, from "flattering the prejudices" of the people only to "betray their interests."[9]

Notes

PREFACE

1. Nicholas F. Jacobs and Sidney M. Milkis, "'I Alone Can Fix It' Donald Trump, the Administrative Presidency, and Hazards of Executive-Centered Partisanship," *The Forum* 15, no. 3 (2017): 583–613.
2. Andrew Restuccia, "The Sanctification of Donald Trump," *Politico*, April 30, 2019, https://www.politico.com/story/2019/04/30/donald-trump-evangelicals-god-1294578.
3. H. H. Gerth and C. Wright Mills, eds., *From Max Weber: Essays in Sociology* (New York: Oxford University Press, 1946), 250.
4. Tim Alberta, *The Kingdom, the Power, and the Glory: American Evangelicals in an Age of Extremism* (New York: HarperCollins, 2023).
5. For example, see Nicholas F. Jacobs and Sidney M. Milkis, *What Happened to the Vital Center? Presidentialism, Populist Revolt, and the Fracturing of America* (New York: Oxford University Press, 2024).
6. On the ideological and political differences among the "deeply engaged," see Yana Krupnikov and John Barry Ryan, *The Other Divide: Polarization and Disengagement in American Politics* (New York: Cambridge University Press, 2022); Eitan Hersh, *Politics Is for Power: How to Move beyond Political Hobbyism, Take Action, and Make Real Change* (New York: Simon & Schuster, 2020).
7. Matt Grossman and David A. Hopkins, *Asymmetric Politics: Ideological Republicans and Group Interest Democrats* (New York: Oxford University Press, 2016).

INTRODUCTION

1. The distinction for military generals accounts for Zachary Taylor, the major figure in the Mexican-American War and Ulysses S. Grant, the commanding general for the Union army during the Civil War. Herbert Hoover's first election was to the presidency.
2. Steven Levitsky and Donald Ziblatt, *How Democracies Die: What History Reveals about Our Future* (New York: Crown, 2019).
3. Charlie Savage, "Incitement to Riot? What Trump Told Supporters before Mob Stormed Capitol," *New York Times*, January 10, 2021.
4. Richard Neustadt, *Presidential Power and the Modern Presidents: The Politics of Leadership from Roosevelt to Reagan*, 4th ed. (New York: Free Press, 1990).
5. Gerald Ford, the House minority leader, was not elected, not even to the vice presidency. Jimmy Carter, the former governor of Georgia, never held a federal office and won largely by demonstrating his outside-Washington credentials. Ronald Reagan, too, never held national office; the former governor of California was the insurgent, anti-Washington candidate for decades before finally capturing the nomination in 1980. Both Bill Clinton

and George W. Bush were popular governors but only built national profiles during their presidential campaigns. And while Barack Obama was a sitting US senator, he was only four years into his first term when he was elected president; before that, he was a local community organizer and state legislator in Illinois.

6. Nicholas Jacobs, Demond King, and Sidney Milkis, "Building a Conservative State: Partisan Polarization and the Redeployment of Administrative Power," *Perspectives on Politics* 17, no. 2 (June 2019): 453–69.

7. Alexander Hamilton, *Federalist* No. 71, in Alexander Hamilton, James Madison, and John Jay, *The Federalist Papers*, ed. Clinton Rossiter, with an introduction and notes by Charles Kessler (New York: Signet Classics, 2003), 431.

8. James David Barber, *The Presidential Character: Predicting Performance in the White House* (Englewood Cliffs, NJ: Prentice-Hall, 1972).

9. Glass quoted in Thomas Edsall, "The Roots of Trump's Rage," *New York Times*, November 22, 2023, https://www.nytimes.com/2023/11/22/opinion/trump-danger-rage-psychology.html?unlocked_article_code=1.AU0.54-2.to8UP5vEu896&smid=em-share.

10. Max Farrand, ed., *The Records of the Federal Convention*, vol. 1 (New Haven, CT: Yale University Press, 1937), 65–66.

11. Alexander Hamilton, *Federalist* No. 70, in Hamilton, Madison, and Jay, *Federalist Papers*, 423, 426.

12. Alexander Hamilton, *Federalist* No. 68, in Hamilton, Madison, and Jay, *Federalist Papers*, 68, 412.

13. Stephen Skowronek, *The Politics Presidents Make* (Cambridge, MA: Harvard University Press, 1993), 20.

14. Skowronek, *The Politics Presidents Make*, chap. 3.

15. William Leuchtenburg, *In the Shadow of FDR: From Harry Truman to Barack Obama*, 4th ed. (Ithaca, NY: Cornell University Press, 2010).

16. Bob Woodward, *Rage* (New York: Simon & Schuster, 2020); Bob Woodward, *Fear: Trump in the White House* (New York: Simon & Schuster, 2018); Bob Woodward and Robert Costa, *Peril* (New York: Simon & Schuster, 2022).

17. Philip Rucker and Carol Leonning, *A Very Stable Genius: Donald Trump's Testing of America* (New York: Penguin, 2020); Philip Rucker and Carol Leonning, *I Alone Can Fix It: Donald Trump's Catastrophic Final Year* (New York: Penguin, 2021).

18. Maggie Haberman, *Confidence Man: The Making of Donald Trump and the Breaking of America* (New York: Penguin, 2022).

19. Jeffrey Tulis, *The Rhetorical Presidency* (Princeton, NJ: Princeton University Press, 1987).

20. On this development, see Nicholas F. Jacobs and Sidney Milkis, *What Happened to the Vital Center? Presidentialism, Populist Revolt, and the Fracturing of America* (New York: Oxford University Press, 2022).

21. Susan Hennessey and Benjamin Wittes, *Unmasking the Presidency: Donald Trump's War on the World's Most Powerful Office* (New York: Farrar, Straus & Giroux, 2020), 8–9.

22. Bob Bauer and Jack Goldsmith, *After Trump: Reconstructing the Presidency* (Washington, DC: Lawfare Press, 2020), 2.

23. Saikrishna Prakash, *Imperial from the Beginning: The Constitution of the Original Executive* (New Haven, CT: Yale University Press, 2015).

24. "From Thomas Jefferson to John Breckinridge, 12 August 1803," Founders Online, National Archives, https://founders.archives.gov/documents/Jefferson/01-41-02-0139.

25. Alexander Hamilton, *Federalist* No. 68, 412.

26. Alexander Hamilton, *Federalist* No. 68, 412; see also Hamilton, *Federalist* No. 70, 423, 426.

27. James Madison, *Federalist* No. 51, in Hamilton, Madison, and Jay, *Federalist Papers*, 319.

28. Thomas P. Slaughter, *The Whiskey Rebellion: Frontier Epilogue to the American Revolution* (New York: Oxford University Press, 1986).

29. Abraham Lincoln, letter to Albert G. Hodges, in *The Evolving Presidency: Landmark Documents*, 6th ed, ed. Michael Nelson (Washington, DC: CQ Press, 2019), 98–99.

30. "Helvidius" Number 4, [14 September] 1793," Founders Online, National Archives, https://founders.archives.gov/documents/Madison/01-15-02-0070.

31. Woodrow Wilson, *Constitutional Government in the United States* (New York: Columbia University Press, 1908), 78–79.

32. Woodrow Wilson, "December 7, 1920: Eighth Annual Message," Miller Center, University of Virginia, https://millercenter.org/the-presidency/presidential-speeches/december-7-1920-eighth-annual-message.

33. Randolph Bourne, "War Is the Health of the State," in *War and the Intellectuals*, ed. Carl Resek (Cambridge, MA: Hackett, 1946, 19–38); William James, "The Moral Equivalent of War" (1910), http://constitution.org/2-Authors/wj/meow.htm.

34. Nicholas F. Jacobs and Sidney M. Milkis, "Extraordinary Isolation? Woodrow Wilson and the Civil Rights Movement," *Studies in American Political Development* 32, no. 2 (2017): 193–217.

35. Michael S. Greve, *The Upside-Down Constitution* (Cambridge, MA: Harvard University Press, 2012).

36. Arthur M. Schlesinger Jr., *The Imperial Presidency* (Boston: Houghton Mifflin, 1973); Theodore Lowi, *The Personal President: Power Invested, Promise Unfulfilled* (Ithaca, NY: Cornell University Press, 1986). The emergence of homeland security as a new federal responsibility in the wake of the war on terror aroused concerns that the post-Watergate guardrails put in place to constrain the dangers of the modern presidency had been breached. See Andrew Rudalevige *The New Imperial Presidency: Renewing Presidential Power after Watergate* (Ann Arbor: University of Michigan Press, 2005).

37. James MacGregor Burns, *Running Alone: Presidential Leadership JFK to Bush II: Why It Has Failed and How We Can Fix It* (New York: Basic Books, 2006).

38. Wilbur J. Cohen, Robert M. Ball, and Robert J. Myers, "Social Security Act Amendments of 1954: A Summary and Legislative History," *Social Security Bulletin* 17 (1954): 3.

39. This was no idle boast. Daniel Patrick Moynihan denominated the national highway program as "the largest public works program in history." David Mayhew, "The Long 1950s as a Policy Era," in *The Politics of Major Policy Reform in Postwar America*, ed. Jeffery A. Jenkins and Sidney M. Milkis (New York: Cambridge University Press, 2014), 35.

40. John F. Kennedy, "Remarks to Members of the White House Conference on National Economic Issues," May 21, 1962, John Woolley and Gerhard Peters, The American Presidency Project, https://www.presidency.ucsb.edu/node/235662.

41. Sidney M. Milkis, *The President and the Parties: The Transformation of the*

American Party System since the New Deal (Oxford: Oxford University Press, 1993), 107; see also Barry D. Karl, *Executive Reorganization and Reform in the New Deal: The Genesis of Administrative Management* (Cambridge, MA: Harvard University Press, 1963).

42. Richard Nathan, *The Administrative Presidency* (New York: Wiley, 1983).

43. Sidney M. Milkis, Jesse H. Rhodes, and Emily J. Charnock, "What Happened to Post-partisanship? Barack Obama and the New American Party System," *Perspectives on Politics* 10, no. 1 (2012): 57–76.

44. Quoted in Daniel K. Williams, *God's Own Party: The Making of the Christian Right* (New York: Oxford University Press, 2012).

45. Richard Nixon, "Remarks on the NBC and CBS Radio Networks: 'The Nature of the Presidency,'" September 19, 1968, John Woolley and Gerhard Peters, The American Presidency Project, https://www.presidency.ucsb.edu/node/326732.

46. Bert Rockman, "The Style and Organization of the Reagan Presidency," in *The Reagan Legacy: Promise and Performance*, ed. Charles O. Jones (Chatham, NJ: Chatham House, 1988), 10.

47. Elizabeth Dias, "Biden and Trump Say They're Fighting for America's 'Soul.' What Does That Mean?," *New York Times*, October 17, 2020, https://www.nytimes.com/2020/10/17/us/biden-trump-soul-nation-country.html.

48. Ali Swenson and Linley Sanders, "Majority of US Adults Say Democracy Is on the Ballot but They Differ on the Threat: AP-NORC Poll," Associated Press, August, 8, 2024.

49. Nicholas F. Jacobs and Connor M. Ewing, "The Promises and Pathologies of Presidential Federalism," *Presidential Studies Quarterly* 48, no. 3 (2018): 552–69.

50. Benjamin Kleinerman, *The Discretionary President: The Promise and Peril of Executive Power* (Baltimore: Johns Hopkins University Press, 2009).

51. Clinton Rossiter, *Constitutional Dictatorship: Crisis Government in the Modern Democracies*, rev. ed. (New York: Routledge, 2002).

1. THE MODERN PRESIDENCY AND EXECUTIVE-CENTERED PARTISANSHIP

1. Morton Keller, *America's Three Regimes: A New Political History* (Oxford: Oxford University Press, 2007).

2. Peri E. Arnold, *Remaking the Presidency: Roosevelt, Taft, and Wilson, 1901–1916* (Lawrence: University Press of Kansas, 2009).

3. Franklin D. Roosevelt, *The Public Papers and Addresses of Franklin D. Roosevelt*, 13 vols., ed. Samuel I. Rosenman (Ann Arbor: University of Michigan Press, 1938–50), 1:751–56.

4. Stephen Skowronek, *Building a New American State: The Expansion of National Administrative Capacities, 1877–1920* (New York: Cambridge University Press, 1982), 40.

5. Skowronek, *Building a New American State*, 752.

6. Woodrow Wilson, *Constitutional Government in the United States* (New York: Columbia University Press, 1908), 68–69.

7. Arthur S. Link, "Woodrow Wilson and the Democratic Party," *Review of Politics*

18 (April 1956): 146–56. Wilson effectively established himself as the principal voice of the Democratic Party, but he accepted traditional partisan practices concerning legislative deliberations and appointments to gain support for his program in Congress, thus failing to strengthen either the party's national organization or its fundamental commitment to progressive principles. After 1914, Wilson embraced many elements of progressive democracy, such as direct leadership of public opinion, national administration of commercial activity, and civil service reform. Wilson thus overcame some of the Democratic Party's antipathy toward national administrative power and showed that with the growing prominence of presidential candidates, party leaders in Congress were willing to sacrifice programmatic principles to win the White House. See Scott James, *Presidents, Parties, and the State: A Party System Perspective on Democratic Regulatory Choice, 1884–1936* (New York: Cambridge University Press, 2000). In the end, however, this conversion to advanced progressivism only exposed the yawning gap between, on the one hand, Wilson's pretense to serving as a national progressive leader and, on the other, his allegiance to a decentralized and patronage-based party. See Daniel Stid, *The President as Statesman: Woodrow Wilson and the Constitution* (Lawrence: University Press of Kansas, 1998), esp. chaps. 6 and 8.

8. Nicholas F. Jacobs and Sidney M. Milkis, "Extraordinary Isolation? Woodrow Wilson and the Civil Rights Movement," *Studies in American Political Development* 32, no. (2017): 193–217.

9. Ernest Cuneo, "The FDR Drama," no date, box 82, folder JAF (James A. Farley), Ernest Cuneo Papers, Franklin D. Roosevelt Library, Hyde Park, New York.

10. Personal and Political Diary of Homer Cummings, January 5, 1933, box 234, no. 2, 90, Homer Cummings Papers (no. 9973), Manuscripts Department, University of Virginia Library, Charlottesville.

11. For a broad critique of electoral realignments, see David R. Mayhew, *Electoral Realignments: A Critique of an American Genre* (New Haven, CT: Yale University Press, 2004).

12. Stanley High, "Whose Party is It?," *Saturday Evening Post*, February 6, 1937, 10–11, 34–37.

13. Edward J. Flynn, *You're the Boss* (New York: Viking Press, 1947), 153.

14. Paul Van Riper, *History of the United States Civil Service* (Westport, CT: Greenwood, 1958), 327.

15. Alfred Phillips Jr. to Franklin D. Roosevelt, June 9, 1937; Roosevelt to Phillips, June 16, 1937, both in President's Personal File, 2666, Franklin D. Roosevelt Library, Hyde Park, New York.

16. Franklin Clarkin, "Two-Thirds Rule Facing Abolition," *New York Times*, January 5, 1936, IV, 10.

17. Thomas Stokes, *Chip Off My Shoulder* (Princeton, NJ: Princeton University Press, 1940), 503. For an assessment of Roosevelt's role in the abolition of the two-thirds rule that also addresses the significance of this party reform, see Harold F. Bass Jr., "Presidential Party Leadership and Party Reform: Franklin D. Roosevelt and the Abrogation of the Two-Thirds Rule" (paper presented at the annual meeting of the Southern Political Science Association, Nashville, Tennessee, November 7–9, 1985).

18. Bailey to R. R. King, August 10, 1936, Josiah Bailey Papers, Senatorial Series, Political National Papers, Box 475, Manuscript Department, William R. Perkins Library, Duke University, Durham North Carolina.

19. James Farley, *Jim Farley's Story* (New York: McGraw-Hill, 1948), 146.

20. On the purge campaign, see Sidney M. Milkis, *The President and the Parties: The Transformation of the American Party System since the New Deal* (New York: Oxford University Press, 1993), chap. 4; Susan Dunn, *Roosevelt's Purge: How FDR Fought to Change the Democratic Party* (Cambridge, MA: Harvard University Press, 2010).

21. Raymond Clapper, "Roosevelt Tries the Primaries," *Current History*, October 1938, 16.

22. When asked whether he thought the solid South would stay Democratic very long, Roosevelt replied: "I think the South is going to be a more intelligent form of democracy than has kept the South, for other reasons, in the democratic column all these years. It will be intelligent thinking, and, in my judgment, because the South is learning, it is going to be a liberal democracy." *Complete Press Conferences of Franklin D. Roosevelt* (New York: Da Capo Press, 1972), April 21, 1938, no. 452-B, 11:338–40. In the end, the New Deal political realignment did not succeed in displacing white supremacy with economic liberalism—and once the New Deal state, pressured by a rising civil rights movement, extended its reach to matters of social justice under Harry Truman, John Kennedy, and especially Lyndon Johnson, the South moved to the Republican Party, which became a solidly right-of-center party by the 1980s.

23. The purge campaign galvanized opposition to Roosevelt throughout the nation, apparently contributing to the heavy losses the Democrats sustained in the 1938 general elections.

24. Ernest Cuneo, "The Eve of the Purge," 23, unpublished manuscript, Ernest Cuneo Papers, box 111, Franklin D. Roosevelt Library, Hyde Park, New York.

25. Morton Frisch, *Franklin D. Roosevelt: The Contribution of the New Deal to American Political Thought and Practice* (Boston: S. T. Wayne, 1975), 79.

26. Frankfurter to Roosevelt, August 9, 1937, box 210, Papers of Thomas G. Corcoran; Roosevelt to Frankfurter, August 12, 1937, reel 60, Felix Frankfurter Papers; both in Manuscript Division, Library of Congress, Washington, DC.

27. The term *benevolent dictatorship* was coined by Herbert Croly. Croly, a fellow Progressive, criticized Wilson's concept of presidential party leadership along these lines. Although he shared Wilson's view that executive power needed to be strengthened, Croly argued that the "necessity of such leadership [was] itself evidence of the decrepitude of the two-party system." Croly believed that Theodore Roosevelt's Progressive Party campaign of 1912, which scorned the two-party system, championed candidate-centered campaigns, and prescribed that presidents seek political support through direct appeals to public opinion, represented the wave of the future. The emergence of a modern executive and the destruction of the two-party system, he wrote, "was an indispensable condition of the success of progressive democracy." Herbert Croly, *Progressive Democracy* (New York: Macmillan, 1914), 345, 348. On the Progressive Party and its legacy, see Sidney M. Milkis and Daniel J. Tichenor, "'Direct Democracy' and Social Justice: The Progressive Party Campaign of 1912," *Studies in American Political Development* 8 (Fall 1994): 282–340;

Sidney M. Milkis, *Theodore Roosevelt, the Progressive Party, and the Transformation of American Democracy* (Lawrence: University Press of Kansas, 2009).

28. The term *second bill of rights* comes from Roosevelt's 1944 State of the Union message, which reaffirmed the New Deal's commitment to an economic constitutional order. Roosevelt, *Public Papers and Addresses*, 13:40.

29. Theodore Lowi, *The End of Liberalism: The Second Republic in the United States*, 2nd ed. (New York: W. W. Norton, 1979).

30. Quoted in Martha Derthick, *Policymaking for Social Security* (Washington, DC: Brookings Institution Press, 1983), 230.

31. Daniel P. Carpenter, *The Forging of Bureaucratic Autonomy: Reputations, Networks, and Policy Innovation, 1862–1928* (Princeton, NJ: Princeton University Press, 2002).

32. Sidney M. Milkis, "Franklin D. Roosevelt, the Economic Constitutional Order, and the New Politics of Presidential Leadership," in *The New Deal and the Triumph of Liberalism*, ed. Sidney M. Milkis and Jerome Mileur (Amherst: University of Massachusetts Press, 2000), 31–72.

33. Gulick quoted in Clinton Rossiter, *The American Presidency* (New York: Mentor, 1963), 129.

34. The term *administrative presidency* is drawn from Richard Nathan's book on the use of administrative strategies by modern presidents to pursue their policy objectives. See Richard Nathan, *The Administrative Presidency* (New York: Wiley, 1993).

35. Sidney M. Milkis, "Ideas, Institutions, and the New Deal Constitutional Order," *American Political Thought* 3, no. 1 (Spring 2014): 167–76.

36. Eric Schickler, *Racial Realignment: The Transformation of American Liberalism, 1932–1965* (Princeton, NJ: Princeton University Press, 2016).

37. Karen Orren and Stephen Skowronek, *The Policy State: An American Predicament* (Cambridge, MA: Harvard University Press, 2017).

38. Hugh Heclo, "Sixties Civics," in *The Great Society and the High Tide of Liberalism*, ed. Sidney M. Milkis and Jerome Mileur (Amherst: University of Massachusetts Press, 2005).

39. Byron Shafer, *Quiet Revolution: The Struggle for the Democratic Party and the Shaping of Post-reform Politics* (New York: Russell Sage Foundation, 1983).

40. John F. Kennedy, "Remarks to Members of the White House Conference on National Economic Issues," May 21, 1962, https://www.presidency.ucsb.edu/node/235662.

41. Daniel Bell, *The End of Ideology* (Cambridge, MA: Harvard University Press, 1962).

42. On the origins of the concept of a Great Society, see Sidney M. Milkis, "Lyndon Johnson, the Great Society and the 'Twilight' of the Modern Presidency," in *The Great Society and the High Tide of Liberalism*, ed. Sidney M. Milkis and Jerome M. Mileur (Amherst: University of Massachusetts Press, 2005).

43. Lyndon B. Johnson, "Remarks at the University of Michigan," May 22, 1964, John T. Woolley and Gerhard Peters, The American Presidency Project, http://www.presidency.ucsb.edu/ws/?pid=26262.

44. Students for a Democratic Society, The Port Huron Statement, 1962.

45. Robert A. Nisbet, *Quest for Community* (New York: Oxford University Press, 1953).

46. Economic Opportunity Act of 1964, Title 2, Part A, Section 202 (a).

47. Allen J. Matusow, *The Unraveling of America: A History of Liberalism in the 1960s* (New York: Harper & Row, 1984), 245.

48. Paul Pierson, "The Rise and Reconfiguration of Activist Government," in *The Transformation of American Politics: Activist Government and the Rise of Conservatism*, ed. Paul Pierson and Theda Skocpol (Princeton, NJ: Princeton University Press, 2007), 19–38.

49. George McGovern, "Address Accepting the Presidential Nomination at the Democratic National Convention, Miami Beach, Florida," July 14, 1972, John Woolley and Gerhard Peters, The American Presidency Project, https://www.presidency.ucsb.edu/node/216662.

50. Ronald Reagan, "Inaugural Address," January 20, 1981, John Woolley and Gerhard Peters, The American Presidency Project, https://www.presidency.ucsb.edu/node/246336.

51. Barry Goldwater, "Address Accepting the Presidential Nomination at the Republican National Convention in San Francisco," July 16, 1964, John Woolley and Gerhard Peters, The American Presidency Project, https://www.presidency.ucsb.edu/node/216657.

52. Charles E. Walcott and Karen M. Hult, "White House Staff Size: Explanations and Implications," *Presidential Studies Quarterly* 29, no. 3 (1999): 638–57.

53. Bert Rockman, "The Style and Organization of the Reagan Presidency," in *The Reagan Legacy: Promise and Performance*, ed. Charles O. Jones (Chatham, NJ: Chatham House, 1988), 10.

54. For a fuller discussion of conservative "redeployment" and its relationship to other theories of American state building, see Nicholas Jacobs, Desmond King, and Sidney Milkis, "Building a Conservative State: Partisan Polarization and the Redeployment of Administrative Power," *Perspectives on Politics* 17, no. 2 (June 2019): 453–69.

55. Carol Felsenthal, *Sweetheart of the Silent Majority* (New York: Doubleday, 1981); John Fund, "Phyllis Schlafly: 'The Sweetheart of the Silent Majority,'" *National Review*, September 6, 2016.

56. Phyllis Schlafly, *A Choice Not an Echo* (Alton, IL: Pere Marquette Press, 1964).

57. On the success of the anti-ERA movement and its influence on public opinion within targeted states, see Donald T. Critchlow and Cynthia L. Stachecki, "The Equal Rights Amendment Reconsidered: Politics, Policy, and Social Mobilization in a Democracy," *Journal of Policy History* 20, no. 1 (2008): 157–76; Jane Mansbridge, "Who's in Charge Here? Decision by Accretion and Gatekeeping in the Struggle for the ERA." *Politics & Society* 13, no. 4 (1984): 343–82.

58. Clyde Wilcox, *Onward Christian Soldiers* (Boulder, CO: Westview Press, 1995).

59. Marjorie J. Spruill, *Divided We Stand: The Battle over Women's Rights and Family Values That Polarized American Politics* (New York: Bloomsbury Press, 2017).

60. Sidney M. Milkis and Daniel J. Tichenor, *Rivalry and Reform: Presidents, Social Movements, and the Transformation of American Politics* (Chicago: University of Chicago Press, 2019), chap. 5.

61. Milkis and Tichenor, *Rivalry and Reform*.

62. Jerry Falwell, "Why the Moral Majority?," *Moral Majority Newsletter*, August 1979, 1, Moral Majority Papers, Series 2, Liberty University Archives, Lynchburg, VA.

63. Joseph Crespino, *In Search of Another Country: Mississippi and the Conservative Counterrevolution* (Princeton, NJ: Princeton University Press, 2009); see also Nancy Burns, *The Formation of American Local Governments: Private Values in Public Institutions* (New York: Oxford University Press, 1994).

64. William Martin, *With God on Our Side: The Rise of the Religious Right in America* (New York: Broadway Books, 1996), 71.

65. Jack White, "Segregation Academies," *Time*, December 15, 1975, 60; David Nevin and Robert Bills, *The Schools That Fear Built: Segregationist Academies in the South* (Atlanta: Acropolis Books, 1976); Peter Skerry, "Christian Schools versus the IRS," *National Affairs*, Fall 1980, https://www.nationalaffairs.com/public_interest/detail/christian-schools-versus-the-irs.

66. Martin, *With God on Our Side*, 70–71.

67. Randall Balmer, *Redeemer: The Life of Jimmy Carter* (New York: Basic Books, 2014), 104–5; Crespino, *In Search of Another* Country, 237–52; Nevin and Bills, *Schools That Fear Built*.

68. In a prescient analysis, the eventual Supreme Court justice and liberal icon Ruth Bader Ginsburg would comment in 1985, "*Roe*, I believe, would have been more acceptable as a judicial decision if it had not gone beyond a ruling on the extreme statute before the Court. The political process was moving in the early 1970s, not swiftly enough for advocates of quick, complete change, but majoritarian institutions were listening and acting. Heavy-handed judicial intervention was difficult to justify and appears to have provoked, not resolved, conflict." See Ruth Bader Ginsburg, "Some Thoughts on Autonomy and Equality in Relation to *Roe v. Wade*," *North Carolina Law Review* 63 (1985): 375–86.

69. Richard M. Nixon, "Address to the Nation on the War in Vietnam," November 3, 1969, John Woolley and Gerhard Peters, The American Presidency Project, http://www.presidency.ucsb.edu/ws/index.php?pid=2303.

70. Goldwater, "Address Accepting the Presidential Nomination."

71. Richard M. Nixon, "Remarks on the NBC and CBS Radio Networks: 'The Nature of the Presidency,'" September 19, 1968, John Woolley and Gerhard Peters, The American Presidency Project, https://www.presidency.ucsb.edu/node/326732.

72. Richard Nixon, "Address Accepting the Presidential Nomination at the Republican National Convention in Miami Beach, Florida," August 8, 1968, John Woolley and Gerhard Peters, The American Presidency Project, https://www.presidency.ucsb.edu/documents/address-accepting-the-presidential-nomination-the-republican-national-convention-miami.

73. *Mapp v. Ohio*, 367 U.S. 643 (1961).

74. *Gideon v. Wainwright*, 372 U.S. 335 (1963).

75. *Miranda v. Arizona*, 384 U.S. 436 (1966).

76. Ronald Kahn and Ken I. Kersch, "Supreme Court Decision Making and American Political Development," in *The Supreme Court and American Political Development*, ed. Ronald Kahn and Ken I. Kersch (Lawrence: University Press of Kansas, 2006).

77. Robert B. Semple Jr., "Warren E. Burger Named Chief Justice by Nixon," *New York Times*, May 22, 1969, 1.

78. *Eugene R. Frazier, Appellant, v. United States of America, Appellee*, 419 F.2d 1161 (D.C. Cir. 1969).

79. Steven M. Teles, *The Rise of the Conservative Legal Movement: The Battle for Control of the Law* (Princeton, NJ: Princeton University Press, 2008).

80. Republican Party Platforms, "Republican Party Platform of 1980," John Woolley and Gerhard Peters, The American Presidency Project, https://www.presidency.ucsb.edu/documents/republican-party-platform-1980.

81. Richard P. Nathan, *The Plot That Failed: Nixon and the Administrative Presidency* (New York: Wiley, 1975), 62.

82. William A. Niskanen, *Bureaucracy and Representative Government* (Chicago: Aldine-Atherton, 1971); E. S. Savas, *Privatizing the Public Sector: How to Shrink Government* (Chatham, NJ: Chatham House, 1982).

83. Kimberly J. Morgan and Andrea Louise Campbell, *The Delegated Welfare State: Medicare, Markets, and the Governance of Social Policy* (Oxford: Oxford University Press, 2011), 4.

84. James Savage, *Balanced Budget and American Politics* (Ithaca, NY: Cornell University Press, 1988).

85. Eric A. Posner and Adrian Vermeule, *The Executive Unbound: After the Madisonian Republic* (Oxford: Oxford University Press, 2011), 11.

86. Mary Dudziak, *War Time: An Idea, Its History, Its Consequences* (Oxford: Oxford University Press, 2012).

87. Grover Norquist, interview by Sidney Milkis and Jesse Rhodes, August 3, 2004.

88. Matthew Dowd, interview by Sidney Milkis and Jesse Rhodes, July 20, 2005.

89. Tad Devine (political strategist, John Kerry–John Edwards 2004), interview by Sidney Milkis, July 26, 2004.

90. Comment by John Kerry on CNN's *Inside Politics*, August 9, 2004.

91. Matthew Dowd, interview, July 20, 2005; Terry Nelson (political director, George W. Bush–Richard Cheney 04), interview by Sidney Milkis and Jesse Rhodes, August 19, 2005.

92. Matthew Dowd, interview, July 20, 2005.

93. Terry Nelson, interview, August 19, 2005.

94. Darrin Klingler, interview by Sidney Milkis and Jesse Rhodes, July 27, 2005.

95. Matthew Dowd, interview by Sidney M. Milkis and Jesse Rhodes, July 26, 2005

96. Karl Rove, interview by Sidney M. Milkis and Jesse Rhodes, November 15, 2001.

97. Sidney M. Milkis, Jesse H. Rhodes, and Emily J. Charnock, "What Happened to Post-Partisanship? Barack Obama and the New American Party System," *Perspectives on Politics* 10, no. 1 (2012): 57–76.

98. Ronald Brownstein, "The Clinton Conundrum," *The Atlantic*, April 17, 2015, https://www.theatlantic.com/politics/archive/2015/04/the-clinton-conundrum/431949/.

99. Roosevelt and Truman had undertaken important initiatives to separate their campaigns from the party, making use of White House operatives and "independent committees." But Citizens for Eisenhower, built for the 1952 campaign, was the first national candidate-centered campaign that operated independently of the regular party apparatus. Theodore Lowi, *The Personal President: Power Invested, Promise Unfulfilled* (Ithaca, NY: Cornell University Press, 1985), 73–79; David Broder, *The Party's Over: The Failure of Politics in America* (New York: Harper & Row, 1972), 1–15.

100. Peter Wallsten, "Retooling Obama's Campaign Machine for the Long Haul," *Los Angeles Times*, January 14, 2008, http://articles.latimes.com/2009/jan/14/nation/na-obama-army14.

101. Adam Nagourney, "Dean Argues His 50-State Strategy Helped Obama Win," *International Herald Tribune*, November 12, 2008.

102. Dana Goldstein and Ezra Klein, "It's His Party," *American Prospect*, August 18, 2008, http://prospect.org/article/its-his-party.

103. Lisa Taddeo, "The Man Who Made Obama," *Esquire*, November 3, 2009, http://www.esquire.com/features/david-plouffe-0309.

104. Alec MacGillis, "Sounds Great but What Does He Really Mean?," *Washington Post*, May 10, 2009, http://articles.washingtonpost.com/2009-05-10/opinions/36845928_1_pragmatism-obama-supporters-president-obama.

105. David Sanger, "Big Win for Obama, but at What Cost?," *New York Times*, March 21, 2010, A1.

106. Remarks by the President on the Economy, Georgetown University, April 14, 2009, Office of the White House Press Secretary, http://www.whitehouse.gov/the-press-office/remarks-president-economy-georgetown-university.

107. In a decision that called into question the president's recess appointments, a federal appeals court ruled that Obama violated the Constitution when he installed three officials on the National Labor Relations Board. Charlie Savage and Steven Greenhouse, "Court Rejects Obama Move to Fill Posts," *New York Times*, January 25, 2013, http://www.nytimes.com/2013/01/26/business/court-rejects-recess-appointments-to-labor-board.html?pagewanted=2&_r=1. For a detailed account of the "We Can't Wait Initiative," see Kenneth Lowande and Sidney M. Milkis, "'We Can't Wait': Barack Obama, Partisan Polarization, and the Administrative Presidency," *The Forum* 12, no. 1 (2014): 3–27.

108. David Klaidman and Andrew Romano, "President Obama's Executive Power Grab," *Daily Beast*, October 22, 2012, http://www.thedailybeast.com/newsweek/2012/10/21/president-obama-s-executive-power-grab.html; Ryan Lizza, "The Party Next Time: The GOP's Demographic Dilemma," *New Yorker*, September 2012, http://www.newyorker.com/reporting/2012/11/19/121119fa_fact_lizza. According to exit polls, Obama won about 70 percent of the Hispanic vote. For example, see Mark Hugo Lopez and Paul Taylor, "Latino Voters in the 2012 Election," Pew Research Hispanic Center, November 7, 2012, http://www.pewhispanic.org/2012/11/07/latino-voters-in-the-2012-election/.

109. OFA volunteer, interview by Sidney Milkis, December 4, 2012. For a detailed account of how the OFA combined sophisticated targeting and old-fashioned canvassing, see Sasha Issenberg, "Obama Does It Better," *Slate*, October 29, 2012, http://www.slate.com/articles/news_and_politics/victory_lab/2012/10/obama_s_secret_weapon_democrats_have_a_massive_advantage_in_targeting_and_single.html.

110. OFA volunteer, interview, December 3, 2012.

111. Email message from OFA volunteer, January 8, 2013, http://www.barackobama.com/about/about-ofa/.

112. Joe Szakos (president, Virginia Organizing), interview by Sidney Milkis and John York, July 21, 2014.

113. Phillip Rucker and Robert Costa, "Battle for the Senate: How the GOP Did It," *Washington Post*, November 5, 2014. The Republicans picked up nine seats in the Senate and thirteen in the House. The GOP majority in the Senate became 54 to 46; its 247 to 188 edge in the House gave the Republicans the largest majority it has enjoyed since 1948.

114. Between 2008 and 2015, Democrats lost thirteen Senate seats, sixty-nine House seats, 913 state legislative seats, 11 governorships, and 32 state legislative chambers. The only president in the past seventy-five years who came close was Dwight Eisenhower, who

witnessed a similar decline for the GOP during his presidency. Juliet Eilperin, "Obama, Who Once Stood as Party Outsider, Now Works to Strengthen Democrats," *Washington Post*, April 25, 2016, https://www.washingtonpost.com/politics/obama-who-once-stood-as-party-outsider-now-works-to-strengthen-democrats/2016/04/25/340b3b0a-0589-11e6-bdcb-0133da18418d_story.html.

115. Immigrants would be eligible to apply for three years of relief from deportation and work permits if they arrived in the United States before 2010 and arrived in the United States under the age of sixteen, or if they arrived in the United States before 2010 and have at least one child who is a US citizen or legal resident.

116. Obama's ambitious immigration initiative was tied up in the federal courts until the Trump administration rescinded it on taking office. Adam Litak and Michael D. Shear, "Supreme Court Tie Blocks Obama Immigration Plan," *New York Times*, June 23, 2016, http://www.nytimes.com/2016/06/24/us/supreme-court-immigration-obama-dapa.html?_r=0. For a detailed case study of OFA and its advance of executive-centered partisanship, see Sidney M. Milkis and John W. York, "Barack Obama, Organizing for Action and Executive-Centered Partisanship," *Studies in American Political Development* 31, no. 1 (April 2017): 1–23.

117. Brownstein, "Clinton Conundrum."

118. Interview by Nicholas Jacobs and Sidney Milkis, May 28, 2019, not for attribution.

119. See Susan B. Glasser, "'I Am the Only One': Trump's Messianic 2024 Message." *New Yorker*, June 15, 2023.

2. TRUMP, THE CONSERVATIVE MOVEMENT, AND THE GRAND OLD PARTY

1. Eli J. Finkel, Christopher A. Bail, Mina Cikara, Peter H. Ditto, Shanto Iyengar, Samara Klar, et al., "Political Sectarianism in America," *Science* 370, no. 6516 (2020): 533–36.

2. Cokie Roberts, "Shutdown Fight Is Not about the Wall. It's about Donald Trump," ABC News, January 9, 2019, https://abcnews.go.com/Politics/shutdown-fight-wall-donald-trump-analysis/story?id=60261637.

3. B. E. Shafer, *Quiet Revolution: Struggle for the Democratic Party and the Shaping of Post-reform Politics* (New York: Russell Sage Foundation, 1983).

4. Morton Keller, *America's Three Regimes: A New Political History* (Oxford: Oxford University Press, 2007).

5. Sidney M. Milkis, *The President and the Parties: The Transformation of the American Party System since the New Deal* (Oxford: Oxford University Press, 1993).

6. Daniel J. Galvin, "Party Domination and Base Mobilization: Donald Trump and Republican Party Building in a Polarized Era," *The Forum* 18, no. 2 (2020): 135–68, https://doi.org/10.1515/for-2020-2003.

7. James Ceaser, *Designing a Polity: America's Constitution in Theory and Practice* (Lanham, MD: Rowman & Littlefield, 2011).

8. Jeremy W. Peters, "Potential G.O.P. Convention Fight Puts Older Hands in Sudden Demand," *New York Times*, April 18, 2016, https://www.nytimes.com/2016/04/19/us/politics/potential-gop-convention-fight-puts-older-hands-in-sudden-demand.html.

9. Robert P. Saldin and Steven M. Teles, *Never Trump: The Revolt of the Conservative Elites* (New York: Oxford University Press, 2020).

10. Ryan Lizza, "Kellyanne Conway's Political Machinations," *New Yorker*, October 8, 2016, https://www.newyorker.com/magazine/2016/10/17/kellyanne-conways-political-machinations.

11. Bill Allison, Brittany Harris, Mira Rojanasakul, and Cedric Sam, "Tracking the 2016 Presidential Money Race," Bloomberg, December 9, 2016, https://www.bloomberg.com/politics/graphics/2016-presidential-campaign-fundraising/.

12. Roderick P. Hart, *Trump and Us: What He Says and Why People Listen*. New York: Cambridge University Press, 2020).

13. Kellyanne Conway, "Transcript: Interview with Jim Gilmore on December 8, 2016," *Frontline*, accessed May 29, 2019, http://apps.frontline.org/trumps-road-white-house-frontline-interviews/transcript/kellyanne-conway.html.

14. "Rush Limbaugh: Romney's Attack on Trump 'Is Nothing New,' 'They Tried to Deny Reagan,'" YouTube, 12:07, posted by "Patriots in the News," March 6, 2016, https://www.realclearpolitics.com/video/2016/03/06/rush_limbaugh_on_trump_much_bigger_up_side_than_down_side.html.

15. Ronald Brownstein, "The Clinton Conundrum," *The Atlantic*, April 17, 2015, https://www.theatlantic.com/politics/archive/2015/04/the-clinton-conundrum/431949/.

16. Odds Shark Staff, "USA Presidential Election: 2016 Odds," Oddsshark, January 10, 2023, https://www.oddsshark.com/entertainment/us-presidential-odds-2016-futures.

17. James E. Campbell, "Introduction," *PS: Political Science & Politics* 49 (2016): 649–54, https://doi.org/10.1017/S1049096516001591.

18. James E. Campbell, Helmut Norpoth, Alan I. Abramowitz, Michael S. Lewis-Beck, Charles Tien, James E. Campbell, et al. "A Recap of the 2016 Election Forecasts," *PS: Political Science & Politics* 50 (2017): 331–38, https://doi.org/10.1017/S1049096516002766.

19. Nicholas Jacobs and James W. Ceaser, "The 2016 Presidential Election by the Numbers and in Historical Perspective," *The Forum* 14, no. 4 (2016): 361–83, https://doi.org/10.1515/for-2016-0032.

20. Maxwell Tani, "'A Complete Earthquake': Joe Scarborough Reacts to Trump Winning the Presidency," *Business Insider*, November 9, 2016, https://www.businessinsider.com/joe-scarborough-donald-trump-2016-11.

21. Lauren Easton, "Calling the Presidential Race State by State," Associated Press, November 9, 2016, https://blog.ap.org/behind-the-news/calling-the-presidential-race-state-by-state.

22. Costas Panagopoulos, *Bases Loaded: How US Presidential Campaigns Are Changing and Why It Matters* (New York: Oxford University Press, 2020), https://doi.org/10.1017/S153759272100133X.

23. Katie Reilly, "Read Hillary Clinton's 'Basket of Deplorables' Remarks about Donald Trump Supporters," *Time*, September 10, 2016, https://time.com/4486502/hillary-clinton-basket-of-deplorables-transcript/.

24. "Clinton's Deplorable Comment Goes Deeper Than a Mere Label for the Right; Reveals Her Contempt for People of Faith," Alex McFarland Ministries, September 22, 2016, https://alexmcfarland.com/media/clintons-deplorables-comment-goes-deeper-than-a-mere-label-for-the-right-reveals-her-contempt-for-people-of-faith/.

25. Trump's vulgar remarks on the so-called Access Hollywood tapes resurfaced as an important issue in the Stormy Daniels trial; Jesse McKinley, "What Is the 'Access Hollywood Tape, and How Does It Factor in Trump's Trial?," *New York Times*, May 28, 2024, https://www.nytimes.com/2024/05/28/nyregion/access-hollywood-tape-trump-trial.html.

26. Katie Glueck, "Christian Leaders See Influence Growing on Trump," *Politico*, November 25, 2016, https://www.politico.com/story/2016/11/christian-evangelicals-donald-trump-influence-231810.

27. Jerry Falwell Jr. interview on Fox Business News, September 27, 2016.

28. Michael Zoorob and Theda Skocpol, "The Overlooked Organizational Basis of Trump's 2016 Victory," in *Upending American Politics: Polarizing Parties, Ideological Elites, and Citizen Activists from the Tea Party to the Anti-Trump Resistance*, ed. Theda Skocpol and Caroline Tervo (New York: Oxford University Press, 2020), 79–100.

29. Republican National Committee, *Growth and Opportunity Project*, March 19, 2013, https://www.documentcloud.org/documents/624581-rnc-autopsy.

30. See Republican National Committee, *Growth and Opportunity Project*, 5.

31. Steven Levitsky and Daniel Ziblatt, *How Democracies Die* (New York: Crown, 2018).

32. Matt Lacombe, *Firepower: How the NRA Turned Gun Owners into a Political Force* (Princeton, NJ: Princeton University Press, 2021).

33. Peter Bachrach and Morton S. Baratz, "Two Faces of Power," *American Political Science Review* 56, no. 4 (1962): 947–52.

34. Dan Roberts and Ben Jacobs, "Donald Trump Proclaims Himself 'Law and Order' Candidate at Republican Convention," *The Guardian*, July 22, 2016, https://www.theguardian.com/us-news/2016/jul/21/donald-trump-republican-national-convention-speech.

35. Donald Trump's full remarks available at "Read: Full Transcript of Trump's Rally Speech in Florida," *Palm Beach Post*, February 18, 2017, https://www.ajc.com/news/national/read-full-transcript-trump-rally-speech-florida/DeDCpoNEKLQmWcIKndWBoM/.

36. Sidney Blumenthal, *The Permanent Campaign: Inside the World of Elite Political Operatives* (Boston: Beacon Press, 1980); Brendon J. Doherty, *The Rise of the President's Permanent Campaign* (Kansas: University Press of Kansas, 2012).

37. Peter Baker, "Trump Returns to Campaign Trail after a Month in Office," *New York Times*, February 18, 2017, https://www.nytimes.com/2017/02/18/us/politics/donald-trump-rally-melbourne-florida.html.

38. Donald Trump's full remarks available at "Read: Full Transcript of Trump's Rally Speech in Florida."

39. Christopher Cadelago, "Trump's Midterm Pitch: Vote for Me," *Politico*, October 10, 2018, https://www.politico.com/story/2018/10/10/trump-midterm-pitch-886196.

40. James E. Campbell, "The Presidential Pulse and the 1994 Midterm Congressional Election," *Journal of Politics* 59, no. 3 (1997): 830–57; Alan I. Abramowitz, "Economic Conditions, Presidential Popularity, and Voting Behavior in Midterm Congressional Elections," *Journal of Politics* 47, no. 1 (1985): 31–43.

41. G. C. Jacobson, "It's Nothing Personal: The Decline of the Incumbency Advantage in US House Elections," *Journal of Politics* 77, no. 3 (2015): 861–73.

42. Nicholas F. Jacobs and James W. Ceaser, "The 2016 Presidential Election by the Numbers and in Historical Perspective," *The Forum* 14, no. 4 (2016): 361–85.

43. Calculations derived from district-level data available at David Leip, "US Presidential Election Data," 2018, David Leip's Atlas of US Presidential Elections, https://uselectionatlas.org/.

44. Alex Thompson, Natasha Korecki, and Christopher Cadelago, "Warren Stumbles with 'Native American' Rollout," *Politico*, October 16, 2018, https://www.politico.com/story/2018/10/16/warren-dna-native-american-905705.

45. Philip Elliott, "Martha McSally, Who Learned to Love Donald Trump, Wins Arizona Primary," *Time*, August 29, 2018; Associated Press, "The Latest: McSally Embraces Trump in Arizona Senate Bid," *Washington Post*, January 12, 2018.

46. Trump backed Moore, even though he faced allegations of sexual abuse.

47. Donald Trump (@realDonaldTrump), "To the great people of West Virginia . . ." Twitter, May 7, 2018.

48. Donald Trump, press conference, CNN, November 7, 2018, https://www.cnn.com/2018/11/07/politics/donald-trump-midterm-election-news-conference/index.html.

49. Dan Balz, "Biden vs. Trump? In 2022, There Was a Clear Winner and a Clear Loser," *Washington Post*, December 17, 2022, https://www.washingtonpost.com/politics/2022/12/17/biden-trump-2024/.

50. Theodore Lowi, *The Personal President: Power Invested, Promise Unfulfilled* (Ithaca, NY: Cornell University Press, 1985).

51. Meredith Conroy, Nathaniel Rakich, and Mai Nguyen, "We Looked at Hundreds of Endorsements. Here's Who Republicans Are Listening To," FiveThirtyEight, September 24, 2018, https://fivethirtyeight.com/features/we-looked-at-hundreds-of-endorsements-heres-who-republicans-are-listening-to/.

52. Stephanie Murray, "Massachusetts Republicans Move to Protect Trump in 2020 Primary," *Politico*, May 6, 2019, https://www.politico.com/story/2019/05/06/massachusetts-republicans-trump-2020-primary-1302875.

53. Donald J. Trump for President, "Donald J. Trump for President Announces Delegate and Party Organization Team for the 2020 Campaign," Democracy in Action, January 18, 2019, https://www.democracyinaction.us/2020/trump/trump022718pr.html.

54. Alex Isenstadt, "Trump Campaign Moves to Stave Off Mayhem at 2020 Convention," *Politico*, January 7, 2019, https://www.politico.com/story/2019/01/07/trump-campaign-2020-convention-1079366.

55. Alex Isenstadt, "How Donald Trump Lost the Summer," *Politico*, August 18, 2016, https://www.politico.eu/article/how-donald-trump-lost-the-summer/.

56. Lachlan Markay, "Scoop: Trump Campaign Boosted by Unsuspecting State GOPs," Axios, April 11, 2021, https://www.axios.com/2021/04/11/republicans-state-gop-trump-campaign.

57. Calculations derived from data available at Federal Election Commission, "Trump Victory, PAC, Non-Qualified, Joint-Fundraising Committee," Campaign Finance Data, 2019, https://www.fec.gov/data/committee/C00618389/.

58. Alex Isenstadt, "Trump Launches Unprecedented Reelection Machine," *Politico*, December 18, 2018, https://www.politico.eu/article/trump-launches-unprecedented-reelection-machine/.

59. Julie Bykowicz and Jill Colvin, "Trump Trashes Media, Cheers Wins at $10 Million Fundraiser," Associated Press, June 29, 2017, https://apnews.com/article/north-america-donald-trump-ap-top-news-elections-barack-obama-9096860f4cd-5499fbd484288fe025a94.

60. Calculations derived from data available at Federal Election Commission, Campaign Finance Data, September 1, 2021, https://www.fec.gov/data/candidates/president/.

61. Galvin, "Party Domination and Base Mobilization."

62. Jeffrey K. Tulis and Nicole Mellow, *Legacies of Losing in American Politics* (Chicago: University of Chicago Press, 2018).

63. Karl Bernstein and Bob Woodward, "Woodward and Bernstein Thought Nixon Defined Corruption. Then Came Trump," *Washington Post*, June 5, 2022, https://www.washingtonpost.com/outlook/2022/06/05/woodward-bernstein-nixon-trump/.

64. "Background on Trump's 'Voter Fraud' Commission," July 18, 2017, Brennan Center for Justice, https://www.brennancenter.org/our-work/analysis-opinion/background-trumps-voter-fraud-commission.

65. Max Greenwood, "Nearly Three-Quarters of GOP Doubt the Legitimacy of Biden's Win: Poll," *The Hill*, December 20, 2021, https://thehill.com/homenews/campaign/587700-nearly-three-quarters-of-gop-doubt-legitimacy-of-bidens-win-poll/.

66. In an ideal world, we would have comparison numbers from 2016 that identified the roughly 51 percent of Republicans who supported Trump in the primary from those who did not, as well their positions on the administrative policies.

67. The White House, "Remarks by President Trump and Members of the Coronavirus Task Force in a Press Briefing," March 30, 2020, https://trumpwhitehouse.archives.gov/briefings-statements/remarks-president-trump-members-coronavirus-task-force-press-briefing/.

68. "Forecasting the US Elections," November 3, 2020, *The Economist*, https://projects.economist.com/us-2020-forecast/president.

69. Helmut Norpoth, "Primary Model Predicts Trump Re-election," Primary Model, 2020, http://primarymodel.com/2020-1.

70. Michael C. Bender, "Trump Rallies Are No Longer Side Shows. They Are the Campaign," *Wall Street Journal*, October 22, 2019, https://www.wsj.com/articles/trumps-rallies-arent-just-part-of-his-campaign-they-are-the-campaign-11571753199.

71. Republican National Committee, "Resolution Regarding the Republican Party Platform," 2020, https://prod-cdn-static.gop.com/docs/Resolution_Platform_2020.pdf?_ga=2.165306300.2055661719.1598124638-455285808.1584478680.

72. Susan Davis, "'Fundraging' Fuels Democratic Money Advantage over GOP in Most Races," NPR, October 22, 2020, https://www.npr.org/2020/10/22/925892007/fundraging-fuels-democratic-money-advantage-over-gop-in-most-races.

73. Kevin Quealy, "The Complete List of Trump's Twitter Insults (2015–2021)," *New York Times*, January 19, 2021, https://www.nytimes.com/interactive/2021/01/19/upshot/trump-complete-insult-list.html.

74. Caitlin O'Kane, "Trump Said Coronavirus 'Affects Virtually Nobody,' as U.S. Surpasses 200,000 Deaths," CBS News, September 22, 2020, https://www.cbsnews.com/news/covid-it-affects-virutally-nobody-trump-coronavirus-rally/.

75. Damian Paletta and Yasmeen Abutaleb, "Inside the Extraordinary Effort to Save

Trump from Covid-19," *Washington Post*, June 25, 2021, https://www.washingtonpost.com/politics/2021/06/24/nightmare-scenario-book-excerpt/.

76. Scott Neuman, "'Maybe I'm Immune': Trump Returns to the White House, Removes Mask Despite Infection," NPR, October 6, 2020, https://www.npr.org/sections/latest-updates-trump-covid-19-results/2020/10/06/920625432/maybe-i-m-immune-trump-returns-to-white-house-removes-mask-after-covid-treatment.

77. Jonathan Martin, Maggie Haberman, and Katie Rogers, "As Protests and Violence Spill Over, Trump Shrinks Back," *New York Times*, June 11, 2020, https://www.nytimes.com/2020/06/11/us/politics/trump-on-race.html.

78. David Siders, "Trump Bets His Presidency on a 'Silent Majority,'" *Politico*, June 3, 2020, https://www.politico.com/news/2020/06/03/trump-suburbs-reelection-nixon-296980.

79. Nicholas F. Jacobs and Daniel M. Shea, *The Rural Voter: The Politics of Place and the Disuniting of America* (New York: Columbia University Press, 2023).

80. Nick Miroff and Matt Zapotosky, "Facing Unrest on American Streets, Trump Turns Homeland Security Powers Inward," *Washington Post*, July 21, 2020, https://www.washingtonpost.com/national/facing-unrest-on-american-streets-trump-turns-homeland-security-powers-inward/2020/07/21/655e7822-cb71-11ea-89ce-ac7d5e4a5a38_story.html.

81. Miles Parks, "Why Is Voting by Mail (Suddenly) Controversial? Here's What You Need to Know," NPR, June 4, 2020, https://www.npr.org/2020/06/04/864899178/why-is-voting-by-mail-suddenly-controversial-heres-what-you-need-to-know.

82. Jack Brewster, "Trump Renews Ballot 'Dump' Conspiracy Theory Claim—Here's Why It's Bogus," *Forbes*, November 30, 2020, https://www.forbes.com/sites/jackbrewster/2020/11/30/trump-renews-ballot-dump-conspiracy-theory-claim-heres-why-its-bogus/?sh=4fbf15531dca.

83. Jacob Shamsian and Sonam Sheth, "Trump and His Allies Filed More Than 40 Lawsuits Challenging the 2020 Election Results. All of Them Failed," *Insider*, February 22, 2021, https://www.businessinsider.com/trump-campaign-lawsuits-election-results-2020-11.

84. Brian Naylor, " Read Trump's Donald Trump, Jan. 6 Speech, a Key Part of Impeachment Trial," NPR, February 10, 2021, https://www.npr.org/2021/02/10/966396848/read-trumps-jan-6-speech-a-key-part-of-impeachment-trial.

85. Charlie Savage, "Incitement to Riot? What Trump Told Supporters before Mob Stormed Capitol," *New York Times*, January 12, 2021, https://www.nytimes.com/2021/01/10/us/trump-speech-riot.html.

86. Jonathan Weisman and Reid J. Epstein, "G.O.P. Declares January 6 Attack 'Legitimate Political Discourse,'" *New York Times*, February 4, 2022, https://www.nytimes.com/2022/02/04/us/politics/republicans-jan-6-cheney-censure.html.

87. John McCormack, "John Eastman vs. the Eastman Memo." *National Review*, October 22, 2021, https://www.nationalreview.com/2021/10/john-eastman-vs-the-eastman-memo/.

88. Paul Bedard, "Exclusive: Trump Urges State Legislators to Reject Electoral Votes, 'You Are the Real Power,'" *Washington Examiner*, January 3, 2021. https://www.washingtonexaminer.com/washington-secrets/exclusive-trump-urges-state-legislators-to-reject-electoral-votes-you-are-the-real-power.

89. Jacqueline Alemany, Emma Brown, Tom Hamburger, and Jon Swaine, "Ahead of Jan. 6, Willard Hotel in Downtown D.C. Was a Trump Team 'Command Center' for Effort to Deny Biden the Presidency," *Washington Post*, October 23, 2021, https://www.washingtonpost.com/investigations/Willard-Trump-Eastman-Giuliani-Bannon/2021/10/23/C45bd2d4-3281-11ec-9241-Aad8e48f01ff_Story.html.

90. Shalini Ramachandran, Alexandra Berzon, and Rebecca Ballhaus, "Jan. 6 Rally Funded by Top Trump Donor, Helped by Alex Jones, Organizers Say," *Wall Street Journal*, February 1, 2021, https://www.wsj.com/articles/jan-6-rally-funded-by-top-trump-donor-helped-by-alex-jones-organizers-say-11612012063.

91. Giuliani Rudy, transcript of speech delivered at Donald Trump's "Save America" rally, January 6, 2021, https://www.rev.com/transcripts/donald-trump-speech-save-america-rally-transcript-january-6.

92. "Capitol 'Mob Calling for the Death of the Vice President,' Plaskett Says," video, PBS News, February 10, 2021, https://www.pbs.org/newshour/politics/watch-video-shows-capitol-mob-calling-for-the-death-of-the-vice-president-plaskett-says.

93. Josh Dawsey, Jacqueline Alemany, Jon Swaine, and Emma Brown, "During Jan. 6 Riot, Trump Attorney Told Pence Team the Vice President's Inaction Caused Attack on Capitol," *Washington Post*, October 29, 2021, https://www.washingtonpost.com/investigations/eastman-pence-email-riot-trump/2021/10/29/59373016-38c1-11ec-91dc-551d44733e2d_story.html.

94. Jacqueline Alemany, Tom Hamburger, Josh Dawsey, and Tyler Remmel, "Texting Through an Insurrection," *Washington Post*, February 16, 2022, https://www.washingtonpost.com/politics/interactive/2022/texting-insurrection/.

95. Zachary Evans, "Trump Turns on GOP Senator for Dismissing 2020 Election Fraud Claims: 'Crazy or Just Stupid?,'" *National Review*, January 10, 2022, https://www.nationalreview.com/news/trump-turns-on-gop-senator-for-dismissing-2020-election-fraud-claims-crazy-or-just-stupid/.

96. Isaac Stanley-Becker and Anu Narayanswamy, "Trump Has More Than $100 Million in Political Cash after First Six Months of 2021," *Washington Post*, August 1, 2021, https://www.washingtonpost.com/politics/2021/07/31/trump-committees-fundraising-2021-fec/.

97. Jason Silverstein, "Trump Posts Flurry of Anti–Fox News Tweets: 'They Forgot What Made Them Successful,'" CBS News, November 13, 2020, https://www.cbsnews.com/news/trump-fox-news-tweets/.

98. Nell Clark, "Trump's Social Media Site Hits the App Store a Year after He Was Banned from Twitter," NPR, February 22, 2022, https://www.npr.org/2022/02/22/1082243094/trumps-social-media-app-launches-year-after-twitter-ban.

3. UNILATERALISM AND THE TRUMP PRESIDENCY

1. Tamara Keith, "How 'Stronger Together' Became Clinton's Response to 'Make America Great Again,'" NPR, August 8, 2016, https://www.npr.org/2016/08/08/489138602/trump-comment-gives-clinton-a-campaign-slogan-with-layered-meaning.

2. Evan Osnos, "Trump's First Term," *New Yorker*, September 19, 2016, https://www.newyorker.com/magazine/2016/09/26/president-trumps-first-term.

3. Phillip Rucker and Robert Costa, "Bannon Promises a Daily Fight for 'Deconstruction of the Administrative State,'" *Washington Post*, February 23, 2017, https://www.washingtonpost.com/politics/top-wh-strategist-vows-a-daily-fight-for-deconstruction-of-the-administrative-state/2017/02/23/03f6b8da-f9ea-11e6-bf01-d47f8cf9b643_story.html.

4. William G. Howell and Terry M. Moe, "The Strongman Presidency and the Two Logics of Presidential Power," *Presidential Studies Quarterly* 53, no. 1 (2023): 145–68.

5. Donald Trump (@realdonaldtrump), "Why is @BarackObama constantly issuing executive orders that are major power grabs of authority?," Twitter, July 10, 2012, 1:11 p.m., https://x.com/realDonaldTrump/status/222739756105207808.

6. Sidney M. Milkis, *The President and the Parties: The Transformation of the American Party System since the New Deal* (New York: Oxford University Press, 1993).

7. Daniel P. Carpenter, *The Forging of Bureaucratic Autonomy: Reputations, Networks, and Policy Innovation in Executive Agencies, 1862–1928* (Princeton, NJ: Princeton University Press, 2001).

8. Rachel Augustine Potter, Andrew Rudalevige, Sharece Thrower, and Adam L. Warber, "Not by the Numbers: Evaluating Trump's Administrative Presidency," *Presidential Studies Quarterly* 52, no. 3 (2022): 596–625.

9. Arthur Meier Schlesinger Jr., "Diary Entry: August 19," in Andrew Schlesinger and Stephen Schlesinger, *The Journals of Arthur M. Schlesinger, Jr: 1952–2000* (New York: Penguin Books, 1962), 163.

10. John Herbers, "Nixon's Presidency: Centralized Control," *New York Times*, March 6, 1973, 1. See also Amy Fried and Douglas Harris, *At War with Government: How Conservatives Weaponized Distrust from Goldwater to Trump* (New York: Columbia University Press, 2021).

11. On transmission belts, see Richard B. Stewart, "The Reformation of American Administrative Law," *Harvard Law Review* 88 (1975): 1684.

12. Rachel Augustine Potter, *Bending the Rules: Procedural Politicking in the Bureaucracy* (Chicago: University of Chicago Press, 2019).

13. Tom Shoop, "Donald Trump's Plan for Cutting Government," Government Executive, February 26, 2016, https://www.govexec.com/federal-news/2016/02/donald-trumps-plan-cutting-government/126242/.

14. Michael A. Livermore and Richard L. Revesz, *Reviving Rationality: Saving Cost-Benefit Analysis for the Sake of the Environment and Our Health* (New York: Oxford University Press, 2020), 15.

15. For a review, see Philip A. Wallach and Kelly Kennedy, "Examining Some of Trump's Deregulation Efforts: Lessons from the Brookings Regulatory Tracker," Brookings Institution, 2022, https://www.brookings.edu/articles/examining-some-of-trumps-deregulation-efforts-lessons-from-the-brookings-regulatory-tracker/.

16. Susan Webb Yackee, "The Politics of Rulemaking in the United States," *Annual Review of Political Science* 22, no. 1 (2019): 37–55; William F. West, "The Institutionalization of Regulatory Review: Organizational Stability and Responsive Competence at OIRA," *Presidential Studies Quarterly* 35, no. 1 (2005): 76–93.

17. Steven Croley, "White House Review of Agency Rulemaking: An Empirical Investigation," *University of Chicago Law Review* 70, no. 3 (2003): 821–85; Alan E.

Wiseman, "Delegation and Positive-Sum Bureaucracies," *Journal of Politics* 71, no. 3 (2009): 998–1014.

18. This applies to rules that "have an annual effect on the economy of $100 million or more or adversely affect in a material way the economy, a sector of the economy, productivity," competition, jobs, the environment, public health or safety, or state, local, or tribal governments or communities.

19. "Regulatory Planning and Review," Executive Order 12866, *Federal Register* 58, no. 190 (October 4, 1993): 51735.

20. Institute for Policy Integrity, New York University School of Law, "Presidential Win Rates," last updated June 21, 2024, https://policyintegrity.org/tracking-major-rules/presidential-win-rates.

21. "Separation of Powers: Legislative-Executive Relations," Markman Memorandum to Edwin Meese III, "Subject: Separation of Powers," April 30, 1986, RG 60, folder OLP, April–May 1986, part 1, box 86, 8, 17, Department of Justice Files, National Archives and Record Administration.

22. Steven G. Calabresi and Kevin H. Rhodes, "The Structural Constitution: Unitary Executive, Plural Judiciary," *Harvard Law Review* 105, no. 6 (1992): 1204.

23. Calabresi and Rhodes, "Structural Constitution," 1216 (emphasis in original).

24. Stephen Skowronek, "The Conservative Insurgency and Presidential Power: A Developmental Perspective on the Unitary Executive," *Harvard Law Review* 122 (2008): 2097–98.

25. J. Richard Piper, "Presidential-Congressional Power Prescriptions in Conservative Political Thought since 1933," *Presidential Studies Quarterly* 21, no. 1 (1991): 35–54; J. Richard Piper, "'Situational Constitutionalism' and Presidential Power: The Rise and Fall of the Liberal Model of Presidential Government," *Presidential Studies Quarterly* 24, no. 3 (1994): 577–94.

26. William P. Barr, "Attorney General William P. Barr Delivers the 19th Annual Barbara K. Olson Memorial Lecture at the Federalist Society's 2019 National Lawyers Convention," Washington, DC, November 15, 2019.

27. US Department of Justice, "Common Legislative Encroachments on Executive Branch Authority," 1989, https://www.justice.gov/olc/opinion/common-legislative-encroachments-executive-branch-authority.

28. Sidney M. Milkis and Nicholas F. Jacobs, "'I Alone Can Fix It': Donald Trump, the Administrative Presidency, and Hazards of Executive-Centered Partisanship," *The Forum* 15, no. 3 (2017): 583–613.

29. Public Law 107-296, November 25, 2002.

30. *Arizona et al. v. United States*, 567 US (2012) (Docket No. 11-182).

31. "Enhancing Public Safety in the Interior of the United States," Executive Order 13768, *Federal Register* 82, no. 18 (January 25, 2017): 8799–803.

32. Maria Sacchetti, "Trump Administration: These Police Agencies Didn't Help Feds with Deportations," *Washington Post*, March 20, 2017, https://www.washingtonpost.com/local/social-issues/trump-administration-these-police-agencies-didnt-help-feds-with-deportations/2017/03/20/67b3767a-0d76-11e7-9b0d-d27c98455440_story.html?utm_term=.c3c731c6b99a; Stephen Dinan, "Sanctuary City List on Hold after 3 Weeks as Homeland Security Acknowledges Errors in Data," *Washington Times*, April 11, 2017,

http://www.washingtontimes.com/news/2017/apr/11/dhs-suspends-sanctuary-city-list-after-3-weeks/.

33. "Supporting Federal, State, Local, and Tribal Law Enforcement," March 31, 2017, Memorandum for Heads of Department Components and United States Attorneys, from the Attorney General, https://www.documentcloud.org/documents/3535148-Consentdecreebaltimore.html.

34. "Restoring State, Tribal, and Local Law Enforcement's Access to Life-Saving Equipment and Resources," Executive Order 13809, *Federal Register* 82, no. 168 (August 28, 2017): 41499–500.

35. "Rescission of Memorandum on Use of Private Prisons," Memorandum for the Acting Director Federal Bureau of Prisons, February 21, 2017, Office of the Attorney General.

36. "Border Security and Immigration Enforcement Improvements," Executive Order 13767, *Federal Register* 82, no. 18 (January 25, 2017): 8793–97.

37. These claims were made in the aftermath of reports that Trump cut a deal with Democrats that would protect the so-called Dreamers in return for strong border measures that did not include funding for the wall—arousing howls of betrayal from anti-immigrant activists and conservative Republicans. Ed O'Keefe and David Nakamura, "Trump, Top Democrats Agree to Work on Deal to Save 'Dreamers' from Deportation," *Washington Post*, September 14, 2017, https://www.washingtonpost.com/news/powerpost/wp/2017/09/13/trump-top-democrats-agree-to-work-on-deal-to-save-daca/?hpid=hp_rhp-top-table-main_daca1013pm%3Ahomepage%2Fstory&utm_term=.16fe3d9f42b9.

38. "Protecting the Nation from Foreign Terrorist Entry into the United States," Executive Order 13769, *Federal Register* 82, no. 20 (January 27, 2017): 8977–82.

39. "President Donald J. Trump Statement Regarding Recent Executive Order Concerning Extreme Vetting," January 29, 2017, The White House: Office of the Press Secretary.

40. The new executive order modified several provisions of the original: those with already-issued visas were excluded; Iraq was taken off the list of banned countries; religious minorities were also included on the new list; and a more straightforward waiver process was established. "Protecting the Nation from Foreign Terrorist Entry into the United States," Executive Order 13780, *Federal Register* 82, no. 56 (March 6, 2017): 13209–19.

41. "In Case You Missed It: McClatchy on Historical Precedent for President's National Security Executive Order," February 7, 2017, The White House: Office of the Press Secretary.

42. *Trump v. Hawaii*, no. 17-965 (2018).

43. *Department of Homeland Security v. Regents of the University of California*, 591 U.S. (2020).

44. Matt Keenley, "Trump Says 'We Won on DACA' at Tulsa Rally after Supreme Court Ruling," *Newsweek*, June 20, 2020, https://www.newsweek.com/trump-says-we-won-daca-tulsa-rally-after-supreme-court-ruling-1512364.

45. Kenneth S. Lowande and Sidney M. Milkis, "'We Can't Wait': Barack Obama, Partisan Polarization and the Administrative Presidency," *The Forum* 12, no. 1 (2014): 3–27.

46. Dana Nakamura, "Trump's Hardline Immigration Rhetoric Runs Into Obstacles—Including Trump," *Washington Post*, February 17, 2017, https://www.washingtonpost.com/politics/trumps-hardline-immigration-rhetoric-runs-into-obstacles--including

-trump/2017/02/17/37ba2218-f537-11e6-b9c9-e83fce42fb61_story.html; Joel Achenbach, "Trump Aides Struggle to Clarify Policy on 'Dreamers' and Deportation," *Washington Post*, April 23, 2017, https://www.washingtonpost.com/news/post-politics/wp/2017/04/23/trump-aides-struggle-to-clarify-policy-on-dreamers-and-deportation/?utm_term=.a6db04872396.

47. "Letter to the Attorney General of the United States: Texas, et al. v. United States, et al., No. 1:14-cv-00254 (S.D. Tex.)," June 29, 2017, Office of the Attorney General of Texas. The attorneys general of Alabama, Arkansas, Idaho, Kansas, Louisiana, Nebraska, South Carolina, Tennessee, and West Virginia joined Texas attorney general Ken Paxton.

48. Maria Sacchetti, "DHS's Kelly: Program Shielding 800,000 Illegal Immigrants May Be in Jeopardy," *Washington Post*, July 12, 2017, https://www.washingtonpost.com/local/social-issues/dhss-kelly-tells-hispanic-caucus-daca-might-not-survive-court-challenge/2017/07/12/b1f19686-672b-11e7-9928-22d00a47778f_story.html?utm_term=.98ffaa1d639a; Editorial Boad, "Secretary Kelly, When Will You Speak Up for 'Dreamers'?," *Washington Post*, July 21, 2017, https://www.washingtonpost.com/opinions/secretary-kelly-when-will-you-speak-up-for-dreamers/2017/07/21/40647476-6d74-11e7-96ab-5f38140b38cc_story.html?utm_term=.e95bb968c2ad.

49. "Border Security and Immigration Enforcement Improvements," Executive Order 13767, January 23, 2017, https://trumpwhitehouse.archives.gov/presidential-actions/executive-order-border-security-immigration-enforcement-improvements/.

50. Julia Edwards Ainsley, "Exclusive: Trump Administration Considering Separating Women, Children at Mexico Border," Reuters, March 3, 2017, https://www.reuters.com/article/us-usa-immigration-children/exclusive-trump-administration-considering-separating-women-children-at-mexico-border-idUSKBN16A2ES.

51. Thai Kopan, "Kelly Says DHS Won't Separate Families at the Border," CNN, March 29, 2017, https://www.cnn.com/2017/03/29/politics/border-families-separation-kelly/index.html.

52. Quoted in Caitlyn Dickerson, "The Secret History of U.S. Government Family-Separation Policy," *The Atlantic*, August 7, 2022, https://www.theatlantic.com/magazine/archive/2022/09/trump-administration-family-separation-policy-immigration/670604/.

53. Dickerson, "Secret History of U.S. Government Family-Separation Policy."

54. DHS Records of Communication with Anti-Immigrant Groups, Francis Cissna memo, March 30, 2018, https://www.documentcloud.org/documents/6821391-DHS-18-0694-K.html#document/p132/a562502.

55. Julia Ainsley and Jacob Soboroff, "Trump Cabinet Officials Voted in 2018 to Separate Migrant Children, Say Officials," NBC News, August 2020, https://www.nbcnews.com/politics/immigration/trump-cabinet-officials-voted-2018-white-house-meeting-separate-migrant-n1237416.

56. Dickerson, "Secret History of U.S. Government Family Separation Policy."

57. Dickerson, "Secret History of U.S. Government Family Separation Policy."

58. Ainsley and Soboroff, "Trump Cabinet Officials Voted in 2018 Meeting."

59. Ginger Thompson, "Listen to Children Who've Just Been Separated from Their Parents at the Border," *ProPublica*, June 18, 2018, https://www.propublica.org/article/children-separated-from-parents-border-patrol-cbp-trump-immigration-policy.

60. Dickerson, "Secret History of the U.S. Government Family-Separation Policy."

61. "Affording Congress an Opportunity to Address Family Separation," Executive Order 1831, June 20, 2018, https://trumpwhitehouse.archives.gov/presidential-actions/affording-congress-opportunity-address-family-separation/.

62. Richard Gonzalez, "Trump's Executive Order on Family Separation: What It Does and Does Not Due," NPR, June 20, 2018, https://www.npr.org/2018/06/20/622095441/trump-executive-order-on-family-separation-what-it-does-and-doesnt-do.

63. A. M. Kurta, "Memorandum: Military Service Suitability Determinations for Foreign Nationals who are Lawful Permanent Residents," Office of the Secretary of Defense, October 13, 2017, https://www.defense.gov/News/Releases/Release/Article/1342317/dod-announces-policy-changes-to-lawful-permanent-residents-and-the-military-acc/; Sarah Holder, "How Rule Changes about Public Benefits Could Affect Immigrants," Bloomberg, City Lab, August 13, 2019, https://www.citylab.com/equity/2019/08/public-charge-rule-legal-immigration-welfare-services-dhs/595987/; Nick Miroff, "Under Secret Stephen Miller Plan, ICE to Use Data on Migrant Children to Expand Deportation Efforts," *Washington Post*, December 20, 2019, https://www.washingtonpost.com/immigration/under-secret-stephen-miller-plan-ice-to-use-data-on-migrant-children-to-expand-deportation-efforts/2019/12/20/36975b34-22a8-11ea-bed5-880264cc91a9_story.html.

64. Immigrant Defense Project, "Safeguarding the Integrity of Our Courts: The Impact of ICE Courthouse Operations in New York State," 2019, https://www.immigrantdefenseproject.org/wp-content/uploads/Safeguarding-the-Integrity-of-Our-Courts-Final-Report.pdf.

65. Debbie Cenziper, Madison Muller, Monique Beals, Rebecca Holland, and Andrew Ba Tran, "Under Trump, ICE Aggressively Recruited Sheriffs as Partners to Question and Detain Undocumented Immigrants," *Washington Post*, November 23, 2021, https://www.washingtonpost.com/investigations/interactive/2021/trump-ice-sheriffs-immigrants-287g/?itid=hp-top-table-main.

66. Paul C. Light, *The Tides of Reform: Making Government Work, 1945–1995* (New Haven, CT: Yale University Press, 1998).

67. Geraldine Baum, Tom Hamburger, and Michael J. Mishak, "Trump Has Thrived with Government's Generosity," *Los Angeles Times*, May 11, 2011, https://www.latimes.com/nation/la-xpm-2011-may-11-la-na-trump-20110511-story.html.

68. Kristina Wong and Rebecca Kheel, "Trump Strikes Fear into Defense Contractors," *The Hill*, December 15, 2016, http://thehill.com/policy/defense/310453-trump-strikes-fear-into-defense-contractors.

69. "Buy American and Hire American," Executive Order 13788, *Federal Register* 93, no. 76 (April 18, 2017): 18837–39.

70. Steven Mufson and David J. Lynch, "Breaking from GOP Orthodoxy, Trump Increasingly Deciding Winners and Losers in the Economy," *Washington Post*, June 1, 2018.

71. Interagency Task Force, "Assessing and Strengthening the Manufacturing and Defense Industrial Base and Supply Chain Resiliency of the United States. Report to President Donald J. Trump by the Interagency Task Force in Fulfillment of Executive Order 13806," September 2018.

72. Immigration and Nationality Act, chap. 477 of the 82nd Cong., 66 Stat. 163; 8 U.S.C. 1101 et seq.

73. Ross Barkan, "Trump Calls Off Tariffs after U.S.-Mexico Deal," *The Guardian*, https://www.theguardian.com/us-news/2019/jun/07/us-mexico-deal-tariffs-trump-says.

74. As with other administrative deployments, Trump did not invent these powers. Rather, his sustained use of tariff adjustment authority confirms a consensus among academics that presidents are increasingly able to strategically distribute economic benefits—including trade protections—to areas needed in the next election. See Kenneth S. Lowande, Jeffery A. Jenkins, and Andrew J. Clarke, "Presidential Particularism and US Trade Politics," *Political Science Research and Methods* 6, no. 2 (2018): 264–81; Douglas L. Kriner and Andrew Reeves, *The Particularistic President: Executive Branch Politics and Political Inequality* (New York: Cambridge University Press, 2015).

75. Chad P. Brown, "Policy Brief 17–21—Steel, Aluminum, Lumber, Solar: Trump's Stealth Trade Protection," 2017, Peterson Institute for International Economics, https://www.piie.com/publications/policy-briefs/steel-aluminum-lumber-solar-trumps-stealth-trade-protection.

76. Jeff Stein, "Trump Signs USMCA, Revamping North American Trade Rules," January 29, 2020, *Washington Post*, https://www.washingtonpost.com/business/2020/01/29/trump-usmca/.

77. Louisa Savage and John F. Harris, "Trump's Method on the Madness of Trade," *Politico*, June 6, 2019, https://www.politico.com/story/2019/06/06/donald-trump-trade-policy-global-translations-1355868.

78. Damian Paletta and Jena McGregor, "Two White House Corporate Advisory Groups Disband amid Charlottesville Fallout," *Washington Post*, August 16, 2017, https://www.washingtonpost.com/business/economy/2017/08/16/bbe888a6-82c5-11e7-ab27-1a21a8e006ab_story.html?utm_term=.8c53d52d9ed6.

79. "Statement by the President on the Keystone XL Pipeline," November 6, 2015, The White House, Office of the Press Secretary.

80. "Construction of the Keystone XL Pipeline," Memorandum for the Secretary of State, the Secretary of the Army, and the Secretary of the Interior, *Federal Register* 82, no. 18 (January 24, 2017): 8663–65; "Construction of the Dakota Access Pipeline," Memorandum for the Secretary of the Army, *Federal Register* 82, no. 18 (January 24, 2017): 8661–62; "Construction of American Pipelines," Memorandum for the Secretary of Commerce, *Federal Register* 82, no. 18 (January 24, 2017): 8659.

81. "Establishing Discipline and Accountability in the Environmental Review and Permitting Process for Infrastructure Projects," Executive Order 13807, *Federal Register* 82, no. 163 (August 15, 2017): 40463–69.

82. "Implementing an America-First Offshore Energy Strategy," Executive Order 13795, *Federal Register* 82, no. 84 (April 28, 2017): 20815–18.

83. Juliet Eilperin, "Trump Administration Working toward Renewed Drilling in Artic National Wildlife Refuge," *Washington Post*, September 15, 2017, https://www.washingtonpost.com/politics/trump-administration-working-toward-renewed-drilling-in-arctic-national-wildlife-refuge/2017/09/15/bfa5765e-97ea-11e7-87fc-c3f7ee4035c9_story.html.

84. "Military Service by Transgender Individuals," Memorandum for the Secretary of Defense and the Secretary of Homeland Security, *Federal Register* 82, no. 167 (August 25, 2017): 41319–20.

85. "Promoting Free Speech and Religious Liberty," Executive Order 13798, *Federal Register* 82, no. 88 (May 4, 2017): 21675–76.

86. Ben Protess, Danielle Ivory, and Steve Eder, "Where Trump's Hands-Off Approach to Governing Does Not Apply," *New York Times*, September 10, 2017, https://www.nytimes.com/2017/09/10/business/trump-regulations-religious-conservatives.html?mcubz=3/.

87. Protess, Ivory, and Eder, "Where Trump's Hands-Off Approach to Governing Does Not Apply."

88. "Hiring Freeze," Memorandum for the Heads of Executive Departments and Agencies, *Federal Register* 82, no. 15 (January 23, 2017): 8493–94.

89. "Comprehensive Plan for Reorganizing the Executive Branch," Executive Order 13781, *Federal Register* 82, no. 50 (March 13, 2017): 13959–60.

90. "Comprehensive Plan for Reforming the Federal Government and Reducing the Federal Civilian Workforce," Memorandum for Heads of Executive Departments and Agencies, April 12, 2017, Executive Office of the President: Office of Management and Budget, M-17-22.

91. "Budget of the U.S. Government: A New Foundation for American Greatness, Fiscal Year 2018," https://www.govinfo.gov/content/pkg/BUDGET-2018-BUD/pdf/BUDGET-2018-BUD-3.pdf.

92. "Reducing Regulation and Controlling Regulatory Costs," Executive Order 13771, *Federal Register* 82, no. 22 (January 30, 2017): 9339–41.

93. "Enforcing the Regulatory Reform Agenda," Executive Order 13777, *Federal Register* 82, no. 39 (February 24, 2017): 12285–87.

94. "Identifying and Reducing Tax Regulatory Burdens," Executive Order 13789, *Federal Register* 82, no. 79 (April 21, 2017): 19317–18.

95. "FY 2018 Regulatory Cost Allowances," Memorandum for Regulatory Reform Officers at Executive Departments and Agencies, September 7, 2017, Executive Office of the President, Office of Management and Budget, M-17-31.

96. Donald Moynihan, "Populism and the Deep State: The Attack on Public Service under Trump," *Democratic Backsliding and Public Administration*, ed. M. W. Bauer, B. G. Peters, J. Pierre, K. Yesilkagit, and S. Becker (New York: Cambridge University Press, 2021), 151–77, https://doi.org/10.1017/9781009023504.008.

97. "Fair Play and Safe Workplaces," Executive Order 13673, *Federal Register* 79, no. 150 (July 31, 2014): 45309–15.

98. "Revocation of Federal Contracting Executive Orders," Executive Order 13782, *Federal Register* 82, no. 60 (March 27, 2017): 15607. See also "The Labor Dept. Wants to Revise a Trump-Era Policy on Handling Discrimination Claims against Contractors," Government Executive, March 23, 2022, https://www.govexec.com/management/2022/03/labor-dept-wants-revise-trump-era-policy-handling-discrimination-claims-against-contractors/363514/.

99. *Coalition for Workforce Innovation, Associated Builders and Contractors of Southeast Texas, Associated Builders and Contractors, Inc., and Financial Services Institute, Inc v. Marty Walsh*, Civil Action No. 1:21-CV-130, Eastern District of Texas.

100. White House Transition Project, "Special Analysis on Pace of Confirmations," September 2017, http://www.whitehousetransitionproject.org/appointments/.

101. On this tension between mobilization and management, readers are encouraged

to consider the arguments of Karen Orren and Stephen Skowronek in *The Policy State: An American Predicament* (Cambridge, MA: Harvard University Press, 2017), 131–35.

102. Michael Brice-Sadler, "While Bemoaning Mueller Probe, Trump Falsely Says the Constitution Gives Him the 'Right to Do Whatever I Want,'" *Washington Post*, July 23, 2019, https://www.washingtonpost.com/politics/2019/07/23/trump-falsely-tells-audi torium-full-teens-constitution-gives-him-right-do-whatever-i-want/.

103. For example, during the 2016 presidential campaign, the Pew Research Center tracked a massive drop in the share of Republicans and Republican-leaning independents claiming that free trade agreements had been a "good thing" for the United States, from 56 percent in early 2015 to 29 percent in October 2016; see Ashley Parker, "A Sturdy Plank in the GOP Platform: Trumpism," *Washington Post*, March 25, 2018, A1, A21, https://www.adn.com/nation-world/2018/03/25/the-gop-platforms-ruling-plank-trumpism/. Trump also managed during his first two years in office to make the wall the core of Republican immigration policy, a partisan symbol of the party's support for border security. Colby Itkowitz, "Republicans Spent Two Years Resisting Trump's Border Wall. What Happened?," *Washington Post*, January 15, 2019, https://www.washingtonpost.com/politics/2019/01/15/republicans-spent-two-years-resisting-trumps-border-wall-what-changed/?utm_term=.2a2eed8bcf78.

104. Kenneth Lowande and Sidney M. Milkis, "'We Can't Wait': Barack Obama, Partisan Polarization, and the Administrative Presidency," *The Forum* 12, no. 1 (2014): 3–27.

4. TRUMP AND THE SEPARATION OF POWERS

1. Robert A. Dahl, "Myth of the Presidential Mandate," *Political Science Quarterly* 105, no. 3 (1990): 355–72.

2. Nicholas F. Jacobs, "Uniquely American: The Inaugural Address of Donald Trump," in *My Fellow Americans: Presidents and Their Inaugural Addresses*, ed. Yuvraj Singh (New York: Oxford University Press, 2024).

3. First Inaugural Address of Andrew Jackson, March 4, 1829, https://avalon.law.yale.edu/19th_century/jackson1.asp#:~:text=A%20diffidence%2C%20perhaps%20too%20just,mind%20that%20reformed%20our%20system.

4. Donald Trump, inauguration speech, January 20, 2017, *Politico*, https://www.politico.com/story/2017/01/full-text-donald-trump-inauguration-speech-transcript-233907.

5. James Madison, *Federalist* No. 51, in Alexander Hamilton, James Madison, and John Jay, *The Federalist Papers*, ed. Clinton Rossiter, with an introduction and notes by Charles R. Kessler (New York: Signet Classics, 2003), 319.

6. Martha Derthick, *Keeping the Compound Republic: Essays on American Federalism* (Washington, DC: Brookings Institution Press, 2001).

7. Nicholas F. Jacobs and James Ceaser, "The 2016 Presidential Election by the Numbers and in Historical Perspective," *The Forum* 14 (2016): 361–83.

8. Jessica M. Steiner, "Review: Charles O. Jones, *The Presidency in a Separated System*," *Journal of Politics* 68 (2005): 479.

9. Sidney M. Milkis, *Political Parties and Constitutional Government: Remaking American Democracy* (Baltimore: Johns Hopkins University Press, 1999).

10. Hugh Heclo, "One Executive Branch or Many," in *Both Ends of the Avenue*, ed. Anthony King (Washington, DC: American Enterprise Institution, 1983), 38–42.

11. Lukas K. Alexander and Nicholas F. Jacobs, "Presidential Partisanship and Legislative Cooperation in the US Senate, 1993–2021," *Congress & the Presidency* 50, no. 3 (2023): 291–316.

12. Philip A. Wallach, *Why Congress* (New York: Oxford University Press, 2023).

13. Greg Goelzhauser and David M. Konisky, "The State of American Federalism 2019–2020: Polarized and Punitive Intergovernmental Relations," *Journal of Federalism* 50 (2020): 311–43.

14. Nicholas F. Jacobs, "Seeing Red and Blue: Assessing How Americans Understand Geographic Polarization, Secession, and the Value of Federalism," *Publius: The Journal of Federalism* 54 (2024): 201–27.

15. John Dinan, "The Institutionalization of State Resistance to Federal Directives in the 21st Century," *The Forum* 18, no. 1 (2020): 3–23; Mikhail Filippov, Peter Ordeshook, and Olga Shvetsova, *Designing Federalism. A Theory of Self-Sustainable Federal Institutions* (New York: Cambridge University Press, 2004).

16. David R. Mayhew, *The Imprint of Congress* (New Haven, CT: Yale University Press, 2017), 6.

17. Sidney M. Milkis, *The President and the Parties: The Transformation of the American Party System since the New Deal* (Oxford: Oxford University Press, 1993), 143; Karen Orren and Stephen Skowronek, *The Policy State: An American Predicament* (Cambridge, MA: Harvard University Press, 2017).

18. R. Shep Melnick, "From Tax and Spend to Mandate and Sue: Liberalism after the Great Society," in *The Great Society and the High Tide of Liberalism*, ed. S. M. Milkis and J. M. Mileur (Amherst: University of Massachusetts Press, 2005), 405.

19. Michael Katz, *The Undeserving Poor: America's Enduring Confrontation with Poverty*, 2nd ed. (New York: Oxford University Press, 2013).

20. Mayhew, *Imprint of Congress*, 114.

21. Frances Lee, *Insecure Majorities: Congress and the Perpetual Campaign* (Chicago: University of Chicago Press, 2016).

22. Much of this discussion is drawn from Nicholas F. Jacobs, "Economic Sectionalism, Executive-Centered Partisanship, and the Politics of the State and Local Tax Deduction," *Political Science Quarterly* 136, no. 2 (2021): 311–38.

23. 26 U.S.C. 164(b)(6).

24. William A. Gamson and Andre Modigliani, "The Changing Culture of Affirmative Action," in *Research in Political Sociology*, vol. 3, ed. Richard D. Braungart (Greenwich, CT: JAI, 1987), 143.

25. Christopher Achen and Larry Bartels, *Democracy for Realists: Why Elections Do Not Produce Responsive Government* (Princeton, NJ: Princeton University Press, 2017).

26. Congressional Budget Office, "Cost Estimate: H.R. 1, A Bill to Provide for Reconciliation Pursuant to Titles II and V of the Concurrent Resolution on the Budget for Fiscal Year 2018," 2017, https://www.cbo.gov/system/files/115th-congress-2017-2018/costestimate/hr1.pdf.

27. Donald J. Trump, "Interview with Fox News, Sean Hannity," Fox News, October 11,

2017, https://www.foxnews.com/transcript/president-trump-vows-largest-tax-cut-in-the-history-of-this-country.

28. Michael Greve, "Governor Cuomo Gets It, Sort Of: So Does The Donald," *Law & Liberty*, January 11, 2018, https://lawliberty.org/governor-cuomo-gets-it-sort-of-so-does-the-donald/.

29. Internal Revenue Service, "Tax Year 2016: Historic Table 2 (SOI Bulletin)," 2018, https://www.irs.gov/statistics/soi-tax-stats-historic-table-2.

30. Jacob S. Hacker and Paul Pierson, "Robbing Blue States to Pay Red," *New York Times*, November 13, 2017.

31. Sarah F. Liebschutz and Irene Lurie, "The Deductibility of State and Local Taxes," *Publius: The Journal of Federalism* 16 (Summer 1986): 51–70; Timothy Conlan, *From New Federalism to Devolution: Twenty-Five Years of Intergovernmental Reform* (Washington, DC: Brookings Institution Press, 1998).

32. Gerald M. Boyd, "Reagan, in Jersey, Defends Tax Plan," *New York Times*, June 14, 1985.

33. Jeffrey H. Birnbaum and Allan S. Murray, *Showdown at Gucci Gulch* (New York: Vintage Books, 1988), 113.

34. John Zaller, *The Nature and Origins of Mass Opinion* (New York: Cambridge University Press, 1992).

35. Maria Bartiromo, Jessica Tarlov, James Freeman, and Howard Kurtz, "Tax Reform Moves to the Senate: Interviews with Kevin Brady, Peter King, Gordon Chang, and Lee Zeldin," *Fox News Sunday*, November 26, 2017.

36. *Meet the Press*, November 4, 2018, https://www.nbcnews.com/meet-the-press/meet-press-november-4-2018-n931056.

37. *Meet the Press*, November 11, 2018, https://www.nbcnews.com/meet-the-press/meet-press-november-11-2018-n934951.

38. Kenneth Scheve and David Stasavage, *Taxing the Rich: A History of Fiscal Fairness in the United States and Europe* (Princeton, NJ: Princeton University Press, 2016); Mark D. Brewer and Jeffrey M. Stonecash, *Polarization and the Politics of Personal Responsibility* (New York: Oxford University Press, 2015).

39. US Congress, Senate, Committee on the Judiciary, *Confirmation Hearing on the Nomination of John G. Roberts, Jr. to Be Chief Justice of the United States*, 115th Cong., 2005.

40. Alexander Hamilton, *Federalist* No. 78, in Hamilton, Madison, and Jay, *Federalist Papers*, 464; David Obrien, *Storm Center: The Supreme Court in American Politics*, 12th ed. (New York: W. W. Norton, 2020).

41. Keither E. Whittington, *Political Foundations of Judicial Supremacy: The Presidency, the Supreme Court, and Constitutional Leadership in U.S. History* (Princeton, NJ: Princeton University Press, 2009).

42. R. Shep Melnick, *The Transformation of Title IX* (Washington, DC: Brookings Institution Press, 2018).

43. Yanna Krupnikov and John Barry Ryan, *The Other Divide* (Cambridge: Cambridge University Press, 2022); David Masci, "The Culture War and the Coming Election," Pew Research Center, April 11, 2007, https://www.pewresearch.org/religion/2007/04/11/the-culture-war-and-the-coming-election/.

44. Mark V. Tushnet, "Constitutional Hardball," Georgetown University Law Center,

2004, https://scholarship.law.georgetown.edu/cgi/viewcontent.cgi?article=1557&context=facpub.

45. Steven Levitsky and Daniel Ziblatt, *How Democracies Die* (New York: Crown, 2018).

46. Adam Liptak and Alicia Parliapiano, "The Supreme Court Aligned with Public Opinion in Most Major Cases This Term," *New York Times*, July 9, 2020, https://www.nytimes.com/interactive/2020/06/15/us/supreme-court-major-cases-2020.html.

47. Robert P. Saldin and Steven M. Teles, *Never Trump: The Revolt of the Conservative Elites* (New York: Oxford University Press, 2020).

48. Nixon, in an essay largely ghostwritten by Pat Buchanan, laid out a lengthy critique of the court's role in abetting lawlessness: Richard Nixon, "What Has Happened to America?," *Reader's Digest*, October 1967. See also Chris Hickman, "Courting the Right: Richard Nixon's 1968 Campaign against the Warren Court," *Journal of Supreme Court History* 36, no. 3 (2011): 287–303.

49. Nick Gass, "Trump Unveils 11 Potential Supreme Court Nominees," *Politico*, May 18, 2016, https://www.politico.com/story/2016/05/trumps-supreme-court-nominees-223331.

50. Steven M. Teles, *The Rise of the Conservative Legal Movement: The Battle for Control of the Law* (Princeton, NJ: Princeton University Press, 2010).

51. US Department of Justice, Office of Legal Counsel, "Using Presidential Signing Statements to Make Fuller Use of the President's Constitutionally Assigned Role in the Process of Enacting Law," February 5, 1986, https://www.archives.gov/files/news/samuel-alito/accession-060-89-269/Acc060-89-269-box6-SG-LSWG-AlitotoLSWG-Feb1986.pdf.

52. Jeremy D. Bailey, "The New Unitary Executive and Democratic Theory: The Problem of Alexander Hamilton," *American Political Science Review* 102, no. 4 (2008): 464.

53. United States Courts, Archive of Judicial Vacancies, https://www.uscourts.gov/judges-judgeships/judicial-vacancies/archive-judicial-vacancies.

54. Thomas Roger Hunter, "Trump and the Judiciary," in *The Unorthodox Presidency of Donald Trump*, ed. Paul E. Rutledge and Chapman Rackaway (Lawrence: University Press of Kansas, 2021), 205–34.

55. Mark A. Theissen, "The 10 Best Things Trump Has Done in 2019," *Washington Post*, December 26, 2019, https://www.washingtonpost.com/opinions/2019/12/26/best-things-trump-has-done/?itid=lk_inline_manual_27; Mark A. Theissen, "The 10 Best Things Trump Has Done in 2018," *Washington Post*, December 31, 2018, https://www.washingtonpost.com/opinions/the-10-best-things-trump-has-done-in-2018/2018/12/31/a2de64b6-0d1b-11e9-84fc-d58c33d6c8c7_story.html?itid=lk_inline_manual_29; Mark A. Theissen, "The 10 Best Things Trump Has Done in 2020," *Washington Post*, December 31, 2020, https://www.washingtonpost.com/opinions/2020/12/31/best-things-trump-did-2020/.

56. "In His Own Words: The President's Attacks on the Courts," Brennan Center for Justice, June 5, 2017, https://www.brennancenter.org/our-work/research-reports/his-own-words-presidents-attacks-courts.

57. Julie Hershfield Davis, "Supreme Court Nominee Calls Trump's Attacks on Judiciary 'Demoralizing,'" *New York Times*, February 9, 2017, https://www.nytimes.com/2017/02/08/us/politics/donald-trump-immigration-ban.html.

58. Alexander Hamilton, *Federalist* No. 78, in Hamilton, Madison, and Jay, *Federalist Papers*, 464.

59. William Howell, *Power without Persuasion: The Politics of Direct Presidential Action* (Princeton, NJ: Princeton University Press, 2003), 174.

60. Julie Hirshfield Davis, "Trump Has the Worst Record at the Supreme Court of Any Modern President," *Washington Post*, July 20, 2020, https://www.washingtonpost.com/outlook/2020/07/20/trump-has-worst-record-supreme-court-any-modern-president/.

61. "Roundup: Trump-Era Agency Policy in the Courts," April 25, 2022, Institute for Policy Integrity, https://policyintegrity.org/trump-court-roundup.

62. Alan Liptak and Alan Rappeport, "Supreme Court Lifts Limits on Trump's Power to Fire Consumer Watchdog," *New York Times*, June 29, 2020, https://www.nytimes.com/2020/06/29/us/politics/cfpb-supreme-court.html.

63. *Department of Homeland Security v. Regents of the University of California*, 591 U.S. (2020).

64. Matt Keenley, "Trump Says 'We Won on DACA' at Tulsa Rally after Supreme Court Ruling," *Newsweek*, June 20, 2020, https://www.newsweek.com/trump-says-we-won-daca-tulsa-rally-after-supreme-court-ruling-1512364.

65. Toluse Olorunnipa, "'A Willingness to Fight': Win or Lose, Trump's Push for Citizenship Question in the Census Is Red Meat for the Base," *Washington Post*, July 6, 2019, https://www.washingtonpost.com/politics/a-willingness-to-fight-win-or-lose-trumps-push-for-a-citizenship-question-in-the-census-is-red-meat-for-his-base/2019/07/06/4950889c-9f5c-11e9-b27f-ed2942f73d70_story.html.

66. US Census Bureau, "Statement from Census Bureau Director Dr. Steven Dillingham," Release Number CB20-RTQ.20, June 23, 2020, https://www.census.gov/newsroom/press-releases/2020/statement-new-staff.html.

67. Dartuinnoro Clark, "Trump Signs Memo to Omit Undocumented Immigrants from Census Apportionment Count," NBC News, July 21, 2020, https://www.nbcnew.com/politics/white-house/trump-sign-executive-order-aimed-omitting-undocumented-immigrants-census-count-n1234228.

68. Nina Totenberg and Hansi Lo Wang, "Supreme Court Punts Census Case, Giving Trump Iffy Chance to Alter Numbers," NPR, December 18, 2020, https://www.npr.org/2020/12/18/946875796/supreme-court-punts-in-census-case-says-its-premature-to-decide-the-issue.

69. Samuel Hutchison Beer, *To Make a Nation: The Rediscovery of American Federalism* (Cambridge, MA: Harvard University Press, 1993).

70. Alexander Hamilton, *Federalist* No. 84, in Hamilton, Madison, and Jay, *Federalist Papers*, 516.

71. James Madison, *Federalist* No. 39, in Hamilton, Madison, and Jay, *Federalist Papers*, 240.

72. Douglas L. Kriner and Andrew Reeves, *The Particularistic President: Executive Branch Politics and Political Inequality* (New York: Cambridge University Press, 2015).

73. John D. Nugent, *Safeguarding Federalism: How States Protect Their Interests in National Policymaking* (Norman: University of Oklahoma Press, 2009).

74. Bruce P. Frohnen, "Waivers, Federalism, and the Rule of Law," *Perspectives on Political Science* 45, no. 1 (2016): 59–67; F. J. Thompson, and C. Burke, "Federalism by

Waiver: MEDICAID and the Transformation of Long-Term Care," *Publius: The Journal of Federalism* 39, no. 1 (2009): 22–46.

75. Jessica Bulman-Pozen, "Executive Federalism Comes to America," *Virginia Law Review* 102 (2016): 953–1030.

76. Martha Derthick, *Keeping the Compound Republic: Essays on American Federalism* (Washington, DC: Brookings Institution Press, 2001), 84.

77. Paul Nolette and Colin Provost, "Change and Continuity in the Role of State Attorneys General in the Obama and Trump Administrations," *Publius: The Journal of Federalism* 48 (Summer 2018): 469–94.

78. Wayne Slater, "Atty Gen Greg Abbott Says His Job Is Simple: Sue the Federal Government, Then Go Home," *Dallas Tribune*, June 7, 2012, https://www.dallasnews.com/news/politics/2012/06/07/updated-atty-gen-greg-abbott-says-his-job-is-simple-sue-the-federal-government-then-go-home/.

79. Nicholas F. Jacobs and Connor M. Ewing, "The Law: The Promises and Pathologies of Presidential Federalism," *Presidential Studies Quarterly* 48, no. 3 (2018): 552–69.

80. Frank J. Thompson, Kenneth K. Wong, and Barry G. Rabe, *Trump, the Administrative Presidency, and Federalism* (Washington, DC: Brookings Institution Press, 2020), 15.

81. Morton Grodzins, *The American System: A New View of Government in the United States* (New Brunswick, NJ: Transaction Publishers, 1966).

82. Jeremy B. White, "Trump Blames California for Wildfires, Tells State 'You Gotta Clean Your Floors,'" *Politico*, August 20, 2020, https://www.politico.com/states/california/story/2020/08/20/trump-blames-california-for-wildfires-tells-state-you-gotta-clean-your-floors-1311059.

83. J. Richard Piper, "'Situational Constitutionalism' and Presidential Power: The Rise and Fall of the Liberal Model of Presidential Government," *Presidential Studies Quarterly* 24, no. 3 (1994): 577–94; J. Richard Piper, "Presidential-Congressional Power Prescriptions in Conservative Political Thought since 1933," *Presidential Studies Quarterly* 21, no. 1 (1991): 35–54.

84. Timothy J. Conlan and Paul L. Posner, "Inflection Point? Federalism and the Obama Administration," *Publius: The Journal of Federalism* 41 (Summer 2011): 421–46.

85. "Minimizing the Economic Burden of the Patient Protection and Affordable Care Act Pending Repeal," Executive Order 13765, *Federal Register* 82, no. 14 (January 20, 2017): 8351–52.

86. Frank J. Thompson, *Medicaid Politics: Federalism, Policy Durability, and Health Reform* (Washington, DC: Georgetown University Press, 2012).

87. Shanna Rose, "Opting In, Opting Out: The Politics of State Medicaid Expansion," *The Forum* 13, no. 1 (2015): 63–82; Bryan Shelly, "The Bigger They Are: Cross-State Variation in Federal Education and Medicaid Waivers, 1991–2008," *Publius: The Journal of Federalism* 43, no. 3 (2013): 452–73.

88. Matthew G. Bevin, "Memorandum of Request for a Section 1115 Demonstration Waiver to Sylvia Burwell," Kentucky Health, August 24, 2016.

89. Kaiser Family Foundation, "Medicaid Waiver Tracker: Approved and Pending Section 1115 Waivers by State," February 2, 2023, https://www.kff.org/medicaid/issue-brief/medicaid-waiver-tracker-approved-and-pending-section-1115-waivers-by-state/.

90. Rick Hess, "Betsy DeVos and the Manichean Impulse," *Education Week Spotlight*, January 17, 2017, http://blogs.edweek.org/edweek/rick_hess_straight_up/2017/01/betsy_devos_and_the_manichean_impulse.html.

91. Erica L. Green, "DeVos's Hard Line on Education Law Surprises States," *New York Times*, July 7, 2017, https://www.nytimes.com/2017/07/07/us/politics/devos-federal-education-law-states.html?mcubz=0.

92. Thompson, Wong, and Rabe, *Trump, the Administrative Presidency, and Federalism*.

93. Martha Derthick, "Presidency," *The Encyclopedia of Federalism*, 2006, https://encyclopedia.federalism.org/index.php/Presidency.

94. "Statement by President Donald J. Trump on the Signing of H.R. 3364," The White House, Office of the Press Secretary, August 2, 2017.

95. Alexander Hamilton, *Federalist* No. 65, in Hamilton, Madison, and Jay, *Federalist Papers*, 395.

96. Mark Nevin, "Nixon Loyalists, Barry Goldwater, and Republican Support for President Nixon during Watergate," *Journal of Policy History* 29, no. 3 (2017): 403–30.

97. Alex Isenstadt, "GOP Cashes in on Impeachment," *Politico*, September 25, 2019.

98. Josh Dawsey and Michelle Ye Hee Lee, "Trump and the RNC Raised Almost Half a Billion Dollars Last Year—And Still Had Nearly $200 Million Heading into 2020," *Washington Post*. January 3, 2020.

99. Toluse Olorunnipa, "'This Lit Up Our Base': Trump Campaign Says Impeachment Will Help Him Win Reelection," *Washington Post*, December 12, 2019.

5. THE PRESIDENCY IN CRISIS: COVID-19, RACIAL JUSTICE, AND THE 2020 PRESIDENTIAL ELECTION

1. For example, Article 16 of the French Constitution explicitly allows the president to take exceptional measures "where the institutions of the Republic, the independence of the Nation, the integrity of its territory or the fulfillment of its international commitments are under serious and immediate threat." https://www.constituteproject.org/constitution/France_2008. This provision was an important template of the Fifth Republic, formed in 1958, which transformed a parliamentary system into a presidential system.

2. Suzanne Mettler, *Soldiers to Citizen: The G.I. Bill and the Making of the Greatest Generation* (New York: Oxford University Press, 2005); William J. Barber, *Designs within Disorder: Franklin D. Roosevelt, the Economists, and the Shaping of American Economic Policy, 1933–1945* (New York: Cambridge University Press, 1996); Karen Orren and Stephen Skowronek, "Regimes and Regime Building in American Government: A Review of Literature on the 1940s," *Political Science Quarterly* 113 (1998): 689–702; Sheldon D. Pollack, *War, Revenue, and State Building; Financing the Development of the American State* (Ithaca, NY: Cornell University Press, 2009).

3. Papers of John F. Kennedy. Pre-Presidential Papers. Senate Files, Box 911, "Coliseum, Raleigh, North Carolina, 17 September 1960." John F. Kennedy Presidential Library

4. Quoted in Joel Achenbach, William Wan, Karin Brulliard, and Chelsea Janes, "The Crisis That Shocked the World: America's Response to the Coronavirus," *Washington Post*, July 19, 2020.

5. Nicholas F. Jacobs and Sidney M. Milkis, "Get Out of the Way: Joe Biden, the U.S. Congress, and Executive-Centered Partisanship during the President's First Year in Office," *The Forum* 19, no. 4 (2021): 709–44.

6. David R. Mayhew, "Wars and American Politics," *Perspectives on Politics* 3 (September 2005): 473.

7. William G. Howell, Saul P. Jackman, and Jon C. Rogowski, *The Wartime President: Executive Influence and the Nationalizing Politics of Threat* (Chicago: University of Chicago Press, 2013).

8. John S. Lapinski, "Policy Substance and Performance in American Lawmaking, 1877–1994," *American Journal of Political Science* 52 (2008): 238.

9. Douglas L. Kriner, *After the Rubicon: Congress, Presidents, and the Politics of Waging War* (Chicago: University of Chicago Press, 2010).

10. Douglas L. Kriner and Andrew Reeves, *The Particularistic President: Executive Branch Politics and Political Inequality* (New York: Cambridge University Press, 2015).

11. Ariel Malka and Mark Adelman, "Expressive Survey Responding: A Closer Look at the Evidence and Its Implications for American Democracy," *Perspectives on Politics* 21 (2023): 1198–209.

12. Toby Green and Thomas Fazi, *The Covid Consensus: The Global Assault on Democracy and the Poor? A Critique from the Left* (New York: Oxford University Press, 2023).

13. Thomas Edsall, "When the Mask You're Wearing 'Tastes Like Socialism,'" *New York Times*, May 20, 2020, https://www.nytimes.com/2020/05/20/opinion/coronavirus-trump-partisanship.html.

14. Laurie McGinley, Yasmeen Abutaleb, Josh Dawsey, and Carolyn Y. Johnson, "Inside Trump's Pressure Campaign on Federal Scientists over a Covid-19 Treatment," *Washington Post*, August 30, 2020, https://www.washingtonpost.com/health/convalescent-plasma-treatment-covid19-fda/2020/08/29/e39a75ec-e935-11ea-bc79-834454439a44_story.html.

15. "Inside Operation Warp Speed," The Choice, *New York Times*, August 17, 2020, https://www.nytimes.com/2020/08/17/podcasts/the-daily/trump-coronavirus-vaccine-covid.html.

16. Michael Wilner, "Urgent Request Sent to States in Push for Coronavirus Delivery by November 1," *McClatchy Report*, September 20, 2020, https://www.mcclatchydc.com/news/coronavirus/article245406245.html.

17. Evan Semones, "Harris Says She Wouldn't Trust Trump on Any Vaccine Released before Election," *Politico*, September 5, 2020, https://www.politico.com/news/2020/09/05/kamala-harris-trump-coronavirus-vaccine-409320; Sean Sullivan, "Biden Questions Whether a Vaccine Approved by Trump Would Be Safe," *Washington Post*, September 16, 2020, https://www.washingtonpost.com/politics/biden-trump-coronavirus-vaccine/2020/09/16/2ffbea6a-f831-11ea-a275-1a2c2d36e1f1_story.html.

18. Andrew Romano, "Yahoo News/YouGov Coronavirus Poll: Number of American Who Plan to Get Vaccinated Falls to 42%—New Low," Yahoo News, August 4, 2020, https://www.yahoo.com/entertainment/yahoo-news-you-gov-coronavirus-poll-number-of-americans-who-plan-to-get-vaccinated-falls-to-42-percent-a-new-low-162000936.html.

19. Caitlin Oprysko and Susannah Luthi, "Trump Labels Himself a 'Wartime President'

Combating Coronavirus," *Politico*, March 18, 2020, https://www.politico.com/news/2020/03/18/trump-administration-self-swab-coronavirus-tests-135590.

20. Colleen Long and Zeke Miller, "Stimulus Checks to Bear Trump's Name in Unprecedented Move," Associated Press, April 15, 2020, https://apnews.com/article/virus-outbreak-donald-trump-us-news-business-ap-top-news-8eafb90e92a676278a5644a2b-72b734c.

21. Donald F. Kettl, "States Divided: The Implications of American Federalism for COVID-19," *Public Administration Review* 80 (July–August 2020): 595–602; Rebecca L. Haffajee and Michelle M. Mello, "Thinking Globally, Acting Locally—The U.S. Response to Covid-19," *New England Journal of Medicine* 382 (2020): e75, https://doi.org/10.1056/NEJMp2006740; Davia Cox Downey and William M. Meyers, "Federalism, Intergovernmental Relationships, and Emergency Response: A Comparison of Australia and the United States," *American Review of Public Administration* 50 (August–October 2020): 526–35.

22. Nicholas F. Jacobs, "Federalism, Polarization, and Policy Responsibility during COVID-19: Experimental and Observational Evidence from the United States," *Publius: The Journal of Federalism* 51, no. 3 (2021): 693–719.

23. Aziz Huq, "States Can Band Together to Fight the Virus—No Matter What Trump Does," *Washington Post*, April 15, 2020, https://www.washingtonpost.com/outlook/2020/04/15/states-coronavirus-agreements-reopen/.

24. Berkeley Lovelace Jr., Noah Higgins-Dunn, and Will Feuer, "Coronavirus: NY, NJ, CT Coordinate Restrictions on Restaurants, Limit Events to Fewer Than 50 People," CNBC, March 15, 2020, https://www.cnbc.com/2020/03/16/new-york-new-jersey-and-connecticut-agree-to-close-restaurants-limit-events-to-less-than-50-people.html.

25. Alexandra Kelley, "Washington State to Return Ventilators for Use in New York for Coronavirus Relief," *The Hill*, April 6, 2020, https://thehill.com/changing-america/well-being/prevention-cures/491310-washington-state-to-return-ventilators-for-use/.

26. Michael S. Greve, "Up with Federalism? A Case for Cautious Optimism," *Law and Liberty*, April 23, 2020, https://lawliberty.org/up-with-federalism-a-case-for-cautious-optimism/?utm_source=LAL+Updates&utm_campaign=a86fcb8987-LAL_Daily_Updates&utm_medium=email&utm_term=0_53ee3e1605-a86fcb8987-72559109.

27. Ari Shapiro, "A Close Look at President Trump's Assertion of 'Absolute' Authority over States," *NPR: All Things Considered*, April 14, 2020, https://www.npr.org/2020/04/14/834460063/a-close-look-at-president-trumps-assertion-of-absolute-authority-over-states.

28. See John Kincaid and J. Wesley Leckrone, "Partisan Fractures in U.S. Federalism's COVID-19 Policy Responses," *State and Local Government Review* 52 (2020): 298–308.

29. Toluse Olorunnipa, Josh Dawsey, Chelsea Janes, and Isaac Stanley-Becker, "Governors Plead for Medical Equipment from Federal Stockpile Plagued by Shortages and Confusion," *Washington Post*, March 31, 2020, https://www.washingtonpost.com/politics/governors-plead-for-medical-equipment-from-federal-stockpile-plagued-by-shortages-and-confusion/2020/03/31/18aadda0-728d-11ea-87da-77a8136c1a6d_story.html.

30. Sarah Mervosh and Katie Rogers, "Governors Fight Back against Coronavirus Chaos: 'It's Like Being on eBay with 50 Other States,'" *New York Times*, March 31, 2020, https://www.nytimes.com/2020/03/31/us/governors-trump-coronavirus.html; Jonathan

Martin, "Trump to Governors on Ventilators: 'Try Getting It Yourselves,'" *New York Times*, March 16, 2020, https://www.nytimes.com/2020/03/16/us/politics/trump-coronavirus-respirators.html.

31. Aaron Blake, "Trump Ties Coronavirus Decisions to Personal Grievances," *Washington Post*, March 28, 2020, https://www.washingtonpost.com/politics/2020/03/27/trump-suggests-personal-grievances-factor-into-his-coronavirus-decisions/.

32. Donald Trump (@realDonaldTrump), "Why should the people and taxpayers of America be bailing out poorly run states . . . ," Twitter, April 27, 2020, 10:41 a.m., https://www.presidency.ucsb.edu/documents/tweets-april-27-2020.

33. Kenneth P. Vogel, Jim Rutenberg, and Lisa Lerer, "The Quiet Hand of Conservative Groups in the Anti-lockdown Protests," *New York Times*, April 21, 2020, https://www.nytimes.com/2020/04/21/us/politics/coronavirus-protests-trump.html.

34. Sidney Tarrow, "There Go the People," *Public Seminar*, April 21, 2020, https://publicseminar.org/essays/there-go-the-people-trump-whitmer.

35. Rona Andrew DeMillo, "GOP Governors in Spiking States Strain for Silver Linings," Associated Press, October 11, 2020, https://apnews.com/article/virus-outbreak-public-health-health-oklahoma-south-dakota-1c355dd08a0b0c455135d9c9af32dec8; Cleve R. Wootson Jr., Issac Stanley-Becker, Lori Rozsa, and Josh Dawsey, "Coronavirus Ravaged Florida, as Ron DeSantis Sidelined Scientists and Followed Trump," *Washington Post*, July 25, 2020, https://www.washingtonpost.com/national/coronavirus-ravaged-florida-as-ron-desantis-sidelined-scientists-and-followed-trump/2020/07/25/0b8008da-c648-11ea-b037-f97111f89ee46_story.html.

36. Ron Brownstein, "An Unprecedented Divide between Red and Blue America," *The Atlantic*, April 16, 2020, https://www.theatlantic.com/politics/archive/2020/04/covid-trump-pandemic/610075/.

37. Michael T. Hartney and Leslie K. Finger, "Politics, Markets, and Pandemics: Public Education's Response to COVID-19," EdWorkingPaper 20-304, Annenberg Institute at Brown University, October 2020, https://doi.org/10.26300/8ff8-3945.

38. Greg Goelzhauser and David M. Konisky, "The State of American Federalism 2019–2020: Polarized and Punitive Intergovernmental Relations," *Publius: The Journal of Federalism* 50 (Summer 2020): 311–43; Nicholas F. Jacobs and Connor M. Ewing, "The Promises and Pathologies of Presidential Federalism," *Presidential Studies Quarterly* 48 (September 2018): 552–69.

39. Burgess Everett, Sarah Ferris, Marianne Levine, and Melanie Nanona, "Trump Backs Down, Signs Stimulus Package," *Politico*, December 27, 2020, https://www.politico.com/news/2020/12/27/congress-stimulus-deal-450380.

40. Jerry Markon, "Watchdogs Are on the Lookout for Obama Appointees Burrowing In," *Washington Post*, November 30, 2015, https://www.washingtonpost.com/news/federal-eye/wp/2015/11/30/whats-that-a-groundhog-no-its-a-federal-worker-burrowing-in/.

41. William Roberts, "Amid the Coronavirus Pandemic, the Trump Administration Targets Government Watchdogs," Center for American Progress, July 1, 2020, https://www.americanprogress.org//issues/democracy/reports/2020/06/01/485656/amid-coronavirus-pandemic-trum-adminstration-targets-government-watchdogs/.

42. Project on Government Oversight, "Inspector General Vacancy Tracker," November 19, 2020, https://www.pogo.org/database/inspector-general-vacancy-tracker/.

43. "Creating Schedule F in the Excepted Service," Executive Order 13957, *Federal Register* 85, no. 207 (October 21, 2020): 67631–35.

44. Zolan Kanno-Youngs and Kirk Semple, "Trump Cites Coronavirus as He Announces a Border Crackdown," *New York Times*, March 20, 2020, https://www.nytimes.com/2020/03/20/us/politics/trump-border-coronavirus.html.

45. Andrea Castillo, "What Is Title 42 and What Happens Now That the Immigration Policy Has Expired?," *Los Angeles Times*, May 11, 2023, https://www.latimes.com/politics/story/2023-05-11/what-is-title-42-and-what-happens-when-the-immigration-border-policy-goes-away.

46. "Suspension of Entry of Immigrants Who Present a Risk to the United States Labor Market during the Economic Recovery Following the 2019 Novel Coronavirus Outbreak," Proclamation 10014, *Federal Register* 85, no. 81 (April 22, 2020): 23441–44; Ilya Somin, "The Danger of America's Coronavirus Immigration Bans," *The Atlantic*, June 28, 2020, https://www.theatlantic.com/ideas/archive/2020/06/danger-americas-coronavirus-immigration-bans/613537/.

47. Rachel Treisman, "ICE Confirms New Foreign Students Can't Take Online-Only Course Loads in the U.S.," NPR, July 24, 2020, https://www.npr.org/sections/coronavirus-live-updates/2020/07/24/895223219/ice-confirms-new-foreign-students-cant-take-online-only-course-loads-in-the-u-s.

48. Toluse Olorunnipa, "Trump Forges Ahead with Broader Agenda Even as Coronavirus Upends the Country," *Washington Post*, April 9, 2020, https://www.washingtonpost.com/politics/trump-coronavirus-immigration-environment-inspectors-general/2020/04/08/bc1590e2-79b9-11ea-b6ff-597f170df8f8_story.html; Caitlin Dickerson and Michael D. Shear, "Before Covid-19, Trump Aide Sought to Use Disease to Close Borders," *New York Times*, May 3, 2020, https://www.nytimes.com/2020/05/03/us/coronavirus-immigration-stephen-miller-public-health.html.

49. Louisa Savage and John F. Harris, "Trump's Method on the Madness of Trade," *Politico*, June 6, 2019, https://www.politico.com/story/2019/06/06/donald-trump-trade-policy-global-translations-1355868.

50. Jeff Stein, Carol D. Leonnig, Josh Dawsey, and Gerry Shih, "U.S. Officials Crafting Retaliatory Actions against China over Coronavirus as President Trump Fumes," *Washington Post*, April 30, 2020, https://www.washingtonpost.com/business/2020/04/30/trump-china-coronavirus-retaliation/.

51. Quoted in Laura Silver, Kat Devlin, and Christin Huang, "Americans Fault China for Its Role in the Spread of COVID-19," Pew Research Center, July 30, 2020, https://www.pewresearch.org/global/2020/07/30/americans-fault-china-for-its-role-in-the-spread-of-covid-19/.

52. Quoted in Rick Gladstone, "How Cold War between U.S. and China Is Intensifying," *New York Times*, July 22, 2020, https://www.nytimes.com/2020/07/22/world/asia/us-china-cold-war.html.

53. Yulin Hswen, Xiang Xu, Anna Hing, Jared B. Hawkins, John S. Brownstein, and Gilbert C. Gee, "Association of '#covid19' versus '#chinesevirus' with Anti-Asian Sentiments on Twitter," *American Journal of Public Health* 111 (May 2021): 956–64; Andrea Salcedo, "Racist Anti-Asian Hashtags Spiked after Trump First Tweeted 'Chinese Virus,' Study Finds," *Washington Post*, March 19, 2021, https://www.washingtonpost.com

/s/nation/2021/03/19/trump-tweets-chinese-virus-racist; Gerda Hooijer and Desmond King, "The Racialized Pandemic: Wave One of COVID-19 and the Reproduction of Global North Inequalities," *Perspectives on Politics*, August 11, 2021, https://doi.org/10.1017 /S153759272100195X.

54. Stuart Anderson, "U.S. International Student Enrollment Dropped as Canada's Soared," *Forbes*, March 3, 2022, https://www.forbes.com/sites/stuartanderson/2022/03/03 /us-international-student-enrollment-dropped-as-canadas-soared/.

55. Donald Moynihan, "Delegitimization, Deconstruction and Control: Undermining the Administrative State," *ANNALS of the American Academy of Political and Social Science* 699, no. 1 (2022): 36–49.

56. Sidney Milkis and Daniel Tichenor, *Rivalry and Reform: Presidents, Social Movements, and the Transformation of American Politics* (Chicago: University of Chicago Press, 2019).

57. Bruce Miroff, "Presidential Leverage over Social Movements: The Johnson White House and Civil Rights," *Journal of Politics* 43, no. 1 (February 1981): 14.

58. Alex Smith, "Showing That It Matters: Mapping the George Floyd or Black Lives Matter Protests," University of Arizona, https://gis.arizona.edu/news/showing-it-matters -mapping-george-floyd-or-black-lives-matter-protests.

59. Monesh Arona, "How the Coronavirus Pandemic Helped the Floyd Protest Become the Biggest in U.S. History," *Washington Post*, August 5, 2020, https://www .washingtonpost.com/politics/2020/08/05/how-coronavirus-pandemic-helped-floyd -protests-become-biggest-us-history/.

60. Max Cohen, "Trump: Black Lives Matter Is a 'Symbol of Hate,'" *Politico*, July 1, 2020, https://www.politico.com/news/2020/07/01/trump-black-lives-matter-347051.

61. David Siders, "Trump Bets His Presidency on a 'Silent Majority,'" *Politico*, June 3, 2020, https://www.politico.com/news/2020/06/03/trump-suburbs-reelection-nixon-296 980.

62. "Protecting American Monuments, Memorials, and Statues and Combating Recent Criminal Violence," Executive Order 13933, *Federal Register* 85, no. 128 (June 26, 2020): 40081–84.

63. Anne Applebaum, "Trump Is Putting on a Show in Portland," *The Atlantic*, July 23, 2020, https://www.theatlantic.com/ideas/archive/2020/07/trump-putting-show-portland /614521/.

64. Nick Miroff, "DHS's Changing Mission Leaves Its Founders Dismayed as Its Critics Call for a Breakup," *Washington Post*, August 13, 2020, https://www.washingtonpost .com/national/dhs-mission-creep-protests/2020/08/13/44a287ce-dc8b-11ea-b4af -72895e22941d_story.html; Tessa Berenson, "'We're Pawns in the Game': Mayors Worry Trump's Operation Legend Is More about Politics Than Law Enforcement," *Time*, August 13, 2020, https://time.com/5878817/operation-legend-mayors-albuquerque-chicago -kansas-city/.

65. Nick Miroff and Matt Zaposky, "Facing Unrest in American Streets, Trump Turns Homeland Security Powers Inward," *Washington Post*, July 21, 2020, https:// www.washingtonpost.com/national/facing-unrest-on-american-streets-trump-turns -homeland-security-powers-inward/2020/07/21/655e7822-cb71-11ea-89ce-ac7d5e4a5a38 _story.html.

66. Movement for Black Lives, "Struggle for Power: The Ongoing Persecution of Black Movement by the U.S. Government," August 18, 2021, https://m4bl.org/struggle-for-power/#about.

67. Peter Baker, Maggie Haberman, Katie Rogers, Zolan Kanno-Youngs, and Katie Benner, "How Trump's Idea for a Photo Op Led to Havoc in a Park," *New York Times*, June 2, 2020, https://www.nytimes.com/2020/06/02/us/politics/trump-walk-lafayette-square.html. An Inspector General report, released a year later, raised doubts that Trump directly ordered federal law enforcement to remove the protesters, but it hints that the order came from Attorney General William Barr. Moreover, whether or not he gave the direct order, Trump praised the show of force in a tweet the following morning. Aaron Rupar, "What the New IG Report about Gassing the Protesters around Lafayette Square Actually Says," *Vox*, June 11, 2021, https://www.vox.com/2021/6/11/22527796/ig-report-trump-bible-lafayette-square-protest.

68. Mia Jankowitz, "Trump's Evangelical Base Is Ecstatic over His Bible Photo-Op," *Insider*, June 4, 2020, https://www.insider.com/the-christian-right-loved-trumps-bible-photo-op-outside-church-2020-6.

69. Antonio Olivo and Nick Miroff, "ICE Flew Detainees from Virginia So That Planes Could Transport Agents to D.C. Protests. A Huge Coronavirus Outbreak Followed," *Washington Post*, September 11, 2020, https://www.washingtonpost.com/coronavirus/ice-air-farmville-protests-covid/2020/09/11/f70ebe1e-e861-11ea-bc79-834454439a44_story.html.

70. Nicholas F. Jacobs and Sidney M. Milkis, "Get Out of the Way: Joe Biden, the U.S. Congress, and Executive-Centered Partisanship during the President's First Year in Office," *The Forum* 19, no. 4 (2021): 709–44.

71. Richard Kreitner, "What History Tells Us about Trump's Implosion and Biden's Opportunity," *The Nation*, October 12, 2020, https://www.thenation.com/article/politics/interview-stephen-skowronek/.

72. Gary C. Jacobson, "The Dimensions, Origins, and Consequences of Belief in Donald Trump's Big Lie," *Political Science Quarterly* 138, no. 2 (2023): 133–66.

73. Benjamin Swasey, "Florida Lawmakers Back the Creation of an Election Crimes Investigative Office," NPR, March 3, 2022, https://www.npr.org/2022/03/10/1085660543/florida-lawmakers-back-the-creation-of-an-election-crimes-investigative-office.

CONCLUSION: THE FUTURE OF THE AMERICAN PRESIDENCY

1. Jonathan Swan, Charlie Savage, and Maggie Haberman, "If Trump Wins, His Allies Want Lawyers Who Will Bless a More Radical Agenda," *New York Times*, November 1, 2023.

2. Paul Dans and Steven Groves, eds., *A Mandate for Leadership: The Conservative Promise* (Washington, DC: Heritage Foundation, 2023).

3. Bill Barrow, "After Trump's Project 2025 Denials, He Is Tapping Its Authors and Influencers for Key Roles," *Associated Press*, November 23, 2024, https://apnews.com/article/trump-project-2025-administration-nominees-843f5ff20131ccba5f056e7ccc5baf23.

4. Jonathan Swan, Charlie Savage, and Maggie Haberman, "Trump and Allies Forge Plans to Increase Presidential Power in 2025," *New York Times*, July 17, 2023.

5. George Packer, "The End of Democratic Delusions: The Trump Reaction and What Comes Next," *The Atlantic*, January 2025, 11–14.

6. Hugh Heclo, *On Thinking Institutionally* (New York: Oxford University Press, 2011).

7. Juan Linz, "The Perils of Presidentialism," *Journal of Democracy* 1, no. 1 (Winter 1990): 51–69.

8. Linz, "Perils of Presidentialism," 53.

9. "From the Archives: President Teddy Roosevelt's New Nationalism Speech," December 6, 2011, https://obamawhitehouse.archives.gov/blog/2011/12/06/archives-president-teddy-roosevelts-new-nationalism-speech.

10. Linz, "Perils of Presidentialism," 64–65.

11. Paul Waldman, "What Biden Means When He Says, 'I Am the Democratic Party,'" *American Prospect*, October 5, 2020, https://prospect.org/politics/biden-debate-i-am-democratic-party/.

12. Elena Schneider, "DNC Shakes Up Presidential Primary Schedule," *Politico*, February 24, 2023, https://www.politico.com/news/2023/02/04/dnc-presidential-primary-calendar-00081206.

13. Martin Van Buren to Thomas Ritchie, January 13, 1827, Teaching American History, https://teachingamericanhistory.org/document/letter-to-thomas-ritchie/.

14. Linz, "Perils of Presidentialism," 69.

15. Donald Trump, "Inauguration Speech," *Politico*, January 20, 2017, https://www.politico.com/story/2017/01/full-text-donald-trump-inauguration-speech-transcript-233907.

16. Max Weber, "The Sociology of Charismatic Authority," in *From Max Weber: Essays in Sociology*, ed. H. H. Gerth and C. Wright Mills (New York: Oxford University Press, 1958), 245–52.

17. About six in ten US registered voters (59 percent) in a September 2023 survey say undocumented immigrants should be allowed to stay in the country legally if certain requirements are met; however, this support is down from 77 percent who said the same in 2017. "Trump and Harris Supporters Differ in Mass Deportation but Favor Border Security, High Skilled Immigration," Pew Research Center, September 27, 2024, https://www.pewresearch.org/.

18. Daniel DiSalvo, *Engines of Change: Party Factions in American Politics, 1868–2010* (New York: Oxford University Press, 2012).

19. "McConnell on Impeachment: 'Disgraceful Dereliction' Cannot Lead Senate to 'Defy Our Own Constitutional Guardrails,'" Mitch McConnell: Republican Leader, February 13, 2021, https://www.republicanleader.senate.gov/newsroom/remarks/mcconnell-on-impeachment-disgraceful-dereliction-cannot-lead-senate-to-defy-our-own-constitutional-guardrails.

20. Nick Niedzwiadek, "McCarthy Says Trump 'Bears Responsibility' for Capitol Riot," *Politico*, January 13, 2021, https://www.politico.com/news/2021/01/13/mccarthy-trump-responsibility-capitol-riot-458975.

21. Jordain Carney, "Graham: Trump's Legacy 'Tarnished,' but Not Supportive Yet of 25th Amendment," *The Hill*, January 7, 2021, https://thehill.com/homenews/senate/533205-graham-trumps-legacy-tarnished-but-not-supportive-yet-of-25th-amendment/.

22. Colby Itkowitz, "'Normal Tourist Visit': Republicans Recast Deadly Jan. 6 Attack by Pro-Trump Mob," *Washington Post*, May 12, 2021, https://www.washingtonpost

.com/politics/trump-riot-capitol-republicans/2021/05/12/dcc03342-b351-11eb-a980-a60af976ed44_story.html.

23. Adam Edelman and Garrett Haake, "Republican Loyal to Trump Claims Capitol Riot Looked More Like 'Normal Tourist Visit,'" *NBC News*, May 12, 2021, https://www.nbcnews.com/politics/congress/republican-loyal-trump-claims-capitol-riot-looked-more-normal-tourist-n1267163.

24. Lisa Mascaro, Mary Clare Jalonick, and Farnoush Amiri, "Tucker Carlson Amplifies Jan. 6 Lies with GOP-Provided Video," Associated Press, March 7, 2023, https://apnews.com/article/jan-6-tucker-carlson-capitol-riot-mccarthy-adc245e22f-50b076925eb72948062808.

25. Josh Dawsey and Felicia Sonmez, "RNC Votes to Condemn Cheney, Kinzinger for Serving on House Committee Investigating Jan. 6 Attack on the Capitol by Pro-Trump Mob," *Washington Post*, February 4, 2022, https://www.washingtonpost.com/nation/2022/02/03/rnc-cheney-trump/.

26. Steve Peoples, "GOP Chair Ronna McDaniel Defeats Rival in Fierce Campaign," Associated Press, January 27, 2023, https://apnews.com/article/politics-republican-national-convention-united-states-government-2022-midterm-elections-donald-trump-ab2a2c94ff0f110e3c45c37cdf695695.

27. Alana Wise, "RNC Votes to Censure Reps. Liz Cheney and Adam Kinzinger over Work with Jan. 6 Panel," NPR, February 4, 2022, https://www.npr.org/2022/02/04/1078316505/rnc-censure-liz-cheney-adam-kinzinger-jan-6-committee-capitol.

28. Zack Beauchamp, "The National GOP Is Broken. State GOPs Might Be Even Worse," *Vox*, January 26, 2021, https://www.vox.com/2021/1/26/22250374/republican-party-gop-oregon-hawaii-arizona.

29. Jonathan J. Cooper, "Arizona Republicans Censure Cindy McCain, GOP Governor," Associated Press, January 23, 2021, https://apnews.com/article/donald-trump-race-and-ethnicity-censures-arizona-lawsuits-a50165b9d5c4468d5d1bb434c5e9c80a.

30. Nicholas Riccardi and Joey Cappelletti, "Failing at Polls, Election Deniers Focus on State GOP Posts," Associated Press, February 26, 2023, https://apnews.com/article/politics-us-republican-party-colorado-6ab686410f80d67b4fe0950a54f16bdb; Nicholas Riccardi, "Colorado GOP Selects Combative, Election-Denying New Leader," Associated Press, March 11, 2023, https://apnews.com/article/republican-party-election-deniers-colorado-trump-biden-d57a4683080ee4de5afd2e76fa8dd619.

31. Michael Scherer, Josh Dawsey, and Maeve Reston, "Trump Works State-by-State to Improve Chances at Republican Convention," *Washington Post*, February 24, 2023, https://www.washingtonpost.com/politics/2023/02/24/trump-states-2024-election/; Alex Isenstadt, "Trump Courts Early-State Republicans at Mar-a-Lago," *Politico*, March 23, 2023, https://www.politico.com/news/2023/03/03/trump-courts-early-state-republicans-at-mar-a-lago-00085488.

32. Richard E. Berg-Andersson, "The Green Papers: Presidential Primaries 2020 Republican Pledged and Unpledged Delegate Summary," 2023, http://www.thegreenpapers.com/P20/R-PU.phtml?sort=t.

33. David Siders and Meredith McGraw, "Just How Big Is the Always Trump Component of the Republican Party?," *Politico*, February 28, https://www.politico.com/news/2023/02/28/trump-voters-republican-primary-00084652.

34. Jazmine Ulloa and Jonathan Weisman, "Haley's Failed Campaign Highlights GOP Rifts and Trump's Dominance," *New York Times*, March 6, 2024, https://www.nytimes.com/2024/03/06/us/politics/nikki-haley-drops-out-trump.html. Like all of Trump's primary rivals, Haley eventually came around, expressing her "strong endorsement for the former president in a speech at the Republican National Convention"; Arit John, Jeff Zeleny, and Kate Sullivan, "Niki Haley Offers Her 'Strong Endorsement' of Trump in Convention Speech," July 16, 2024, https://www.cnn.com/2024/07/16/politics/nikki-haley-trump-rnc-speech/index.html.

35. Quoted in Tom Phillips, "Judges Ban Bolsonaro for Running for Office for Eight Years over 'Appalling Lies,'" *The Guardian*, June 30, 2023, https://www.theguardian.com/world/2023/jun/30/jair-bolsonaro-judges-vote-ban-running-for-office.

36. Quoted in Jack Nicas, "Why Trump Was Barred in Brazil but Trump Can Run in the United States," *New York Times*, July 8, 2023, https://www.nytimes.com/2023/07/01/world/americas/trump-bolsonaro-brazil-us.html.

37. Sidney M. Milkis and Daniel J. Tichenor, *Rivalry and Reform: Presidents, Social Movements, and the Transformation of American Politics* (Chicago: University of Chicago Press, 2019).

38. Linz, "Perils of Presidentialism," 57.

39. Joe Biden, "My message to Republicans: If you don't want to help save the country, get out of the way," Twitter, October 5, 2021, 15:21, https://x.com/JoeBiden/status/1445469237468749841.

40. Joe Biden, "Campaign Speech, Warms Springs, Georgia," October 27, 2020, https://www.rev.com/blog/transcripts/joe-biden-campaign-speech-transcript-warm-springs-ga-october-27.

41. Joe Biden, campaign speech transcript, Milwaukee, Wisconsin, October 30, 2020, https://rollcall.com/factbase/biden/transcript/joe-biden-speech-milwaukee-wisconsin-october-30-2020/.

42. Laura Barrón-López and Christopher Cadelgo, "How Biden's Sherpa, Steve Ricchetti, Scored the Big Deal," *Politico*, July 30, 2021, https://www.politico.com/news/2021/07/30/biden-sherpa-richetti-501730.

43. Matt Viser and Cleve Wootson, "Embracing 'Bidenomics,' President Seeks to Turn Insult into Strength," *Washington Post*, June 28, 2023, https://www.washingtonpost.com/politics/2023/06/28/bidenomics-biden-economy-campaign/.

44. Geoffrey Skelly, "Biden's First Hundred Days Shows How Partisan Things Have Become," April 28, 2021, FiveThirtyEight, https://fivethirtyeight.com/features/bidens-first-100-days-show-how-partisan-things-have-become/.

45. David Leonhardt, "Recent Immigration Surge Has Been Largest in History," *New York Times*, December 11, 2024, https://www.nytimes.com/2024/12/11/briefing/us-immigration-surge.html.

46. Jennifer Kates, Jennifer Tolbert, and Kendal Orgera, "The Red/Blue Divide in COVID-19 Vaccination Rates," Kaiser Family Foundation, September 14, 2021, https://www.kff.org/policy-watch/the-red-blue-divide-in-covid-19-vaccination-rates/; Philip Bump, "Republicans Are Still a Bigger Obstacle to Vaccination Than Black Americans," *Washington Post*, September 15, 2021.

47. Arnav Shah, Shanoor Seervai, and Eric C. Schneider, "How Can the U.S. Catch Up

with Other Countries on COVID-19 Vaccination?," The Commonwealth Fund, December 15, 2021, https://www.commonwealthfund.org/blog/2021/how-can-us-catch-other-countries-covid-19-vaccination.

48. Greg Sargent, "Biden's Sharp Rebuke of GOP Governors Should Prompt a Democratic Rethink," *Washington Post*, August 4, 2021.

49. Apoorva Mandavilli and Benjamin Mueller, "C.D.C. Chief Overrules Agency Panel and Recommends Pfizer-BioNTech Boosters for Workers at Risk," *New York Times*, September 24, 2021.

50. Carla K. Johnson and Hannah Fingerhut, "Biden Vaccine Mandate Splits US on Party Lines: AP-NORC Poll," AP News, September 30, 2021, https://apnews.com/article/coronavirus-pandemic-joe-biden-business-health-5b62c8e442ea495c58ed51d9f50d7c0d.

51. "COVID–19 Vaccination and Testing; Emergency Temporary Standard," Occupational Safety and Health Administration, Interim Final Rule, *Federal Register* 86, no. 212 (November 5, 2021): 61402–555.

52. Margaret Talev, "Axios-Ipsos Poll: 60% of Voters Back Biden Vaccine Mandates," Axios, September 14, 2021, https://www.axios.com/axios-ipsos-poll-covid-vaccine-mandates-biden-c0b7af63-6de0-4ec2-82bf-fb85e3e021ea.html.

53. Maeve Reston, "Republicans Seize on Federal Vaccine Mandates to Fire Up Their Base and Try to Court New Voters Worried about the Economy," CNN, November 12, 2021, https://www.cnn.com/2021/11/12/politics/republicans-covid-vaccine-mandates/index.html.

54. Adam Liptak, "Supreme Court Blocks Biden's Virus Mandate for Large Employees," *New York Times*, January 13, 2022, https://www.nytimes.com/2022/01/13/us/politics/supreme-court-biden-vaccine-mandate.html.

55. Scott Bomboy, "Current Constitutional Issues Related to Vaccine Mandates," The National Constitution Center, August 6, 2021, https://constitutioncenter.org/blog/current-constitutional-issues-related-to-vaccine-mandates.

56. *National Federation of Independent Business v. Occupational Safety and Health Administration*, 595 U.S. (2022).

57. Adam Liptack, "Supreme Court Rejects Biden's Student Loan Forgiveness Plan," *New York Times*, June 30, 2023, https://www.nytimes.com/2023/06/30/us/student-loan-forgiveness-supreme-court-biden.html.

58. Ryan Cooper, "President Biden's Most Powerful Student Loan Tool," American Prospect, July 17, 2023, https://prospect.org/education/2023-07-17-bidens-most-powerful-student-loan-tool/.

59. "Harris vs. Trump on Student Loans, Education: Where They Stand," September 10, 2024, *Washington Post*, https://www.washingtonpost.com/politics/interactive/2024/trump-harris-student-loans-education/.

60. Karl Rove, "Trump Invited This Indictment," *Wall Street Journal*, June 14, 2023, https://www.wsj.com/articles/trump-indictment-news-arrest-arraignment-jail-national-security-2024-presidential-race-9230357b?mod=opinion_lead_pos9.

61. Just as we were finishing this concluding chapter, Fulton County district attorney Fani Willis brought a fourth highly ambitious indictment against former president Trump, charging him and eighteen others with criminal activity in connection with efforts to overturn Joe Biden's win in Georgia. Trump and his alleged fellow conspirators, including Chief of Staff Mark Meadows and Trump attorney Rudy Giuliani, were charged

under Georgia's Racketeer Influenced and Corrupt Organization Act (RICO). Although RICO is patterned after a federal law to fight organized crime, it has recently been used effectively to prosecute white-collar crime and political corruption. This case was certainly a threat to Trump and his "accomplices," especially as it involved state law, not subject to a presidential pardon, the Georgia case would have required the prosecutors to prove the existence of an "enterprise" and a "pattern of racketeering activity." Whether this sprawling case would have proven more effective than Jack Smith's more focused indictment became a moot issue with the outcome of the 2024 election. Danny Hakim and Richard Fausset, "Inside a Georgia Prosecutor's Investigation of a Former President," *New York Times*, August 15, 2023, https://www.nytimes.com/2023/08/15/us/fani-willis-donald-trump-georgia-investigation.html.

62. *United States of America v. Donald J. Trump*, https://int.nyt.com/data/documenttools/trump-jan-6-indictment-2020-election/1f1c76972b25c802/full.pdf.

63. Peter Baker, "Trump's Case Has Broad Implications for American Democracy," *New York Times*, August 1, 2023, https://www.nytimes.com/2023/08/01/us/politics/trump-charged-jan-6-election-democracy.html?searchResultPosition=2.

64. Michael D. Shear and Zolan Kanno-Youngs, "Biden Issues a 'Full and Unconditional Pardon' of His Son Hunter Biden," *New York Times*, December 3, 2024, https://www.nytimes.com/2024/12/01/us/politics/biden-pardon-son-hunter.html.

65. Donald P. Green, Bradley Palmquist, and Eric Schickler, *Partisan Hearts and Minds: Political Parties and the Social Identities of Voters* (New Haven, CT: Yale University Press, 2004).

66. Sidney M. Milkis, *The President and the Parties: The Transformation of the American Party System since the New Deal* (New York: Oxford University Press, 1993).

67. William G. Howell and Terry M. Moe, *Relic: How Our Constitution Undermines Effective Government—and Why We Need a More Powerful Presidency* (New York: Basic Books, 2016).

68. Frances Lee, review of William Howell and Terry Moe, *Relic: How Our Constitution Undermines Effective Government and Why We Need a More Powerful Presidency*, *Journal of Politics* 79, no. 4 (September 2015): 278–87.

69. Donald Trump, remarks at Mount Rushmore, July 4, 2020, https://trumpwhitehouse.archives.gov/briefings-statements/remarks-president-trump-south-dakotas-2020-mount-rushmore-fireworks-celebration-keystone-south-dakota/.

70. "Remarks by President Biden on the Continued Battle for the Soul of the Nation," Philadelphia, PA, September 1, 2022, https://www.whitehouse.gov/briefing-room/speeches-remarks/2022/09/01/remarks-by-president-bidenon-the-continued-battle-for-the-soul-of-the-nation/.

POSTSCRIPT

1. Domenico Montanaro, "Trump Claims a 'Massive' Mandate, but Presidents Often Overread Their Victories," NPR, December 16, 2024, https://www.npr.org/2024/12/16/g-s1-38003/trump-mandate-presidents.

2. George Packer, "The End of Democratic Delusions: The Trump Reaction and What Comes Next," *The Atlantic*, January 2025, 12.

3. Packer, "End of Democratic Delusions," 13; Nate Cohen, "Trump's Re-election

Defines a New Era of American Politics," *New York Times*, December 25, 2024, https://www.nytimes.com/2024/12/25/upshot/trump-era-republicans-democrats.html?unlocked_article_code=1.kE4.xU6G.GBvkgOTU3MXq&smid=em-share.

4. Jessie Blaeser, Benjamin Storrow, and Kelsey Tamborino, "What Has Biden Wrought?," *Politico*, December 23, 2024, https://www.politico.com/news/2024/12/23/biden-spending-unfinished-business-00195256.

5. "Spending on Infrastructure Has Fallen in Real Terms in America," *The Economist*, November 22, 2023, https://www.economist.com/united-states/2023/11/22/spending-on-infrastructure-has-fallen-in-real-terms-in-america.

6. Ben Gittleson, "Biden Takes Victory Lap on Inflation Reduction Act amid 2024 'Bidenomics' Push," ABC News, August 16, 2023, https://abcnews.go.com/Politics/biden-takes-victory-lap-inflation-reduction-act-amid/story?id=102319410.

7. Piper Hudspeth, Abby Turner, Way Mullery, Kenneth Uzquiano, Katherine Sullivan, and Kit Maher, "Here's What Trump Has Promised to Do in a Second Term," CNN, December 26, 2024, https://www.cnn.com/interactive/2024/04/politics/trump-campaign-promises-dg/.

8. Tom Dreisbach, "Donald Trump Calls January 6th a 'Day of Love': Here Are the Facts," NPR, October 29, 2024, https://www.npr.org/2024/10/29/nx-s1-5159868/2024-election-trump-harris-capitol-riot.

9. Alexander Hamilton, *Federalist* No. 71, in Alexander Hamilton, James Madison, and John Jay, *The Federalist Papers*, ed. Clinton Rossiter, with an introduction and notes by Charles Kessler (New York: Signet Classics, 2003), 431.

Index

Note: page numbers in italics refer to figures or tables. Those followed by n refer to notes, with note number.

Abbott, Greg, 186
abortion, as conservative rallying point, 48
activists and interest groups
   disdain for pragmatism and political norms, xiii
   and federal government turn to activist state, 43
   increased influence of, xi, 28, 66, 79
   influence on Democratic Party, xiii
   influence on presidents, xii, 3, 28–29, 43–44, 222, 246
   Johnson's failed effort to harness, 42–43
   judiciary and, 171
   and nationalization of politics, 18, 56
   and political polarization, xii
Adams, John, 10, 11
administrative presidency
   definition of, 109
   and sharpening of partisanship, 148–149
   unitary executive doctrine and, 117–119
administrative presidency of Trump
   bureaucracy reduction and reshaping, 141–145
   conservative intellectuals supporting, 116–119
   courts' blocking of agenda, 116
   federal hiring freeze, 141–142
   and labor law, 143–144
   long-term effects of, 141, 143–144
   partisan control of bureaucracy, 108, 113–114, 141–142, 144–145, 232–233
   politics of fear underlying, 120
   precedents for, 108, 110, 112–113, *114*, *115*, 119, 122, 138–139
   and regulation-making process, 114–115
   rejection of bureaucratic management, 114
   rejection of norms, 113, 119
   rules finalized *vs.* other presidents, 115, 116, *116*
   rules limiting new regulations, 142–143
   tools to control administrative state, 109–110
   values and goals of, 108
Administrative Procedures Act of 1946, 17–18, 157
administrative state
   autonomy of, 38, 110
   balance with presidential power, 111, 112
   as brake on presidential action, 95–96
   Congress's loss of control over, 157
   conservatives' repurposing of, 44–56, 116–117, 145
   conservatives' traditional opposition to, 117
   establishment of, 15–18
   executive-centered partisanship and, 108
   FDR's consolidation of control over, 38
   and government by experts, 16, 38, 111
   and growth of presidential power, 17–18, 37–39
   political oversight *vs.* Europe, 111–112
   postwar subordination of party politics to, 39–40
   power to obstruct outside influences, 112
   traditional role of, 111
   Trump's attacks on, 133–134
   Trump's control of, 108, 113–114, 141–142, 144–145, 232–233
   Trump's damage to public faith in, 221–222
   Trump's impounding of funds of, 232
   Trump's promise to dismantle, 108, 113
   turn to "democratic" state, under Lyndon Johnson, 41–43
Affordable Care Act of 2010. *See* Patient Protection and Affordable Care Act (Obamacare)
Albence, Matt, 130–131
Alberta, Tim, x

Alito, Samuel, 174
America First Action, 92
American Rescue Plan, 250
Arpaio, Joe, 84, 127
Atkinson, Michael, 197, 218

Babbitt, Ashli, 241
Bailey, Jeremy, 174
Bannon, Steve, 77, 103, 108, 144, 151, 178
Barr, William, 116–117, 118–119, 225, 230
Barrett, Amy Coney, 99, 172, 178
Bauer, Bob, 8
Bell, Daniel, 41
Biden, Joseph
    approval ratings, 252
    and COVID-19, 202–203, 210, 248–249, 253–255
    and Democrats' 2024 primary, 237
    and election of 2020, 21, 93
    and election of 2024, 237
    and federalism, 194
    immigration policy, 221, 252
    and inflation, 268
    legislative successes of, 251–252
    and national unity, attempts at, 247–248, 251, 253, 255, 256, 258
    and Obamacare, 190–191
    pardoning of son, 261
    policies unresponsive to public needs, 267–268
    as pragmatic centrist, 247
    progressives' influence on, xiii, 248
    slim margin in Congress, 85
    and Trump indictments, 260, 261
    and Trump policies, effect of, 221, 228–229
    See also executive-centered partisanship of Biden
Blackburn, Marsha, 83
Black Lives Matter protests
    broad support for, 222, *223*
    clearing of Lafayette Park, 225–226
    COVID-19 and, 222
    election of 2020 and, 97, 100–101
    as mostly peaceful, 224
    motives driving Trump's response, 222, 223, 224–225
    as one of several crises in 2020, 200
    Trump's law-and-order response to, 201, 222–227
    Trump supporters' views on, 223, *223*
    Trump's use as distraction, 227
    use of federal agents against, 225–227, 308n67
Bolsonaro, Jair, 245, 259
Bossie, David, 69
Bragg, Alvin, 259
Brazil, election of 2022, 245
Bredesen, Phil, 83
Brownlow Committee, 17
Buchanan, Pat, 90, 164–165
bureaucracy, federal. *See* administrative state
Burger, Warren, 50–51
Burns, James MacGregor, 15
Burr, Richard, 243
Bush, George H. W., 2, 52, 90
Bush, George W.
    and administrative presidency, 122
    and conservative activism, 120
    and election of 2002, 81, *82*
    and executive-centered partisanship, 53–55, 149
    fundraising by, 93
    grassroots campaign of, 57, 58
    and Homeland Security Department, 53
    judicial appointments, 176, *176*
    and Republican statism, 108
    repurposing of administrative state, 53, 56
    and war on terror, 52

Calabresi, Steven, 117
California, emission standards, 188, 193–194
CARES Act. *See* Coronavirus Aid, Relief, and Economic Security Act
Carpenter, Daniel, 38
Carter, Jimmy, 44, 90, 271n5
census, Trump and, *181*, 182–184
Charlottesville incident, and business leaders' criticism of Trump, 137–138
Chauvin, Derek, 99–100
Cheney, Liz, 242, 270
Chips and Science Act of 2022, 251
A Choice Not an Echo (Schlafly), 19, 46
Christian right
    alliance with Republicans, 20, 56, 246

Trump and, 77–78, 140–141, 173, 246
See also evangelical Christians
Clapper, Raymond, 35
Clean Power Plan, 188, 192
Clinton, Bill, 2, 44, 115, 176, *176*, 197, 271n5
Clinton, Hillary
   and election of 2016, 70–71, 75–76, 77, 91, 239
   FBI treatment *vs.* Trump, 178
   private email server scandal, 261–262
   Republican attacks on, 69
   on Trump's unilateralism, 108
Collins, Susan, 196
Comey, James, 261
community action programs (CAPS), 42–43
Condray, Richard, 180
Congress
   electoral success tied to president, 161
   and executive-centered partisanship, 154, 156–158, 161–168
   growth in partisanship in, 160
   and national representation, 156
   presidents' evasion of control by, 52
   and president's power over bureaucracy, 17–18
   and Russian election interference, 195–196
   Senate, in constitutional design, 184–185
   Trump's relationship with, 159–161, 195–196
   universal fast track proposal for, 263
   votes supporting president, by party, 1954–2022, 158, *159*, 160
conservatism, modern
   and administrative state, 44–56, 108, 116, 120, 238
   coalition supporting, 239
   components of, 68
   and executive-centered partisanship, 44–56, 174–175
   free market beliefs, Trump and, 134, 135
   opposition to New Left, 19, 47–48, 52, 56, 120
   platform *vs.* traditional conservatism, 237–238
   Trump's capture of, 238, 239–240
   turn from pragmatism and political norms, 45
   See also New Right

Constitution
   constraints on president's power, 8
   diseased, Trump as symptom of, 2, 4
   and moderate consensus, 235, 262
   survival of first Trump administration, 228
   Trump administration's impact on, 195–199
constitutional government
   checks and balances in, 152
   cooperation necessary in, 152
   dependence on norms, 171–172
   executive-centered partisanship and, 151–161, 234–237
   and factionalism, framers on, 153
   role of political parties in, 153
   Roosevelt and, 14
Consumer Financial and Protection Bureau (CFPB), 180–182
Conway, Kellyanne, 69, 70, 71
Coolidge, Calvin, 81, *82*
Cooperative Election Study, 146, *147*
Coronavirus Aid, Relief, and Economic Security Act (CARES Act), 211, 217
corporate leaders' relations with Trump, 138
COVID-19, 203–222
   Biden and, 202–203, 210, 227, 248–249, 253–255
   and Black Lives Matter protests, 222, 227
   and competence of administrative state, 111
   deaths in, 230
   and deportations, 219
   economic stimulus packages, 211, 217
   and hydroxychloroquine, 206, *207*
   impact on 2020 election, 98–99, 100–101
   lockdowns, right-wing protests against, 214–215
   mishandling of, and accountability, 228, 229
   as one of several crises in 2020, 200
   public opinion on response, 98, 204–208, *205*, *207*
   states' early response to, 211–213
   and Trump's abuses of power, 217–222
   and Trump's anti-China rhetoric, 220–221
   Trump's campaigning despite, 97–98
   Trump's focus on economy, 206–207, 211, 213, 215–216
   Trump's infection and recovery, 99
   Trump's lack of leadership on, 212–213

COVID-19 (cont.)
  Trump's partisan response, 201, 202,
    207–208, 213–216, 217, 219
  Trump's policy changes, impact of, 220–222
  Trump's resistance to public health
    measures, 207–209, 211
  Trump's war on bureaucracy and, 217–219
  vaccine development, 209–210
crises
  effect of partisan president on, 202–203
  as increasingly common, 227–228
  multiple, in 2020, 200–202
  president's power and, 12–16, 30, 39, 200,
    203–204, 211, 227–230
Croly, Herbert, 276–277n27
Cruz, Ted, 104, 131–132
Cuccinelli, Ken, 225, 233
culture wars
  and battle for national identity, xii, 4, 20
  and judicial legitimacy, 171
  origin in 1960s, 267
  Trump's action on, 140–141
Cuomo, Andrew, 164–165

DACA. *See* Deferred Action for Childhood
    Arrivals
Dahl, Robert, 151
Dakota Access Pipeline, 138–139
D'Amato, Alfonse, 165
Daniels, Stormy, 259
Deferred Action for Childhood Arrivals
    (DACA), 60, 124–127, 133, *181*, 183, 252
Deferred Action for Parents of Americans
    (DAPA), 125
deficit, Tax Cuts and Jobs Act of 2017 and, 162
Delegate and Party Organization, 89
Democratic Party
  and executive-centered partisanship, 234,
    236–237, 258–259
  FDR's battle for control of, 33–34
  interest group influence on, xiii
  loss of white working class support, 238
  as national programmatic party, 30–36,
    37–39
  as pragmatic and diverse party, xii–xiii
  presumed dominance before 2024, 267
Derthick, Martha, 185–186

DeSantis, Ron, 212–213, 229, 244–245
DeVos, Betsy, 191–192
DHS. *See* Homeland Security, Department of
Dodd-Frank Act of 2010, 180
Donilon, Mike, 250
donors, increased influence of, xi, 28
Dowd, Matthew, 53–54, 55
Ducey, Doug, 243
Durbin, Richard, 128

Eagle Forum, 46, 48
Eastman, John, 103, 104–105, 119
Economic Opportunity Act of 1964, 42
economic policies of Trump administration
  energy policy, 134, 138–140
  precedents for, 294n74
  support for American manufacturing, 134
  See also trade policies of Trump
    administration
Edsall, Thomas, 208
education, and federalism under Trump,
    191–192
Eisenhower, Dwight D., 16, 280n99,
    281–282n114
election of 1936, 32
election of 1984, 75
election of 2004, 53–55
election of 2010, 59
election of 2012, 60, 78
election of 2014, 62, 281–282nn113–114
election of 2016
  and change in institution of presidency, 1
  and Clinton's private server scandal,
    261–262
  Republican congressional bids in, 82–83
  Russian interference in, 195–196
  Trump's claim of voter fraud in, 95, 230
  Trump's margin of victory, 75, 76
  Trump supporters in, 267
  Trump victory as unexpected, 74–75
  See also Trump campaign for 2016
election of 2018
  Republican gains and losses in, 65, 81–82,
    82, 83
  Trump's effort to influence, 80, 83–85
election of 2020
  down-ticket candidates and, 85, 86–87, 228

and executive-centered partisanship, 20–21
as free and fair, ix, 2, 172, 217
large number of mail-in ballots in, 101
multiple crises affecting, 200–201
number of votes in, 229
projections of Trump victory, 97
and Republican calls for election security, 229
Republican support for America-First agenda, 98
split-ticket voting in, 86–87, *87*
Supreme Court ruling on, 172
Trump's claim of victory in 2020 Election, 94–95, 234
  as accurate, in many Republicans' view, 95, 106–107, 229, 243–244
  and claimed illegal voting, 101–102, 229
  as effort to overturn free and fair election, 1–2, 3, 95, 101–106, 217, 270
  peaceful transfer of power and, 231
  as preeminent fact characterizing Trump, 262
  as Republican litmus test, 262
  as threat to democracy, 95, 102
  and undermining of election system, 201
Trump's loss as relief to many, 228
Trump's strategy in, 98
tumultuous events surrounding, 93–94, 96–100
See also Trump campaign for 2020
election of 2024
  appeal of Trump's strong leadership, 268
  and executive-centered partisanship, 21
  and identity politics, 269
  novel features of, 266
  partisan realignment in, 246, 267
  Trump's popular vote victory in, 236
  Trump's victory in, 231
Electoral College, 10–11, 75, 131, 185
Encarnacion, Omar, 245
environmental policy of Trump administration
  deregulation in, 138–140
  federalism and, 192–194
  Paris Climate Accord and, 139, 187
  public opinion on, *147*, 148
Environmental Protection Agency (EPA), 111

Epstein, Lee, 180
Equal Rights Amendment (ERA), 46–47
Espers, Mark, 224
evangelical Christians
  and conservative movement, 47
  and executive-centered partisanship, 19–20
  and political polarization, xii
  support for Trump, x, 77–78
  as tradition Republican base, 68
  Trump's law and order policies and, 226
executive-centered partisanship
  acceleration after 1960s, 19–20
  appointment of federal judges and, 50–51
  and battle for national identity, 20
  bipartisan legitimacy of, 52
  and claim to govern for "the people," 153
  as consequence of national polarization, 159
  conservatives and, 44–56, 174–175
  and control of administrative state, 108
  crises of 2020 and, 201–202
  and cult of personality, 245–246
  Democrats' embrace of, 234, 236–237
  and federalism under Trump, 194
  growth of executive power and, xi–xii, 7–9, 18
  Johnson's Great Society and, 40–44
  and judiciary, 154–155, 170–173
  and leadership in crisis, 202–203
  midterm elections and, 82, 86
  as new norm for presidents, 149–150
  Obama as culmination of, 56–62
  origin with FDR, 262–263
  and president as leader of party, 66
  and presidential influence in states, 185–186
  and president's *vs.* nation's goals, 216–217
  public's support for, 9
  and subordination of legislature, 154, 156–158
  as symptom of diseased system, 2–4
  and temptation to rule by unilateral action, 154
  as threat to Constitution, 18, 20, 153–161, 234–237
  universal fast track as proposed remedy for, 263
  and weakening of federalism, 155

executive-centered partisanship *(cont.)*
    weakening of party system and, xi, 7, 9, 28, 44–45, 54–55, 56, 153, 236
    See also presidentialism; presidential power
executive-centered partisanship of Biden, xiii, 203, 227, 236–237, 246–258, 264–265
    COVID-19 policies and, 253–255
    and new spending (Bidenomics), 249–251, 268
    progressive executive actions, 252–253, 257
    as reaction to Trump, 246–248, 258, 264–265
    reluctant turn to, 248–249
    reversal of Trump policies, 252
    speech condemning Trump supporters, 264–265
    and spending on Democratic priorities, 250
    and student loan forgiveness, 256–258
    and widening of partisan divide, 257–258
executive-centered partisanship of Trump
    crisis created by, 19–21
    as dangerous culmination of historical trend, xi, xii, 62–64, 107, 119, 145, 149, 153–154, 155–156, 197–199, 203, 232, 233–234, 235, 246–247, 259, 265
    and Democrats' reactive partisanship, 246–248, 258, 264–265
    false promise of, 149–150
    as harsh and unfiltered, 120
    messianic fervor of, as unprecedented, 63–64
    and partisan fracturing of nation, 151–152, 236
    precedents for, 125
    and president as center of political movement, 63
    resistance from courts, states, and Congress, 63
    as threat to Constitution, 234–237
    widening of partisan divide by, 247–248
    See also unilateralism of Trump
Executive Office of the President (EOP), xii, 17, 38–39
executive orders, by Trump *vs.* other presidents, 112–113, *114*, *115*
executive prerogative. *See* presidential power
Executive Reorganization Act of 1939, xii, 17, 28, 38–39

Farley, James, 32, 34
Fauci, Anthony, 99, 218
federalism
    in constitutional design, 184–185
    and executive-centered partisanship, 155, 185–186
    and state lawsuits against federal policy, 186–187, *187*
federalism under Trump, 186–194
    Affordable Care Act and, 188–191
    and education policy, 191–192
    and environmental policy, 192–194
    and executive-centered partisanship, 194
    immigration policies and, 188
    impact of Trump policies on states, 187–194
    state attorneys general lawsuits, 186–187, *187*
Federalist Papers, 152, 179, 197
Federalist Society, 51, 117, 118–119, 173, 174
Federation for American Immigration Reform (FAIR), 132–133
Flake, Jeff, 83, 243
Flores Agreement, 127
Floyd, George, murder of, 93, 99–100, 200, 201, 222
Flynn, Michael, 144, 178
Frankfurter, Felix, 36
Freedom from Fear
    Roosevelt on, 15–16, 39, 40, 52, 121
    Trump policies in support of, 120–121, *121*
Freedom from Want
    Roosevelt on, 15–16, 39–40, 52, 121
    Trump policies in support of, 120–121, *121*

Galvin, Daniel, 93
Garland, Merrick, 124, 171–172, 175–177, *177*, 259–260
Gideon v. Wainwright (1963), 49–50
Ginsburg, Ruth Bader, 172, 176–177, *177*, 279n68
Giuliani, Rudy, 69, 103, 104, 312–313n61
Goldsmith, Jack, 8
Goldwater, Barry, 19, 45, 46, 49, 52, 94
Goodwin, Richard, 41, 42
Gorka, Sebastian, 144
Gorsuch, Neil, 124, 173
government, reduction of
    modern conservatives' rejection of, 116–117

as traditional conservative value, 108, 116, 120
Trump's failure to accomplish, 108, 116, 120
Graham, Billy, 19
Graham, Lindsey, 65–66, 240
Grant, Ulysses S., 12
Great Depression, and presidential power, 14–16, 30
Great Society, and presidential power, 40–44
Greve, Michael, 14, 212
Gulick, Luther, 38–39

Hacker, Jacob, 164
Hahn, Stephen, 209
Haley, Nikki, 243, 244–245, 311n34
Hamilton, Alexander, 4, 6, 10, 168, 179, 184, 197
Hamilton, Gene, 122, 129
Hannity, Sean, 105
Harding, Warren G., 14
Harris, Kamala, 21, 210, 236, 237, 267, 268, 269
Haslam, Bill, 166–167
Hawley, Josh, 104
Heclo, Hugh, 40, 56, 153
Hennessey, Susan, 8
Heritage Foundation, 173, 232–233
Hice, Jody, 241
High, Stanley, 32–33
Hogan, Larry, 88, 215
Homan, Tom, 130, 233
Homeland Security, Department of (DHS), 52, 53, 122, 224–225, 273n36
homeland security policies
    conservative focus on, after 9/11 attack, 56
    as threat to civil liberties and rule of law, 52
    of Trump, 120–121, 121
    See also immigration policies of Trump administration
Hoover, Herbert, 30–31
Howell, William, 179, 263

immigration
    DHS and, 122
    presidentialism's polarization of debate on, 269
    undocumented, as conservative concern, 56
    undocumented, public opinion on, 309n17
immigration policies of Trump administration, 121, 121–133, 291n37
    and administrative presidency, 122
    border wall, resistance to, 123–124
    Child Separation Policy, 127–132
    compelling of cooperation from subnational jurisdictions, 123, 133
    court rulings against, 124–125, 126, 133, 178–179
    COVID-19 and, 219
    DACA and DAPA and, 124–127, 133
    damage to government legitimacy, 133
    as draconian, 109, 129, 233, 262
    exaggerated fear underlying, 121, 131
    family separation policy and, 127–132
    impact of many small changes, 132–133
    lack of public support, 239
    media coverage of, 132
    Migration Protection Protocols (Remain in Mexico policy), 135–136
    Muslim ban, 124, 148, 180, 187–188, 291n40
    officials leading, 122
    political considerations underlying, 131
    refugees and, 124
    and sanctuary cities, 123, 188
    in second term, 233
    tariffs as leverage in, 135
    unilateral action on, 122–123, 125–126
    zero-tolerance policy, 127–132
Inflation Reduction Act of 2022, 250, 268
Infrastructure Investment and Jobs Act, 250, 268
Islamic terrorism, as conservative concern, 56

Jackson, Andrew, 6, 151, 170–171
Jacobson, Gary, 229
January 6, 2021, Capital riot
    congressional investigation of, 105
    as constitutional crisis, 102, 231, 245
    deaths in, 241
    as effort to destroy democracy, 1–2, 3
    indictments of Trump for, 105, 260–261
    limited impact on Trump's support, 105–106
    nation's horror at, 156
    Republicans' views on, 95, 243
    Trump's lack of accountability for, 239–242
    Trump's pardon of participants, 269, 270
    Trump's speech prior to, 102, 103

Jefferson, Thomas, 6, 10, 11
Johnson, Andrew, 94, 197
Johnson, Lyndon B., 19, 40–44, 48, 50, 111
Jones, Alex, 103
judiciary
    challenges to Trump's authority, 178
    confidence in, by party and year, *169*, 169–170
    dependence on executive for enforcement, 179
    executive-centered partisanship and, 154–155, 170–173
    and expansion of criminals' rights, 49–50
    impartiality expected of, 168–169
    and limits of presidential power, 172
    necessary political awareness of, 179–180
    and partisan battle for nation's soul, 171
    and signing statements, 174
    Trump appointments *vs.* other presidents, 175–178, *176*
    Trump's attacks on, 173–184
    Trump's judges and reproductive rights, 173, 177
    See also Supreme Court

Kaine, Timothy, 57
Kasich, John, 71, 88
Kavanaugh, Brett, 84, 177–178, 255
Kelly, John, 122, 126, 127, 129
Kennedy, John F., 16–17, 40–43, 50, 112, 200
Kerry, John, 54, 139
Keystone XL Pipeline, 138–139
King, Peter, 165–166
Kinzinger, Adam, 242–243
Koch network, and election of 2020, 91–92
Kushner, Jared, 144

Land, Richard, 141
Lapinski, John, 204
law and order
    Nixon and, 49–50, 121, 223–224
    Trump's support for, 100, 121, 123, 137–138, 226
Lee, Frances, 159–160, 263
legal system, US, Trump's damage to, 261–262
Legislative Reorganization Act of 1946, 17–18, 117, 157

Levitsky, Steven, 172
Limbaugh, Rush, 74
Lincoln, Abraham, 6, 12, 153, 171
Linz, Juan, 234–237, 245, 247, 257, 262
Livermore, Michael, 113
Locke, John, 30
Lockheed Martin, Trump negotiations with, 134
Lowi, Theodore, 17, 37
Lula da Silva, Luiz Inácio, 245
Lyons, Jim, 89

Madison, James, 10, 152
Manafort, Paul, 69, 178
Manchin, Joe, 84
mandate claimed by presidents, 2, 14, 151, 152
    Trump's assertion of, 151–152
A Mandate for Leadership (Heritage Foundation), 232–233
Matusow, Allen, 43
Mayhew, David, 156, 158, 204
McAleenan, Kevin, 129, 130
McCain, Cindy, 243
McCain, John, 84, 120
McCarthy, Kevin, 240–242
McConnell, Mitch, 124, 171–172, 175, 240–241
McDaniel, Ronna, 88, 91–92, 105–106, 242–243
McGovern, George, 44
McGovern-Fraser reforms, xi, 28, 66
McKinley, William, 12
Meadows, Mark, 105, 312–313n61
media
    and federalism, 155
    Trump and, 79, 80
Medicare, 53, 249, 254
Meese, Edwin III, 174
Melnick, R. Shep, 157
midterm elections
    changes in Congressional seats, 81, *82*
    executive-centered partisanship and, 82, 86
    factors affecting, 82
Miller, Stephen, 122, 127–129, 131, 144, 219, 233
Miranda rights, 50
Moe, Terry, 263
Moore, Roy, 84
Morgan, Mark, 225

Mount Rushmore, 264, 265
Moyers, Bill, 41
Moynihan, Donald, 143
Mueller, Robert, 118–119
Mulvaney, Mick, 142
Musk, Elon, 267

NAFTA. *See* North American Free Trade Agreement
Napolitano, Janet, 124–125
National Review, 74
National Rifle Association (NRA), 79
national security state, 16, 18
NCIB v. Sebelius (2012), 190
Neustadt, Richard, 2
Never Trumpers, 65, 69–70, 88, 93, 114, 238, 259
New Deal
  centralization of policy and party control, 30–36
  as nonpartisan issue, in Roosevelt's view, 36
  and reappraisal of rights, 30–31, 36–37
  and weakening of party system, 29–37
New Left
  conservative opposition to, 19, 47, 49–50
  and executive-centered partisanship, 19–20
  expansion of criminals' rights, 49–50
  Johnson and, 42
New Right
  groups joining, 47, 48
  opposition to Leftist policies, 49–50, 239
  populism of, 45
  Reagan's agenda and, 51
Nielsen, Kirstjen, 129–131, 135
Nisbet, Robert A., 42
Nixon, Richard M.
  abuse of power by, 94
  and administrative state, 111, 112, 117, 145
  attacks on Supreme Court, 173
  and big government conservatism, 238
  Burger's appointment as chief justice, 50–51
  conservative state as goal of, 233
  devolution and decentralization by, 52
  and election of 1972, 44
  and executive-centered partisanship, 19–20
  judicial appointments, 176, *176*
  law and order platform of, 49–50, 121, 223–224
  resignation of, 94, 259
  and "silent majority," 48
  use of administrative state, 45–46, 49, 51–52
  and Vietnam War, 48
  Watergate and, 50–51
No Child Left Behind Act of 2002, 191
Noem, Kristi, 264
North American Free Trade Agreement (NAFTA), 136–137, 220

Oath Keepers, 104
Obama, Barack
  and administrative presidency, 122, 149
  campaign strategy, 57
  and election of 2010, 59
  and election of 2012, 60
  and election of 2014, 62
  and environmental regulations, 138–139
  and executive-centered partisanship, 56–62, 125–126, 149
  fundraising by, 93
  immigration policy, 60, 62, 124–125, 252, 282nn115–116
  judicial appointments, 175–176, *176*
  and labor law, 143–144
  legacy, Trump's erasure of, 108
  midterm elections and, 82
  and OFA organization, 57–59, 60–61, 71, 80
  partisan unilateral actions by, 58–59, 60–61, 62, 108, 138–139, 281n107
  as political outsider, 271n6
  progressive coalition supporting, 44, 57, 59–60, 266–267
  and Republican anti-intellectualism, 79
  subordination of party to personal goals, 61–62
  and Trump, similarity of political styles, 63, 71
  and war on terror, 52–53
  and weakening of party system, 57–58
  We Can't Wait campaign, 59, 60
Obamacare. *See* Patient Protection and Affordable Care Act
Obama for America (OFA), 57, 80

OFA. *See* Obama for America; Organizing for Action; Organizing for America
Office of Management and Budget (OMB), xii, 28, 45, 114–115, 233
O'Neill, Tip, 18
Organizing for Action (OFA), 60–61
Organizing for America (OFA), 57–58

Paris Climate Accords, 139, 187
partisan polarization
    Biden's partisanship and, 257–258
    and cold civil war, 65, 107
    and erosion of trust in government, 247
    presidentialism and, 262
    radicalization of Republican Party and, xii
    as threat to Constitution, x
    Trump and, ix, 109, 247–248, 251, 262
    See also executive-centered partisanship
party system
    G. W. Bush's grassroots campaign and, 55
    origin of, 11, 28
    polarization of society and, 262
    and pragmatic moderation, 247, 262
    role in constitutional government, 153
    success of Constitution and, 235, 262
    tension between presidency and, 29–30
party system, weakening of, 29–40
    donors and activists and, xi, 28, 43–44, 66
    establishment of administrative state and, 39–40
    executive-centered partisanship and, xi, 7, 9, 28, 44–45, 54–55, 56, 153, 236
    FDR's New Deal and, 29–37
    nationalizing of policy debate and, 56
    national welfare state and, 37–40
    Obama and, 57–58
    populism of 1960s and, 40–44
    returning power to people as goal of, xi, 28, 66
    and Trump's capture of party apparatus, 66, 79
Patient Protection and Affordable Care Act (Obamacare), 162, 180, 188–191, 194
Pence, Mike, 102–105, 140, 189, 210, 213, 244, 261
"The Perils of Presidentialism" (Linz), 234–235

Perot, H. Ross, 69, 79
Pierson, Paul, 43, 164
Piper, J. Richard, 188
police brutality, public opinion on, 222–223, 223
politics, nationalization of, 18, 56
populism
    of 1960s, and presidential power, 40–44
    in Brazil, 245
    damage to US institutions, 270
    Democrats' denigration of, 267
    of Jackson, 170
    of New Right, 45
    of Republicans in 2016, 78
    of Trump
        appeal of, 238, 268
        and COVID-19, 208–209
        DeSantis and, 245
        and distrust of law enforcement and electoral system, 261–262
        and election of 2016, 74, 76–77, 78–79, 92
        and election of 2020, 90
        and immigration policy, 120–121
        and January 6th Capitol riot, 90
        as reaction against Democratic policies, 266
        Republican loyalty to, 110, 239–240, 243, 246
        resistance to, 217
Port Huron Statement, 42
Posner, Eric, 180
Potter, Rachel, 112
presidency, as institution
    complexity of, 7
    Founders' design of, 5–6, 9–12
    as inherently hostile to status quo, 6
    and power of president's personality, 10
presidentialism
    as driver of polarization, 262
    historical development of, 6–18
    politicians' lack of incentives to curtail, 8
    and stability/rigidity of executive, 235–236
    as unlikely to be addressed, 259
    vagueness of constraints on, 8
    See also executive-centered partisanship
presidential power
    activists and, xii, 3, 28–29

administrative state and, 15–18, 37–39
demands of global power and, 12–13
and executive-centered partisanship, xi–xii, 7–9
expansion in crises, 12–16, 30, 39, 200, 203–204, 211, 227–230
FDR and, xii, 6–7, 14–17, 29, 30–37, 38
guardrails, failure to restore, 198–199
increase over time, 6–18
as issue since founding, 9–11
national welfare state and, 37–40
party system and, 11
scholars defending necessity of, 263
vagueness of constraints on, 8
presidential systems, Linz on, 234–237, 247, 257
presidents
idealized expectations for, 1, 2, 9
influence of activists and interest groups on, xii, 3, 28–29, 43–44, 222, 246
modern, as "outsiders," 2, 271–272n5
Priebus, Reince, 144
private schools, desegregation and, 47
Proud Boys, 103–104
Provost, Colin and Nolette, 186
Pruitt, Scott, 192–193

Rabe, Barry, 187
racial justice. *See* Black Lives Matter protests; Floyd, George, murder of
Reagan, Ronald W.
and administrative presidency, 117
and administrative state, 51–52, 112
and Christian right, 140, 246
denunciations of communism, 51
and devolution and decentralization, 52
and election of 1976, 90
and election of 1984, 75
and executive-centered partisanship, 19, 51, 149
on government as the problem, 44
and "Make American Great Again" slogan, 238
as "outsider," 271n5
and presidential power, 18
and radicalization of Republican Party, xii
and Republican statism, 108

and tax reform, 161, 164–165
and unitary executive doctrine, 174
Redfield, Robert, 99, 210
Reed, Ralph, 77
Rehnquist, William, 168
Republican National Committee (RNC), Trump and, 65, 85–86, 88, 90–91
Republican Party
anti-intellectualism of base, 79
as charismatic leader, x. *See also* Weber, Max
and "election security" push, 94
militant conservative base, 56
opposition to Obamacare, 58–59
presidential nomination process, 72–73
primary election of 2024, 243, 244–245
radicalization of, xii
Republican Party, Trump's takeover of, 80–93
continued influence after 2020 election, 85, 89–90, 110
and cult of personality, 245–246
election of 2024 as confirmation of, 266
elimination or conversion of opposition, 65–66, 82–83, 88, 93, 242–243
and endurance of Trumpism, 239
fundraising control, 88–89, 90–92
as grave danger to democracy, 258
at national level, 65, 67–68, 79, 80–88, 90–93
and Party's abandonment of its conservative principles, 106
and right-wing policies, 238–240
at state level, 65, 67, 89–90, 243–245
supporters' capture of party structures, 239, 243
support of Republican voters for Trump and congressional candidates, 87–88
and Trump's claim of victory in 2020, 94–95
and Trump's lack of accountability, 239–242
and vapidity of Party, 262
Revesz, Richard, 113
Revolution of 1800, 106
Rhodes, Kevin, 117
rights, New Deal and, 15, 30–31, 36–37, 39
RNC. *See* Republican National Committee
Robart, James, 124
Roberts, John, 168, 178, 180–184, 190, 255, 256

Rockman, Bert, 20
Roe v. Wade (1973), 48, 51, 173, 279n68
Romney, Mitt, 60, 78, 88, 120, 196
Roosevelt, Franklin D. (FDR)
   and administrative presidency, 110
   and battle for control of Democratic Party, 33–35
   centralization of policy and party control, 30–36
   and centralized welfare state, 37–40
   direct public support for, 35–36, 280n99
   and election of 1934, 81, 82
   and establishment of administrative state, 15–17
   and executive-centered partisanship, 262–263
   and Four Freedoms, 15–16, 39, 52
   and Freedom from Fear, 15–16, 39, 40, 52, 121
   and Freedom from Want, 15–16, 39–40, 52, 121
   and growth of presidential power, xii, 6–7, 14–17, 29, 30–37, 38
   as last president to achieve a full-scale party realignment, 2, 14
   and radio, 36
   and reappraisal of rights, 15, 30–31, 36–37, 39
   on South and liberal agenda, 276n22
Roosevelt, Theodore ("Teddy"), 6, 13, 29, 31, 235
Rosenstein, Rod, 118–119
Rove, Karl, 55, 260

Saldin, Robert, 70
Sanders, Bernie, 78–79, 257, 392
Scalia, Antonin, 117, 171, 173, 176
Schattschneider, E. E., 43–44
Schiff, Adam, 166
Schlafly, Phyllis, 19, 46–47, 48
Schlesinger, Arthur Jr., 14–15, 112
Scott, Tim, 244
Self, Jeff, 128
September 11th terrorist attacks, 52, 56
Sessions, Jeff, 118–119, 122, 127, 129, 140
Shriver, Sargent, 42
signing statements, 113, *114*, *115*, 174
Sinema, Kyrsten, 84
situational constitutionalism, 188

Skocpol, Theda, 77
Skowronek, Stephen, 6, 30–31, 118
Smith, Jack, 105, 259–261
Southern Democrats, FDR and, 34–35
Spicer, Sean, 144
split-ticket voting, 86–87, *87*
state and local tax (SALT) deduction, 162–167
Stokes, Thomas, 34
Stone, Roger, 69, 178
Supreme Court
   appointments, partisan battles over, 171–172, 176–177, *177*
   and Biden's COVID vaccine mandate, 254–255
   and Biden's student loan forgiveness, 256
   and expansion of criminals' rights, 49–50
   impartiality expected of, 168–169
   legitimacy of, partisan attacks and, 170–171
   Nixon's attacks on, 173
   on presidential immunity, 258
   and pressure from partisan executive, 255
   rulings on Trump policies, 124–125, 126, 133, 172–173, 180–183, *181–182*
   on unitary executive doctrine, 180–182, *181–182*
Szakos, Joe, 61

Tax Cuts and Jobs Act of 2017 (TCJA), 109, 161–167
Tax Reform Act of 1986, 161
Tea Party, 56, 145, 215
Teles, Steven, 70
Tennessee Valley Authority, 35, 52
Thiessen, Marc, 177–178
Thompson, Frank, 187
Tigar, Jon, 178
Tomasulo, Gary, 131
trade policies of Trump administration
   China and, 137
   and NAFTA, replacement with USMCA, 136–137
   performative aspects of, 134
   precedents for, 294n74
   tariffs, 135–137
   unilateral action on, 134, 136
Trainer, Nick, 89, 90
Truman, Harry, 2, 16, 69, 280n99

Trump, Donald J.
  as authoritarian demagogue, 270
  bases' uncritical support of, 236
  and battle for national identity, 20
  campaign style, 63
  as charismatic leader, x, 80, 107
  coalition supporting, 63, 74, 108–109, 137, 267
  contempt for political opposition, 264
  disruption of American politics and society, 107
  impeachments of, 8, 94, 196–198, 218, 231, 241, 247
  indictments of, xiii, 63–64, 105, 231, 258–261, 312–313n61
  influence after leaving office, 238, 239
  Jackson's influence on, 151
  as not elected by majority, 161
  and Obama, similarity of political styles, 63, 71
  parallels to Louis XIV, 64
  pathological personality of, 5
  and populist conservatism, 110
  similar strongmen in US history, x
  skill in branding policy positions, 70
  sowing of discord and rancor, 3, 4, 20
  success of candidates endorsed by, 86–87
  transgressions of, as irrelevant to supporters, 239
  and US cold civil war, 65, 107
  See also executive-centered partisanship of Trump
Trump, Donald Jr., 105
Trump, Ivanka, 144, 210
Trump, Lara, 243
Trump administration, first
  abuses of power by, 197–198
  appeal of policies to right wing, 120–121
  appointments to Supreme Court, 173
  approval rating, by party, 65, 67
  and constitution, impact on, 195–199, 228
  court challenges to authority of, 178
  disregard of core institutions and norms, 236
  and election of 2018, effort to influence, 83–85
  elimination of Republican critics, 65–66
  end in disgrace for Trump, 239
  inaugural address, 81, 151
  journalists' stories on palace intrigues, 7
  judicial appointments, 175–178, *176*
  legislative achievements, lack of, 108, 109
  low level of success on most traditional measures, 109
  mass rallies of supporters, 80
  numerous investigations of figures in, 178
  partisan divisiveness of, 109, 162–163, 166–167, 227, 251, 262, 264–265
  policies, public opinion on, 95–96, *97*, 110, 146–148, *147*, 239
  presidents' accumulation of power and, 7
  relations with Congress, 159–161
  reshaping of Republican Party, 146–149, 296n103
  and Russian interference investigation, 118–119
  significant policy legacy of, 109–110
  strained relations with Congress, 195–196
  Supreme Court rulings on policies, 124–125, 126, 133, 172–173, 180–183, *181–182*
  as symptom of diseased political system, 2–4
  as threat to democracy, ix–x, 1, 230
  Trump's continued campaigning during, 80–81, 95
  Trump's deceit and wrongdoing, 196
  Trump's direct connection to public, 80–81
  Trump's political influence after, 228–229, 231
  See also Republican Party, Trump's takeover of; unilateralism of Trump
Trump administration, second
  control of bureaucracy as goal of, 232–233
  as new political era, 266
  ongoing disruption of, 266, 268–270
  policies of, 232–233, 269–270
  potential for backlash against, 270
  as reaction to changes of past half century, 266
  as recrudescence, ix, 3
  as threat to democracy, x, xiii, 3–4, 234–235
Trump campaign for 2016
  campaign staff, 69
  capture of Republican Party apparatuses, 65, 79

Trump campaign for 2016 (*cont.*)
   connection with Republican base, 70, 71
   mass rallies in, 63, 70, 71
   mobilization of Republican base, 63, 67–68, 70
   outsider image of, 70
   populism of, 74, 76–77, 78–79
   and presidential nominee as leader of party, 66
   primary strategy, 71–74, 72
   promise to appoint antiabortion judges, 173, 177
   Republican opposition to, 69–70, 74, 78
   strategy for, 76–77
   and struggle for American identity, 65, 79
   unification of diverse Republican elements, 68
Trump campaign for 2020
   campaign's takeover of RNC, 85–86, 90–91
   control of Republican fundraising, 88–89, 90–93
   focus on law and order, 100
   force of presidency behind, 94, 95
   mass rallies, 98–99
   pandemic and, 89–90
   super PACs supporting, 91–92
Trump Victory Leadership Team, 90–91
Truth Social, 105–106
Tulis, Jeffrey, 7, 13
Tumlin, Karen, 132
Twelfth Amendment, 11

unilateralism of Trump
   on environmental deregulation, 138–139
   and erasure of Obama's legacy, 108
   and modern presidential leadership, 149–150
   politics of fear underlying, 120
   as threat to democracy, 110
   in trade policy, 134, 136
   See also administrative presidency of Trump
unitary executive doctrine
   and administrative presidency, 117–119
   Congress's efforts to hamstring Trump and, 119
   debate on, 174–175
   and Obamacare, 194
   as pillar of conservative movement, 173–174
   and president as only representative of all the people, 118
   Supreme Court on, 180–182
   and Trump's war on federal bureaucracy, 218–219
United States-Mexico-Canada Agreement (USMCA), 137
Urban, David, 69
USMCA. *See* United States-Mexico-Canada Agreement (USMCA)

Van Riper, Paul, 33
Vietnam War, 48
Vought, Russell, 233

Walensky, Rochelle, 253–254
Wallace, George, x, 69, 79
war on terror, 52–53
Warren, Earl, 49–50
Warren, Elizabeth, 180, 257
Washington, George, 9–10, 11, 28
Weber, Max, x, 239
Weld, Bill, 89, 97, 244
welfare state
   establishment of, 15–16, 37
   and executive-centered government, 37–40
   and nationalization of politics, 18
   Trump policies on, *121*
Whatley, Michael, 243
White, Paula, 140
White House Office of Information and regulatory Affairs (OIRA), 114–115
Whitmer, Gretchen, 214, 215
Willis, Fani, 105, 312–313n61
Wilson, Woodrow, 6, 12–14, 29, 31, 274–275n7, 276–277n27
Wittes, Benjamin, 8
Wolf, Chad, 129, 219, 225
Wong, Kenneth, 187
World Health Organization, 221
World War II, and presidential power, 15–16, 30, 39

Yoo, John, 179

Ziblatt, Daniel, 172
Zoorob, Michael, 77

www.ingramcontent.com/pod-product-compliance
Lightning Source LLC
Chambersburg PA
CBHW030521230426
43665CB00010B/704